WILLIAM SHAKESPEARE
The Tempest

A Case Study in Critical Controversy

Second Edition

EDITED BY

Gerald Graff
University of Illinois at Chicago

James Phelan
Ohio State University

Bedford/St. Martin's
BOSTON • NEW YORK

For Bedford/St. Martin's

Executive Editor: Stephen A. Scipione
Editorial Assistant: Marisa Feinstein
Senior Production Supervisor: Joe Ford
Production Associate: Ashley Chalmers
Marketing Manager: Adrienne Petsick
Text Design: Sandra Rigney
Project Management: DeMasi Design and Publishing Service
Cover Design: Joy Linn
Cover Art: Jacques Le Moyne de Morgues (1530–1588). Laudonnierus and King Athore (detail) from *Laudonnierus et rex athore ante columnam a praefecto prima navigatione locatam quamque venerantur floridenses* ("The inhabitants of Florida present a decorated column to the French"). Gouache drawing, 1564. The New York Public Library/Art Resource, NY
Composition: TexTech International
Printing and Binding: RR Donnelley & Sons Company

President: Joan E. Feinberg
Editorial Director: Denise B. Wydra
Director of Marketing: Karen R. Soeltz
Director of Editing, Design, and Production: Marcia Cohen
Assistant Director of Editing, Design, and Production: Elise S. Kaiser
Manager, Publishing Services: Emily Berleth

Library of Congress Control Number: 2008934228

For information, write: Bedford/St. Martin's
75 Arlington Street, Boston, MA 02116   (617-399-4000)

ISBN-10: 0-312-45752-9
ISBN-13: 978-0-312-45752-5

Published and distributed outside North America by

PALGRAVE MACMILLAN
Houndmills, Basingstoke, Hampshire RG21 6XS
Companies and representatives throughout the world.

ISBN-10: 0-230-22211-0
ISBN-13: 978-0-230-22211-3

A catalogue record for this book is available from the British Library.

Acknowledgments

Acknowledgments and copyrights are continued at the back of the book on pages 421–22, which constitute an extension of the copyright page.

Preface

ABOUT THE SERIES

Each volume in the *Case Studies in Critical Controversy* series reprints an authoritative text of a classic literary work, along with documents and critical essays that have been selected and organized to introduce the major critical debates and cultural conflicts concerning the work.

THE CASE OF *THE TEMPEST*

Is Shakespeare's *The Tempest* a colonialist play or a disinterested work of art? Can it be both at once? How should it be taught and studied? Helping students participate in the lively critical and cultural debates generated by such questions is the purpose of this case study. It consists of the complete text of *The Tempest*, in the authoritative version edited and annotated by David Bevington, and twenty-four documents and essays, the latter representing a range of different positions on several important controversies about the play. We also include our own editorial commentary that prepares students to consider *The Tempest* in relation to the current critical conversation about it. Finally, we include a portfolio of images of Caliban that themselves indicate radically different takes on his character.

Like the first volume in this series, Mark Twain's *Adventures of Huckleberry Finn: A Case Study in Critical Controversy* (2004), this book emphasizes debate and controversy because we believe that reading with absorption and enjoyment and talking, even arguing, with others about what we read are deeply interdependent activities. All of us most fruitfully read a book (or watch a film, or look at a painting, or, indeed, experience almost any event) when our attention is directed and intensified by our awareness of others' responses, an awareness that can also inspire us to make our own contributions to the ongoing discussion. Thus, this case study emphasizes controversy, which, increasingly, is the form contemporary discourse about books and culture takes.

Our approach as editors of this volume grows out of our own undergraduate experiences, coming to college from families where book talk and intellectual discussions were not everyday events. Like many of our students today, we wondered why the academy put so much emphasis on reading literature for its "hidden meanings" when, from our perspectives, literature was something primarily to be enjoyed, not elaborately analyzed. We each eventually found that exposure to pertinent critical controversies in the classroom helped greatly to dispel our initial fear and confusion, and to show us why the "meanings" of texts, and the debates about those meanings, can indeed matter.[1]

The problems we had in getting socialized into the conversations of literary study are also faced by today's students. When students in literature courses are shy and silent in class discussions and find critical essays a struggle to write, the reason often lies in the mysterious and intimidating nature of literary critical discourse.

To be sure, an instructor can alleviate the problem by telling such students to forget academic intellectual talk and just respond in their own voices: "Never mind how the critics say you should feel about *The Tempest;* tell us how you feel." Though such a tactic is understandable — perhaps even essential — at the beginning stages of literary study, it is not a long-term solution. It deepens rather than closes the already large gulf between the discourse of the teacher and that of the student. More important, it deepens the gulf between those students who "talk the talk" of the academy — the ones who get the As

---

[1] See Gerald Graff's *Beyond the Culture Wars* (New York: Norton, 1992, pp. 67–68) for an account of how his awareness of controversies about *Huckleberry Finn* helped him begin to like books.

and are destined for professional career tracks — and those who settle for lesser awards and ambitions.

Closing the gap between literary critical discourse and student discourse is important if higher education in the humanities is to be effective. And the best way to close this gap is to think of reading, discussing, and writing about literature as a process of entering into a critical conversation about it.

Learning by controversy offers a practical classroom solution to the angrily polarized debates of our time. Indeed, this strategy presents a model of how the quality of cultural debate in our society at large might be improved. It is a common prediction that the culture of the twenty-first century will continue to put a premium on people's ability to deal productively with conflict and cultural difference. Learning by controversy is sound training for citizenship in that future.

ABOUT THE SECOND EDITION

Part One begins with "The Life and Work of William Shakespeare," an essay that locates *The Tempest* in the larger context of his life and other writings, and addresses the debate about the authorship of those writings. The rest of Part One reprints David Bevington's text of *The Tempest*, first published in his edition of *The Complete Works of Shakespeare* in 1973. The version here is from the Updated Fourth Edition of 1997. Bevington's impeccable scholarship and thorough notes render his text an extraordinarily useful one for students — and his essay on Shakespeare's life has been helpful in composing ours.

Part Two includes our essay "Why Study Critical Controversies about *The Tempest*?" which explains and illustrates the principles underlying this edition; twenty-one essays that locate *The Tempest* in both critical and cultural contexts; and — new to this edition — a portfolio of seven images of Caliban, some by painters, others by performers. Collectively, these images capture a good stretch of the spectrum of critical interpretations of his character. Part Two concludes with our new essay addressing the issue of "Writing about Critical Controversy and *The Tempest*."

The readings begin with a debate between George Will and Stephen Greenblatt that marks the eruption of Shakespeare and *The Tempest* into the high profile "culture wars" of the early 1990s. From there, we take students back to Shakespeare's own time through cultural documents believed to have had an influence on the play. We then move to two new documents that highlight some other important elements of context: Daniel Wilson's essay "The Monster Caliban" from his 1873 book, *Caliban: The Missing Link,* and an excerpt from E. M. W. Tillyard's 1944 book, *The Elizabethan World Picture.* Wilson's essay provides a glimpse at how Caliban was perceived during the period when England was an imperial power, and Tillyard's places *The Tempest* itself within an account of the Elizabethan sense of the hierarchy among God's creatures. This section ends with sociologist Ronald Takaki's 1993 essay that helps place the earlier documents into the context of early European colonial practices and attitudes.

Part Two then presents modern and recent critical controversies about *The Tempest,* beginning with traditional historical and New Critical readings and moving through recent postcolonial and feminist writings in response to earlier criticism (and, in the case of Aimé Césaire, a rewriting of the play itself). The new materials in this section are an additional except from Césaire's *A Tempest* and an excerpt from Leah Marcus's 1996 essay on the larger interpretive consequences of different ways of glossing Prospero's reference to Sycorax, Caliban's mother, as a "blue-eyed hag" (page 23 in this volume). In order to orient students to the larger critical and cultural issues at stake in the controversies, we have organized the essays into several larger groups and written introductions to each group.

Given the enormous body of Shakespeare scholarship and criticism, we have had, of necessity, to limit ourselves to a few exemplary selections that we hope will model for students how academic and cultural controversies unfold over time. Particular kinds of criticism may only be possible at particular cultural moments; earlier controversies are recast in light of later critical developments. Above all, we want students to recognize that no reading is sacrosanct, and that they, too, can enter the conversation.

ACKNOWLEDGMENTS

The collaboration necessary to bring this book into existence extends beyond that between the editors, and we would like to express our thanks to some of our other collaborators: To the students to whom we taught the first edition. To David Richter, whose *Falling into Theory* provided a model of how to turn the theory of learning by controversy into an effective textbook. To Sylvan Barnet, Kristen McDermott, Russ McDonald, James Shapiro, James Siemon, Jyotsna

Singh, Frank Whigham, and Paul Yachnin, whose reviews of our prospectus and materials were extremely helpful and influential as we prepared the first edition. To numerous reviewers, whose comments on the first edition and recommendations for the second were just as valuable: John Black, David Blake, James Dutcher, David Humphries, Parmita Kapadia, Revathi Krishnaswamy, Lawrence McCauley, Kathryn E. Morris, Linda Reesman, and Theresa Winterhalter.

We also want to extend our appreciation to those at Bedford/ St. Martin's who brought their expertise to bear on the book: To Chuck Christensen and Joan Feinberg, who saw the usefulness of this series, and who provided crucial encouragement and support throughout the course of the project. To Karen Henry, whose knowledge of Shakespeare backstopped us at every stage. To Marisa Feinstein, who orchestrated the review program for the second edition. To Elizabeth Schaaf and Emily Berleth, who oversaw the production of the first and second editions. To the production team, Linda DeMasi of DeMasi Design and Publishing Service and Ashley Chalmers of Bedford/ St. Martin's, who turned the manuscript into a book. To Sandy Schechter and Helene Proteras, who cleared permissions for the essays and images in the book. To Edward Maloney, Jim Phelan's research assistant during much of the preparation of the first edition, who found materials on short notice and even endured Phelan's dramatic reading of the play. To Molly Youngkin, who succeeded Edward Maloney, and carefully proofread the entire manuscript of the first edition. To Paul McCormick, who did similar work for this edition. To Elizabeth Marsch, who located the images of Caliban. And especially to Steve Scipione of Bedford/St. Martin's, whose commitment to the book has been unwavering, whose critical judgment is unerring, and whose overall editorial skills — including the skill of motivating his authors — are unparalleled. Without him, this book would be a lesser thing.

Any remaining signs that this book is the work of mooncalves with an ague are the sole responsibility of the editors.

Gerald Graff
University of Illinois at Chicago

James Phelan
Ohio State University

Contents

Preface   iii

PART ONE

Shakespeare and *The Tempest*

The Life and Work of William Shakespeare   3

The Text of *The Tempest*   10

PART TWO

A Case Study in Critical Controversy

Why Study Critical Controversies about *The Tempest*?   91

Literary Study, Politics, and Shakespeare: A Debate   109

    GEORGE WILL, Literary Politics   110
    STEPHEN GREENBLATT, The Best Way to Kill Our Literary
    Inheritance Is to Turn It into a Decorous Celebration
    of the New World Order   113

Sources and Contexts   116

    MICHEL DE MONTAIGNE, from Of the Cannibals   120
    WILLIAM STRACHEY, from True Repertory of the Wrack   122
    SYLVESTER JOURDAIN, from A Discovery of the Barmudas   124

RICHARD HAKLUYT, Reasons for Colonization   126
BARTOLOMÉ DE LAS CASAS, from Letter to Philip, Great Prince
of Spain   136
DANIEL WILSON, The Monster Caliban   141
A Portfolio of Images of Caliban   161
E. M. W. TILLYARD, from The Elizabethan World Picture   168
RONALD TAKAKI, The "Tempest" in the Wilderness   180

Shakespeare and the Power of Order   213

FRANK KERMODE, from Shakespeare: The Final Plays   215
REUBEN A. BROWER, The Mirror of Analogy: *The Tempest*   224
LEAH MARCUS, The Blue-Eyed Witch   244

The Challenge of Postcolonial Criticism   265

PAUL BROWN, "This Thing of Darkness I Acknowledge Mine":
The Tempest and the Discourse of Colonialism   268
FRANCIS BARKER AND PETER HULME, Nymphs and Reapers
Heavily Vanish: The Discursive Con-texts of *The Tempest*   292
AIMÉ CÉSAIRE, from *A Tempest*   309

Responding to the Challenge   320

DEBORAH WILLIS, Shakespeare's *Tempest* and the Discourse
of Colonialism   321
DAVID SCOTT KASTAN, "The Duke of Milan / And His Brave Son":
Old Histories and New in *The Tempest*   333
MEREDITH ANNE SKURA, Discourse and the Individual:
The Case of Colonialism in *The Tempest*   351

The Challenge of Feminist Criticism   388

ANIA LOOMBA, from Gender, race, Renaissance Drama   389
ANN THOMPSON, "Miranda, Where's Your Sister?": Reading
Shakespeare's *The Tempest*   402

Writing about Critical Controversy and *The Tempest*   413

About the Editors   419

PART ONE

Shakespeare and *The Tempest*

The Life and Work
of William Shakespeare

William Shakespeare became the greatest writer in the history of the English language, but nothing in the unexceptional facts of his life seems to explain how he did so. Shakespeare's 38 plays, 154 sonnets, and 5 other poems, including the long narratives *Venus and Adonis* and *The Rape of Lucrece,* are remarkable for their formal artistry, their range, and their quality. The poems, especially the sonnets, display a mastery of Renaissance poetic style as well as keen insight into friendship, poetry, mutability, loss, and love. The plays include such rich comedies as *A Midsummer Night's Dream* and *Twelfth Night,* such powerful tragedies as *Macbeth* and *King Lear,* such vivid and astute histories as *Richard III* and *Henry IV, Part I,* and such imaginative romances as *A Winter's Tale* and *The Tempest.* Furthermore, the plays display considerable awareness of their own theatricality, even as they encompass a stunningly wide scope of human action, emotion, and character. Shakespeare is as accomplished in his creation and depiction of farce, verbal by-play, and sexual innuendo as he is in his treatment of passionate love, mature friendship, dark despair, and irredeemable madness. As the study of Shakespeare's sources has shown, among his greatest gifts is a rare ability to take an existing version of a story and reimagine it so completely as to transform its meaning and effect.

Shakespeare's remarkable achievements as a writer are puzzling because they are not explainable from what we know of the rest of his life. Over the years, the puzzle has led many, including such notable figures as Mark Twain, Walt Whitman, and Sigmund Freud, to conclude that someone other than Will (the nickname that appears in the sonnets) must have written the plays. These doubters (called anti-Stratfordians) have proposed many rivals — including Francis Bacon, Christopher Marlowe, and most recently, Edward de Vere, the seventeenth earl of Oxford — but the doubters have not been able to make a fully persuasive case for any of them. Nevertheless, many continue to look at the life of William Shakespeare and wonder how that life could have led to the works we attribute to him. Let us look, then, at that life, and at the significance of the persistent skepticism that such a life was the preparation for such works as *Hamlet,* "The expense of spirit in a waste of shame" (Sonnet 129), and *The Tempest.*

William Shakespeare was born in Stratford-upon-Avon, a town in Warwickshire, England, in 1564. His exact birthdate has not been established, but we do know that he was baptized on April 26, and that in 1564, children were baptized very soon after birth. As a result, Shakespeare's birthday is celebrated on April 23, which is also the feast of St. George, the patron saint of England, and the date of Shakespeare's death. His parents, Mary Arden and John, were important people in Stratford. Mary was the daughter of a large landholder, and John was a merchant who bought and sold leather goods and produce, and became, for a time, a holder of various civic offices, including high bailiff, a position roughly equivalent to mayor. Around 1576, John applied for the right to have a coat of arms, which also meant the right to be called a gentleman. John's petition was not granted at the time, perhaps because he did not have the financial resources to get it through the system. Around 1577, for reasons that are not entirely clear, John began to experience financial difficulty, and he eventually withdrew from public office. In 1596, however, Will renewed John's petition for the right to be called a gentleman, and this time the petition was granted. It is likely that Will succeeded where his father had not, because by 1596 he had made a name — and some fortune — for himself in the London theater. The applications of both John and Will show a desire for upward mobility that is evident also in John's office holding and in Will's later land purchases.

As a child, Will attended the King's New School in Stratford, one of the best country schools of its day. It employed well-trained teachers and took its students through a rigorous curriculum that focused first on the reading and writing of English, and then moved rather swiftly to the reading and writing of Greek and especially Latin. Among the classical authors Will would have studied at school are Virgil, Ovid, Horace, Plautus, Terence, and Seneca. Ben Jonson's remark that Shakespeare had "small Latin and less Greek" has often been quoted — and almost as often disputed, because the plays themselves suggest he was more learned than that (and because Jonson's own classical learning went far beyond that offered by the grammar school curriculum).

In November 1582, at the age of eighteen, Shakespeare married Anne Hathaway, a twenty-six-year-old woman from the nearby town of Shottery. Just six months later, in May of 1583, Anne gave birth to their first child, Susanna. There is considerable speculation but not much hard evidence about whether William and Anne were happily married, speculation fueled by their significant difference in age and our uncertainty about whether they got married only because of Anne's pregnancy. In Shakespeare's day, a formal engagement had the force of marriage, but we do not know whether William and Anne made a formal announcement of their betrothal. If they had, the date of Susanna's birth would not be cause for speculation about their marital happiness. William and Anne settled in Stratford and became parents again in February of 1585, this time to fraternal twins, Hamnet and Judith.

No records of Shakespeare's life between 1585 and 1592 have been found, leaving the field open to speculation about his activities. Some believe that he spent these years as a country schoolteacher, a theory that helps explain why his early works, such as *The Comedy of Errors* and *Titus Andronicus*, clearly show the influence of Roman literature. Others believe that he apprenticed himself to a butcher in Stratford until he ran away to London. One legend has it that Shakespeare was often caught stealing game from Sir Thomas Lucy, who punished him so severely (by whipping or imprisonment) that he eventually left Warwickshire for London.

Despite the gaps in the record of Shakespeare's life in Stratford from 1564 until about 1590, we can reach several conclusions about his first twenty-five years: He had the fundamentals of a classical education; the experience of living in a family that was first on the rise socially and financially and then on the decline; firsthand knowledge of older women, marriage, and parenthood; and, whatever his actual employment from 1585 to 1592, a direct understanding of middle-class country existence.

Exactly when and why Shakespeare left Stratford for London and the theater is not known, but once he began his career, his rise as both actor and playwright was swift. The first sign of his success is a written attack in Robert Greene's 1592 book *Greene's Groatsworth of Wit Bought with a Million of Repentance*. Greene calls him "an upstart crow" who "supposes he is as well able to bombast out a blank verse as the best of you, and . . . is in his own conceit the only Shake-scene in a country." In the decade from about 1590 to 1600, Shakespeare wrote most of his comedies (starting with *A Comedy of Errors* and ending with *All's Well That Ends Well*) and histories (starting with the three plays about *Henry VI* and ending with *Henry V*), and the first few tragedies (including *Romeo and Juliet* and *Julius Caesar*). During this period he also wrote the narrative poems *Venus and Adonis* and *The Rape of Lucrece* and most of his sequence of 154 sonnets. From 1594 to 1603, Shakespeare was a member of a dramatic company called the Lord Chamberlain's Men, participating as actor, playwright, and shareholder, a situation that allowed him, in a sense, to invest in his own success. The company first performed at a playhouse called the Theatre northeast of London, and then, after 1599, at the Globe on the south side of the Thames River. During this period, Shakespeare received greater acclaim as a playwright than as an actor, and he played his last known part in Ben Jonson's *Sejanus* in 1603. Once King James took the throne in 1603, the Lord Chamberlain's Men became the King's Men, and its most important members, including Shakespeare, were given the title Grooms of the Royal Chamber. By 1603, then, Shakespeare had risen to the very top of his profession.

From about 1600 to 1611, Shakespeare wrote the major tragedies (including *Hamlet, Othello, King Lear,* and *Macbeth*), a set of plays about classical figures (including *Timon of Athens, Antony and Cleopatra,* and *Coriolanus*), and the romances, ending with *The Tempest* in 1611. His last two dramatic works were *Henry VIII* (1613) and a collaboration with John Fletcher in 1613–14, *The Two Noble Kinsmen.*

Despite all that he was doing in London, Shakespeare continued to return to Stratford, to take care of his family, and to display his own version of his father's aspiration to gentility. In 1596, he endured the loss of his only son, Hamnet. That same year, as noted above, he successfully renewed his father's application for a coat of arms. In 1597, he bought one of the two largest houses in the town, an edifice called New Place, which remained the family home until the death of his last direct descendant, a granddaughter, in 1670. In the early 1600s, he began to purchase additional real estate in Stratford, buying a farm of 127 acres as well as a cottage and garden across from New Place in 1602. In 1605, he purchased tithes in Stratford and adjacent villages, an acquisition that entitled him to collect taxes from the villagers.

In 1608, Shakespeare's acting company entered into a long-term lease for the use of Blackfriars Theater, and his late plays were acted there, at the Globe, and at court. His romances (written between 1608 and 1611) were part of a vogue of such plays, but by the time he wrote *The Tempest,* he was withdrawing from active involvement in the company and in the London theater scene. After 1610, he spent more and more time in Stratford, and by 1612, he had given up his residence in London. His collaboration with Fletcher in *The Two Noble Kinsmen* can be seen as a significant transitional moment, because Fletcher succeeded Shakespeare as the principal playwright for the King's Men. Shakespeare's last years in Stratford were relatively uneventful, and he died on April 23, 1616.

As we hope you can see, there is nothing in this account of Will's life that is inconsistent with the view that he wrote the works we call Shakespeare's. But there is also nothing that unquestionably ties the life to the work or even allows us to say, "the seeds of the career were planted in experience X." Consequently, those who desire such connections continue to look for an author other than Will, and the current favored rival is, as we noted above, Edward de Vere, the seventeenth earl of Oxford (1550–1604). His supporters (called Oxfordians), like other anti-Stratfordians, point both to the lack of positive evidence in Will's life and to various kinds of circumstantial evidence in the life of their rival. For example, anti-Stratfordians note that there is no acknowledgment in Stratford of Will's achievements as a playwright — nothing mentioned in his will, on his tombstone, or in any town monument. The one contemporary monument, erected in the wall of the church, showed him not as a man of letters but as a grain dealer. They also claim that the learning and worldly experience required to produce the plays are both more than Will probably had, since, in their view, the playwright had to know French, Italian, Latin, and Greek and to have had some firsthand knowledge of life at court and life in European cities. In addition, they contend that Will's gradual withdrawal from London to Stratford after 1605 or so is unlikely for a man who was only forty-one years old, at the height of his powers, and the top of his profession.

De Vere's champions go on to argue that his education and experiences as a privileged nobleman, including travel to France and Italy, are more in keeping with the deep learning and broad scope of knowledge in the work. They also claim that the works are filled with allusions to people and events important in de Vere's life. For example, the narrative poems were dedicated to Henry Wriothesley, the third earl of Southampton, who has also been identified as the "youth" to whom many of the sonnets, including several urging him to marry, are addressed. Since de Vere's father-in-law, Lord Burghley, is known to have wanted Southampton to marry de Vere's daughter Elizabeth the Oxfordians argue that the sonnets urging the youth to marry show de Vere echoing his father-in-law's advice. The First Folio edition of the plays (1623) was dedicated to the earl of Pembroke and the earl of Montgomery, who were married to de Vere's other two daughters. *Hamlet,* argue the Oxfordians, is almost a dramatic *roman à clef* (literally, a novel with a key; more generally, a novel in which the characters are thinly disguised real people), with the protagonist being a figure of de Vere himself, and Ophelia and Polonius, figures of his wife, Anne Cecil, and Lord Burghley, whose nickname was Polus.

Furthermore, de Vere's champions maintain that he would need a screen for his literary production, because such production was seen as beneath a nobleman, and because de Vere, whose father-in-law was a special counselor to Queen Elizabeth, could not risk having his plays read as being critical of the court. According to the Oxfordians, de Vere chose Will Shakespeare as his screen because the name could be linked both to his family and to the theater: the de Vere family crest displayed a lion shaking a lance, and the goddess of the theater, Pallas Athena, was known as the "spear shaker."

As this summary suggests, the arguments for de Vere depend more on fancy footwork than on airtight reasoning. These arguments also have difficulty with recalcitrant evidence, such as the facts that de Vere died in 1604 and that internal allusions to contemporary events in some of the later plays indicate they were written after 1604. From our perspective, what is significant here is not that the Oxfordians have a compelling case, but that their position is the latest in a long line of anti-Stratfordian arguments and that anti-Stratfordian sentiment shows no signs of going away. The April 1999 issue of *Harper's Magazine* devotes twenty-five full pages to the debate, in which ten scholars, five "for Oxford" and five "for Shakespeare," argue their cases. Some Stratfordians have set up a Web site (www.clark.net/pub/tross/ws/will.html) called "The Shakespeare Authorship Page: Dedicated to the Proposition that Shakespeare Wrote Shakespeare." Such dedication would of course be unnecessary if the Stratfordians were comfortable regarding the Oxfordians (who have their own Web site at www.shakespeare-oxford.com/) and other anti-Stratfordians as harmless speculators.

The persistence of the debate suggests, first of all, that, despite some recent theoretical claims that the concept of the author is obsolete, most readers and critics do care about the connection between the life and the works of our important writers. Behind that caring — and behind the controversy over the authorship of Shakespeare's plays — is the assumption that the life and the works will be mutually illuminating. Perhaps what is most at stake in today's opposition between William Shakespeare and Edward de Vere is where to locate Shakespeare's social sympathies in the plays: was he a man of the middle class with aspirations toward gentility or an aristocrat?

Most important for our purposes in this edition, how we decide this question can have consequences for how we interpret his works. Nevertheless, the specific move from fact to interpretation is not automatic, since facts about the life may complicate rather than settle debates about the work; the plays themselves must be the ultimate source of evidence. As you will see, one of the major controversies about *The Tempest* is whether the audience should be sympathetic toward Caliban or should regard him, as Prospero does for the most part, as an almost subhuman monster. If we think that *The Tempest* was written by the seventeenth earl of Oxford, we may conclude that the aristocratic Prospero reliably expresses Shakespeare's attitude. On the other hand, if we emphasize de Vere's secret rather than his aristocratic status, we may suppose that by time he wrote *The Tempest*, de Vere was resentful of having to hide behind the identity of Shakespeare and that he occasionally gives voice to that resentment through Caliban. Similarly, if we think that *The Tempest* was written by William Shakespeare of Stratford, we may conclude that Shakespeare's experience of looking up at the aristocracy leads him to create an occasionally sympathetic Caliban. On the other hand, we may also argue that Shakespeare's aspiration toward gentility would lead him to want to distance himself from the Calibans of the world and, therefore, to side with Prospero.

At this point, you may be wondering whether the authorship question will ever be settled. Although we are reluctant to say it never will, we doubt that it will be settled soon. Shakespeare's identity as the greatest writer in the history of the English language makes him a central figure in our culture, and, thus, a figure whose identity matters. As our image of Shakespeare changes, so too does our image of our cultural tradition, and, thus, of ourselves. "We" of course are not all one and the same but rather plural and diverse, and so "we" will continue to argue with each other about who Shakespeare was — or even who he could have been. And, as you will see in the critical selections in this book, what goes for the writer also goes for the works. It is our hope that as you study some of the controversies about *The Tempest*, you will become more interested in the play itself, in the life behind it, and in questions about the connection between the two.

The Tempest

NAMES OF THE ACTORS

ALONSO, *King of Naples*
SEBASTIAN, *his brother*
PROSPERO, *the right Duke of Milan*
ANTONIO, *his brother, the usurping Duke of Milan*
FERDINAND, *son to the King of Naples*
GONZALO, *an honest old councillor*
ADRIAN *and* ⎱ *lords*
FRANCISCO, ⎰
CALIBAN, *a salvage° and deformed slave*
TRINCULO, *a jester*
STEPHANO, *a drunken butler*

MASTER *of a ship*
BOATSWAIN
MARINERS

MIRANDA, *daughter to Prospero*

ARIEL, *an airy spirit*
IRIS,
CERES,
JUNO, ⎱ [*presented by*] *spirits*
NYMPHS,
REAPERS, ⎰

[*Other Spirits attending on Prospero*]

SCENE: *An uninhabited island*

salvage: savage.

ACT 1, Scene 1°

A tempestuous noise of thunder and lightning heard. Enter a Ship-master and a Boatswain.

MASTER: Boatswain!
BOATSWAIN: Here, Master. What cheer?
MASTER: Good,° speak to the mariners. Fall to 't yarely,° or we
  run ourselves aground. Bestir, bestir!   *Exit.*

Enter Mariners.

BOATSWAIN: Heigh, my hearts! Cheerly, cheerly, my hearts!   5
  Yare, yare! Take in the topsail. Tend° to the Master's
  whistle. — Blow° till thou burst thy wind, if room enough!°

Enter Alonso, Sebastian, Antonio, Ferdinand, Gonzalo, and others.

ALONSO: Good Boatswain, have care. Where's the Master? Play
  the men.°
BOATSWAIN: I pray now, keep below.   10
ANTONIO: Where is the Master, Boatswain?
BOATSWAIN: Do you not hear him? You mar our labor. Keep°
  your cabins! You do assist the storm.
GONZALO: Nay, good,° be patient.
BOATSWAIN: When the sea is. Hence! What cares these roarers°   15
  for the name of king? To cabin! Silence! Trouble us not.
GONZALO: Good, yet remember whom thou hast aboard.
BOATSWAIN: None that I more love than myself. You are a councillor; if you can command these elements to silence and
  work the peace of the present,° we will not hand° a rope   20
  more. Use your authority. If you cannot, give thanks you
  have lived so long and make yourself ready in your cabin
  for the mischance of the hours, if it so hap° — Cheerly,
  good hearts! — Out of our way, I say.   *Exit.*
GONZALO: I have great comfort from this fellow. Methinks he   25
  hath no drowning mark upon him; his complexion is

1.1. Location: on board ship, off the island's coast.   **3. Good:** i.e., it's good you've
come, or, my good fellow.   **yarely:** nimbly.   **6. Tend:** attend.   **7. Blow:**
(Addressed to the wind.)   **if room enough:** as long as we have sea room enough.
8–9. Play the men: act like men (?) ply, urge the men to exert themselves (?).   **12. Keep:**
remain in.   **14. good:** good fellow.   **15. roarers:** waves or winds, or both; spoken
to as though they were "bullies" or "blusterers."   **20. work . . . present:** bring calm to
our present circumstances.   **hand:** handle.   **23. hap:** happen.

perfect gallows.° Stand fast, good Fate, to his hanging!
Make the rope of his destiny our cable, for our own doth
little advantage.° If he be not born to be hanged, our case
is miserable.°   *Exeunt [courtiers].*   30

Enter Boatswain.

BOATSWAIN: Down with the topmast! Yare! Lower, lower! Bring
her to try wi' the main course.° (*A cry within.*) A plague
upon this howling! They are louder than the weather or
our office.°

Enter Sebastian, Antonio, and Gonzalo.

Yet again? What do you here? Shall we give o'er° and   35
drown? Have you a mind to sink?
SEBASTIAN: A pox o' your throat, you bawling, blasphemous,
incharitable dog!
BOATSWAIN: Work you, then.
ANTONIO: Hang, cur! Hang, you whoreson, insolent noise-   40
maker! We are less afraid to be drowned than thou art.
GONZALO: I'll warrant him for drowning,° though the ship
were no stronger than a nutshell and as leaky as an
unstanched° wench.
BOATSWAIN: Lay her ahold, ahold!° Set her two courses.° Off to   45
sea again! Lay her off!

Enter Mariners, wet.

Mariners: All lost! To prayers, to prayers! All lost!
  [*The Mariners run about in confusion, exiting at random.*]
BOATSWAIN: What, must our mouths be cold?°
GONZALO: The King and Prince at prayers! Let's assist them,
  For our case is as theirs.
SEBASTIAN: I am out of patience.   50

26–27. complexion . . . gallows: appearance shows he was born to be hanged (and therefore, according to the proverb, in no danger of drowning).   **28–29. our . . . advantage:** our own cable is of little benefit.   **29–30. case is miserable:** circumstances are
desperate.   **31–32. Bring . . . course:** sail her close to the wind by means of the
mainsail.   **34. our office:** i.e., the noise we make at our work.   **35. give o'er:** give
up.   **42. warrant him for drowning:** guarantee that he will never be drowned.
44. unstanched: insatiable, loose, unrestrained (suggesting also "incontinent" and "men-
strual").   **45. ahold:** ahull, close to the wind.   **courses:** sails, i.e., foresail as well as
mainsail, set in an attempt to get the ship back out into open water.   **48. must . . .
cold:** i.e., must we drown in the cold sea, or, let us heat up our mouths with liquor.

ANTONIO: We are merely° cheated of our lives by drunkards.
This wide-chapped° rascal! Would thou mightst lie
    drowning
The washing of ten tides!°
GONZALO: He'll be hanged yet,
Though every drop of water swear against it
And gape at wid'st° to glut° him.
(*A confused noise within:*)   "Mercy on us!"—   55
"We split, we split!"° —"Farewell my wife and children!"—
"Farewell, brother!"—"We split, we split, we split!"
                              [*Exit Boatswain.*]
ANTONIO: Let's all sink wi' the King.
SEBASTIAN: Let's take leave of him.
                              Exit [*with Antonio*].
GONZALO: Now would I give a thousand furlongs of sea for   60
an acre of barren ground: long heath,° brown furze,° any-
thing. The wills above be done! But I would fain° die a dry
death.   *Exit.*

Scene 2°

Enter Prospero [*in his magic cloak*] *and Miranda.*

MIRANDA: If by your art,° my dearest father, you have
Put the wild waters in this roar, allay° them.
The sky, it seems, would pour down stinking pitch,
But that the sea, mounting to th' welkin's cheek,°
Dashes the fire out. O, I have suffered   5
With those that I saw suffer! A brave° vessel,
Who had, no doubt, some noble creature in her,
Dashed all to pieces. O, the cry did knock
Against my very heart! Poor souls, they perished.
Had I been any god of power, I would   10

---

51. **merely:** utterly.   52. **wide-chapped:** with mouth wide open.   52–53. **lie . . .
tides:** (Pirates were hanged on the shore and left until three tides had come in.)   55. **at
wid'st:** wide open.   **glut:** swallow.   56. **split:** break apart.   61. **heath:** heather.
furze: gorse, a weed growing on wasteland.   62. **fain:** rather.   1.2. **Location:** The
island, near Prospero's cell. On the Elizabethan stage, this cell is implicitly at hand
throughout the play, although in some scenes the convention of flexible distance allows us
to imagine characters in other parts of the island.   1. **art:** magic.   2. **allay:** pacify.
4. **welkin's cheek:** sky's face.   6. **brave:** gallant, splendid.

Have sunk the sea within the earth or ere°
It should the good ship so have swallowed and
The freighting° souls within her.
PROSPERO: Be collected.°
No more amazement.° Tell your piteous° heart
There's no harm done.
MIRANDA: O, woe the day!
PROSPERO: No harm.   15
I have done nothing but° in care of thee,
Of thee, my dear one, thee, my daughter, who
Art ignorant of what thou art, naught knowing
Of whence I am, nor that I am more better°
Than Prospero, master of a full° poor cell,   20
And thy no greater father.
MIRANDA: More to know
Did never meddle° with my thoughts.
PROSPERO: 'Tis time
I should inform thee farther. Lend thy hand
And pluck my magic garment from me. So,
                    [*laying down his magic cloak and staff*]
Lie there, my art. — Wipe thou thine eyes. Have comfort.   25
The direful spectacle of the wreck,° which touched
The very virtue° of compassion in thee,
I have with such provision° in mine art
So safely ordered that there is no soul —
No, not so much perdition° as an hair   30
Betid° to any creature in the vessel
Which° thou heard'st cry, which thou saw'st sink. Sit
      down,
For thou must now know farther.
MIRANDA [*sitting*]:   You have often
Begun to tell me what I am, but stopped
And left me to a bootless inquisition,°   35
Concluding, "Stay, not yet."
PROSPERO: The hour's now come;
The very minute bids thee ope thine ear.

---

11. or ere: before.   13. freighting: forming the cargo.   collected: calm, composed.
14. amazement: consternation.   piteous: pitying.   16. but: except.   19. more
better: of higher rank.   20. full: very.   22. meddle: mingle.   26. wreck: shipwreck.   27. virtue: essence.   28. provision: foresight.   30. perdition: loss.
31. Betid: happened.   32. Which: whom.   35. bootless inquisition: profitless
inquiry.

Obey, and be attentive. Canst thou remember
A time before we came unto this cell?
I do not think thou canst, for then thou wast not   40
Out° three years old.
MIRANDA: Certainly, sir, I can.
PROSPERO: By what? By any other house or person?
Of anything the image, tell me, that
Hath kept with thy remembrance.
MIRANDA: 'Tis far off,
And rather like a dream than an assurance   45
That my remembrance warrants.° Had I not
Four or five women once that tended me?
PROSPERO: Thou hadst, and more, Miranda. But how is it
That this lives in thy mind? What seest thou else
In the dark backward and abysm of time?°   50
If thou rememberest aught° ere thou cam'st here,
How thou cam'st here thou mayst.
MIRANDA: But that I do not.
PROSPERO: Twelve year since, Miranda, twelve year since,
Thy father was the Duke of Milan and
A prince of power.
MIRANDA: Sir, are not you my father?   55
PROSPERO: Thy mother was a piece° of virtue, and
She said thou wast my daughter; and thy father
Was Duke of Milan, and his only heir
And princess no worse issued.°
MIRANDA: O the heavens!
What foul play had we, that we came from thence?   60
Or blessèd was 't we did?
PROSPERO: Both, both, my girl.
By foul play, as thou sayst, were we heaved thence,
But blessedly holp° hither.
MIRANDA: O, my heart bleeds
To think o' the teen that I have turned you to,°
Which is from° my remembrance! Please you, farther.   65
PROSPERO: My brother and thy uncle, called Antonio —

---

41. Out: fully.   **45–46. assurance . . . warrants:** certainty that my memory guaran-
tees.   **50. backward . . . time:** abyss of the past.   **51. aught:** anything.   **56. piece:**
masterpiece, exemplar.   **59. no worse issued:** no less nobly born, descended.
63. holp: helped.   **64. teen . . . to:** trouble I've caused you to remember or put
you to.   **65. from:** out of.

I pray thee mark me — that a brother should
Be so perfidious! — he whom next° thyself
Of all the world I loved, and to him put
The manage° of my state, as at that time   70
Through all the seigniories° it was the first,
And Prospero the prime° duke, being so reputed
In dignity, and for the liberal arts
Without a parallel; those being all my study,
The government I cast upon my brother   75
And to my state grew stranger,° being transported°
And rapt in secret studies. Thy false uncle —
Dost thou attend me?
MIRANDA: Sir, most heedfully.
PROSPERO: Being once perfected° how to grant suits,
How to deny them, who t' advance and who   80
To trash° for overtopping,° new created
The creatures° that were mine, I say, or changed 'em,
Or else new formed 'em;° having both the key°
Of officer and office, set all hearts i' the state
To what tune pleased his ear, that° now he was   85
The ivy which had hid my princely trunk
And sucked my verdure° out on 't.° Thou attend'st not.
MIRANDA: O, good sir, I do.
PROSPERO: I pray thee, mark me.
I, thus neglecting worldly ends, all dedicated
To closeness° and the bettering of my mind   90
With that which, but by being so retired,
O'erprized all popular rate,° in my false brother
Awaked an evil nature; and my trust,
Like a good parent,° did beget of° him

---

68. next: next to.   **70. manage:** management, administration.   **71. seigniories:**
i.e., city-states of northern Italy.   **72. prime:** first in rank and importance.   **76. to . . .
stranger:** i.e., withdrew from my responsibilities as duke.   **transported:** carried away.
79. perfected: grown skillful.   **81. trash:** check a hound by tying a cord or weight to its
neck.   **overtopping:** running too far ahead of the pack; surmounting, exceeding one's
authority.   **82. creatures:** dependents.   **82–83. or changed . . . formed 'em:** i.e.,
either changed their loyalties and duties or else created new ones.   **83. key:** (1) key for
unlocking (2) tool for tuning stringed instruments.   **85. that:** so that.   **87. verdure:**
vitality.   **on 't:** of it.   **90. closeness:** retirement, seclusion.   **91–92. but . . . rate:**
i.e., were it not that its private nature caused me to neglect my public responsibilities, had
a value far beyond what public opinion could appreciate, or, simply because it was done in
such seclusion, had a value not appreciated by popular opinion.   **94. good parent:** (Alludes to the proverb that good parents often bear bad children; see also line 120.)   **of:** in.

A falsehood in its contrary as great   95
As my trust was, which had indeed no limit,
A confidence sans° bound. He being thus lorded°
Not only with what my revenue yielded
But what my power might else° exact, like one
Who, having into° truth by telling of it,   100
Made such a sinner of his memory
To° credit his own lie,° he did believe
He was indeed the Duke, out o'° the substitution
And executing th' outward face of royalty°
With all prerogative. Hence his ambition growing —   105
Dost thou hear?
MIRANDA: Your tale, sir, would cure deafness.
PROSPERO: To have no screen between this part he played
And him he played it for,° he needs will be°
Absolute Milan.° Me, poor man, my library
Was dukedom large enough. Of temporal royalties°   110
He thinks me now incapable; confederates° —
So dry° he was for sway° — wi' the King of Naples
To give him° annual tribute, do him homage,
Subject his coronet to his° crown, and bend°
The dukedom yet° unbowed — alas, poor Milan! —   115
To most ignoble stooping.
MIRANDA: O the heavens!
PROSPERO: Mark his condition° and th' event,° then tell me
If this might be a brother.
MIRANDA: I should sin
To think but° nobly of my grandmother.
Good wombs have borne bad sons.

97. sans: without.   **lorded:** raised to lordship, with power and wealth.   **99. else:** otherwise, additionally.   **100–02. Who . . . lie:** i.e., who, by repeatedly telling the lie (that he was indeed Duke of Milan), made his memory such a confirmed sinner against truth that he began to believe his own lie.   **100. into:** unto, against.   **102. To:** so as to.   **103. out o':** as a result of.   **104. And . . . royalty:** and (as a result of) his carrying out all the visible functions of royalty.   **107–08. To have . . . it for:** to have no separation or barrier between his role and himself. (Antonio wanted to act in his own person, not as substitute.)   **108. needs will be:** insisted on becoming.   **109. Absolute Milan:** unconditional Duke of Milan.   **110. temporal royalties:** practical prerogatives and responsibilities of a sovereign.   **111. confederates:** conspires, allies himself.   **112. dry:** thirsty.   **sway:** power.   **113. him:** i.e., the King of Naples.   **114. his . . . his:** Antonio's . . . the King of Naples'.   **bend:** make bow down.   **115. yet:** hitherto.   **117. condition:** pact.   **event:** outcome.   **119. but:** other than.

PROSPERO: Now the condition.   120
  This King of Naples, being an enemy
To me inveterate, hearkens° my brother's suit,
Which was that he,° in lieu o' the premises°
Of homage and I know not how much tribute,
Should presently extirpate° me and mine   125
Out of the dukedom and confer fair Milan,
With all the honors, on my brother. Whereon,
A treacherous army levied, one midnight
Fated to th' purpose did Antonio open
The gates of Milan, and, i' the dead of darkness,   130
The ministers for the purpose° hurried thence°
Me and thy crying self.
MIRANDA: Alack, for pity!
  I, not remembering how I cried out then,
Will cry it o'er again. It is a hint°
That wrings° mine eyes to 't.
PROSPERO: Hear a little further,   135
And then I'll bring thee to the present business
Which now's upon 's, without the which this story
Were most impertinent.°
MIRANDA: Wherefore° did they not
  That hour destroy us?
PROSPERO: Well demanded,° wench.°
  My tale provokes that question. Dear, they durst not,   140
So dear the love my people bore me, nor set
A mark so bloody° on the business, but
With colors fairer° painted their foul ends.
In few,° they hurried us aboard a bark,°
Bore us some leagues to sea, where they prepared   145
A rotten carcass of a butt,° not rigged,
Nor tackle,° sail, nor mast; the very rats

---

122. hearkens: listens to.   **123. he:** the King of Naples.   **in . . . premises:** in return for the stipulation.   **125. presently extirpate:** at once remove.   **131. ministers . . . purpose:** agents employed to do this.   **thence:** from there.   **134. hint:** occasion.   **135. wrings:** (1) constrains (2) wrings tears from.   **138. impertinent:** irrelevant.   **Wherefore:** why.   **139. demanded:** asked.   **wench:** (Here a term of endearment.)   **141–42. set . . . bloody:** i.e., make obvious their murderous intent. (From the practice of marking with the blood of the prey those who have participated in a successful hunt.)   **143. fairer:** apparently more attractive.   **144. few:** few words.   **bark:** ship.   **146. butt:** cask, tub.   **147. Nor tackle:** neither rigging.

Instinctively have quit° it. There they hoist us,
To cry to th' sea that roared to us, to sigh
To th' winds whose pity, sighing back again,   150
Did us but loving wrong.°
MIRANDA: Alack, what trouble
Was I then to you!
PROSPERO: O, a cherubin
Thou wast that did preserve me. Thou didst smile,
Infusèd with a fortitude from heaven,
When I have decked° the sea with drops full salt,   155
Under my burden groaned, which° raised in me
An undergoing stomach,° to bear up
Against what should ensue.
MIRANDA: How came we ashore?
PROSPERO: By Providence divine.
Some food we had, and some fresh water, that   160
A noble Neapolitan, Gonzalo,
Out of his charity, who being then appointed
Master of this design, did give us, with
Rich garments, linens, stuffs,° and necessaries,
Which since have steaded much.° So, of° his gentleness,   165
Knowing I loved my books, he furnished me
From mine own library with volumes that
I prize above my dukedom.
MIRANDA: Would° I might
But ever° see that man!
PROSPERO: Now I arise.
                        [*He puts on his magic cloak.*]
Sit still, and hear the last of our sea sorrow.°   170
Here in this island we arrived; and here
Have I, thy schoolmaster, made thee more profit°
Than other princess'° can, that have more time
For vainer° hours and tutors not so careful.

---

148. quit: abandoned.   **151. Did . . . wrong:** (i.e., the winds pitied Prospero and
Miranda, though of necessity they blew them from shore).   **155. decked:** covered
(with salt tears), adorned.   **156. which:** i.e., the smile.   **157. undergoing stomach:**
courage to go on.   **164. stuffs:** supplies.   **165. steaded much:** been of much use.
So, of: similarly, out of.   **168. Would:** I wish.   **169. But ever:** i.e., someday.
170. sea sorrow: sorrowful adventure at sea.   **172. more profit:** profit more.
173. princess': princesses. (Or the word may be *princes*, referring to royal children both
male and female.)   **174. vainer:** more foolishly spent.

MIRANDA: Heavens thank you for 't! And now, I pray you, sir —   175
    For still 'tis beating in my mind — your reason
    For raising this sea storm?
PROSPERO: Know thus far forth:
    By accident most strange, bountiful Fortune,
    Now my dear lady,° hath mine enemies
    Brought to this shore; and by my prescience   180
    I find my zenith° doth depend upon
    A most auspicious star, whose influence°
    If now I court not, but omit,° my fortunes
    Will ever after droop. Here cease more questions.
    Thou art inclined to sleep. 'Tis a good dullness,°   185
    And give it way.° I know thou canst not choose.
                                    [*Miranda sleeps.*]
    Come away,° servant, come! I am ready now.
    Approach, my Ariel, come.

Enter Ariel.

ARIEL: All hail, great master, grave sir, hail! I come
    To answer thy best pleasure; be 't to fly,   190
    To swim, to dive into the fire, to ride
    On the curled clouds, to thy strong bidding task°
    Ariel and all his quality.°
PROSPERO: Hast thou, spirit,
    Performed to point° the tempest that I bade thee?
ARIEL: To every article.   195
    I boarded the King's ship. Now on the beak,°
    Now in the waist,° the deck,° in every cabin,
    I flamed amazement.° Sometimes I'd divide
    And burn in many places; on the topmast,
    The yards, and bowsprit would I flame distinctly,°   200
    Then meet and join. Jove's lightning, the precursors

---

179. **my dear lady:** (Refers to Fortune, not Miranda.)   181. **zenith:** height of
fortune. (Astrological term.)   182. **influence:** astrological power.   183. **omit:**
ignore.   185. **dullness:** drowsiness.   186. **give it way:** let it happen (i.e., don't fight
it).   187. **Come away:** come.   192. **task:** make demands upon.   193. **quality:**
(1) fellow spirits (2) abilities.   194. **to point:** to the smallest detail.   196. **beak:**
prow.   197. **waist:** midships.   **deck:** poop deck at the stern.   198. **flamed amazement:** struck terror in the guise of fire, i.e., Saint Elmo's fire.   200. **distinctly:** in different places.

O' the dreadful thunderclaps, more momentary
And sight-outrunning° were not.° The fire and cracks
Of sulfurous roaring the most mighty Neptune°
Seem to besiege and make his bold waves tremble,   205
Yea, his dread trident shake.

PROSPERO: My brave spirit!
Who was so firm, so constant, that this coil°
Would not infect his reason?

ARIEL: Not a soul
But felt a fever of the mad° and played
Some tricks of desperation. All but mariners   210
Plunged in the foaming brine and quit the vessel,
Then all afire with me. The King's son, Ferdinand,
With hair up-staring° — then like reeds, not hair —
Was the first man that leapt; cried, "Hell is empty,
And all the devils are here!"

PROSPERO: Why, that's my spirit!   215
But was not this nigh shore?

ARIEL: Close by, my master.

PROSPERO: But are they, Ariel, safe?

ARIEL: Not a hair perished.
On their sustaining garments° not a blemish,
But fresher than before; and, as thou bad'st° me,
In troops° I have dispersed them, 'bout the isle.   220
The King's son have I landed by himself,
Whom I left cooling of° the air with sighs
In an odd angle° of the isle, and sitting,
His arms in this sad knot.°   [*He folds his arms.*]

PROSPERO: Of the King's ship,
The mariners, say how thou hast disposed,   225
And all the rest o' the fleet.

ARIEL: Safely in harbor
Is the King's ship; in the deep nook,° where once
Thou called'st me up at midnight to fetch dew°

---

203. sight-outrunning: swifter than sight.   **were not:** could not have been.
204. Neptune: Roman god of the sea.   **207. coil:** tumult.   **209. of the mad:**
i.e., such as madmen feel.   **213. up-staring:** standing on end.   **218. sustaining gar-**
ments: garments that buoyed them up in the sea.   **219. bad'st:** ordered.
220. troops: groups.   **222. cooling of:** cooling.   **223. angle:** corner.   **224. sad**
knot: (Folded arms are indicative of melancholy.)   **227. nook:** bay.   **228. dew:**
(Collected at midnight for magical purposes; compare with line 324.)

From the still-vexed Bermudas,° there she's hid;
The mariners all under hatches stowed,   230
Who, with a charm joined to their suffered labor,°
I have left asleep. And for the rest o' the fleet,
Which I dispersed, they all have met again
And are upon the Mediterranean float°
Bound sadly home for Naples,   235
Supposing that they saw the King's ship wrecked
And his great person perish.
PROSPERO: Ariel, thy charge
Exactly is performed. But there's more work.
What is the time o' the day?
ARIEL: Past the mid season.°
PROSPERO: At least two glasses.° The time twixt six and now   240
Must by us both be spent most preciously.
ARIEL: Is there more toil? Since thou dost give me pains,°
Let me remember° thee what thou hast promised,
Which is not yet performed me.
PROSPERO: How now? Moody?
What is 't thou canst demand?
ARIEL: My liberty.   245
PROSPERO: Before the time be out? No more!
ARIEL: I prithee,
Remember I have done thee worthy service,
Told thee no lies, made thee no mistakings, served
Without or grudge or grumblings. Thou did promise
To bate° me a full year.
PROSPERO: Dost thou forget   250
From what a torment I did free thee?
ARIEL: No.
PROSPERO: Thou dost, and think'st it much to tread the ooze
Of the salt deep,
To run upon the sharp wind of the north,

---

229. **still-vexed Bermudas:** ever stormy Bermudas. (Perhaps refers to the then recent Bermuda shipwreck. The Folio text reads "Bermoothes.") **231. with . . . labor:** by means of a spell added to all the labor they have undergone. **234. float:** sea. **239. mid season:** noon. **240. glasses:** hourglasses. **242. pains:** labors. **243. remember:** remind. **250. bate:** remit, deduct.

To do me° business in the veins° o' the earth   255
    When it is baked° with frost.
ARIEL: I do not, sir.
PROSPERO: Thou liest, malignant thing! Hast thou forgot
    The foul witch Sycorax, who with age and envy°
    Was grown into a hoop?° Hast thou forgot her?
ARIEL: No, sir.   260
PROSPERO: Thou hast. Where was she born? Speak. Tell me.
ARIEL: Sir, in Argier.°
PROSPERO: O, was she so? I must
    Once in a month recount what thou hast been,
    Which thou forgett'st. This damned witch Sycorax,
    For mischiefs manifold and sorceries terrible   265
    To enter human hearing, from Argier,
    Thou know'st, was banished. For one thing she did°
    They would not take her life. Is not this true?
ARIEL: Ay, sir.
PROSPERO: This blue-eyed° hag was hither brought with child°   270
    And here was left by the sailors. Thou, my slave,
    As thou report'st thyself, was then her servant;
    And, for° thou wast a spirit too delicate
    To act her earthy and abhorred commands,
    Refusing her grand hests,° she did confine thee,   275
    By help of her more potent ministers
    And in her most unmitigable rage,
    Into a cloven pine, within which rift
    Imprisoned thou didst painfully remain
    A dozen years; within which space she died   280
    And left thee there, where thou didst vent thy groans
    As fast as mill wheels strike.° Then was this island —
    Save° for the son that she did litter° here,

---

255. do me: do for me.   **veins:** veins of minerals, or, underground streams, thought
to be analogous to the veins of the human body.   **256. baked:** hardened.
258. envy: malice.   **259. grown into a hoop:** i.e., so bent over with age as to
resemble a hoop.   **262. Argier:** Algiers.   **267. one . . . did:** (Perhaps a reference to her pregnancy, for which her life would be spared.)   **270. blue-eyed:** with
dark circles under the eyes or with blue eyelids, implying pregnancy.   **with child:**
pregnant.   **273. for:** because.   **275. hests:** commands.   **282. as mill wheels
strike:** as the blades of a mill wheel strike the water.   **283. Save:** except.   **litter:**
give birth to.

A freckled whelp,° hag-born° — not honored with
A human shape.
ARIEL: Yes, Caliban her son.°   285
PROSPERO: Dull thing, I say so:° he, that Caliban
    Whom now I keep in service. Thou best know'st
    What torment I did find thee in. Thy groans
    Did make wolves howl, and penetrate the breasts
    Of ever-angry bears. It was a torment   290
    To lay upon the damned, which Sycorax
    Could not gain undo. It was mine art,
    When I arrived and heard thee, that made gape°
    The pine and let thee out.
ARIEL: I thank thee, master.
PROSPERO: If thou more murmur'st, I will rend an oak   295
    And peg thee in his° knotty entrails till
    Thou hast howled away twelve winters.
ARIEL: Pardon, master.
    I will be correspondent° to command
    And do my spriting° gently.°
PROSPERO: Do so, and after two days   300
    I will discharge thee.
ARIEL: That's my noble master!
    What shall I do? Say what? What shall I do?
PROSPERO: Go make thyself like a nymph o' the sea. Be subject
    To no sight but thine and mine, invisible
    To every eyeball else. Go take this shape   305
    And hither come in 't. Go, hence with diligence!
                                              Exit [*Ariel*].
    Awake, dear heart, awake! Thou hast slept well.
    Awake!
MIRANDA: The strangeness of your story put
    Heaviness° in me.
PROSPERO: Shake it off. Come on,   310
    We'll visit Caliban, my slave, who never
    Yields us kind answer.

---

284. whelp: offspring. (Used of animals.)   **hag-born:** born of a female demon.
285. Yes . . . son: (Ariel is probably concurring with Prospero's comment about a
"freckled whelp," not contradicting the point about a "human shape.")
286. Dull . . . so: i.e., exactly, that's what I said, you dullard.   **293. gape:** open wide.
296. his: its.   **298. correspondent:** responsive, submissive.   **299. spriting:** duties
as a spirit.   **gently:** willingly, ungrudgingly.   **310. Heaviness:** drowsiness.

MIRANDA: 'Tis a villain, sir,
   I do not love to look on.
PROSPERO: But, as 'tis,
   We cannot miss° him. He does make our fire,
   Fetch in our wood, and serves in offices°   315
   That profit us. — What ho! Slave! Caliban!
   Thou earth, thou! Speak.
CALIBAN (*within*):   There's wood enough within.
PROSPERO: Come forth, I say! There's other business for thee.
   Come, thou tortoise! When?°

Enter Ariel like a water nymph.

   Fine apparition! My quaint° Ariel,   320
   Hark in thine ear.   [*He whispers.*]
ARIEL: My lord, it shall be done.   *Exit.*
PROSPERO: Thou poisonous slave, got° by the devil himself
   Upon thy wicked dam,° come forth!

Enter Caliban.

CALIBAN: As wicked° dew as e'er my mother brushed
   With raven's feather from unwholesome fen°   325
   Drop on you both! A southwest° blow on ye
   And blister you all o'er!
PROSPERO: For this, be sure, tonight thou shalt have cramps,
   Side-stitches that shall pen thy breath up. Urchins°
   Shall forth at vast° of night that they may work   330
   All exercise on thee. Thou shalt be pinched
   As thick as honeycomb,° each pinch more stinging
   Than bees that made 'em.°
CALIBAN: I must eat my dinner.
   This island's mine, by Sycorax my mother,
   Which thou tak'st from me. When thou cam'st first,   335
   Thou strok'st me and made much of me, wouldst give me

314. miss: do without.   **315. offices:** functions, duties.   **319. When:** (An exclamation of impatience.)   **320. quaint:** ingenious.   **322. got:** begotten, sired.
323. dam: mother. (Used of animals.)   **324. wicked:** mischievous, harmful.
325. fen: marsh, bog.   **326. southwest:** i.e., wind thought to bring disease.
329. Urchins: hedgehogs; here, suggesting goblins in the guise of hedgehogs.
330. vast: lengthy, desolate time. (Malignant spirits were thought to be restricted to the hours of darkness.)   **332. As thick as honeycomb:** i.e., all over, with as many pinches as a honeycomb has cells.   **333. 'em:** i.e., the honeycomb.

Water with berries in 't, and teach me how
To name the bigger light, and how the less,°
That burn by day and night. And then I loved thee
And showed thee all the qualities o' th' isle,   340
The fresh springs, brine pits, barren place and fertile.
Cursed be I that did so! All the charms°
Of Sycorax, toads, beetles, bats, light on you!
For I am all the subjects that you have,
Which first was mine own king; and here you sty° me   345
In this hard rock, whiles you do keep from me
The rest o' th' island.
PROSPERO: Thou most lying slave,
Whom stripes° may move, not kindness! I have used thee,
Filth as thou art, with humane° care, and lodged thee
In mine own cell, till thou didst seek to violate   350
The honor of my child.
CALIBAN: O ho! O ho! Would 't had been done!
Thou didst prevent me; I had peopled else°
This isle with Calibans.
MIRANDA: Abhorrèd° slave,
Which any print° of goodness wilt not take,   355
Being capable of all ill! I pitied thee,
Took pains to make thee speak, taught thee each hour
One thing or other. When thou didst not, savage,
Know thine own meaning, but wouldst gabble like
A thing most brutish, I endowed thy purposes°   360
With words that made them known. But thy vile race,°
Though thou didst learn, had that in 't which good natures
Could not abide to be with; therefore wast thou
Deservedly confined into this rock,
Who hadst deserved more than a prison.   365
CALIBAN: You taught me language, and my profit on 't

---

338. the bigger . . . less: i.e., the sun and the moon (see Genesis 1:16: "God then
made two great lights: the greater light to rule the day, and the less light to rule the
night").   342. charms: spells.   345. sty: confine as in a sty.   348. stripes:
lashes.   349. humane: (Not distinguished as a word from *human*.)   353. peopled
else: otherwise populated.   354–65. Abhorrèd . . . prison: (Sometimes assigned by
editors to Prospero.)   355. print: imprint, impression.   360. purposes: meanings, desires.   361. race: natural disposition; species, nature.

Is I know how to curse. The red plague° rid° you
For learning° me your language!
PROSPERO: Hagseed,° hence!
Fetch us in fuel, and be quick, thou'rt best,°
To answer other business.° Shrugg'st thou, malice?   370
If thou neglect'st or dost unwillingly
What I command, I'll rack thee with old° cramps,
Fill all thy bones with aches,° make thee roar
That beasts shall tremble at thy din.
CALIBAN: No, pray thee.
[*Aside.*] I must obey. His art is of such power   375
It would control my dam's god, Setebos,°
And make a vassal of him.
PROSPERO: So, slave, hence!
                                        Exit Caliban.

Enter Ferdinand; and Ariel, invisible,° playing and singing.
[*Ferdinand does not see Prospero and Miranda.*]

                         Ariel's Song.
ARIEL: Come unto these yellow sands,
                 And then take hands;
              Curtsied when you have,° and kissed   380
                 The wild waves whist,°
              Foot it featly° here and there,
                 And, sweet sprites,° bear
              The burden.° Hark, hark!
                    Burden, dispersedly° [*within*]. Bow-wow.   385
              The watchdogs bark.
                    [*Burden, dispersedly within.*] Bow-wow.
              Hark, hark! I hear

367. **red plague:** plague characterized by red sores and evacuation of blood.
rid: destroy.   368. **learning:** teaching.   **Hagseed:** offspring of a female demon.
369. **thou'rt best:** you'd be well advised.   370. **answer other business:** perform
other tasks.   372. **old:** such as old people suffer, or, plenty of.   373. **aches:** (Pronounced "aitches.")   376. **Setebos:** (A god of the Patagonians, named in Robert
Eden's *History of Travel,* 1577.)   377. s.d. *Ariel, invisible:* (Ariel wears a garment
that by convention indicates he is invisible to the other characters.)
380. **Curtsied . . . have:** when you have curtsied.   380–81. **kissed . . . whist:**
kissed the waves into silence, or, kissed while the waves are being hushed.   382. **Foot
it featly:** dance nimbly.   383. **sprites:** spirits.   384. **burden:** refrain, undersong.
385. s.d. *dispersedly:* i.e., from all directions, not in unison.

The strain of strutting chanticleer
            Cry Cock-a-diddle-dow.   390
FERDINAND: Where should this music be? I' th' air or th' earth?
    It sounds no more; and sure it waits upon°
    Some god o' th' island. Sitting on a bank,°
    Weeping again the King my father's wreck,
    This music crept by me upon the waters,   395
    Allaying both their fury and my passion°
    With its sweet air. Thence° I have followed it,
    Or it hath drawn me rather. But 'tis gone.
    No, it begins again.
                        Ariel's Song.
ARIEL: Full fathom five thy father lies.   400
                Of his bones are coral made.
            Those are pearls that were his eyes.
                Nothing of him that doth fade
            But doth suffer a sea change
            Into something rich and strange.   405
            Sea nymphs hourly ring his knell.°
                        Burden [*within*]. Ding dong.
            Hark, now I hear them, ding dong bell.
FERDINAND: The ditty does remember° my drowned father.
    This is no mortal business, nor no sound   410
    That the earth owes.° I hear it now above me.
PROSPERO [*to Miranda*]: The fringèd curtains of thine eye
        advance°
    And say what thou seest yond.
MIRANDA: What is 't? A spirit?
    Lord, how it looks about! Believe me, sir,
    It carries a brave° form. But 'tis a spirit.   415
PROSPERO: No, wench, it eats and sleeps and hath such senses
    As we have, such. This gallant which thou seest
    Was in the wreck; and, but° he's something stained°
    With grief, that's beauty's canker,° thou mightst call him

---

392. **waits upon:** serves, attends.   393. **bank:** sandbank.   396. **passion:** grief.
397. **Thence:** i.e., from the bank on which I sat.   406. **knell:** announcement of a
death by the tolling of a bell.   409. **remember:** commemorate.   411. **owes:**
owns.   412. **advance:** raise.   415. **brave:** excellent.   418. **but:** except that.
something stained: somewhat disfigured.   419. **canker:** cankerworm (feeding on
buds and leaves).

A goodly person. He hath lost his fellows   420
And strays about to find 'em.
MIRANDA: I might call him
A thing divine, for nothing natural
I ever saw so noble.
PROSPERO [*aside*]:   It goes on,° I see,
As my soul prompts it. — Spirit, fine spirit, I'll free thee
Within two days for this.
FERDINAND [*seeing Miranda*]: Most sure, the goddess   425
On whom these airs° attend! — Vouchsafe° my prayer
May know° if you remain° upon this island,
And that you will some good instruction give
How I may bear me° here. My prime° request,
Which I do last pronounce, is — O you wonder!° —   430
If you be maid or no?°
MIRANDA: No wonder, sir,
But certainly a maid.
FERDINAND: My language? Heavens!
I am the best° of them that speak this speech,
Were I but where 'tis spoken.
PROSPERO [*coming forward*]:   How? The best?
What wert thou if the King of Naples heard thee?   435
FERDINAND: A single° thing, as I am now, that wonders
To hear thee speak of Naples.° He does hear me,°
And that he does I weep.° Myself am Naples,°
Who with mine eyes, never since at ebb,° beheld
The King my father wrecked.
MIRANDA: Alack, for mercy!   440
FERDINAND: Yes, faith, and all his lords, the Duke of Milan
And his brave son° being twain.
PROSPERO [*aside*]:   The Duke of Milan

---

423. It goes on: i.e., my plan works.   **426. airs:** songs.   **Vouchsafe:** grant.
427. May know: i.e., that I may know.   **remain:** dwell.   **429. bear me:** conduct
myself.   **prime:** chief.   **430. wonder:** (Miranda's name means "to be wondered
at.")   **431. maid or no:** i.e., a human maiden as opposed to a goddess or married
woman.   **433. best:** i.e., in birth.   **436. single:** (1) solitary, being at once King of
Naples and myself (2) feeble.   **437, 438. Naples:** the King of Naples.   **437. He
does hear me:** i.e., the King of Naples does hear my words, for I am King of Naples.
438. And . . . weep: i.e., and I weep at this reminder that my father is seemingly dead,
leaving me heir.   **439. at ebb:** i.e., dry, not weeping.   **442. son:** (The only reference in the play to a son of Antonio.)

And his more braver° daughter could control° thee,
If now 'twere fit to do 't. At the first sight
They have changed eyes.° — Delicate Ariel,   445
I'll set thee free for this. [*To Ferdinand.*] A word, good sir.
I fear you have done yourself some wrong.° A word!
MIRANDA [*aside*]: Why speaks my father so urgently? This
Is the third man that e'er I saw, the first
That e'er I sighed for. Pity move my father   450
To be inclined my way!
FERDINAND: O, if a virgin,
And your affection not gone forth, I'll make you
The Queen of Naples.
PROSPERO: Soft, sir! One word more.
[*Aside.*] They are both in either's° powers; but this swift
    business
I must uneasy° make, lest too light winning   455
Make the prize light.° [*To Ferdinand.*] One word more: I
    charge thee
That thou attend° me. Thou dost here usurp
The name thou ow'st° not, and hast put thyself
Upon this island as a spy, to win it
From me, the lord on 't.°
FERDINAND: No, as I am a man.   460
MIRANDA: There's nothing ill can dwell in such a temple.
If the ill spirit have so fair a house,
Good things will strive to dwell with 't.°
PROSPERO: Follow me. —
Speak not you for him; he's a traitor. — Come,
I'll manacle thy neck and feet together.   465
Seawater shalt thou drink; thy food shall be
The fresh-brook mussels, withered roots, and husks
Wherein the acorn cradled. Follow.
FERDINAND: No!
I will resist such entertainment° till
Mine enemy has more power.

---

443. more braver: more splendid. **control:** refute. **445. changed eyes:** exchanged amorous glances. **447. done . . . wrong:** i.e., spoken falsely. **454. both in either's:** each in the other's. **455. uneasy:** difficult. **455–56. light . . . light:** easy . . . cheap. **457. attend:** follow, obey. **458. ow'st:** ownest. **460. on 't:** of it. **463. strive . . . with 't:** i.e., expel the evil and occupy the *temple*, the body. **469. entertainment:** treatment.

He draws, and is charmed° from moving.

MIRANDA: O dear father,   470
Make not too rash° a trial of him, for
He's gentle,° and not fearful.°
PROSPERO: What, I say,
My foot° my tutor? — Put thy sword up, traitor,
Who mak'st a show but dar'st not strike, thy conscience
Is so possessed with guilt. Come, from thy ward,°   475
For I can here disarm thee with this stick
And make thy weapon drop.   [*He brandishes his staff.*]
MIRANDA [*trying to hinder him*]: Beseech you, father!
PROSPERO: Hence! Hang not on my garments.
MIRANDA: Sir, have pity!
I'll be his surety.°
PROSPERO: Silence! One word more
Shall make me chide thee, if not hate thee. What,   480
An advocate for an impostor? Hush!
Thou think'st there is no more such shapes as he,
Having seen but him and Caliban. Foolish wench,
To° the most of men this is a Caliban,
And they to him are angels.
MIRANDA: My affections   485
Are then most humble; I have no ambition
To see a goodlier man.
PROSPERO [*to Ferdinand*]: Come on, obey.
Thy nerves° are in their infancy again
And have no vigor in them.
FERDINAND: So they are.
My spirits,° as in a dream, are all bound up.   490
My father's loss, the weakness which I feel,
The wreck of all my friends, nor this man's threats
To whom I am subdued, are but light° to me,
Might I but through my prison once a day
Behold this maid. All corners else° o' th' earth   495

---

470 s.d. *charmed:* magically prevented.   **471. rash:** harsh.   **472. gentle:** well-born.   **fearful:** frightening, dangerous, or perhaps, cowardly.   **473. foot:** subordinate (Miranda, the foot, presumes to instruct Prospero, the head).   **475. ward:** defensive posture (in fencing).   **479. surety:** guarantee.   **484. To:** compared to.   **488. nerves:** sinews.   **490. spirits:** vital powers.   **493. light:** unimportant.   **495. corners else:** other corners, regions.

Let liberty make use of; space enough
Have I in such a prison.
PROSPERO [*aside*]:   It works. [*To Ferdinand.*] Come
    on. —
Thou hast done well, fine Ariel! [*To Ferdinand.*] Follow
    me.
[*To Ariel.*] Hark what thou else shalt do me.°
MIRANDA [*to Ferdinand*]:   Be of comfort.
My father's of a better nature, sir,   500
Than he appears by speech. This is unwonted°
Which now came from him.
PROSPERO [*to Ariel*]:   Thou shalt be as free
As mountain winds; but then° exactly do
All points of my command.
ARIEL: To th' syllable.
PROSPERO [*to Ferdinand*]: Come, follow. [*To Miranda.*] Speak   505
    not for him.

                                         Exeunt.

ACT 2, Scene 1°

*Enter Alonso, Sebastian, Antonio, Gonzalo, Adrian, Francisco,
and others.*

GONZALO [*to Alonso*]: Beseech you, sir, be merry. You have
    cause,
So have we all, of joy, for our escape
Is much beyond our loss. Our hint° of woe
Is common; every day some sailor's wife,
The masters of some merchant, and the merchant,°   5
Have just our theme of woe. But for the miracle,
I mean our preservation, few in millions
Can speak like us. Then wisely, good sir, weigh
Our sorrow with° our comfort.
ALONSO: Prithee, peace.

---

499. me: for me.   **501. unwonted:** unusual.   **503. then:** until then, or, if that is
to be so.   **2.1. Location:** Another part of the island.   **3. hint:** occasion.   **5. masters . . . the merchant:** officers of some merchant vessel and the merchant himself, the
owner.   **9. with:** against.

SEBASTIAN [*aside to Antonio*]: He receives comfort like cold   10
    porridge.°
ANTONIO [*aside to Sebastian*]: The visitor° will not give him
    o'er° so.
SEBASTIAN: Look, he's winding up the watch of his wit; by and
    by it will strike.   15
GONZALO [*to Alonso*]: Sir —
SEBASTIAN [*aside to Antonio*]: One. Tell.°
GONZALO: When every grief is entertained
    That's offered, comes to th' entertainer° —
SEBASTIAN: A dollar.°   20
GONZALO: Dolor comes to him, indeed. You have spoken truer
    than you purposed.
SEBASTIAN: You have taken it wiselier than I meant you should.
GONZALO [*to Alonso*]: Therefore, my lord —
ANTONIO: Fie, what a spendthrift is he of his tongue!   25
ALONSO [*to Gonzalo*]: I prithee, spare.°
GONZALO: Well, I have done. But yet —
SEBASTIAN [*aside to Antonio*]: He will be talking.
ANTONIO [*aside to Sebastian*]: Which, of he or Adrian, for a
    good wager, first begins to crow?°   30
SEBASTIAN: The old cock.°
ANTONIO: The cockerel.°
SEBASTIAN: Done. The wager?
ANTONIO: A laughter.°
SEBASTIAN: A match!°   35
ADRIAN: Though this island seem to be desert° —

---

11. porridge: (punningly suggested by *peace,* i.e., "peas" or "pease," a common ingre-
dient of porridge).   **12. visitor:** one taking nourishment and comfort to the sick, as
Gonzalo is doing.   **12–13. give him o'er:** abandon him.   **17. Tell:** keep count.
18–19. When . . . entertainer: when every sorrow that presents itself is accepted without resistance, there comes to the recipient.   **20. dollar:** widely circulated coin, the
German thaler and the Spanish piece of eight. (Sebastian puns on *entertainer* in the sense
of innkeeper; to Gonzalo, *dollar* suggests "dolor," grief.)   **26. spare:** forbear, cease.
29–30. Which . . . crow: which of the two, Gonzalo or Adrian, do you bet will speak
(crow) first?   **31. old cock:** i.e., Gonzalo.   **32. cockerel:** i.e., Adrian.
34. laughter: (1) burst of laughter (2) sitting of eggs. (When Adrian, the *cockerel,* begins
to speak two lines later, Sebastian loses the bet. The Folio speech prefixes in lines 37–38
are here reversed so that Antonio enjoys his laugh as the prize for winning, as in the
proverb "He who laughs last laughs best" or "He laughs that wins." The Folio assignment can work in the theater, however, if Sebastian pays for losing with a sardonic laugh
of concession.)   **35. A match:** a bargain; agreed.   **36. desert:** uninhabited.

ANTONIO: Ha, ha, ha!

SEBASTIAN: So, you're paid.°

ADRIAN: Uninhabitable and almost inaccessible —

SEBASTIAN: Yet —   40

ADRIAN: Yet —

ANTONIO: He could not miss 't.°

ADRIAN: It must needs be° of subtle, tender, and delicate temperance.°

ANTONIO: Temperance° was a delicate° wench.   45

SEBASTIAN: Ay, and a subtle,° as he most learnedly delivered.°

ADRIAN: The air breathes upon us here most sweetly.

SEBASTIAN: As if it had lungs, and rotten ones.

ANTONIO: Or as 'twere perfumed by a fen.

GONZALO: Here is everything advantageous to life.   50

ANTONIO: True, save° means to live.

SEBASTIAN: Of that there's none, or little.

GONZALO: How lush and lusty° the grass looks! How green!

ANTONIO: The ground indeed is tawny.°

SEBASTIAN: With an eye° of green in 't.   55

ANTONIO: He misses not much.

SEBASTIAN: No. He doth but° mistake the truth totally.

GONZALO: But the rarity of it is — which is indeed almost beyond credit —

SEBASTIAN: As many vouched rarities° are.   60

GONZALO: That our garments, being, as they were, drenched in the sea, hold notwithstanding their freshness and glosses, being rather new-dyed than stained with salt water.

ANTONIO: If but one of his pockets° could speak, would it not say he lies?   65

---

38. you're paid: i.e., you've had your laugh.   **42. miss 't:** (1) avoid saying "Yet" (2) miss the island.   **43. must needs be:** has to be.   **44. temperance:** mildness of climate.   **45. Temperance:** a girl's name.   **delicate:** (Here it means "given to pleasure, voluptuous"; in line 43, "pleasant." Antonio is evidently suggesting that *tender, and delicate temperance* sounds like a Puritan phrase, which Antonio then mocks by applying the words to a woman rather than an island. He began this bawdy comparison with a double entendre on *inaccessible,* line 39.)   **46. subtle:** (Here it means "tricky, sexually crafty"; in line 43, "delicate.")   **delivered:** uttered. (Sebastian joins Antonio in baiting the Puritans with his use of the pious cant phrase *learnedly delivered.*) **51. save:** except.   **53. lusty:** healthy.   **54. tawny:** dull brown, yellowish. **55. eye:** tinge, or spot (perhaps with reference to Gonzalo's eye or judgment). **57. but:** merely.   **60. vouched rarities:** allegedly real though strange sights. **64. pockets:** i.e., because they are muddy.

SEBASTIAN: Ay, or very falsely pocket up° his report.°

GONZALO: Methinks our garments are now as fresh as when we
    put them on first in Afric, at the marriage of the King's fair
    daughter Claribel to the King of Tunis.

SEBASTIAN: 'Twas a sweet marriage, and we prosper well in our   70
    return.

ADRIAN: Tunis was never graced before with such a paragon to°
    their queen.

GONZALO: Not since widow Dido's° time.

ANTONIO [*aside to Sebastian*]: Widow? A pox o' that! How   75
    came that "widow" in? Widow Dido!

SEBASTIAN: What if he had said "widower Aeneas" too? Good
    Lord, how you take° it!

ADRIAN [*to Gonzalo*]: "Widow Dido" said you? You make me
    study of° that. She was of Carthage, not of Tunis.   80

GONZALO: This Tunis, sir, was Carthage.

ADRIAN: Carthage?

GONZALO: I assure you, Carthage.

ANTONIO: His word is more than the miraculous harp.°

SEBASTIAN: He hath raised the wall, and houses too.   85

ANTONIO: What impossible matter will he make easy next?

SEBASTIAN: I think he will carry this island home in his pocket
    and give it his son for an apple.

ANTONIO: And, sowing the kernels° of it in the sea, bring forth
    more islands.   90

GONZALO: Ay.°

ANTONIO: Why, in good time.°

GONZALO [*to Alonso*]: Sir, we were talking° that our garments

---

66. pocket up: i.e., conceal, suppress; often used in the sense of "receive unprotestingly,
fail to respond to a challenge."   **his report:** (Sebastian's jest is that the evidence of
Gonzalo's soggy and sea-stained pockets would confute Gonzalo's speech and his reputation for truth telling.)   **72. to:** for.   **74. widow Dido's:** queen of Carthage,
deserted by Aeneas. (She was, in fact, a widow when Aeneas, a widower, met her, but
Antonio may be amused at Gonzalo's prudish use of the term "widow" to describe a
woman deserted by her lover.)   **78. take:** understand, respond to, interpret.
80. study of: think about.   **84. miraculous harp:** (Alludes to Amphion's harp, with
which he raised the walls of Thebes; Gonzalo has exceeded that deed by recreating
ancient Carthage — *wall and houses* — mistakenly on the site of modern-day Tunis.
Some Renaissance commentators believed, like Gonzalo, that the two sites were near
each other.)   **89. kernels:** seeds.   **91. Ay:** (Gonzalo may be reasserting his point
about Carthage, or he may be responding ironically to Antonio, who, in turn, answers
sarcastically.)   **92. in good time:** (An expression of ironical acquiescence or amazement, i.e., "sure, right away.")   **93. talking:** saying.

seem now as fresh as when we were at Tunis at the marriage
of your daughter, who is now queen.   95
ANTONIO: And the rarest° that e'er came there.
SEBASTIAN: Bate,° I beseech you, widow Dido.
ANTONIO: O, widow Dido! Ay, widow Dido.
GONZALO: Is not, sir, my doublet° as fresh as the first day I wore
it? I mean, in a sort.°   100
ANTONIO: That "sort"° was well fished for.
GONZALO: When I wore it at your daughter's marriage.
ALONSO: You cram these words into mine ears against
    The stomach of my sense.° Would I had never
    Married° my daughter there! For, coming thence,   105
    My son is lost and, in my rate,° she too,
    Who is so far from Italy removed
    I ne'er again shall see her. O thou mine heir
    Of Naples and of Milan, what strange fish
    Hath made his meal on thee?
FRANCISCO: Sir, he may live.   110
    I saw him beat the surges° under him
    And ride upon their backs. He trod the water,
    Whose enmity he flung aside, and breasted
    The surge most swoll'n that met him. His bold head
    'Bove the contentious waves he kept, and oared   115
    Himself with his good arms in lusty° stroke
    To th' shore, that o'er his° wave-worn basis bowed,°
    As° stooping to relieve him. I not doubt
    He came alive to land.
ALONSO: No, no, he's gone.
SEBASTIAN [*to Alonso*]: Sir, you may thank yourself for this great
    loss,   120
    That° would not bless our Europe with your daughter,
    But rather° loose° her to an African,

---

96. rarest: most remarkable, beautiful.   **97. Bate:** abate, except, leave out. (Sebastian
says sardonically, surely you should allow widow Dido to be an exception.)   **99. dou-
blet:** close-fitting jacket.   **100. in a sort:** in a way.   **101. "sort":** (Antonio plays
on the idea of drawing lots and on "fishing" for something to say.)   **104. The stomach . . . sense:** my appetite for hearing them.   **105. Married:** given in marriage.
106. rate: estimation, opinion.   **111. surges:** waves.   **116. lusty:** vigorous.
117. his: its.   **that . . . bowed:** i.e., that projected out over the base of the cliff that
had been eroded by the surf, thus seeming to bend down toward the sea.   **118. As:** as
if.   **121. That:** you who.   **122. rather:** would rather.   **loose:** (1) release, let
loose (2) lose.

Where she at least is banished from your eye,°
Who hath cause to wet the grief on 't.°

ALONSO: Prithee, peace.

SEBASTIAN: You were kneeled to and importuned° otherwise   125
    By all of us, and the fair soul herself
    Weighed between loathness and obedience at
    Which end o' the beam should bow.° We have lost your
        son,
    I fear, forever. Milan and Naples have
    More widows in them of this business' making°   130
    Than we bring men to comfort them.
    The fault's your own.

ALONSO: So is the dear'st° o' the loss.

GONZALO: My lord Sebastian,
    The truth you speak doth lack some gentleness
    And time° to speak it in. You rub the sore   135
    When you should bring the plaster.°

SEBASTIAN: Very well.

ANTONIO: And most chirurgeonly.°

GONZALO [to Alonso]: It is foul weather in us all, good sir,
    When you are cloudy.

SEBASTIAN [to Antonio]:   Fowl° weather?

ANTONIO [to Sebastian]:   Very foul.

GONZALO: Had I plantation° of this isle, my lord —   140

ANTONIO [to Sebastian]: He'd sow 't with nettle seed.

SEBASTIAN: Or docks,
    or mallows.°

GONZALO: And were the king on 't, what would I do?

---

123. is banished from your eye: is not constantly before your eye to serve as a reproachful reminder of what you have done.   **124. Who . . . on 't:** i.e., your eye, which has good reason to weep because of this, or, Claribel, who has good reason to weep for it.   **125. importuned:** urged, implored.   **126–28. the fair . . . bow:** Claribel herself was poised uncertainly between unwillingness to marry and obedience to her father as to which end of the scales should sink, which should prevail.   **130. of . . . making:** on account of this marriage and subsequent shipwreck.   **132. dear'st:** heaviest, most costly.   **135. time:** appropriate time.   **136. plaster:** (A medical application.)   **137. chirurgeonly:** like a skilled surgeon. (Antonio mocks Gonzalo's medical analogy of a *plaster* applied curatively to a wound.)   **139. Fowl:** (with a pun on *foul,* returning to the imagery of lines 29–34.)   **140. plantation:** colonization (with subsequent wordplay on the literal meaning, "planting").   **141. docks, or mallows:** (Weeds used as antidotes for nettle stings.)

SEBASTIAN: Scape° being drunk for want° of wine.
GONZALO: I' the commonwealth I would by contraries°
 Execute all things; for no kind of traffic,°   145
 Would I admit; no name of magistrate,
 Letters° should not be known; riches, poverty,
 And use of service,° none; contract, succession,°
 Bourn, bound of land, tilth,° vineyard, none;
 No use of metal, corn,° or wine, or oil;   150
 No occupation; all men idle, all,
 And women too, but innocent and pure;
 No sovereignty —
SEBASTIAN: Yet he would be king on 't.
ANTONIO: The latter end of his commonwealth forgets the
 beginning.   155
GONZALO: All things in common nature should produce
 Without sweat or endeavor. Treason, felony,
 Sword, pike,° knife, gun, or need of any engine°
 Would I not have; but nature should bring forth,
 Of its own kind, all foison,° all abundance,   160
 To feed my innocent people.
SEBASTIAN: No marrying 'mong his subjects?
ANTONIO: None, man, all idle — whores and knaves.
GONZALO: I would with such perfection govern, sir,
 T' excel the Golden Age.°
SEBASTIAN: 'Save° His Majesty!   165
ANTONIO: Long live Gonzalo!
GONZALO: And — do you mark me, sir?
ALONSO: Prithee, no more. Thou dost talk nothing to me.
GONZALO: I do well believe Your Highness, and did it to minister
 occasion° to these gentlemen, who are of such sensible° and
 nimble lungs that they always use° to laugh at nothing.   170
ANTONIO: 'Twas you we laughed at.

---

143. Scape: escape. want: lack. (Sebastian jokes sarcastically that this hypothetical
ruler would be saved from dissipation only by the barrenness of the island.) 144. by
contraries: by what is directly opposite to usual custom. 145. traffic: trade.
147. Letters: learning. 148. use of service: custom of employing servants. succession: holding of property by right of inheritance. 149. Bourn . . . tilth: boundaries, property limits, tillage of soil. 150. corn: grain. 158. pike: lance.
engine: instrument of warfare. 160. foison: plenty. 165. the Golden Age: the
age, according to Hesiod, when Cronus, or Saturn, ruled the world; an age of innocence
and abundance. 'Save: God save. 168–69. minister occasion: furnish opportunity. 169. sensible: sensitive. 170. use: are accustomed.

GONZALO: Who in this kind of merry fooling am nothing to
    you; so you may continue, and laugh at nothing still.
ANTONIO: What a blow was there given!
SEBASTIAN: An° it had not fallen flat-long.°   175
GONZALO: You are gentlemen of brave mettle;° you would lift
    the moon out of her sphere° if she would continue in it five
    weeks without changing.

Enter Ariel [invisible] playing solemn music.

SEBASTIAN: We would so, and then go a-batfowling.°
ANTONIO: Nay, good my lord, be not angry.   180
GONZALO: No, I warrant you, I will not adventure my
    discretion so weakly.° Will you laugh me asleep? For I am
    very heavy.°
ANTONIO: Go sleep, and hear us.°
        [*All sleep except Alonso, Sebastian, and Antonio.*]
ALONSO: What, all so soon asleep? I wish mine eyes   185
    Would, with themselves, shut up my thoughts.° I find
    They are inclined to do so.
SEBASTIAN: Please you, sir,
    Do not omit° the heavy° offer of it.
    It seldom visits sorrow; when it doth,
    It is a comforter.
ANTONIO: We two, my lord,   190
    Will guard your person while you take your rest,
    And watch your safety.
ALONSO: Thank you. Wondrous heavy.
           [*Alonso sleeps. Exit Ariel.*]
SEBASTIAN: What a strange drowsiness possesses them!
ANTONIO: It is the quality o' the climate.
SEBASTIAN: Why

---

175. An: if.   **flat-long:** with the flat of the sword, i.e., ineffectually. (Compare with
"fallen flat.")   **176. mettle:** temperament, courage. (The sense of *metal,* indistinguishable as a form from *mettle,* continues the metaphor of the sword.)   **177. sphere:**
orbit. (Literally, one of the concentric zones occupied by planets in Ptolemaic astron-
omy.)   **179. a-batfowling:** hunting birds at night with lantern and *bat,* or "stick";
also, gulling a simpleton. (Gonzalo is the simpleton, or fowl, and Sebastian will use the
moon as his lantern.)   **181–82. adventure . . . weakly:** risk my reputation for discre-
tion for so trivial a cause (by getting angry at these sarcastic fellows).   **183. heavy:**
sleepy.   **184. Go . . . us:** i.e., get ready for sleep, and we'll do our part by laughing.
186. Would . . . thoughts: would shut off my melancholy brooding when they close
themselves in sleep.   **188. omit:** neglect.   **heavy:** drowsy.

Doth it not then our eyelids sink? I find not   195
Myself disposed to sleep.
ANTONIO: Nor I. My spirits are nimble.
They° fell together all, as by consent;°
They dropped, as by a thunderstroke. What might,
Worthy Sebastian, O, what might — ? No more.
And yet methinks I see it in thy face,   200
What thou shouldst be. Th' occasion speaks thee,° and
My strong imagination sees a crown
Dropping upon thy head.
SEBASTIAN: What, art thou waking?
ANTONIO: Do you not hear me speak?
SEBASTIAN: I do, and surely
It is a sleepy° language, and thou speak'st   205
Out of thy sleep. What is it thou didst say?
This is a strange repose, to be asleep
With eyes wide open — standing, speaking, moving —
And yet so fast asleep.
ANTONIO: Noble Sebastian,
Thou lett'st thy fortune sleep — die, rather; wink'st°   210
Whiles thou art waking.
SEBASTIAN: Thou dost snore distinctly;°
There's meaning in thy snores.
ANTONIO: I am more serious than my custom. You
Must be so too if heed° me, which to do
Trebles thee o'er.°
SEBASTIAN: Well, I am standing water.°   215
ANTONIO: I'll teach you how to flow.
SEBASTIAN: Do so. To ebb°
Hereditary sloth° instructs me.
ANTONIO: O,
If you but knew how you the purpose cherish
Whiles thus you mock it!° How, in stripping it,

---

197. They: the sleepers.   **consent:** common agreement.   **201. occasion speaks
thee:** opportunity of the moment calls upon you, i.e., proclaims you usurper of Alonso's
crown.   **205. sleepy:** dreamlike, fantastic.   **210. wink'st:** (you) shut your eyes.
211. distinctly: articulately.   **214. if heed:** if you heed.   **215. Trebles thee o'er:**
makes you three times as great and rich.   **standing water:** water that neither ebbs nor
flows, at a standstill.   **216. ebb:** recede, decline.   **217. Hereditary sloth:** natural
laziness and the position of younger brother, one who cannot inherit.   **218–19. If . . .
mock it:** if you only knew how much you really enhance the value of ambition even
while your words mock your purpose.

You more invest° it!° Ebbing men, indeed,   220
Most often do so near the bottom° run
By their own fear or sloth.
SEBASTIAN: Prithee, say on.
The setting° of thine eye and cheek proclaim
A matter° from thee, and a birth indeed
Which throes° thee much to yield.°
ANTONIO: Thus, sir: 225
Although this lord° of weak remembrance,° this
Who shall be of as little memory
When he is earthed,° hath here almost persuaded —
For he's a spirit of persuasion, only
Professes to persuade° — the King his son's alive,   230
'Tis as impossible that he's undrowned
As he that sleeps here swims.
SEBASTIAN: I have no hope
That he's undrowned.
ANTONIO: O, out of that "no hope"
What great hope have you! No hope that way° is
Another way so high a hope that even   235
Ambition cannot pierce a wink° beyond,
But doubt discovery there.° Will you grant with me
That Ferdinand is drowned?
SEBASTIAN: He's gone.
ANTONIO: Then tell me,
Who's the next heir of Naples?
SEBASTIAN: Claribel.
ANTONIO: She that is Queen of Tunis; she that dwells   240
Ten leagues beyond man's life;° she that from Naples

219–20. How . . . invest it: i.e., how the more you speak flippantly of ambition, the more you, in effect, affirm it.   **220. invest:** clothe. (Antonio's paradox is that, by skeptically stripping away illusions, Sebastian can see the essence of a situation and the opportunity it presents or that, by disclaiming and deriding his purpose, Sebastian shows how valuable it really is.)   **221. the bottom:** i.e., on which unadventurous men may go aground and miss the tide of fortune.   **223. setting:** set expression (of earnestness).   **224. matter:** matter of importance.   **225. throes:** causes pain, as in giving birth.   **yield:** give forth, speak about.   **226. this lord:** i.e., Gonzalo.   **remembrance:** (1) power of remembering (2) being remembered after his death.   **228. earthed:** buried.   **229–30. only . . . persuade:** whose whole function (as a privy councillor) is to persuade.   **234. that way:** i.e., in regard to Ferdinand's being saved.   **236. wink:** glimpse.   **236–37. Ambition . . . there:** ambition itself cannot see any further than that hope (of the crown), is unsure of finding anything to achieve beyond it or even there.   **241. Ten . . . life:** i.e., further than the journey of a lifetime.

Can have no note,° unless the sun were post° —
The Man i' the Moon's too slow — till newborn chins
Be rough and razorable;° she that from° whom
We all were sea-swallowed, though some cast° again,   245
And by that destiny to perform an act
Whereof what's past is prologue, what to come
In yours and my discharge.°

SEBASTIAN: What stuff is this? How say you?
  'Tis true my brother's daughter's Queen of Tunis,   250
  So is she heir of Naples, twixt which regions
  There is some space.

ANTONIO: A space whose every cubit°
  Seems to cry out, "How shall that Claribel
  Measure us° back to Naples? Keep° in Tunis,
  And let Sebastian wake."° Say this were death   255
  That now hath seized them, why, they were no worse
  Than now they are. There be° that can rule Naples
  As well as he that sleeps, lords that can prate°
  As amply and unnecessarily
  As this Gonzalo. I myself could make   260
  A chough of as deep chat.° O, that you bore
  The mind that I do! What a sleep were this
  For your advancement! Do you understand me?

SEBASTIAN: Methinks I do.

ANTONIO: And how does your content°
  Tender° your own good fortune?

SEBASTIAN: I remember   265
  You did supplant your brother Prospero.

ANTONIO: True.
  And look how well my garments sit upon me,
  Much feater° than before. My brother's servants
  Were then my fellows. Now they are my men.

---

242. **note:** news, intimation.   **post:** messenger.   **244. razorable:** ready for shav-
ing.   **from:** on our voyage from.   **245. cast:** were disgorged (with a pun on *casting*
of parts for a play).   **248. discharge:** performance.   **252. cubit:** ancient measure of
length of about twenty inches.   **254. Measure us:** i.e., traverse the cubits, find her
way.   **Keep:** stay (addressed to Claribel).   **255. wake:** i.e., to his good fortune.
257. There be: there are those.   **258. prate:** speak foolishly.   **260–61. I . . .
chat:** I could teach a jackdaw to talk as wisely, or, be such a garrulous talker myself.
264. content: desire, inclination.   **265. Tender:** regard, look after.   **268. feater:**
more becomingly, fittingly.

SEBASTIAN: But, for your conscience?   270
ANTONIO: Ay, sir, where lies that? If 'twere a kibe,°
    'Twould put me to° my slipper; but I feel not
    This deity in my bosom. Twenty consciences
    That stand twixt me and Milan,° candied° be they°
    And melt ere they molest!° Here lies your brother,   275
    No better than the earth he lies upon,
    If he were that which now he's like — that's dead,
    Whom I, with this obedient steel, three inches of it,
    Can lay to bed forever; whiles you, doing thus,°
    To the perpetual wink° for aye° might put   280
    This ancient morsel, this Sir Prudence, who
    Should not° upbraid our course. For all the rest,
    They'll take suggestion° as a cat laps milk;
    They'll tell the clock° to any business that
    We say befits the hour.
SEBASTIAN: Thy case, dear friend,   285
    Shall be my precedent. As thou gott'st Milan,
    I'll come by Naples. Draw thy sword. One stroke
    Shall free thee from the tribute° which thou payest,
    And I the king shall love thee.
ANTONIO: Draw together;
    And when I rear my hand, do you the like   290
    To fall it° on Gonzalo.   *[They draw.]*
SEBASTIAN: O, but one word.
                              [They talk apart.]

Enter Ariel [invisible], with music and song.

ARIEL [*to Gonzalo*]: My master through his art foresees the
      danger
    That you, his friend, are in, and sends me forth —
    For else his project dies — to keep them living.
                    Sings in Gonzalo's ear.

---

271. **kibe:** chilblain, here a sore on the heel.   272. **put me to:** oblige me to wear. 274. **Milan:** the dukedom of Milan.   **candied:** frozen, congealed in crystalline form.   **be they:** may they be.   275. **molest:** interfere.   279. **thus:** similarly. (The actor makes a stabbing gesture.)   280. **wink:** sleep, closing of eyes.   **aye:** ever.   282. **Should not:** would not then be able to.   283. **take suggestion:** respond to prompting.   284. **tell the clock:** i.e., agree, answer appropriately, chime. 288. **tribute:** (see 1.2.113–24).   291. **fall it:** let it fall.

While you here do snoring lie,   295
Open-eyed conspiracy
    His time° doth take.
If of life you keep a care,
Shake off slumber, and beware.
    Awake, awake!   300

ANTONIO: Then let us both be sudden.°

GONZALO [*waking*]: Now, good angels preserve the King!
                                [*The others wake.*]

ALONSO: Why, how now, ho, awake? Why are you drawn?
    Wherefore this ghastly looking?

GONZALO: What's the matter?

SEBASTIAN: Whiles we stood here securing° your repose,   305
    Even now, we heard a hollow burst of bellowing
    Like bulls, or rather lions. Did 't not wake you?
    It struck mine ear most terribly.

ALONSO: I heard nothing.

ANTONIO: O, 'twas a din to fright a monster's ear,
    To make an earthquake! Sure it was the roar   310
    Of a whole herd of lions.

ALONSO: Heard you this, Gonzalo?

GONZALO: Upon mine honor, sir, I heard a humming,
    And that a strange one too, which did awake me.
    I shaked you, sir, and cried.° As mine eyes opened,
    I saw their weapons drawn. There was a noise,   315
    That's verily.° 'Tis best we stand upon our guard,
    Or that we quit this place. Let's draw our weapons.

ALONSO: Lead off this ground, and let's make further search
    For my poor son.

GONZALO: Heavens keep him from these beasts!
    For he is, sure, i' th' island.

ALONSO: Lead away.   320

ARIEL [*aside*]: Prospero my lord shall know what I have done.
    So, King, go safely on to seek thy son.
                                Exeunt [*separately*].

---

297. **time:** opportunity.   301. **sudden:** quick.   305. **securing:** standing guard
over.   314. **cried:** called out.   316. **verily:** true.

Scene 2°

Enter Caliban with a burden of wood. A noise of thunder heard.

CALIBAN: All the infections that the sun sucks up
From bogs, fens, flats,° on Prosper fall, and make him
By inchmeal° a disease! His spirits hear me,
And yet I needs must° curse. But they'll nor° pinch,
Fright me with urchin shows,° pitch me i' the mire,   5
Nor lead me, like a firebrand,° in the dark
Out of my way, unless he bid 'em. But
For every trifle are they set upon me,
Sometimes like apes, that mow° and chatter at me
And after bite me; then like hedgehogs, which   10
Lie tumbling in my barefoot way and mount
Their pricks at my footfall. Sometimes am I
All wound with° adders, who with cloven tongues
Do hiss me into madness.

Enter Trinculo.

                         Lo, now, lo!
Here comes a spirit of his, and to torment me   15
For bringing wood in slowly. I'll fall flat.
Perchance he will not mind° me.   [*He lies down.*]
TRINCULO: Here's neither bush nor shrub to bear off° any
weather at all. And another storm brewing; I hear it sing i'
the wind. Yond same black cloud, yond huge one, looks   20
like a foul bombard° that would shed his° liquor. If it
should thunder as it did before, I know not where to hide
my head. Yond same cloud cannot choose but fall by pail-
fuls. [*Seeing Caliban.*] What have we here, a man or a fish?
Dead or alive? A fish, he smells like a fish; a very ancient   25
and fishlike smell; a kind of not-of-the-newest Poor John.°
A strange fish! Were I in England now, as once I was, and

2.2. Location: Another part of the island.   **2. flats:** swamps.   **3. By inchmeal:**
inch by inch.   **4. needs must:** have to.   **nor:** neither.   **5. urchin shows:** elvish
apparitions shaped like hedgehogs.   **6. like a firebrand:** they in the guise of a will-o'-
the-wisp.   **9. mow:** make faces.   **13. wound with:** entwined by.   **17. mind:**
notice.   **18. bear off:** keep off.   **21. foul bombard:** dirty leather jug.   **his:** its.
26. Poor John: salted fish, type of poor fare.

had but this fish painted,° not a holiday fool there but
would give a piece of silver. There would this monster
make a man.° Any strange beast there makes a man. When   30
they will not give a doit° to relieve a lame beggar, they will
lay out ten to see a dead Indian. Legged like a man, and his
fins like arms! Warm, o' my troth!° I do now let loose my
opinion, hold it° no longer: this is no fish, but an islander,
that hath lately suffered° by a thunderbolt. [*Thunder.*]   35
Alas, the storm is come again! My best way is to creep
under his gaberdine.° There is no other shelter hereabout.
Misery acquaints a man with strange bedfellows. I will here
shroud° till the dregs° of the storm be past.
                    [*He creeps under Caliban's garment.*]

Enter Stephano, singing, [a bottle in his hand].

STEPHANO: "I shall no more to sea, to sea,   40
            Here shall I die ashore —"
This is a very scurvy tune to sing at a man's funeral. Well,
here's my comfort.   *Drinks.*
(*Sings.*)
            "The master, the swabber,° the boatswain, and I,
                The gunner and his mate,   45
            Loved Mall, Meg, and Marian, and Margery,
                But none of us cared for Kate.
                    For she had a tongue with a tang,°
                    Would cry to a sailor, 'Go hang!'
            She loved not the savor of tar nor of pitch,   50
            Yet a tailor might scratch her where'er she did itch.°
                Then to sea, boys, and let her go hang!"
This is a scurvy tune too. But here's my comfort.
                                                     Drinks.
CALIBAN: Do not torment me!° O!

---

28. painted: i.e., painted on a sign set up outside a booth or tent at a fair.   **30. make
a man:** (1) make one's fortune (2) be indistinguishable from an Englishman.
31. doit: small coin.   **33. o' my troth:** by my faith.   **34. hold it:** hold it in.
35.   suffered: i.e., died.   **37.   gaberdine:** cloak,   loose   upper   garment.
39. shroud: take shelter.   **dregs:** i.e., last remains (as in a *bombard* or jug, line 21).
44. swabber: crew member whose job is to wash the decks.   **48. tang:** sting.
51. tailor . . . itch: (A dig at tailors for their supposed effeminacy and a bawdy suggestion of satisfying a sexual craving.)   **54. Do . . . me:** (Caliban assumes that one of
Prospero's spirits has come to punish him.)

STEPHANO: What's the matter?° Have we devils here? Do you   55
  put tricks upon 's° with savages and men of Ind,° ha? I have
  not scaped drowning to be afeard now of your four legs.
  For it hath been said, "As proper° a man as ever went on
  four legs° cannot make him give ground"; and it shall be
  said so again while Stephano breathes at'° nostrils.   60
CALIBAN: This spirit torments me! O!
STEPHANO: This is some monster of the isle with four legs, who
  hath got, as I take it, an ague.° Where the devil should he
  learn° our language? I will give him some relief, if it be but
  for that.° If I can recover° him and keep him tame and get   65
  to Naples with him, he's a present for any emperor that
  ever trod on neat's leather.°
CALIBAN: Do not torment me, prithee. I'll bring my wood
  home faster.
STEPHANO: He's in his fit now and does not talk after the   70
  wisest.° He shall taste of my bottle. If he have never drunk
  wine afore,° it will go near to° remove his fit. If I can
  recover° him and keep him tame, I will not take too much°
  for him. He shall pay for him that hath° him,° and that
  soundly.   75
CALIBAN: Thou dost me yet but little hurt; thou wilt anon,° I
  know it by thy trembling. Now Prosper works upon thee.
STEPHANO: Come on your ways. Open your mouth. Here is that
  which will give language to you, cat. Open your mouth.°
  This will shake your shaking, I can tell you, and that   80
  soundly. [*Giving Caliban a drink.*] You cannot tell who's
  your friend. Open your chaps° again.
TRINCULO: I should know that voice. It should be — but he is
  drowned, and these are devils. O, defend me!

55. What's the matter?: what's going on here?   **56. put tricks upon 's:** trick us
with conjuring shows.   **Ind:** India.   **58. proper:** handsome.   **59. four legs:**
(The conventional phrase would supply *two legs*, but the creature Stephano thinks he sees
has four.)   **60. at':** at the.   **63. ague:** fever. (Probably both Caliban and Trinculo
are quaking; see lines 54 and 77.)   **63–64. should he learn:** could he have learned.
65. for that: i.e., for knowing our language.   **recover:** restore.   **67. neat's
leather:** cowhide.   **70–71. after the wisest:** in the wisest fashion.   **72. afore:**
before.   **go near to:** be in a fair way to.   **73. recover:** restore.   **I will . . . much:**
i.e., no sum can be too much.   **74. hath:** possesses, receives.   **He shall . . . hath
him:** i.e., anyone who wants him will have to pay dearly for him.   **76. anon:**
presently.   **78–79. Here . . . mouth:** (Allusion to the proverb "Good liquor will
make a cat speak.")   **82. chaps:** jaws.

STEPHANO: Four legs and two voices — a most delicate°   85
   monster! His forward voice now is to speak well of his
   friend; his backward voice° is to utter foul speeches and to
   detract. If all the wine in my bottle will recover him,° I will
   help° his ague. Come. [*Giving a drink.*] Amen! I will pour
   some in thy other mouth.   90
TRINCULO: Stephano!
STEPHANO: Doth thy other mouth call me?° Mercy, mercy! This
   is a devil, and no monster. I will leave him. I have no long
   spoon.°
TRINCULO: Stephano! If thou beest Stephano, touch me and   95
   speak to me, for I am Trinculo — be not afeard — thy
   good friend Trinculo.
STEPHANO: If thou beest Trinculo, come forth. I'll pull thee by
   the lesser legs. If any be Trinculo's legs, these are they.
   [*Pulling him out.*] Thou art very Trinculo indeed! How   100
   cam'st thou to be the siege° of this mooncalf?° Can he
   vent° Trinculos?
TRINCULO: I took him to be killed with a thunderstroke. But art
   thou not drowned, Stephano? I hope now thou art not
   drowned. Is the storm overblown?° I hid me under the   105
   dead mooncalf's gaberdine for fear of the storm. And art
   thou living, Stephano? O Stephano, two Neapolitans
   scaped!   [*He capers with Stephano.*]
STEPHANO: Prithee, do not turn me about. My stomach is not
   constant.°   110
CALIBAN: These be fine things, an if° they be not spirits.
   That's a brave° god, and bears° celestial liquor.
   I will kneel to him.
STEPHANO: How didst thou scape? How cam'st thou hither?
   Swear by this bottle how thou cam'st hither. I escaped   115
   upon a butt of sack° which the sailors heaved o'erboard —

---

85. delicate: ingenious.   **87. backward voice:** (Trinculo and Caliban are facing in
opposite directions. Stephano supposes the monster to have a rear end that can emit *foul
speeches* or foul-smelling wind at the monster's *other mouth,* line 90.)   **88. If . . . him:**
even if it takes all the wine in my bottle to cure him.   **89. help:** cure.   **92. call me:**
i.e., call me by name, know supernaturally who I am.   **93–94. long spoon:** (Allusion to
the proverb "He that sups with the devil has need of a long spoon.")   **101. siege:** excrement.   **mooncalf:** monstrous or misshapen creature (whose deformity is caused by the
malignant influence of the moon).   **102. vent:** excrete, defecate.   **105. overblown:**
blown over.   **109–10. not constant:** unsteady.   **111. an if:** if.   **112. brave:** fine,
magnificent.   **bears:** he carries.   **116. butt of sack:** barrel of Canary wine.

by this bottle,° which I made of the bark of a tree with
mine own hands since° I was cast ashore.

CALIBAN [*kneeling*]: I'll swear upon that bottle to be thy true
    subject, for the liquor is not earthly.   120

STEPHANO: Here. Swear then how thou escapedst.

TRINCULO: Swum ashore, man, like a duck. I can swim like a
    duck, I'll be sworn.

STEPHANO: Here, kiss the book.° Though thou canst swim like a
    duck, thou art made like a goose.   125

                       [*Giving him a drink.*]

TRINCULO: O Stephano, hast any more of this?

STEPHANO: The whole butt, man. My cellar is in a rock by the
    seaside, where my wine is hid. — How now, mooncalf?
    How does thine ague?

CALIBAN: Hast thou not dropped from heaven?   130

STEPHANO: Out o' the moon, I do assure thee. I was the Man i'
    the Moon when time was.°

CALIBAN: I have seen thee in her, and I do adore thee.
    My mistress showed me thee, and thy dog, and thy bush.°

STEPHANO: Come, swear to that. Kiss the book. I will furnish it   135
    anon with new contents. Swear.

                       [*Giving him a drink.*]

TRINCULO: By this good light,° this is a very shallow monster! I
    afeard of him? A very weak monster! The Man i' the
    Moon? A most poor credulous monster! Well drawn,°
    monster, in good sooth!°   140

CALIBAN [*to Stephano*]: I'll show thee every fertile inch o' th'
    island,
    And I will kiss thy foot. I prithee, be my god.

TRINCULO: By this light, a most perfidious and drunken
    monster! When 's god's asleep, he'll rob his bottle.°

CALIBAN: I'll kiss thy foot. I'll swear myself thy subject.   145

STEPHANO: Come on then. Down, and swear.

                       [*Caliban kneels.*]

---

117. by this bottle: i.e., I swear by this bottle.   **118. since:** after.   **124. book:**
i.e., bottle (but with ironic reference to the practice of kissing the Bible in swearing
an oath; see *I'll be sworn* in line 123).   **132. when time was:** once upon a time.
134. dog . . . bush: (The Man in the Moon was popularly imagined to have with him a
dog and a bush of thorn.)   **137. By . . . light:** by God's light, by this good light from
heaven.   **139. Well drawn:** well pulled (on the bottle).   **140. in good sooth:**
truly, indeed.   **144. When . . . bottle:** i.e., Caliban wouldn't even stop at robbing his
god of his bottle if he could catch him asleep.

TRINCULO: I shall laugh myself to death at this puppy-headed
    monster. A most scurvy monster! I could find in my heart
    to beat him —

STEPHANO: Come, kiss.   150

TRINCULO: But that the poor monster's in drink.° An abominable
    monster!

CALIBAN: I'll show thee the best springs. I'll pluck thee berries.
    I'll fish for thee and get thee wood enough.
    A plague upon the tyrant that I serve!   155
    I'll bear him no more sticks, but follow thee,
    Thou wondrous man.

TRINCULO: A most ridiculous monster, to make a wonder of a
    poor drunkard!

CALIBAN: I prithee, let me bring thee where crabs° grow,   160
    And I with my long nails will dig thee pignuts,°
    Show thee a jay's nest, and instruct thee how
    To snare the nimble marmoset.° I'll bring thee
    To clustering filberts, and sometimes I'll get thee
    Young scamels° from the rock. Wilt thou go with me?   165

STEPHANO: I prithee now, lead the way without any more
    talking. — Trinculo, the King and all our company else°
    being drowned, we will inherit° here. — Here, bear my
    bottle. — Fellow Trinculo, we'll fill him by and by again.

CALIBAN (*sings drunkenly*): Farewell, master, farewell, farewell!   170

TRINCULO: A howling monster; a drunken monster!

CALIBAN: No more dams I'll make for fish,
        Nor fetch in firing°
        At requiring,
        Nor scrape trenchering,° nor wash dish.   175
        'Ban, 'Ban, Ca–Caliban
        Has a new master. Get a new man!°
    Freedom, high-day!° High-day, freedom! Freedom, high-
    day, freedom!

STEPHANO: O brave monster! Lead the way.   *Exeunt.*   180

---

151. in drink: drunk.   **160. crabs:** crab apples, or perhaps crabs.   **161. pignuts:**
earthnuts, edible tuberous roots.   **163. marmoset:** small monkey.   **165. scamels:**
(Possibly *seamews,* mentioned in Strachey's letter, or shellfish, or perhaps from *squamelle,*
"furnished with little scales." Contemporary French and Italian travel accounts report
that the natives of Patagonia in South America ate small fish described as *fort scameux* and
squame.)   **167. else:** in addition, besides ourselves.   **168. inherit:** take possession.
173. firing: firewood.   **175. trenchering:** trenchers, wooden plates.   **177. Get a
new man:** (Addressed to Prospero.)   **178. high-day:** holiday.

ACT 3, Scene 1°

Enter Ferdinand, bearing a log.

FERDINAND: There be some sports are painful, and their labor
    Delight in them sets off.° Some kinds of baseness°
    Are nobly undergone,° and most poor° matters
    Point to rich ends. This my mean° task
    Would be as heavy to me as odious, but°   5
    The mistress which I serve quickens° what's dead
    And makes my labors pleasures. O, she is
    Ten times more gentle than her father's crabbed,
    And he's composed of harshness. I must remove
    Some thousands of these logs and pile them up,   10
    Upon a sore injunction.° My sweet mistress
    Weeps when she sees me work and says such baseness
    Had never like executor.° I forget;°
    But these sweet thoughts do even refresh my labors,
    Most busy lest when I do it.°

Enter Miranda; and Prospero [at a distance, unseen].

MIRANDA: Alas now, pray you,   15
    Work not so hard. I would the lightning had
    Burnt up those logs that you are enjoined° to pile!
    Pray, set it down and rest you. When this° burns,
    'Twill weep° for having wearied you. My father
    Is hard at study. Pray now, rest yourself.   20
    He's safe for these° three hours.
FERDINAND: O most dear mistress,
    The sun will set before I shall discharge°
    What I must strive to do.

3.1. Location: Before Prospero's cell.   **1–2: There . . . sets off:** some pastimes
are laborious, but the pleasure we get from them compensates for the effort. (Pleasure
is *set off* by labor as a jewel is set off by its foil.)   **2. baseness:** menial activity.
3. undergone: undertaken.   **most poor:** poorest.   **4. mean:** lowly.   **5. but:**
were it not that.   **6. quickens:** gives life to.   **11. sore injunction:** severe command.
13. Had . . . executor: i.e., was never before undertaken by so noble a being.   **I forget:**
i.e., I forget that I'm supposed to be working, or, I forget my happiness, oppressed by
my labor.   **15. Most . . . it:** i.e., busy at my labor but with my mind on other things (?)
(the line may be in need of emendation).   **17. enjoined:** commanded.   **18. this:** i.e.,
the log.   **19. weep:** i.e., exude resin.   **21. these:** the next.   **22. discharge:**
complete.

MIRANDA: If you'll sit down,
  I'll bear your logs the while. Pray, give me that.
  I'll carry it to the pile.
FERDINAND: No, precious creature,   25
  I had rather crack my sinews, break my back,
  Than you should such dishonor undergo
  While I sit lazy by.
MIRANDA: It would become me
  As well as it does you; and I should do it
  With much more ease, for my good will is to it,   30
  And yours it is against.
PROSPERO [*aside*]:   Poor worm, thou art infected!
  This visitation° shows it.
MIRANDA: You look wearily.
FERDINAND: No, noble mistress, 'tis fresh morning with me
  When you are by° at night. I do beseech you —
  Chiefly that I might set it in my prayers —   35
  What is your name?
MIRANDA: Miranda. — O my father,
  I have broke your hest° to say so.
FERDINAND: Admired Miranda!°
  Indeed the top of admiration, worth
  What's dearest° to the world! Full many a lady
  I have eyed with best regard,° and many a time   40
  The harmony of their tongues hath into bondage
  Brought my too diligent° ear. For several° virtues
  Have I liked several women, never any
  With so full soul but some defect in her
  Did quarrel with the noblest grace she owed°   45
  And put it to the foil.° But you, O you,
  So perfect and so peerless, are created
  Of° every creature's best!
MIRANDA: I do not know

---

32. visitation: (1) Miranda's visit to Ferdinand (2) visitation of the plague, i.e., infection
of love.   **34. by:** nearby.   **37. hest:** command.   **Admired Miranda:** (Her name
means "to be admired or wondered at.")   **39. dearest:** most treasured.   **40. best
regard:** thoughtful and approving attention.   **42. diligent:** attentive.   **several:**
various (also on line 43).   **45. owed:** owned.   **46. put . . . foil:** (1) overthrew it (as
in wrestling) (2) served as a *foil,* or "contrast," to set it off.   **48. Of:** out of.

One of my sex; no woman's face remember,
Save, from my glass, mine own. Nor have I seen   50
More that I may call men than you, good friend,
And my dear father. How features are abroad°
I am skilless° of; but, by my modesty,°
The jewel in my dower, I would not wish
Any companion in the world but you;   55
Nor can imagination form a shape,
Besides yourself, to like of.° But I prattle
Something° too wildly, and my father's precepts
I therein do forget.

FERDINAND: I am in my condition°
A prince, Miranda; I do think, a king —   60
I would,° not so! — and would no more endure
This wooden slavery° than to suffer
The flesh-fly° blow° my mouth. Hear my soul speak:
The very instant that I saw you did
My heart fly to your service, there resides   65
To make me slave to it, and for your sake
Am I this patient log-man.

MIRANDA: Do you love me?

FERDINAND: O heaven, O earth, bear witness to this sound,
And crown what I profess with kind event°
If I speak true! If hollowly,° invert°   70
What best is boded° me to mischief!° I
Beyond all limit of what° else i' the world
Do love, prize, honor you.

MIRANDA [*weeping*]:   I am a fool
To weep at what I am glad of.

PROSPERO [*aside*]:   Fair encounter
Of two most rare affections! Heavens rain grace   75
On that which breeds between 'em!

FERDINAND: Wherefore weep you?

---

52. How . . . abroad: what people look like in other places.   **53. skilless:** ignorant.
modesty: virginity.   **57. like of:** be pleased with, be fond of.   **58. Something:**
somewhat.   **59. condition:** rank.   **61. would:** wish (it were).   **62. wooden
slavery:** being compelled to carry wood.   **63. flesh-fly:** insect that deposits its eggs
in dead flesh.   **blow:** befoul with fly eggs.   **69. kind event:** favorable outcome.
70. hollowly: insincerely, falsely.   **invert:** turn.   **71. boded:** in store for.
mischief: harm.   **72. what:** whatever.

MIRANDA: At mine unworthiness, that dare not offer
  What I desire to give, and much less take
  What I shall die° to want.° But this is trifling,
  And all the more it seeks to hide itself   80
  The bigger bulk it shows. Hence, bashful cunning,°
  And prompt me, plain and holy innocence!
  I am your wife, if you will marry me;
  If not, I'll die your maid.° To be your fellow°
  You may deny me, but I'll be your servant   85
  Whether you will° or no.
FERDINAND: My mistress,° dearest,
  And I thus humble ever.
MIRANDA: My husband, then?
FERDINAND: Ay, with a heart as willing°
  As bondage e'er of freedom. Here's my hand.
MIRANDA [clasping his hand]: And mine, with my heart in 't.
  And now farewell   90
  Till half an hour hence.
FERDINAND: A thousand thousand!°
                  Exeunt [Ferdinand and Miranda, separately].
PROSPERO: So glad of this as they I cannot be,
  Who are surprised with all;° but my rejoicing
  At nothing can be more. I'll to my book,
  For yet ere suppertime must I perform   95
  Much business appertaining.°   Exit.

Scene 2°

Enter Caliban, Stephano, and Trinculo.

STEPHANO: Tell not me. When the butt is out,° we will drink
  water, not a drop before. Therefore bear up and board
  'em.° Servant monster, drink to me.

---

79. die: (Probably with an unconscious sexual meaning that underlies all of lines 77–81.)
to want: through lacking.   **81. bashful cunning:** coyness.   **84. maid:** hand-
maiden, servant.   **fellow:** mate, equal.   **86. will:** desire it.   **My mistress:** i.e., the
woman I adore and serve (not an illicit sexual partner).   **88. willing:** desirous.   **91. A
thousand thousand:** i.e., a thousand thousand farewells.   **93. with all:** by everything
that has happened, or, *withal,* "with it."   **96. appertaining:** related to this.   **3.2.
Location:** Another part of the island.   **1. out:** empty.   **2–3. bear . . . 'em:**
(Stephano uses the terminology of maneuvering at sea and boarding a vessel under attack as
a way of urging an assault on the liquor supply.)

TRINCULO: Servant monster? The folly of° this island! They say
    there's but five upon this isle. We are three of them; if th'   5
    other two be brained° like us, the state totters.

STEPHANO: Drink, servant monster, when I bid thee. Thy eyes
    are almost set° in thy head.   [*Giving a drink.*]

TRINCULO: Where should they be set° else? He were a brave°
    monster indeed if they were set in his tail.   10

STEPHANO: My man-monster hath drowned his tongue in sack.
    For my part, the sea cannot drown me. I swam, ere I could
    recover° the shore, five and thirty leagues° off and on.° By
    this light,° thou shalt be my lieutenant, monster, or my
    standard.°   15

TRINCULO: Your lieutenant, if you list;° he's no standard.°

STEPHANO: We'll not run,° Monsieur Monster.

TRINCULO: Nor go° neither, but you'll lie° like dogs and yet say
    nothing neither.

STEPHANO: Mooncalf, speak once in thy life, if thou beest a   20
    good mooncalf.

CALIBAN: How does thy honor? Let me lick thy shoe.
    I'll not serve him. He is not valiant.

TRINCULO: Thou liest, most ignorant monster, I am in case to
    jostle a constable.° Why, thou debauched° fish, thou, was   25
    there ever man a coward that hath drunk so much sack° as I
    today? Wilt thou tell a monstrous lie, being but half a fish
    and half a monster?

CALIBAN: Lo, how he mocks me! Wilt thou let him, my lord?

TRINCULO: "Lord," quoth he? That a monster should be such a   30
    natural!°

CALIBAN: Lo, lo, again! Bite him to death, I prithee.

STEPHANO: Trinculo, keep a good tongue in your head. If you

---

4. folly of: i.e., stupidity found on.   **6. be brained:** are endowed with intelligence.
8. set: fixed in a drunken stare, or, sunk, like the sun.   **9. set:** placed.   **brave:** fine,
splendid.   **13. recover:** gain, reach.   **leagues:** units of distance, each equaling
about three miles.   **off and on:** intermittently.   **13–14. By this light:** (An oath:
by the light of the sun.)   **15. standard:** standard-bearer, ensign (as distinguished from
lieutenant, lines 14 and 16).   **16. list:** prefer.   **no standard:** i.e., not able to stand
up.   **17. run:** (1) retreat (2) urinate (taking Trinculo's *standard,* line 16, in the old
sense of "conduit").   **18. go:** walk.   **lie:** (1) tell lies, (2) lie prostrate, (3) excrete.
24–25. in case ... constable: i.e., in fit condition, made valiant by drink, to taunt or
challenge the police.   **25. debauched:** (1) seduced away from proper service and
allegiance (2) depraved.   **26. sack:** Spanish white wine.   **31. natural:** (1) idiot
(2) natural as opposed to unnatural, monsterlike.

prove a mutineer — the next tree!° The poor monster's my
   subject, and he shall not suffer indignity.   35
CALIBAN: I thank my noble lord. Wilt thou be pleased
   To hearken once again to the suit I made to thee?
STEPHANO: Marry,° will I. Kneel and repeat it. I will stand, and
   so shall Trinculo.   [*Caliban kneels.*]

Enter Ariel, invisible.°

CALIBAN: As I told thee before, I am subject to a tyrant,   40
   A sorcerer, that by his cunning hath
   Cheated me of the island.
ARIEL [*mimicking Trinculo*]: Thou liest.
CALIBAN: Thou liest, thou
      jesting monkey, thou!
   I would my valiant master would destroy thee.
   I do not lie.   45
STEPHANO: Trinculo, if you trouble him any more in 's tale, by
   this hand, I will supplant° some of your teeth.
TRINCULO: Why, I said nothing.
STEPHANO: Mum, then, and no more. — Proceed.
CALIBAN: I say by sorcery he got this isle;   50
   From me he got it. If thy greatness will
   Revenge it on him — for I know thou dar'st,
   But this thing° dare not —
STEPHANO: That's most certain.
CALIBAN: Thou shalt be lord of it, and I'll serve thee.   55
STEPHANO: How now shall this be compassed?° Canst thou
   bring me to the party?
CALIBAN: Yea, yea, my lord. I'll yield him thee asleep,
   Where thou mayst knock a nail into his head.
ARIEL: Thou liest; thou canst not.   60
CALIBAN: What a pied ninny's° this! Thou scurvy patch!° —
   I do beseech thy greatness, give him blows
   And take his bottle from him. When that's gone
   He shall drink naught but brine, for I'll not show him
   Where the quick freshes° are.   65

---

34. the next tree: i.e., you'll hang.   **38. Marry:** i.e., indeed. (Originally an oath,
"by the Virgin Mary.")   **39 s.d.** *invisible:* i.e., wearing a garment to connote
invisibility, as at 1.2.377.   **47. supplant:** uproot, displace.   **53. this thing:** i.e.,
Trinculo.   **56. compassed:** achieved.   **61. pied ninny:** fool in motley.   **patch:**
fool.   **65. quick freshes:** running springs.

STEPHANO: Trinculo, run into no further danger. Interrupt the
    monster one word further° and, by this hand, I'll turn my
    mercy out o' doors° and make a stockfish° of thee.
TRINCULO: Why, what did I? I did nothing. I'll go farther off.°
STEPHANO: Didst thou not say he lied?   70
ARIEL: Thou liest.
STEPHANO: Do I so? Take thou that. [*He beats Trinculo.*] As you
    like this, give me the lie° another time.
TRINCULO: I did not give the lie. Out o' your wits and hearing
    too? A pox o' your bottle! This can sack and drinking do. A   75
    murrain° on your monster, and the devil take your fingers!
CALIBAN: Ha, ha, ha!
STEPHANO: Now, forward with your tale. [*To Trinculo.*] Prithee,
    stand further off.
CALIBAN: Beat him enough. After a little time   80
    I'll beat him too.
STEPHANO: Stand farther. — Come, proceed.
CALIBAN: Why, as I told thee, 'tis a custom with him
    I' th' afternoon to sleep. There thou mayst brain him,
    Having first seized his books; or with a log
    Batter his skull, or paunch° him with a stake,   85
    Or cut his weasand° with thy knife. Remember
    First to possess his books, for without them
    He's but a sot,° as I am, nor hath not
    One spirit to command. They all do hate him
    As rootedly as I. Burn but his books.   90
    He has brave utensils° — for so he calls them —
    Which, when he has a house, he'll deck withal.°
    And that most deeply to consider is
    The beauty of his daughter. He himself
    Calls her a nonpareil. I never saw a woman   95
    But only Sycorax my dam and she;
    But she as far surpasseth Sycorax
    As great'st does least.
STEPHANO: Is it so brave° a lass?

---

67. one word further: i.e., one more time.   **67–68. turn . . . doors:** i.e., forget
about being merciful.   **68. stockfish:** dried cod beaten before cooking.   **69. off:**
away.   **73. give me the lie:** call me a liar to my face.   **76. murrain:** plague. (Literally, a cattle disease.)   **85. paunch:** stab in the belly.   **86. weasand:** windpipe.
88. sot: fool.   **91. brave utensils:** fine furnishings.   **92. deck withal:** furnish it
with.   **98. brave:** splendid, attractive.

CALIBAN: Ay, lord. She will become° thy bed, I warrant,
  And bring thee forth brave brood.   100
STEPHANO: Monster, I will kill this man. His daughter and I will
  be king and queen — save Our Graces! — and Trinculo and
  thyself shall be viceroys. Dost thou like the plot, Trinculo?
TRINCULO: Excellent.
STEPHANO: Give me thy hand. I am sorry I beat thee; but, while   105
  thou liv'st, keep a good tongue in thy head.
CALIBAN: Within this half hour will he be asleep.
  Wilt thou destroy him then?
STEPHANO: Ay, on mine honor.
ARIEL [aside]: This will I tell my master.   110
CALIBAN: Thou mak'st me merry; I am full of pleasure.
  Let us be jocund.° Will you troll the catch°
  You taught me but whilere?°
STEPHANO: At thy request, monster, I will do reason, any
  reason.° — Come on, Trinculo, let us sing.   Sings.   115
    "Flout° 'em and scout° 'em
    And scout 'em and flout 'em!
    Thought is free."
CALIBAN: That's not the tune.
                  Ariel plays the tune on a tabor° and pipe.
STEPHANO: What is this same?   120
TRINCULO: This is the tune of our catch, played by the picture
  of Nobody.°
STEPHANO: If thou beest a man, show thyself in thy likeness. If
  thou beest a devil, take 't as thou list.°
TRINCULO: O, forgive me my sins!   125
STEPHANO: He that dies pays all debts.° I defy thee. Mercy
  upon us!
CALIBAN: Art thou afeard?
STEPHANO: No, monster, not I.
CALIBAN: Be not afeard. The isle is full of noises,   130
  Sounds, and sweet airs, that give delight and hurt not.

---

99. become: suit (sexually).   **112. jocund:** jovial, merry.   **troll the catch:** sing the
round.   **113. but whilere:** only a short time ago.   **114–15. reason, any reason:**
anything reasonable.   **116. Flout:** scoff at.   **scout:** deride.   **119. s.d.** *tabor:*
small drum.   **121–22. picture of Nobody:** (Refers to a familiar figure with head, arms,
and legs but no trunk.)   **124. take 't . . . list:** i.e., take my defiance as you please, as
best you can.   **126. He . . . debts:** i.e., if I have to die, at least that will be the end of all
my woes and obligations.

Sometimes a thousand twangling instruments
Will hum about mine ears, and sometimes voices
That, if I then had waked after long sleep,
Will make me sleep again; and then, in dreaming,   135
The clouds methought would open and show riches
Ready to drop upon me, that when I waked
I cried to dream° again.
STEPHANO: This will prove a brave kingdom to me, where I shall
have my music for nothing.   140
CALIBAN: When Prospero is destroyed.
STEPHANO: That shall be by and by.° I remember the story.
TRINCULO: The sound is going away. Let's follow it, and after
do our work.
STEPHANO: Lead, monster; we'll follow. I would I could see this   145
taborer! He lays it on.°
TRINCULO: Wilt come? I'll follow, Stephano.
                              Exeunt [*following Ariel's music*].

Scene 3°

*Enter Alonso, Sebastian, Antonio, Gonzalo, Adrian, Francisco,
etc.*

GONZALO: By 'r lakin,° I can go no further, sir.
My old bones aches. Here's a maze trod indeed
Through forthrights and meanders!° By your patience,
I needs must° rest me.
ALONSO: Old lord, I cannot blame thee,
Who am myself attached° with weariness,   5
To th' dulling of my spirits.° Sit down and rest.
Even here I will put off my hope, and keep it
No longer for° my flatterer. He is drowned
Whom thus we stray to find, and the sea mocks
Our frustrate° search on land. Well, let him go.   10
                              [*Alonso and Gonzalo sit.*]

---

138. to dream: desirous of dreaming.   **142. by and by:** very soon.   **146. lays it on:**
i.e., plays the drum vigorously.   **3.3. Location:** Another part of the island.
1. By 'r lakin: by our Ladykin, by our Lady.   **3. forthrights and meanders:** paths
straight and crooked.   **4. needs must:** have to.   **5. attached:** seized.   **6. To . . .
spirits:** to the point of being dull-spirited.   **8. for:** as.   **10. frustrate:** frustrated.

ANTONIO [*aside to Sebastian*]: I am right° glad that he's so out
    of hope.
  Do not, for° one repulse, forgo the purpose
  That you resolved t' effect.
SEBASTIAN [*to Antonio*]:   The next advantage
  Will we take throughly.°
ANTONIO [*to Sebastian*]:   Let it be tonight,
  For, now° they are oppressed with travel,° they   15
  Will not, nor cannot, use° such vigilance
  As when they are fresh.
SEBASTIAN [*to Antonio*]:   I say tonight. No more.

Solemn and strange music; and Prospero on the top,° invisible.

ALONSO: What harmony is this? My good friends, hark!
GONZALO: Marvelous sweet music!

*Enter several strange shapes, bringing in a banquet, and dance
about it with gentle actions of salutations; and, inviting the
King, etc., to eat, they depart.*

ALONSO: Give us kind keepers,° heavens! What were these?   20
SEBASTIAN: A living° drollery.° Now I will believe
  That there are unicorns; that in Arabia
  There is one tree, the phoenix' throne, one phoenix°
  At this hour reigning there.
ANTONIO: I'll believe both;
  And what does else want credit,° come to me   25
  And I'll be sworn 'tis true. Travelers ne'er did lie,
  Though fools at home condemn 'em.
GONZALO: If in Naples
  I should report this now, would they believe me
  If I should say I saw such islanders?
  For, certes,° these are people of the island,   30
  Who, though they are of monstrous° shape, yet note,

---

11. right: very.   **12. for:** because of.   **14. throughly:** thoroughly.   **15. now:**
now that.   **travel:** (Spelled *trauaile* in the Folio and carrying the sense of labor as well
as traveling.)   **16. use:** apply.   **17. s.d.** *on the top:* at some high point of the tiring-
house or the theater, on a third level above the gallery.   **20. kind keepers:** guardian
angels.   **21. living:** with live actors.   **drollery:** comic entertainment, caricature,
puppet show.   **23. phoenix:** mythical bird consumed to ashes every five hundred to
six hundred years, only to be renewed into another cycle.   **25. want credit:** lack credence.   **30. certes:** certainly.   **31. monstrous:** unnatural.

Their manners are more gentle, kind, than of
Our human generation you shall find
Many, nay, almost any.
PROSPERO [*aside*]:   Honest lord,
Thou hast said well, for some of you there present   35
Are worse than devils.
ALONSO: I cannot too much muse°
Such shapes, such gesture, and such sound, expressing —
Although they want° the use of tongue — a kind
Of excellent dumb discourse.
PROSPERO [*aside*]:   Praise in departing.°
FRANCISCO: They vanished strangely.
SEBASTIAN: No matter, since   40
They have left their viands° behind, for we have stomachs.°
Will 't please you taste of what is here?
ALONSO: Not I.
GONZALO: Faith, sir, you need not fear. When we were boys,
Who would believe that there were mountaineers°
Dewlapped° like bulls, whose throats had hanging at 'em   45
Wallets° of flesh? Or that there were such men
Whose heads stood in their breasts? Which now we find
Each putter-out of five for one° will bring us
Good warrant° of.
ALONSO: I will stand to° and feed,
Although my last° — no matter, since I feel   50
The best° is past. Brother, my lord the Duke,
Stand to, and do as we.   [*They approach the table.*]

*Thunder and lightning. Enter Ariel, like a harpy,° claps his wings
upon the table, and with a quaint device° the banquet vanishes.°*

36. muse: wonder at.   38. want: lack.   39. Praise in departing: i.e., save your
praise until the end of the performance (proverbial).   41. viands: provisions.
stomachs: appetites.   44. mountaineers: mountain dwellers.   45. Dewlapped:
having a dewlap, or fold of skin hanging from the neck, like cattle.   46. Wallets:
pendent folds of skin, wattles.   48. putter-out . . . one: one who invests money or
gambles on the risks of travel on the condition that the traveler who returns safely is to
receive five times the amount deposited; hence, any traveler.   49. Good warrant:
assurance.   stand to: fall to, take the risk.   50. Although my last: even if this were
to be my last meal.   51. best: best part of life.   52. s.d. harpy: a fabulous monster
with a woman's face and breasts and a vulture's body, supposed to be a minister of divine
vengeance.   s.d. quaint device: ingenious stage contrivance.   s.d. the banquet
vanishes: i.e., the food vanishes; the table remains until line 82.

ARIEL: You are three men of sin, whom Destiny —
          That hath to instrument this lower world
          And what is in 't — the never-surfeited sea   55
          Hath caused to belch up you,° and on this island
          Where man doth not inhabit, you 'mongst men
          Being most unfit to live. I have made you mad;
          And even with suchlike valor° men hang and drown
          Their proper° selves.
                    [*Alonso, Sebastian, and Antonio draw their swords.*]
                              You fools! I and my fellows   60
          Are ministers of Fate. The elements
          Of whom° your swords are tempered° may as well
          Wound the loud winds, or with bemocked-at° stabs
          Kill the still-closing° waters, as diminish
          One dowl° that's in my plume. My fellow ministers   65
          Are like° invulnerable. If° you could hurt,
          Your swords are now too massy° for your strengths
          And will not be uplifted. But remember —
          For that's my business to you — that you three
          From Milan did supplant good Prospero;   70
          Exposed unto the sea, which hath requit° it,
          Him and his innocent child; for which foul deed
          The powers, delaying, not forgetting, have
          Incensed the seas and shores, yea, all the creatures,
          Against your peace. Thee of thy son, Alonso,   75
          They have bereft; and to pronounce by me
          Ling'ring perdition,° worse than any death
          Can be at once, shall step by step attend
          You and your ways; whose° wraths to guard you from —
          Which here, in this most desolate isle, else° falls   80
          Upon your heads — is nothing° but heart's sorrow
          And a clear° life ensuing.

53–56. whom . . . up you: you whom Destiny, controller of the sublunary world as
its instrument, has caused the ever-hungry sea to belch up.   59. suchlike valor:
i.e., the reckless valor derived from madness.   60. proper: own.   62. whom:
which.   tempered: composed and hardened.   63.   bemocked-at: scorned.
64. still-closing: always closing again when parted.   65. dowl: soft, fine feather.
66. like: likewise, similarly.   If: even if.   67. massy: heavy.   71. requit: requited,
avenged.   77. perdition: ruin, destruction.   79. whose: (Refers to the heavenly
powers.)   80. else: otherwise.   81. is nothing: there is no way.   82. clear:
unspotted, innocent.

He vanishes in thunder; then, to soft music, enter the shapes again,
and dance, with mocks and mows,° and carrying out the table.

PROSPERO: Bravely° the figure of this harpy hast thou
    Performed, my Ariel; a grace it had devouring.°
    Of my instruction hast thou nothing bated°   85
    In what thou hadst to say. So,° with good life°
    And observation strange,° my meaner° ministers
    Their several kinds° have done. My high charms work,
    And these mine enemies are all knit up
    In their distractions.° They now are in my power;   90
    And in these fits I leave them, while I visit
    Young Ferdinand, whom they suppose is drowned,
    And his and mine loved darling.   [*Exit above.*]
GONZALO: I' the name of something holy, sir, why° stand you
    In this strange stare?
ALONSO: O, it° is monstrous, monstrous!   95
    Methought the billows° spoke and told me of it;
    The winds did sing it to me, and the thunder,
    That deep and dreadful organ pipe, pronounced
    The name of Prosper; it did bass my trespass.°
    Therefor° my son i' th' ooze is bedded; and   100
    I'll seek him deeper than e'er plummet° sounded,°
    And with him there lie mudded.   *Exit.*
SEBASTIAN: But one fiend at a time,
    I'll fight their legions o'er.°
ANTONIO: I'll be thy second.
         Exeunt [*Sebastian and Antonio*].
GONZALO: All three of them are desperate.° Their great guilt,

---

82. s.d. *mocks and mows:* mocking gestures and grimaces.   **83. Bravely:** finely, dashingly.   **84. a grace . . . devouring:** i.e., you gracefully caused the banquet to disappear as if you had consumed it (with puns on *grace*, meaning "gracefulness" and "a blessing on the meal," and on *devouring*, meaning "a literal eating" and "an all-consuming or ravishing grace").   **85. bated:** abated, omitted.   **86. So:** in the same fashion.   **good life:** faithful reproduction.   **87. observation strange:** exceptional attention to detail.   **meaner:** i.e., subordinate to Ariel.   **88. several kinds:** individual parts.   **90. distractions:** trancelike state.   **94. why:** (Gonzalo was not addressed in Ariel's speech to the *three men of sin*, line 53, and is not, as they are, in a maddened state; see lines 104–06.)   **95. it:** i.e., my sin (also in line 96).   **96. billows:** waves.   **99. bass my trespass:** proclaim my trespass like a bass note in music.   **100. Therefor:** in consequence of that.   **101. plummet:** a lead weight attached to a line for testing depth.   **sounded:** probed, tested the depth of.   **103. o'er:** one after another.   **104. desperate:** despairing and reckless.

Like poison given to work a great time after,   105
Now 'gins to bite the spirits.° I do beseech you,
That are of suppler joints, follow them swiftly
And hinder them from what this ecstasy°
May now provoke them to.

ADRIAN: Follow, I pray you.

Exeunt omnes.

ACT 4, Scene 1°

Enter Prospero, Ferdinand, and Miranda.

PROSPERO: If I have too austerely punished you,
Your compensation makes amends, for I
Have given you here a third° of mine own life,
Or that for which I live; who once again
I tender° to thy hand. All thy vexations   5
Were but my trials of thy love, and thou
Hast strangely° stood the test. Here, afore heaven,
I ratify this my rich gift. O Ferdinand,
Do not smile at me that I boast her off,°
For thou shalt find she will outstrip all praise   10
And make it halt° behind her.

FERDINAND: I do believe it.
Against an oracle.°

PROSPERO: Then, as my gift and thine own acquisition
Worthily purchased, take my daughter. But
If thou dost break her virgin-knot before   15
All sanctimonious° ceremonies may
With full and holy rite be ministered,
No sweet aspersion° shall the heavens let fall
To make this contract grow; but barren hate,
Sour-eyed disdain, and discord shall bestrew   20

---

106. bite the spirits: sap their vital powers through anguish.   **108. ecstasy:** mad
frenzy.   **4.1. Location:** Before Prospero's cell.   **3. a third:** i.e., Miranda, into whose
education Prospero has put a third of his life (?) or who represents a large part of what
he cares about, along with his dukedom and his learned study (?).   **5. tender:** offer.
7. strangely: extraordinarily.   **9. boast her off:** i.e., praise her so, or, perhaps an error
for "boast of her"; the Folio reads "boast her of."   **11. halt:** limp.   **12. Against an
oracle:** even if an oracle should declare otherwise.   **16. sanctimonious:** sacred.
18. aspersion: dew, shower.

The union of your bed with weeds° so loathly
That you shall hate it both. Therefore take heed,
As Hymen's lamps shall light you.°
FERDINAND: As I hope
For quiet days, fair issue,° and long life,
With such love as 'tis now, the murkiest den,   25
The most opportune place, the strong'st suggestion°
Our worser genius° can,° shall never melt
Mine honor into lust, to° take away
The edge° of that day's celebration
When I shall think or° Phoebus' steeds are foundered°   30
Or Night kept chained below.
PROSPERO: Fairly spoke.
Sit then and talk with her. She is thine own.
        [*Ferdinand and Miranda sit and talk together.*]
What,° Ariel! My industrious servant, Ariel!

Enter Ariel.

ARIEL: What would my potent master? Here I am.
PROSPERO: Thou and thy meaner fellows° your last service   35
Did worthily perform, and I must use you
In such another trick.° Go bring the rabble,°
O'er whom I give thee power, here to this place.
Incite them to quick motion, for I must
Bestow upon the eyes of this young couple   40
Some vanity° of mine art. It is my promise,
And they expect it from me.
ARIEL: Presently?°
PROSPERO: Ay, with a twink.°
ARIEL: Before you can say "Come" and "Go,"
                And breathe twice, and cry "So, so,"   45

---

21. weeds: (in place of the flowers customarily strewn on the marriage bed).   **23. As . . . you:** i.e., as you long for happiness and concord in your marriage. (Hymen was the Greek and Roman god of marriage; his symbolic torches, the wedding torches, were supposed to burn brightly for a happy marriage and smokily for a troubled one.)   **24. issue:** offspring.   **26. suggestion:** temptation.   **27. worser genius:** evil genius, or, evil attendant spirit.   **can:** is capable of.   **28. to:** so as to.   **29. edge:** keen enjoyment, sexual ardor.   **30. or:** either.   **foundered:** broken down, made lame. (Ferdinand will wait impatiently for the bridal night.)   **33. What:** now then.   **35. meaner fellows:** subordinates.   **37. trick:** device.   **rabble:** band, i.e., the *meaner fellows* of line 35.   **41. vanity:** (1) illusion (2) trifle (3) desire for admiration, conceit.   **42. Presently:** immediately.   **43. with a twink:** in the twinkling of an eye.

Each one, tripping on his toe,
Will be here with mop and mow.°
Do you love me, master? No?
PROSPERO: Dearly, my delicate Ariel. Do not approach
    Till thou dost hear me call.
ARIEL: Well; I conceive.°   *Exit.*   50
PROSPERO: Look thou be true;° do not give dalliance
    Too much the rein. The strongest oaths are straw
    To the fire i' the blood. Be more abstemious,
    Or else good night° your vow!
FERDINAND: I warrant° you, sir,
    The white cold virgin snow upon my heart°   55
    Abates the ardor of my liver.°
PROSPERO: Well.
    Now come, my Ariel! Bring a corollary,°
    Rather than want° a spirit. Appear, and pertly!° —
    No tongue!° All eyes! Be silent.   *Soft music.*

Enter Iris.°

IRIS: Ceres,° most bounteous lady, thy rich leas°   60
    Of wheat, rye, barley, vetches,° oats, and peas;
    Thy turfy mountains, where live nibbling sheep,
    And flat meads° thatched with stover,° them to keep;
    Thy banks with pionèd and twillèd° brims,
    Which spongy° April at thy hest° betrims   65
    To make cold nymphs chaste crowns; and thy broom
        groves,°
    Whose shadow the dismissèd bachelor° loves,
    Being lass-lorn; thy poll-clipped° vineyard;

---

47. mop and mow: gestures and grimaces.   **50. conceive:** understand.   **51. true:**
true to your promise.   **54. good night:** i.e., say good-bye to.   **warrant:** guarantee.
55. The white . . . heart: i.e., the ideal of chastity and consciousness of Miranda's chaste
innocence enshrined in my heart.   **56. liver:** (as the presumed seat of the passions.)
57. corollary: surplus, extra supply.   **58. want:** lack.   **pertly:** briskly.   **59. No
tongue:** all the beholders are to be silent (lest the spirits vanish).   **s.d. Iris:** goddess of
the rainbow and Juno's messenger.   **60. Ceres:** goddess of the generative power of
nature.   **leas:** meadows.   **61. vetches:** plants for forage, fodder.   **63. meads:**
meadows.   **stover:** winter fodder for cattle.   **64. pionèd and twillèd:** undercut
by the swift current and protected by roots and branches that tangle to form a barricade.
65. spongy: wet.   **hest:** command.   **66. broom groves:** clumps of broom, gorse,
yellow-flowered   shrubs.   **67.   dismissèd   bachelor:** rejected   male   lover.
68. poll-clipped: pruned, lopped at the top, or *pole-clipped*, "hedged in with poles."

And thy sea marge,° sterile and rocky hard,
Where thou thyself dost air:° the queen o' the sky,°   70
Whose watery arch° and messenger am I,
Bids thee leave these, and with her sovereign grace,
                    Juno descends° [*slowly in her car*].
Here on this grass plot, in this very place,
To come and sport. Her peacocks° fly amain.°
Approach, rich Ceres, her to entertain.°   75

Enter Ceres.

CERES: Hail, many-colored messenger, that ne'er
        Dost disobey the wife of Jupiter,
        Who with thy saffron° wings upon my flowers
        Diffusest honeydrops, refreshing showers,
        And with each end of thy blue bow° dost crown   80
        My bosky° acres and my unshrubbed down,°
        Rich scarf° to my proud earth. Why hath thy queen
        Summoned me hither to this short-grassed green?
IRIS: A contract of true love to celebrate,
        And some donation freely to estate°   85
        On the blest lovers.
CERES: Tell me, heavenly bow,
        If Venus or her son,° as° thou dost know,
        Do now attend the Queen? Since they did plot
        The means that° dusky° Dis my daughter got,°
        Her° and her blind boy's scandaled° company   90
        I have forsworn.
IRIS: Of her society°
        Be not afraid. I met her deity°
        Cutting the clouds towards Paphos,° and her son

---

69. sea marge: shore.   **70. thou ... air:** you take the air, go for walks.   **queen o'
the sky:** i.e., Juno.   **71. watery arch:** rainbow.   **72. s.d.** *Juno descends:* i.e., starts
her descent from the "heavens" above the stage (?).   **74. peacocks:** birds sacred to Juno
and used to pull her chariot.   **amain:** with full speed.   **75. entertain:** receive.
78. saffron: yellow.   **80. bow:** i.e., rainbow.   **81. bosky:** wooded.   **unshrubbed
down:** open upland.   **82. scarf:** (The rainbow is like a colored silk band adorning the
earth.)   **85. estate:** bestow.   **87. son:** i.e., Cupid.   **as:** as far as.   **89. that:**
whereby.   **dusky:** dark.   **Dis ... got:** (Pluto, or *Dis*, god of the infernal regions,
carried off Proserpina, daughter of Ceres, to be his bride in Hades.)   **90. her:** i.e.,
Venus's.   **scandaled:** scandalous.   **91. society:** company.   **92. her deity:** i.e., Her
Highness.   **93. Paphos:** place on the island of Cyprus, sacred to Venus.

Dove-drawn° with her. Here thought they to have done°
Some wanton charm° upon this man and maid,   95
Whose vows are that no bed-right shall be paid
Till Hymen's torch be lighted; but in vain.
Mars's hot minion° is returned° again;
Her waspish-headed° son has broke his arrows,
Swears he will shoot no more, but play with sparrows°   100
And be a boy right out.°

[*Juno alights.*]

CERES: Highest Queen of state,°
    Great Juno, comes; I know her by her gait.°
JUNO: How does my bounteous sister?° Go with me
    To bless this twain, that they may prosperous be,
    And honored in their issue.°   *They sing:*   105
JUNO: Honor, riches, marriage blessing,
             Long continuance, and increasing,
             Hourly joys be still° upon you!
             Juno sings her blessings on you.
CERES: Earth's increase, foison plenty,°   110
             Barns and garners° never empty,
             Vines with clustering bunches growing,
             Plants with goodly burden bowing;

             Spring come to you at the farthest
             In the very end of harvest!°   115
             Scarcity and want shall shun you;
             Ceres' blessing so is on you.
FERDINAND: This is a most majestic vision, and
    Harmonious charmingly.° May I be bold
    To think these spirits?
PROSPERO: Spirits, which by mine art   120
    I have from their confines called to enact
    My present fancies.

---

94. Dove-drawn: (Venus's chariot was drawn by doves.)   **done:** placed.   **95. wanton charm:** lustful spell.   **98. Mars's hot minion:** i.e., Venus, the beloved of Mars. **returned:** i.e., returned to Paphos.   **99. waspish-headed:** hotheaded, peevish. **100. sparrows:** (Supposed lustful, and sacred to Venus.)   **101. right out:** outright. **Highest . . . state:** most majestic Queen.   **102. gait:** i.e., majestic bearing.   **103. sister:** i.e., fellow goddess (?).   **105. issue:** offspring.   **108. still:** always.   **110. foison plenty:** plentiful harvest.   **111. garners:** granaries.   **115. In . . . harvest:** i.e., with no winter in between.   **119. charmingly:** enchantingly.

FERDINAND: Let me live here ever!
    So rare a wondered° father and a wife
    Makes this place Paradise.
       Juno and Ceres whisper, and send Iris on employment.
PROSPERO: Sweet now, silence!
    Juno and Ceres whisper seriously;   125
    There's something else to do. Hush and be mute,
    Or else our spell is marred.
IRIS [*calling offstage*]: You nymphs, called naiads,° of the
       windring° brooks,
    With your sedged° crowns and ever-harmless° looks,
    Leave your crisp° channels, and on this green land   130
    Answer your summons; Juno does command.
    Come, temperate° nymphs, and help to celebrate
    A contract of true love. Be not too late.

Enter certain nymphs.

    You sunburned sicklemen,° of August weary,°
    Come hither from the furrow° and be merry.   135
    Make holiday; your rye-straw hats put on,
    And these fresh nymphs encounter° every one
    In country footing.°

Enter certain reapers, properly° habited. They join with the nymphs in a graceful dance, towards the end whereof Prospero starts suddenly, and speaks; after which, to a strange, hollow, and confused noise, they heavily° vanish.

PROSPERO [*aside*]: I had forgot that foul conspiracy
    Of the beast Caliban and his confederates   140
    Against my life. The minute of their plot
    Is almost come. [*To the Spirits.*] Well done! Avoid;° no
       more!
FERDINAND [*to Miranda*]: This is strange. Your father's in some
       passion

---

123. **wondered:** wonder-performing, wondrous.   128. **naiads:** nymphs of springs, rivers, or lakes.   **windring:** wandering, winding (?).   129. **sedged:** made of reeds. **ever-harmless:** ever-innocent.   130. **crisp:** curled, rippled.   132. **temperate:** chaste.   134. **sicklemen:** harvesters, fieldworkers who cut down grain and grass.   **of August weary:** i.e., weary of the hard work of the harvest.   135. **furrow:** i.e., plowed fields.   137. **encounter:** join.   138. **country footing:** country dancing.   **s.d. properly:** suitably.   **s.d. heavily:** slowly, dejectedly.   142. **Avoid:** withdraw.

That works° him strongly.

MIRANDA: Never till this day
   Saw I him touched with anger so distempered.   145

PROSPERO: You do look, my son, in a moved sort,°
   As if you were dismayed. Be cheerful, sir.
   Our revels° now are ended. These our actors,
   As I foretold you, were all spirits and
   Are melted into air, into thin air;   150
   And, like the baseless fabric° of this vision,
   The cloud-capped towers, the gorgeous palaces,
   The solemn temples, the great globe° itself,
   Yea, all which it inherit,° shall dissolve,
   And, like this insubstantial pageant faded,   155
   Leave not a rack° behind. We are such stuff
   As dreams are made on,° and our little life
   Is rounded° with a sleep. Sir, I am vexed.
   Bear with my weakness. My old brain is troubled.
   Be not disturbed with° my infirmity.   160
   If you be pleased, retire° into my cell
   And there repose. A turn or two I'll walk
   To still my beating° mind.

FERDINAND, MIRANDA: We wish your peace.
                        Exeunt [Ferdinand and Miranda].

PROSPERO: Come with a thought!° I thank thee, Ariel. Come.

Enter Ariel.

ARIEL: Thy thoughts I cleave° to. What's thy pleasure?

PROSPERO: Spirit,   165
   We must prepare to meet with Caliban.

ARIEL: Ay, my commander. When I presented° Ceres,
   I thought to have told thee of it, but I feared
   Lest I might anger thee.

PROSPERO: Say again, where didst thou leave these varlets?   170

---

144. works: affects, agitates.   **146. moved sort:** troubled state, condition.
148. revels: entertainment, pageant.   **151. baseless fabric:** unsubstantial theatrical
edifice or contrivance.   **153. great globe:** (With a glance at the Globe Theatre.)
154. which it inherit: who subsequently occupy it.   **156. rack:** wisp of cloud.
157. on: of.   **158. rounded:** surrounded (before birth and after death), or crowned,
rounded off.   **160. with:** by.   **161. retire:** withdraw, go.   **163. beating:** agitated.   **164. with a thought:** i.e., on the instant, or, summoned by my thought, no
sooner thought of than here.   **165. cleave:** cling, adhere.   **167. presented:** acted
the part of, or, introduced.

ARIEL: I told you, sir, they were red-hot with drinking;
   So full of valor that they smote the air
   For breathing in their faces, beat the ground
   For kissing of their feet; yet always bending°
   Towards their project. Then I beat my tabor,   175
   At which, like unbacked° colts, they pricked their ears,
   Advanced° their eyelids, lifted up their noses
   As° they smelt music. So I charmed their ears
   That calflike they my lowing° followed through
   Toothed briers, sharp furzes, pricking gorse,° and thorns,   180
   Which entered their frail shins. At last I left them
   I' the filthy-mantled° pool beyond your cell,
   There dancing up to the chins, that the foul lake
   O'erstunk° their feet.
PROSPERO: This was well done, my bird.
   Thy shape invisible retain thou still.   185
   The trumpery° in my house, go bring it hither,
   For stale° to catch these thieves.
ARIEL: I go, I go.   *Exit.*
PROSPERO: A devil, a born devil, on whose nature
   Nurture can never stick; on whom my pains,
   Humanely taken, all, all lost, quite lost!   190
   And as with age his body uglier grows,
   So his mind cankers.° I will plague them all,
   Even to roaring.

Enter Ariel, loaden with glistering apparel, etc.

   Come, hang them on this line.°

[*Ariel hangs up the showy finery; Prospero and Ariel remain,°
invisible.*] *Enter Caliban, Stephano, and Trinculo, all wet.*

---

174. bending: aiming.   **176. unbacked:** unbroken, unridden.   **177. Advanced:**
lifted up.   **178. As:** as if.   **179. lowing:** mooing.   **180. furzes, . . . gorse:** prickly
shrubs.   **182. filthy-mantled:** covered with a slimy coating.   **184. O'erstunk:**
smelled worse than, or, caused to stink terribly.   **186. trumpery:** cheap goods, the
glistering apparel mentioned in the following stage direction.   **187. stale:** (1) decoy
(2) out-of-fashion garments (with possible further suggestions of "horse piss," as in line
198, and "steal," pronounced like *stale*). *For stale* could also mean "fit for a prostitute."
192. cankers: festers, grows malignant.   **193. line:** lime tree or linden.   **s.d. Prospero and Ariel remain:** (The staging is uncertain. They may instead exit here and return
with the spirits at line 253.)

CALIBAN: Pray you, tread softly, that the blind mole may
    Not hear a foot fall. We now are near his cell.   195

STEPHANO: Monster, your fairy, which you say is a harmless
    fairy, has done little better than played the jack° with us.

TRINCULO: Monster, I do smell all horse piss, at which my nose
    is in great indignation.

STEPHANO: So is mine. Do you hear, monster? If I should take a   200
    displeasure against you, look you —

TRINCULO: Thou wert but a lost monster.

CALIBAN: Good my lord, give me thy favor still.
    Be patient, for the prize I'll bring thee to
    Shall hoodwink this mischance.° Therefore speak softly.   205
    All's hushed as midnight yet.

TRINCULO: Ay, but to lose our bottles in the pool —

STEPHANO: There is not only disgrace and dishonor in that,
    monster, but an infinite loss.

TRINCULO: That's more to me than my wetting. Yet this is your   210
    harmless fairy, monster!

STEPHANO: I will fetch off my bottle, though I be o'er ears° for
    my labor.

CALIBAN: Prithee, my king, be quiet. Seest thou here,
    This is the mouth o' the cell. No noise, and enter.   215
    Do that good mischief which may make this island
    Thine own forever, and I thy Caliban
    For aye thy footlicker.

STEPHANO: Give me thy hand. I do begin to have bloody
    thoughts.   220

TRINCULO [*seeing the finery*]: O King Stephano! O peer!° O
    worthy Stephano! Look what a wardrobe here is for thee!

CALIBAN: Let it alone, thou fool, it is but trash.

TRINCULO: O ho, monster! We know what belongs to a
    frippery.° O King Stephano!   [*He puts on a gown.*]   225

STEPHANO: Put off° that gown, Trinculo. By this hand, I'll have
    that gown.

---

197. **jack:** (1) knave (2) will-o'-the-wisp.   **205. hoodwink this mischance:**
(Misfortune is to be prevented from doing further harm by being hooded like a hawk and
also put out of remembrance.)   **212. o'er ears:** i.e., totally submerged and perhaps
drowned.   **221. King . . . peer:** (Alludes to the old ballad beginning, "King Stephen
was a worthy peer.")   **225. frippery:** place where cast-off clothes are sold.   **226. Put
off:** put down, or, take off.

TRINCULO: Thy Grace shall have it.

CALIBAN: The dropsy° drown this fool! What do you mean
    To dote thus on such luggage?° Let 't alone   230
    And do the murder first. If he awake,
    From toe to crown° he'll fill our skins with pinches,
    Make us strange stuff.

STEPHANO: Be you quiet, monster. — Mistress line,° is not this
    my jerkin?° [*He takes it down.*] Now is the jerkin under the   235
    line.° Now, jerkin, you are like° to lose your hair and prove
    a bald° jerkin.

TRINCULO: Do, do!° We steal by line and level,° an 't like° Your
    Grace.

STEPHANO: I thank thee for that jest. Here's a garment for 't.   240
    [*He gives a garment.*] Wit shall not go unrewarded while I
    am king of this country. "Steal by line and level" is an
    excellent pass of pate.° There's another garment for 't.

TRINCULO: Monster, come, put some lime° upon your fingers,
    and away with the rest.   245

CALIBAN: I will have none on 't. We shall lose our time,
    And all be turned to barnacles,° or to apes
    With foreheads villainous° low.

STEPHANO: Monster, lay to° your fingers. Help to bear this°
    away where my hogshead° of wine is, or I'll turn you out of   250
    my kingdom. Go to,° carry this.

TRINCULO: And this.

STEPHANO: Ay, and this.

---

229. dropsy: disease characterized by the accumulation of fluid in the connective tissue of the body.   **230. luggage:** cumbersome trash.   **232. crown:** head.   **234. Mistress line:** (Addressed to the linden or lime tree upon which, at line 193, Ariel hung the *glistering apparel.*)   **235. jerkin:** jacket made of leather.   **235–36. under the line:** under the lime tree. (With punning sense of being south of the equinoctial line or equator; sailors on long voyages to the southern regions were popularly supposed to lose their hair from scurvy or other diseases. Stephano also quibbles bawdily on losing hair through syphilis, and in *Mistress* and *jerkin*.)   **236. like:** likely.   **237. bald:** (1) hairless, napless (2) meager.   **238. Do, do:** i.e., bravo. (Said in response to the jesting or to the taking of the jerkin, or both.)   **by line and level:** i.e., by means of plumb line and carpenter's level, methodically (with pun on *line,* "lime tree," line 236, and *steal,* pronounced like *stale,* i.e., prostitute, continuing Stephano's bawdy quibble).   **an 't like:** if it please.   **243. pass of pate:** sally of wit. (The metaphor is from fencing.)   **244. lime:** birdlime, sticky substance (to give Caliban sticky fingers).   **247. barnacles:** barnacle geese, formerly supposed to be hatched from barnacles attached to trees or to rotting timber; here, evidently used, like *apes,* as types of simpletons.   **248. villainous:** miserably.   **249. lay to:** start using.   **this:** i.e., the *glistering apparel.*   **250. hogshead:** large cask.   **251. Go to:** (An expression of exhortation or remonstrance.)

[*They load Caliban with more and more garments.*]

A noise of hunters heard. Enter divers spirits, in shape of dogs
and hounds, hunting them about, Prospero and Ariel setting
them on.

PROSPERO: Hey, Mountain, hey!
ARIEL: Silver! There it goes, Silver!   255
PROSPERO: Fury, Fury! There, Tyrant, there! Hark! Hark!
          [*Caliban, Stephano, and Trinculo are driven out.*]
    Go, charge my goblins that they grind their joints
    With dry° convulsions,° shorten up their sinews
    With agèd° cramps, and more pinch-spotted make them
    Than pard° or cat o' mountain.°
ARIEL: Hark, they roar!   260
PROSPERO: Let them be hunted soundly.° At this hour
    Lies at my mercy all mine enemies.
    Shortly shall all my labors end, and thou
    Shalt have the air at freedom. For a little°
    Follow, and do me service.   *Exeunt.*   265

ACT 5, Scene 1°

Enter Prospero in his magic robes, [with his staff,] and Ariel.

PROSPERO: Now does my project gather to a head.
    My charms crack° not, my spirits obey, and Time
    Goes upright with his carriage.° How's the day?
ARIEL: On° the sixth hour, at which time, my lord,
    You said our work should cease.
PROSPERO: I did say so,   5
    When first I raised the tempest. Say, my spirit,
    How fares the King and 's followers?
ARIEL: Confined together
    In the same fashion as you gave in charge,

---

258. dry: associated with age, arthritic (?). **convulsions:** cramps. **259. agèd:**
characteristic of old age. **260. pard:** panther or leopard. **cat o' mountain:** wildcat.
261. soundly: thoroughly (and suggesting the sounds of the hunt). **264. little:** little
while longer. **5.1. Location:** Before Prospero's cell. **2. crack:** collapse, fail. (The
metaphor is probably alchemical, as in *project* and *gather to a head*, line 1.) **3. his
carriage:** its burden (time is no longer heavily burdened and so can go *upright*, "standing
straight and unimpeded"). **4. On:** approaching.

Just as you left them; all prisoners, sir,
In the line grove° which weather-fends° your cell.   10
They cannot budge till your release.° The King,
His brother, and yours abide all three distracted,°
And the remainder mourning over them,
Brim full of sorrow and dismay; but chiefly
Him that you termed, sir, the good old lord, Gonzalo.   15
His tears run down his beard like winter's drops
From eaves of reeds.° Your charm so strongly works 'em
That if you now beheld them your affections°
Would become tender.

PROSPERO: Dost thou think so, spirit?

ARIEL: Mine would, sir, were I human.°

PROSPERO: And mine shall.   20
Hast thou, which art but air, a touch,° a feeling
Of their afflictions, and shall not myself,
One of their kind, that relish all as sharply
Passion as they,° be kindlier° moved than thou art?
Though with their high wrongs I am struck to the quick,   25
Yet with my nobler reason 'gainst my fury
Do I take part. The rarer° action is
In virtue than in vengeance. They being penitent,
The sole drift of my purpose doth extend
Not a frown further. Go release them, Ariel.   30
My charms I'll break, their senses I'll restore,
And they shall be themselves.

ARIEL: I'll fetch them, sir.

Exit.

[*Prospero traces a charmed circle with his staff.*]

PROSPERO: Ye elves of hills, brooks, standing lakes, and groves,
And ye that on the sands with printless foot
Do chase the ebbing Neptune, and do fly him   35
When he comes back; you demi-puppets° that

---

10. line grove: grove of lime trees.   **weather-fends:** protects from the weather.
11. your release: you release them.   **12. distracted:** out of their wits.   **17. eaves
of reeds:** thatched roofs.   **18. affections:** disposition, feelings.   **20. human:**
(Spelled *humane* in the Folio and encompassing both senses.)   **21. touch:** sense,
apprehension.   **23–24. that . . . they:** I who experience human passions as acutely as
they.   **24. kindlier:** (1) more sympathetically (2) more naturally, humanly.
27. rarer: nobler.   **33–50. Ye . . . art:** (This famous passage is an embellished para-
phrase of Golding's translation of Ovid's *Metamorphoses,* 7.197–219.)   **36. demi-
puppets:** puppets of half size, i.e., elves and fairies.

By moonshine do the green sour ringlets° make,
Whereof the ewe not bites; and you whose pastime
Is to make midnight mushrooms,° that rejoice
To hear the solemn curfew;° by whose aid,   40
Weak masters° though ye be, I have bedimmed
The noontide sun, called forth the mutinous winds,
And twixt the green sea and the azured vault°
Set roaring war; to the dread rattling thunder
Have I given fire,° and rifted° Jove's stout oak°   45
With his own bolt;° the strong-based promontory
Have I made shake, and by the spurs° plucked up
The pine and cedar; graves at my command
Have waked their sleepers, oped, and let 'em forth
By my so potent art. But this rough° magic   50
I here abjure, and when I have required°
Some heavenly music — which even now I do —
To work mine end upon their senses that°
This airy charm° is for, I'll break my staff,
Bury it certain fathoms in the earth,   55
And deeper than did ever plummet sound
I'll drown my book.   *Solemn music.*

Here enters Ariel before; then Alonso, with a frantic gesture,
attended by Gonzalo; Sebastian and Antonio in like manner,
attended by Adrian and Francisco. They all enter the circle which
Prospero had made, and there stand charmed; which Prospero
observing, speaks:

    [*To Alonso.*] A solemn air,° and° the best comforter
    To an unsettled fancy,° cure thy brains,
    Now useless, boiled° within thy skull! [*To Sebastian and*
       Antonio.] There stand,   60

---

37. green sour ringlets: fairy rings, circles in grass (actually produced by mushrooms).
39. midnight mushrooms: mushrooms appearing overnight. **40. curfew:**
evening bell, usually rung at nine o'clock, ushering in the time when spirits are abroad.
41. Weak masters: i.e., subordinate spirits, as in 4.1.35 (?). **43. the azured vault:**
i.e., the sky. **44-45. to . . . fire:** I have discharged the dread rattling thunderbolt.
45. rifted: riven, split. **oak:** a tree that was sacred to Jove. **46. bolt:** lightning
bolt. **47. spurs:** roots. **50. rough:** violent. **51. required:** requested.
53. their senses that: the senses of those whom. **54. airy charm:** i.e., music.
58. air: song. **and:** i.e., which is. **59. fancy:** imagination. **60. boiled:** i.e.,
extremely agitated.

For you are spell-stopped. —
Holy Gonzalo, honorable man,
Mine eyes, e'en sociable° to the show° of thine,
Fall° fellowly drops. [*Aside.*] The charm dissolves apace,
And as the morning steals upon the night,   65
Melting the darkness, so their rising senses
Begin to chase the ignorant fumes° that mantle°
Their clearer° reason. — O good Gonzalo,
My true preserver, and a loyal sir
To him thou follow'st! I will pay thy graces°   70
Home° both in word and deed. — Most cruelly
Didst thou, Alonso, use me and my daughter.
Thy brother was a furtherer° in the act. —
Thou art pinched° for 't now, Sebastian. [*To Antonio.*]
      Flesh and blood,
You, brother mine, that entertained ambition,   75
Expelled remorse° and nature,° whom,° with Sebastian,
Whose inward pinches therefore are most strong,
Would here have killed your king, I do forgive thee,
Unnatural though thou art. — Their understanding
Begins to swell, and the approaching tide   80
Will shortly fill the reasonable shore°
That now lies foul and muddy. Not one of them
That yet looks on me, or would know me. — Ariel,
Fetch me the hat and rapier in my cell.
      [*Ariel goes to the cell and returns immediately.*]
I will disease° me and myself present   85
As I was sometime Milan.° Quickly, spirit!
Thou shalt ere long be free.
                        Ariel sings and helps to attire him.
ARIEL: Where the bee sucks, there suck I.
            In a cowslip's bell I lie;
            There I couch° when owls do cry.   90

---

63. sociable: sympathetic. **show:** appearance. **64. Fall:** let fall. **67. ignorant fumes:** fumes that render them incapable of comprehension. **mantle:** envelop.
68. clearer: growing clearer. **70. pay thy graces:** requite your favors and virtues.
71. Home: fully. **73. furtherer:** accomplice. **74. pinched:** punished, afflicted.
76. remorse: pity. **nature:** natural feeling. **whom:** i.e., who. **81. reasonable
shore:** shores of reason, i.e., minds. (Their reason returns, like the incoming tide.)
85. disease: disrobe. **86. As . . . Milan:** in my former appearance as Duke of Milan.
90. couch: lie.

On the bat's back I do fly
After° summer merrily.
Merrily, merrily shall I live now
Under the blossom that hangs on the bough.

PROSPERO: Why, that's my dainty Ariel! I shall miss thee,   95
But yet thou shalt have freedom. So, so, so.°
To the King's ship, invisible as thou art!
There shalt thou find the mariners asleep
Under the hatches. The Master and the Boatswain
Being awake, enforce them to this place,   100
And presently,° I prithee.

ARIEL: I drink the air before me and return
Or ere° your pulse twice beat.   *Exit.*

GONZALO: All torment, trouble, wonder, and amazement
Inhabits here. Some heavenly power guide us   105
Out of this fearful° country!

PROSPERO: Behold, sir King,
The wrongèd Duke of Milan, Prospero.
For more assurance that a living prince
Does now speak to thee, I embrace thy body;
And to thee and thy company I bid   110
A hearty welcome.   [*Embracing him.*]

ALONSO: Whe'er thou be'st he or no,
Or some enchanted trifle° to abuse° me,
As late° I have been, I not know. Thy pulse
Beats as of flesh and blood; and, since I saw thee,
Th' affliction of my mind amends, with which   115
I fear a madness held me. This must crave° —
An if this be at all° — a most strange story.°
Thy dukedom I resign,° and do entreat
Thou pardon me my wrongs.° But how should Prospero
Be living, and be here?

PROSPERO [*to Gonzalo*]:   First, noble friend,   120
Let me embrace thine age,° whose honor cannot

---

92. After: i.e., pursuing.   **96. So, so, so:** (Expresses approval of Ariel's help as valet.)
101. presently: immediately.   **103. Or ere:** before.   **106. fearful:** frightening.
112. trifle: trick of magic.   **abuse:** deceive.   **113. late:** lately.   **116. crave:**
require.   **117. An . . . all:** if this is actually happening.   **story:** i.e., explanation.
118. Thy . . . resign: (Alonso made arrangements with Antonio at the time of Prospero's banishment for Milan to pay tribute to Naples; see 1.2.113–27.)   **119. wrongs:**
wrongdoings.   **121. thine age:** your venerable self.

Be measured or confined.   [*Embracing him.*]
GONZALO: Whether this be
  Or be not, I'll not swear.
PROSPERO: You do yet taste
  Some subtleties° o' th' isle, that will not let you
  Believe things certain. Welcome, my friends all!   125
  [*Aside to Sebastian and Antonio.*] But you, my brace° of
    lords, were I so minded,
  I here could pluck His Highness' frown upon you
  And justify you° traitors. At this time
  I will tell no tales.
SEBASTIAN: The devil speaks in him.
PROSPERO: No.
  [*To Antonio.*] For you, most wicked sir, whom to call
    brother   130
  Would even infect my mouth, I do forgive
  Thy rankest fault — all of them; and require
  My dukedom of thee, which perforce° I know
  Thou must restore.
ALONSO: If thou be'st Prospero,
  Give us particulars of thy preservation,   135
  How thou hast met us here, whom° three hours since
  Were wrecked upon this shore; where I have lost —
  How sharp the point of this remembrance is! —
  My dear son Ferdinand.
PROSPERO: I am woe° for 't, sir.
ALONSO: Irreparable is the loss, and Patience   140
  Says it is past her cure.
PROSPERO: I rather think
  You have not sought her help, of whose soft grace°
  For the like loss I have her sovereign° aid
  And rest myself content.
ALONSO: You the like loss?
PROSPERO: As great to me as late,° and supportable   145
  To make the dear loss, have I° means much weaker

---

124. subtleties: illusions, magical powers (playing on the idea of "pastries, concoctions").
126. brace: pair.   **128. justify you:** prove you to be.   **133. perforce:** necessarily.
136. whom: i.e., who.   **139. woe:** sorry.   **142. of . . . grace:** by whose mercy.
143. sovereign: efficacious.   **145. late:** recent.   **145–46. supportable . . . have I:**
to make the deeply felt loss bearable, I have.

Than you may call to comfort you; for I
Have lost my daughter.

ALONSO: A daughter?
O heavens, that they were living both in Naples,
The king and queen there! That° they were, I wish   150
Myself were mudded° in that oozy bed
Where my son lies. When did you lose your daughter?

PROSPERO: In this last tempest. I perceive these lords
At this encounter do so much admire°
That they devour their reason° and scarce think   155
Their eyes do offices of truth, their words
Are natural breath.° But, howsoever you have
Been jostled from your senses, know for certain
That I am Prospero and that very duke
Which was thrust forth of° Milan, who most strangely   160
Upon this shore, where you were wrecked, was landed
To be the lord on 't. No more yet of this,
For 'tis a chronicle of day by day,°
Not a relation for a breakfast nor
Befitting this first meeting. Welcome, sir.   165
This cell's my court. Here have I few attendants,
And subjects none abroad.° Pray you, look in.
My dukedom since you have given me again,
I will requite° you with as good a thing,
At least bring forth a wonder to content ye   170
As much as me my dukedom.

Here Prospero discovers° Ferdinand and Miranda, playing at chess.

MIRANDA: Sweet lord, you play me false.°
FERDINAND: No, my dearest love,
I would not for the world.

---

150. **That:** so that.   151. **mudded:** buried in the mud.   154. **admire:** wonder.
155. **devour their reason:** i.e., are openmouthed, dumbfounded.   155–57. **scarce . . .
breath:** scarcely believe that their eyes inform them accurately as to what they see or
that their words are naturally spoken.   160. **of:** from.   163. **of day by day:**
requiring days to tell.   167. **abroad:** away from here, anywhere else.   169. **requite:**
repay.   171 s.d. *discovers:* i.e., by opening a curtain, presumably rearstage.   172. **play
me false:** i.e., press your advantage.

MIRANDA: Yes, for a score of kingdoms you should wrangle,
    And I would call it fair play.°
ALONSO: If this prove   175
    A vision° of the island, one dear son
    Shall I twice lose.
SEBASTIAN: A most high miracle!
FERDINAND [*approaching his father*]: Though the seas threaten,
    they are merciful;
    I have cursed them without cause.   [*He kneels.*]
ALONSO: Now all the blessings
    Of a glad father compass° thee about!   180
    Arise, and say how thou cam'st here.
                      [*Ferdinand rises.*]
MIRANDA: O, wonder!
    How many goodly creatures are there here!
    How beauteous mankind is! O brave° new world
    That has such people in 't!
PROSPERO: 'Tis new to thee.
ALONSO: What is this maid with whom thou wast at play?   185
    Your eld'st° acquaintance cannot be three hours.
    Is she the goddess that hath severed us,
    And brought us thus together?
FERDINAND: Sir, she is mortal;
    But by immortal Providence she's mine.
    I chose her when I could not ask my father   190
    For his advice, nor thought I had one. She
    Is daughter to this famous Duke of Milan,
    Of whom so often I have heard renown,
    But never saw before; of whom I have
    Received a second life; and second father   195
    This lady makes him to me.
ALONSO: I am hers.

174–75. Yes . . . play: i.e., yes, even if we were playing for only twenty kingdoms, you would still press your advantage against me, and I would lovingly let you do it as though it were fair play, or if you were to play not just for stakes but literally for kingdoms, my complaint would be out of order in that your "wrangling" would be proper. **176. vision:** illusion. **180. compass:** encompass, embrace. **183. brave:** splendid, gorgeously appareled, handsome. **186. eld'st:** longest.

But O, how oddly will it sound that I
Must ask my child forgiveness!
PROSPERO: There, sir, stop.
  Let us not burden our remembrances with
  A heaviness° that's gone.
GONZALO: I have inly° wept,   200
  Or should have spoke ere this. Look down, you gods,
  And on this couple drop a blessèd crown!
  For it is you that have chalked forth the way°
  Which brought us hither.
ALONSO: I say amen, Gonzalo!
GONZALO: Was Milan° thrust from Milan, that his issue   205
  Should become kings of Naples? O, rejoice
  Beyond a common joy, and set it down
  With gold on lasting pillars: In one voyage
  Did Claribel her husband find at Tunis,
  And Ferdinand, her brother, found a wife   210
  Where he himself was lost; Prospero his dukedom
  In a poor isle; and all of us ourselves
  When no man was his own.°
ALONSO [to Ferdinand and Miranda]: Give me your hands.
  Let grief and sorrow still° embrace his° heart
  That° doth not wish you joy!
GONZALO: Be it so! Amen!   215

Enter Ariel, with the Master and Boatswain amazedly following.

  O, look, sir, look, sir! Here is more of us.
  I prophesied, if a gallows were on land,
  This fellow could not drown. — Now, blasphemy,°
  That swear'st grace o'erboard,° not an oath° on shore?
  Hast thou no mouth by land? What is the news?   220
BOATSWAIN: The best news is that we have safely found
  Our King and company; the next, our ship —

---

200. heaviness: sadness.   **inly:** inwardly.   **203. chalked . . . way:** marked, as with a
piece of chalk, the pathway.   **205. Was Milan:** was the Duke of Milan.   **212–13. all
. . . own:** all of us have found ourselves and our sanity when we all had lost our senses.
214. still: always.   **his:** that person's.   **215. That:** who.   **218. blasphemy:** i.e.,
blasphemer.   **219. That swear'st grace o'erboard:** i.e., you who banish heavenly
grace from the ship by your blasphemies.   **not an oath:** aren't you going to swear an
oath.

Which, but three glasses° since, we gave out° split —
Is tight and yare° and bravely° rigged as when
We first put out to sea.
ARIEL [*aside to Prospero*]:   Sir, all this service   225
Have I done since I went.
PROSPERO [*aside to Ariel*]:   My tricksy° spirit!
ALONSO: These are not natural events; they strengthen°
From strange to stranger. Say, how came you hither?
BOATSWAIN: If I did think, sir, I were well awake,
I'd strive to tell you. We were dead of sleep,°   230
And — how we know not — all clapped under hatches,
Where but even now, with strange and several° noises
Of roaring, shrieking, howling, jingling chains,
And more diversity of sounds, all horrible,
We were awaked; straightway at liberty;   235
Where we, in all her trim, freshly beheld
Our royal, good, and gallant ship, our Master
Cap'ring to eye° her. On a trice,° so please you,
Even in a dream, were we divided from them°
And were brought moping° hither.
ARIEL [*aside to Prospero*]:   Was 't well done?   240
PROSPERO [*aside to Ariel*]: Bravely, my diligence. Thou shalt be
free.
ALONSO: This is as strange a maze as e'er men trod,
And there is in this business more than nature
Was ever conduct° of. Some oracle
Must rectify our knowledge.
PROSPERO: Sir, my liege,   245
Do not infest° your mind with beating on°
The strangeness of this business. At picked° leisure,
Which shall be shortly, single° I'll resolve° you,
Which to you shall seem probable,° of every

---

223. glasses: i.e., hours.   **gave out:** reported, professed to be.   **224. yare:** ready.
bravely: splendidly.   **226.   tricksy:** ingenious,   sportive.   **227.   strengthen:**
increase.   **230. dead of sleep:** deep in sleep.   **232. several:** diverse.   **238. Cap'ring
to eye:** dancing for joy to see.   **On a trice:** in an instant.   **239. them:** i.e., the other
crew members.   **240. moping:** in a daze.   **244. conduct:** guide.   **246. infest:**
harass, disturb.   **beating on:** worrying about.   **247. picked:** chosen, convenient.
248. single: privately, by my own human powers.   **resolve:** satisfy, explain to.
249. probable: plausible.

These° happened accidents;° till when, be cheerful   250
And think of each thing well.° [*Aside to Ariel.*] Come
    hither, spirit.
Set Caliban and his companions free.
Untie the spell. [*Exit Ariel.*] How fares my gracious sir?
There are yet missing of your company
Some few odd° lads that you remember not.   255

*Enter Ariel, driving in Caliban, Stephano, and Trinculo, in
their stolen apparel.*

STEPHANO: Every man shift° for all the rest,° and let no man
    take care for himself; for all is but fortune. Coragio,° bully
    monster,° coragio!
TRINCULO: If these be true spies° which I wear in my head,
    here's a goodly sight.   260
CALIBAN: O Setebos, these be brave° spirits indeed!
    How fine° my master is! I am afraid
    He will chastise me.
SEBASTIAN: Ha, ha!
    What things are these, my lord Antonio?
    Will money buy 'em?
ANTONIO: Very like. One of them   265
    Is a plain fish, and no doubt marketable.
PROSPERO: Mark but the badges° of these men, my lords,
    Then say if they be true.° This misshapen knave,
    His mother was a witch, and one so strong
    That could control the moon, make flows and ebbs,   270
    And deal in her command without her power.°
    These three have robbed me, and this demidevil —
    For he's a bastard° one — had plotted with them
    To take my life. Two of these fellows you

249–50. of every These: about every one of these.   250. accidents: occurrences.
251. well: favorably.   255. odd: unaccounted for.   256. shift: provide.   for
all the rest: (Stephano drunkenly gets wrong the saying "Every man for himself.")
257. Coragio: courage.   257–58. bully monster: gallant monster (ironical).
259. true spies: accurate observers (i.e., sharp eyes).   261. brave: handsome.
262. fine: splendidly attired.   267. badges: emblems of cloth or silver worn by
retainers to indicate whom they serve. (Prospero refers here to the stolen clothes as
emblems of their villainy.)   268. true: honest.   271. deal . . . power: wield the
moon's power, either without her authority or beyond her influence, or, even though to
do so was beyond Sycorax's own power.   273. bastard: counterfeit.

Must know and own.° This thing of darkness I   275
    Acknowledge mine.

CALIBAN: I shall be pinched to death.

ALONSO: Is not this Stephano, my drunken butler?

SEBASTIAN: He is drunk now. Where had he wine?

ALONSO: And Trinculo is reeling ripe.° Where should they
    Find this grand liquor that hath gilded° 'em?   280
    [*To Trinculo.*] How cam'st thou in this pickle?°

TRINCULO: I have been in such a pickle since I saw you last that,
    I fear me, will never out of my bones. I shall not fear
    flyblowing.°

SEBASTIAN: Why, how now, Stephano?   285

STEPHANO: O, touch me not! I am not Stephano, but a cramp.

PROSPERO: You'd be king o' the isle, sirrah?°

STEPHANO: I should have been a sore° one, then.

ALONSO [*pointing to Caliban*]: This is a strange thing as e'er I
    looked on.

PROSPERO: He is as disproportioned in his manners   290
    As in his shape. — Go, sirrah, to my cell.
    Take with you your companions. As you look
    To have my pardon, trim° it handsomely.

CALIBAN: Ay, that I will; and I'll be wise hereafter
    And seek for grace.° What a thrice-double ass   295
    Was I to take this drunkard for a god
    And worship this dull fool!

PROSPERO: Go to. Away!

ALONSO: Hence, and bestow your luggage where you found it.

SEBASTIAN: Or stole it, rather.

      [*Exeunt Caliban, Stephano, and Trinculo.*]

PROSPERO: Sir, I invite Your Highness and your train   300
    To my poor cell, where you shall take your rest
    For this one night; which, part of it, I'll waste°
    With such discourse as, I not doubt, shall make it

---

275. own: recognize, admit as belonging to you.   **279. reeling ripe:** stumbling drunk.   **280. gilded:** (1) flushed, made drunk (2) covered with gilt (suggesting the horse urine).   **281. pickle:** (1) fix, predicament (2) pickling brine (in this case, horse urine).   **284. flyblowing:** i.e., being fouled by fly eggs (from which he is saved by being pickled).   **287. sirrah:** (Standard form of address to an inferior, here expressing reprimand.)   **288. sore:** (1) tyrannical (2) sorry, inept (3) wracked by pain. **293. trim:** prepare, decorate.   **295. grace:** pardon, favor.   **302. waste:** spend.

Go quick away: the story of my life,
And the particular accidents° gone by   305
Since I came to this isle. And in the morn
I'll bring you to your ship, and so to Naples,
Where I have hope to see the nuptial
Of these our dear-belovèd solemnized;
And thence retire me° to my Milan, where   310
Every third thought shall be my grave.
ALONSO: I long
To hear the story of your life, which must
Take° the ear strangely.
PROSPERO: I'll deliver° all;
And promise you calm seas, auspicious gales,
And sail so expeditious that shall catch   315
Your royal fleet far off.° [*Aside to Ariel.*] My Ariel, chick,
That is thy charge. Then to the elements
Be free, and fare thou well! — Please you, draw near.°
                              Exeunt omnes [*except Prospero*].

EPILOGUE

Spoken by PROSPERO.

Now my charms are all o'erthrown,
And what strength I have 's mine own,
Which is most faint. Now, 'tis true,
I must be here confined by you
Or sent to Naples. Let me not,   5
Since I have my dukedom got
And pardoned the deceiver, dwell
In this bare island by your spell,
But release me from my bands°
With the help of your good hands.°   10
Gentle breath° of yours my sails

---

305. **accidents:** occurrences.   **310. retire me:** return.   **313. Take:** take effect
upon, enchant.   **deliver:** declare, relate.   **315–16. catch . . . far off:** enable you to
catch up with the main part of your royal fleet, now afar off en route to Naples (see
1.2.234–35).   **318. draw near:** i.e., enter my cell.   **9. bands:** bonds.   **10. hands:**
i.e., applause (the noise of which would break the spell of silence).   **11. Gentle breath:**
favorable breeze (produced by hands clapping or favorable comment).

Must fill, or else my project fails,
Which was to please. Now I want°
Spirits to enforce,° art to enchant,
And my ending is despair,   15
Unless I be relieved by prayer,°
Which pierces so that it assaults°
Mercy itself, and frees° all faults.
As you from crimes° would pardoned be,
Let your indulgence° set me free.   *Exit.*   20

---

13. want: lack.   **14. enforce:** control.   **16. prayer:** i.e., Prospero's petition to the
audience.   **17. assaults:** rightfully gains the attention of.   **18. frees:** obtains
forgiveness for.   **19. crimes:** sins.   **20. indulgence:** (1) humoring, lenient approval
(2) remission of punishment for sin.

TEXTUAL NOTES

Copy text: the First Folio. Characters' names are grouped at the heads of scenes throughout. Act and scene divisions are as marked in the Folio.

Names of the Actors: [printed in F at the end of the play].
ACT 1, SCENE 1. **7. s.d. *Ferdinand: Ferdinando.* 30.** s.d. *Exeunt: Exit.*
32. [and elsewhere] wi' the: with. **34. s.d.:** [at line 37 in F].
ACT 1, SCENE 2. **99. exact, like:** exact. Like. **165. steaded much:** steeded much.
200. bowsprit: Bore-spritt. **212. me. The:** me the. **229. Bermudas:**
Bermoothes. **283. she:** he. **287. service. Thou:** service, thou. **330. forth at:**
for that. **377, 399. s.d. *Ariel's:*** Ariel (or Ariell). **385. s.d. *Burden, dispers-***
edly: [before "Hark, hark!" in line 384 in F]. **387.** [F provides a speech prefix,
Ar.]. **399. s.p. Ariel:** [not in F].
ACT 2, SCENE 1. **28. s.p. Antonio:** *Seb.* **29. s.p. Sebastian:** *Ant.* **225. throes:**
throwes.
ACT 2, SCENE 2. **9. mow:** moe. **111. spirits:** sprights.
ACT 3, SCENE 1. **2. sets:** set.
ACT 3, SCENE 2. **25. debauched:** debosh'd. **50–51. isle; From me he:** Isle /
From me, he. **116. scout:** *cout*
ACT 3, SCENE 3. **15. travel:** trauaile. **17. s.d. *Solemn . . . invisible:*** [after "they
are fresh" in F, and followed by the s.d. at line 19, *Enter . . . depart*]. **28. me:** me?
29. islanders: Islands. **33. human:** humaine. **65. plume:** plumbe.
ACT 4, SCENE 1. **9. off:** of. **13. gift:** guest. **25. love as 'tis now, the:** loue, as
'tis now the. **61. vetches:** Fetches. **68. poll-clipped:** pole-clipt. **74. Her:**
here. **110. s.p. Ceres:** [not in F]. **123. wife:** wise. **124. s.d.:** [after line 127
in F]. **163. s.d., *Exeunt: Exit.* 193. s.d. *Enter Ariel . . . etc.:*** [after "on this
line" in F, and followed by *Enter Caliban . . . all wet*]. **193. them on:** on them.
230. Let 't: let's.
ACT 5, SCENE 1. **60. boiled:** boile. **72. Didst:** Did. **75. entertained:**
entertaine. **82. lies:** ly. **88. s.p. Ariel:** [not in F]. **234. horrible,:** horrible.
236. her: our. **247. business. At:** businesse, at. **248. Which . . . single:**
(Which shall be shortly single). **257–58. Coragio:** Corasio.

PART TWO

A Case Study
in Critical Controversy

Why Study Critical Controversies about *The Tempest*?

CONTROVERSY SUPPRESSED: ONE STUDENT'S EXPERIENCE

A student we know relates the following story about studying Shakespeare's *The Tempest* in two different college courses:

> In my freshman year, I took a course in which we read Shakespeare's *Tempest*. The professor took a very different approach to Shakespeare than my high school teachers had. For her, Shakespeare was not a transcendent genius we were supposed to worship but a historical figure implicated in the politics of his time. She presented *The Tempest* as a play concerned with colonialism and the European domination of the New World natives. For her, Caliban was not a monstrous villain but a heroic rebel against Prospero's unjust oppression. The experience was a real eye-opener.
>
> The very next semester, however, I took the regular Shakespeare course, and when our class took up *The Tempest,* the professor announced that he would have no patience with political readings of the play. He warned us that *The Tempest* should be regarded as a literary work of genius — that it is reductive to read it as a document about racism, oppression, and other current "politically

correct" issues. The play's greatness, he emphasized, lies in its ability to speak beyond its particular historical moment or ours. And after the warning, he went on to develop his own persuasive reading of the play in which Prospero is a spokesman for legitimate authority and Caliban a comic malcontent who at the end gets the humiliation he deserves.

We asked our student how she had managed to cope with these starkly different versions of *The Tempest*. She replied that she never had any direct conflict with her teachers, but by the end of the year she felt bewildered by the question of how she might choose between their diametrically opposed readings.

We suspect you may recognize this kind of situation from your own experience of classes, in which two or more of your teachers present dramatically conflicting views on the same text or issue. We think exposure to such a diversity of views is of great educational benefit, but we also think the lack of direct debate between these views can limit this benefit. Exposure to opposing interpretations of literature can help you think not only about different ways to read a given work, but also about such larger issues as the relation between literature and history or art and politics. In the absence of debate, however, you may find it hard to measure the differences between divergent views or even to be sure that they really are differences of substance rather than different ways of saying the same thing. Furthermore, when there is no direct engagement between differing views, teachers can become too easily convinced of the unassailable truth of their analyses and students can end up frustrated and confused.

This edition of *The Tempest* is designed to help you make the most of the opportunity presented by the debates about this play, a play that has become especially controversial in today's climate of increased multicultural awareness. As cultural historian Ronald Takaki points out in one of the selections reprinted below, it was in *The Tempest* more than any other work that Shakespeare confronted the European encounter with the New World. "This was an era," Takaki writes, "when the English were encountering 'other' peoples and delineating the boundary between 'civilization' and 'savagery'" (p. 183 in this volume). We call the approach behind this edition "learning by controversy," and we want in this chapter to explain what we mean by such an approach, and to explore some aspects of it that may themselves be controversial.

CONTROVERSY DEVELOPED: DEBATING *THE TEMPEST*

Let us imagine how our two professors might have defended their readings had they come together and presented their main points to our perplexed student. What follows is one hypothetical version of what each would say, a version that connects their positions to several of the critical selections in this book. In the interest of clarity, we have made the oppositions between the sides rather stark in this hypothetical debate. We hope, though, that complications will appear as we probe more deeply into the issues, and even that a measure of agreement will emerge.

POSTCOLONIALIST PROFESSOR: "I see no problem in reading *The Tempest* as a play very much concerned with colonialism and politics. Shakespeare's concerns with colonialism, as Stephen Greenblatt points out (p. 114), were very much alive in the period and are announced very early in the play. *The Tempest*'s preoccupation with questions of usurpation and appropriate government in Milan invites its audience to draw parallels with the situation of Europe in the New World. That invitation becomes explicit through Shakespeare's complex representation of Caliban. Though he is a comic figure, too easily taken in by Trinculo and Stephano, Shakespeare gives him some of the best lines in the play, lines that show him protesting eloquently and convincingly about what Prospero has done to him. In act 1, scene 2, Caliban movingly protests against Prospero's imperialism: 'This island's mine, by Sycorax my mother, / Which thou tak'st from me' (1.2.334–35). Later he accuses Prospero of having 'cheated me of the island' by sorcery (3.2.42), a claim that is difficult to refute.

"Such moments indicate that Shakespeare, despite having Caliban accept his punishment at the end of the play, finds some legitimacy in Caliban's defiance of Prospero. As Greenblatt puts it, Caliban's claim against Prospero — in which he 'bitterly challenges the European's right to sovereignty' — 'is not upheld in *The Tempest*, but neither is it simply dismissed' (p. 114). Similarly, it is this undercurrent in the play to which Aimé Césaire is responding when he rewrites *The Tempest* as *A Tempest* and shows Caliban successfully rebelling against Prospero (p. 309).

"Furthermore, we should remember that secondary characters like Caliban often shed light on questions that a work's main action raises but doesn't directly answer. In this play, the struggles of rival interest groups are virtually everywhere. They're in the very situation that gives rise to the play, the conflict between Prospero and Antonio; they're in the opening scene where aristocrats and sailors bicker over who is running the ship; they're in the relations between Prospero and his daughter Miranda; they're just under the surface of the Prospero-Ariel relationship (see act 1, scene 2, where the issue breaks through the surface). Reading these struggles in connection with Caliban's rebellion shows us how much Shakespeare is thematizing questions of power and legitimate rule that are, of course, key to any depiction of colonialism.

"But what of the ending? I know that the traditional view of the play, which my colleague will defend in a moment, emphasizes Shakespeare's representation of Prospero's success in bringing about an apparently happy restoration of order and harmony at the end. And I concede that Caliban does seem to accept the justice of Prospero's punishment of him. But why do we as readers or spectators have to accept it? It's easy for the Prosperos of the world, in their culturally dominant positions, to identify with Prospero's victory, but doing so is much harder for the Calibans, those who are culturally marginalized or aware of the plight of the marginalized. The first question, in other words, is whose story we readers and viewers of the play should identify with: Prospero's or Caliban's? The winner's or the loser's? The second, and more encompassing, question is, does either story quite get the last word? I'll grant that Shakespeare tries to resolve the conflicts on the side of Prospero, but I don't think he fully succeeds — and that's one of the reasons I like the play."

TRADITIONALIST PROFESSOR: "My colleague's reading exemplifies just about everything I object to in the current emphasis on political readings of literature. Although she is more respectful of the play itself than some recent critics, she nevertheless is clearly trying to use *The Tempest* to advance her own political agenda. I agree with George Will that it's simply absurd to impose our contemporary concern with "the imperialist rape of the Third World" (p. 111) on Shakespeare's *Tempest*. Such readings may be politically correct — for what it's worth, I sympathize with their politics — but they are neither historically accurate nor responsive to the details of the work.

"I agree that Caliban is an important, though secondary, character in the play, but I disagree that the play is primarily about imperialism and that Caliban's main function is to focus our attention on those issues. In the past, it was common to see the relation between Prospero and Caliban as an expression of the Renaissance idea of the Great Chain of Being, which held that the world's creatures existed in a divinely ordered hierarchy from plants to animals to humans to God at the top. In this view, Caliban occupied a lower rung on the chain than

Prospero and so Prospero's domination was right and proper. Although contemporary Renaissance scholars now regard the Great Chain of Being as an overly simplistic view of Renaissance beliefs, their rejection of that theory doesn't mean that we need to reach different conclusions about the relation between Prospero and Caliban.

"What I'm trying to say here is summed up beautifully by Frank Kermode, who notes that the play positions Caliban as a creature of nature and Prospero as a creature of art and culture, and that it ultimately demonstrates the superiority of art and culture to nature. As Kermode puts it,

> If Aristotle was right in arguing that "men . . . who are as much inferior to others as the body is to the soul . . . are slaves by nature, and it is advantageous to be always under government . . ." then the black and mutilated cannibal must be the natural slave of the European gentleman, and *a fortiori,* the salvage and deformed Caliban of the learned Prospero.[1]

As Kermode goes on to argue, Caliban's attempted rape of Miranda is a good example of how he acts according to impulse, without the control of civilization. Prospero, according to Kermode, is, by contrast, a figure of civilized man, rightly establishing and maintaining order on the island and in the small community of himself, Miranda, Ariel, and Caliban; he is also, quite clearly, a figure of the artist. He uses his imagination and his magic to orchestrate the action of the play and bring it to successful resolution. Caliban's excesses, including his participation in the rebellion against Prospero, indicate that, for Shakespeare, his humiliation at the end of the play, when he gets dunked in horse urine, is just. Indeed, as you concede, Shakespeare has Caliban himself admit at the end that his rebellion was wrong, a clear signal that we should see it that way too. Shakespeare has Caliban acquiesce to the rule of culture over nature, saying 'I'll be wise hereafter / And seek for grace. What a thrice-double ass / Was I' (5.1.294–96). In other words, in accepting Prospero's judgment, Caliban is affirming the values that have guided the play all along, values that elevate civilization and art over brute impulses.

"Prospero exhibits both the power of reason and the power of the imagination. I agree with your point that the play is shot through with concerns about political struggle and about appropriate power, but in

---

[1]William Shakespeare, *The Tempest,* ed. Frank Kermode (Cambridge: Harvard UP, 1954), xlii.

identifying with Prospero's careful and successful orchestration of the action, Shakespeare is presenting us with a model of the good ruler rather than a model of the imperialist colonizer. Prospero remains in control, and he pursues reconciliation rather than revenge. Indeed, Prospero's own orchestration of the action is a figure for Shakespeare's. What does the successful playwright do, after all, but what Prospero has done, namely, employ reason and imagination in the service of a careful arrangement of diverse elements into a larger harmony? Rather than being a play about imperialism, stuck tar-baby-like in the politics of its own time, *The Tempest* speaks to us across the ages about the superiority of civilization and culture to untrammeled nature — and about the redeeming power of art. In this sense, the play transcends politics."

CONTROVERSY EXPLORED: ANALYZING THE DEBATE

What are the major points of disagreement here? As in most significant interpretive disputes, they involve both specific meanings in the text and more general theories about the nature of literature, art, and reading. TRADITIONALIST PROFESSOR argues that POSTCOLONIALIST PROFESSOR and similar critics are guilty of forcing political issues on the play in order to advance their preferred social agenda. For TRADITIONALIST PROFESSOR, POSTCOLONIALIST PROFESSOR's reading is anachronistic, attributing modern political attitudes about the evils of European expansion and colonization to a work written centuries before such attitudes had come into existence. For him, the reading ends up distorting the play.

According to POSTCOLONIALIST PROFESSOR, however, these attitudes *did* exist in Shakespeare's time. She builds her case in part by referring to specific passages in the text and in part by referring to the historical situation at the time the play was written. Since Shakespeare and his audience were aware of the domination of native peoples accompanying European explorations of the globe, she argues, we can assume that Caliban's protest against Prospero's rule refers to this domination and expresses a degree of protest against it on Shakespeare's part.

Countering this argument, TRADITIONALIST PROFESSOR concedes that Prospero has enslaved Caliban, but he maintains that Shakespeare and his age would have approved of such enslavement as part of his exploration of the relation between nature and civilization, an exploration that finds untrammeled nature inferior to nature curbed by civilization and enhanced by art. POSTCOLONIALIST PROFESSOR misreads the play,

TRADITIONALIST PROFESSOR suggests, when she construes Prospero's enslavement of Caliban as an instance of unjustified oppression, an interpretation that, according to him, improperly substitutes a modern liberal standard of values for the values Shakespeare was working with in the play. TRADITIONALIST PROFESSOR calls specific attention to Caliban's own acceptance of his punishment as key evidence for his view.

POSTCOLONIALIST PROFESSOR in turn concedes that Caliban accepts his punishment, but she questions whether this is the whole story of the play. Her closing comments complicate the issue by suggesting that there may be a conflict or contradiction in Shakespeare's attitude toward the competing claims of Prospero and Caliban. As it happens, recent critics and cultural historians (represented in this book by Paul Brown, Francis Barker and Peter Hulme, and Ronald Takaki) have suggested that Shakespeare's culture was marked by a conflict of attitudes over how European adventurers should treat natives, and whether colonization was moral or immoral. If Shakespeare is ambivalent toward Caliban and Prospero, he may be reflecting this clash of attitudes in the culture at the time. Indeed, this is a view that predated the arrival of postcolonial criticism; earlier scholars had argued that, as James Shapiro notes, the Elizabethan theater often reflected the contradiction "between the medieval and the modern" views of the world.[2]

CAN WE KNOW WHAT SHAKESPEARE MEANT?

But here the debate is further complicated by another issue. When we suggest, as we just did, that "Shakespeare is ambivalent toward Caliban and Prospero," some may ask, "how can you claim to know what Shakespeare felt? He's been dead, after all, for nearly four hundred years." What kind of access we as readers and critics can legitimately claim to the intentions of authors has itself been the subject of an intense debate among literary theorists. Few of these theorists deny the difficulty of determining an author's intention with any certainty and some categorically deny that we can have any knowledge of such an intention. Others, however (and we tend to side with their position), argue that while it may be true that we never know anyone's intentions with certainty, we can and do make inferences about each

---

[2] James Shapiro, "Soul of the Age," rev. of *Shakespeare: The Invention of the Human*, by Harold Bloom, *New York Times Book Review*, Nov. 1, 1998: 8.

other's intentions all the time and could hardly communicate if we did not. A case in point is our ability to identify verbal mistakes: in one of the funniest scenes in Woody Allen's film *Take the Money and Run*, Allen in his role as a would-be bank robber pushes a note demanding money at a bank teller. With his less than perfect handwriting, however, Allen has scrawled on the note what looks like "I've got a gub." The teller immediately gets into a discussion with Allen, asking him, "What does this say? I've got a gub?" The humor lies not just in the ineptness of Allen's character, but also in the teller's absurd literal-mindedness. Allen relies on his audience to recognize that, in a real-life bank robbery, the teller would readily infer that a man in a mask who handed him such a note must intend "gub" to mean "gun." The intention, in short, counts more than what is literally written.

READING WITH AND AGAINST THE GRAIN

Further complicating the question of intention, however, is the fact that our utterances carry meanings we are not aware of, and may even deny when they are pointed out to us, but are part of the assumptions of our culture. Thus, a man may be telling the truth when he says he never intended to offend anyone by using the word *babes* to denote women. In this case, the demeaning intention comes not from the speaker but from the culture whose traditional sexist assumptions he is reflecting. No matter how suspicious we may be of psychoanalyzing other people, virtually all of us have at times read "between the lines" of their utterances and found meanings there that the speakers may not have intended but which betrayed assumptions they had absorbed from their culture or upbringing. In literary interpretation, this kind of reading that looks for what a text betrays rather than what it intends or explicitly says has come to be known as "reading against the grain." Critics oppose this kind of reading to "reading with the grain," or (more commonly) reading the text "on its own terms."

The debate between TRADITIONALIST PROFESSOR and POSTCOLONIALIST PROFESSOR is in part an example of a disagreement about how to read with the grain of *The Tempest*. In one sense, TRADITIONALIST PROFESSOR tries to counter POSTCOLONIALIST PROFESSOR's political interpretation by treating it as an anachronistic reading against the grain, while POSTCOLONIALIST PROFESSOR insists that she is reading with the grain to the extent that conflicts over colonialism are part of Shakespeare's concern. But POSTCOLONIALIST PROFESSOR's argument also shows what it means to read against the grain when she emphasizes the scenes and lines that betray a sympathy toward Caliban that the larger action of the play, especially the ending, works against. Furthermore, as her argument develops, it illustrates another meaning of "reading against the grain." When she acknowledges that the play indicates that Caliban's punishment is just, you might think that she has conceded so much to TRADITIONALIST PROFESSOR that she ought to give up the argument. She doesn't give up, however, because in addition to asking about the meanings of the play (intentional and unintentional), she also asks how we should judge those meanings. Thus, when she acknowledges the play's concluding condemnation of Caliban, she goes on to question the condemnation itself and to ask whether we should side with the Calibans or the Prosperos of the world.

LITERATURE OR POLITICS?

POSTCOLONIALIST PROFESSOR's responses here highlight another aspect of the debate. TRADITIONALIST PROFESSOR contends that POSTCOLONIALIST PROFESSOR's interpretation of the play ignores or violates the nature of literature. TRADITIONALIST PROFESSOR might grant that if the events of *The Tempest* were recounted in a historical document — in a letter, let's imagine, from an English explorer to his trading company — it would be perfectly proper to see the politics of colonialist exploitation as central in such an account. Furthermore, TRADITIONALIST PROFESSOR might concede that since *The Tempest* can always be read as a historical document — as Takaki in fact reads it for his particular purposes as a social historian — we can use the play as a source of information about the politics of its time. But TRADITIONALIST PROFESSOR would then insist that *The Tempest* is not a mere historical document but an important work of literature. Consequently, the student of literature ought not to be concerned with passing judgment on the long-forgotten politics of Shakespeare's time, but instead should attend to the concerns about nature, civilization, and the power of art through which the play still speaks to us. To reduce literature to politics, as TRADITIONALIST PROFESSOR believes POSTCOLONIALIST PROFESSOR does, is to narrow and limit its universal appeal.

Again POSTCOLONIALIST PROFESSOR would have a response. She would point out that while TRADITIONALIST PROFESSOR accuses her of imposing an anachronistic agenda on the play, his concern with how the play "still speaks to us" runs that risk even more dangerously because it masks its own contemporary concerns under a false guise of "universality." The failure to recognize this mask is evident, POSTCOLONIALIST PROFESSOR would argue, in TRADITIONALIST PROFESSOR's mistaken claim that her reading is political and his is not. To celebrate the redeeming power of art when the play shows that Caliban is punished by Prospero rather than reconciled to him privileges the experience of the European characters over that of Caliban — and this privileging, POSTCOLONIALIST PROFESSOR would point out, is inescapably political. POSTCOLONIALIST PROFESSOR would also question TRADITIONALIST PROFESSOR's views about the nature of great literature and their relevance to the debate. Her questions would once again be historical ones: Did Shakespeare believe that the proper function of literature was to escape its own historical moment and tell timeless truths? Shakespeare's history plays, whose explorations of ideas of kingship appear to be very relevant to Queen Elizabeth's reign, would suggest otherwise. If TRADITIONALIST PROFESSOR accuses POSTCOLONIALIST PROFESSOR of imposing a contemporary political agenda on the play, POSTCOLONIALIST PROFESSOR can accuse TRADITIONALIST PROFESSOR of imposing a contemporary belief about the nature of literature on it.

Furthermore, POSTCOLONIALIST PROFESSOR would ask, on what grounds should we deliberately limit the relevance of literature by denying its uses for our contemporary political debates? Since the politics of colonialism are very much with us in the twenty-first century, why not see how Shakespeare treated these politics in his play? Great literature passes "the test of time," POSTCOLONIALIST PROFESSOR would argue, not because it transcends politics but because its treatment of the political issues of its own day has relevance to future situations.

Perhaps we can make our point more concretely if we go back to a comment TRADITIONALIST PROFESSOR cites approvingly from Frank Kermode, that the "black and mutilated cannibal must be the natural slave of the European gentleman." On the one hand, Kermode and TRADITIONALIST PROFESSOR advance this view of Prospero's natural superiority to Caliban not as one they agree with but as a description of Shakespeare and his culture's dominant message. Taken this way, as a "with the grain" reading, such a description seems to us partly right, though an oversimplification. On the other hand, can we as readers and critics be content to stop with such a description, as Kermode and TRADITIONALIST PROFESSOR seem to do? Is it not fair to argue that insofar as the play endorses such a view of the natural superiority of masters over slaves we are obligated to resist it — that is, to read the play "against the grain"? And is it not fair to look for countertendencies in the play, suggesting that the grain itself does not run in only one direction?

OKAY, OKAY, BUT WHO'S RIGHT?

We anticipate that some of you will reply to what we've been arguing so far by saying "yes, studying controversy may be all well and good, but what about the truth? What about the conclusions and results that controversy is supposed to be the means to? As you two describe it so far, teaching by controversy seems to assume that all values, interpretations, and teaching methods are equally valid — is that its guiding assumption?"

By no means. We would not be offering this edition of *The Tempest* if we did not think that Shakespeare's play possesses genuine literary value, and we would have been unable to select from the mass of critical writing on the play if we did not think that some interpretations (and debates) are more productive than others. Our premise is not that literary value and interpretive truth are merely arbitrary matters of opinion or that debates should proliferate without ever reaching resolution. Our premise is that it is only by going through the process of reasoned and passionate debate about questions of value and truth that we can ever hope to resolve such questions. Controversy for us is not the opposite of reaching resolution but a precondition of doing so.

In our view, the best debates are ones in which it is not obvious who is right but in which it is nevertheless possible to take a stand. We would not enter into debates unless we believed there were some chance that they could reach some resolution, if only temporarily and provisionally. Where, then, do *we* stand in the debate between TRADITIONALIST PROFESSOR and POSTCOLONIALIST PROFESSOR?

Our own answer, for what it is worth, has just been suggested in our comments on reading with and against the grain. But let us start by asking if something cannot be learned from the continued persistence of debates about the play like that between our two professors. Does not the division, for example, over whether Caliban or Prospero has justice on his side point to the likelihood that there is some merit to both positions, that legitimate evidence exists for both? When TRADITIONALIST PROFESSOR points to Caliban's meek acquiescence at the end of the play to the judgment and punishment Prospero metes out to him, it is hard to disagree with his conclusion that at this point in the play we are supposed to accept Prospero's view of things as correct and just. On the other hand, when POSTCOLONIALIST PROFESSOR points to the apparent accuracy of Caliban's protests against Prospero's mistreatment of him, it is hard to disagree with her conclusion that at this point the play solicits at least partial sympathy for Caliban.

To make such an argument is to agree with POSTCOLONIALIST PROFESSOR and others who argue that *The Tempest* is not a unified text but a contradictory and conflicted one. If we accept the view of Ronald Takaki and other earlier historical critics that Shakespeare was writing at a moment of transition between the hierarchical worldview of the Middle Ages and the more individualistic and libertarian worldview emerging in the Renaissance, then it would not be surprising to find internal conflicts and contradictions in the play.

By this point we hope you can see how critical debates like the one between TRADITIONALIST PROFESSOR and POSTCOLONIALIST PROFESSOR can deepen our engagement with literature. We want now to step back from this debate about *The Tempest* and consider some of the objections that might be lodged against "learning by controversy" itself.

AN OBJECTION FROM TEACHERS; OR, THE INEVITABILITY OF CRITICISM

Some teachers maintain that asking students to attend to arguments between critics is counterproductive. According to them, reading what critics have said about a literary text only distracts students from the primary and immediate experience of reading the text itself, replacing the students' responses to it with somebody else's opinions. These teachers maintain that exposure to criticism — and to the debates among the critics — is proper and necessary at the graduate level, where students are being trained as professionals in a discipline, but it has no place in undergraduate courses, where the goal is to teach students to understand and appreciate literature itself. These teachers, then, implicitly distinguish between a student's "direct" and "unmediated" response to the text and the formal academic analyses done by professional critics, which they see as at best an overlay on more primary responses and at worst a distorting attempt to advance the critic's agenda.

We respectfully disagree with these teachers. First of all, we think that the distinction between a direct and a mediated response does not hold up, since all responses are mediated. It is not possible, for example, to read Shakespeare today without the mediating filter of his reputation as the greatest writer in the history of English literature. It is not possible for any class approaching *The Tempest* to escape the mediation established by the context of the whole course and by the instructor's particular approach to the material. The choice is not between direct and mediated reading but between different kinds of mediation.

Second, as students you have an obvious stake in being exposed to the kind of discourse you are asked to produce. In most undergraduate courses you are asked to do literary criticism, in the written form of papers and/or in the oral discourse of class discussion. It seems contradictory for us teachers to expect you to produce effective literary criticism if we don't provide you with examples of such criticism. Just as it would be strange to ask you to shoot free throws while discouraging you from ever seeing a basketball game, or to play a piano sonata without your ever having watched and responded to a pianist play one, it seems strange to expect you to learn the "moves" critics make without giving you the chance to watch and listen to some critics in action.

Third, we believe that debates between critics can help to make literary works more intelligible and interesting. Far from interfering with your spontaneous reactions to *The Tempest*, reading a debate such as the one between POSTCOLONIALIST PROFESSOR and TRADITIONALIST PROFESSOR will help you engage more deeply with its themes, language, and structure. The debate enables you to connect these elements of the play with larger issues and to see some of what is at stake in analyzing the play. The moves made by literary critics, like those made by basketball players or pianists, become more meaningful and interesting when you watch them actually performing rather than doing drills in isolation.

In other words, we believe that, as with basketball or piano playing, you learn by doing. You learn how to make the moves on the court or the keyboard when you cease being a spectator and start playing games and pieces yourself. This is why we have organized our book in a way that enables you to enter the game of *Tempest* criticism by jumping into the critical fray and joining some of the debates that have gone on and continue to go on over the play.

AN OBJECTION FROM STUDENTS; OR, THE HIDDEN MEANING PROBLEM

Some students have doubts about our approach on other grounds. From their perspective, the two professors seem quite similar, despite the vast difference between their readings of the play and their apparent political slants. Both professors expect you not just to read and enjoy the play, but to interpret and analyze it in a way that probes deeply for complex meanings not immediately evident to the casual playgoer. Both professors, in other words, want their students to look for and articulate "hidden meanings" or "symbolism" in the play.

The question students often ask is, why can't we just enjoy literature? Why do we always have to probe for deep and complex significance? Doesn't such searching for hidden meanings under every line or in every scene often spoil the pure pleasure of a good story and exciting drama? Did Shakespeare himself expect us to pick over his plays for elaborate networks of symbolism and "themes"? In short, isn't there something excessive about this whole academic process of reading everything — not only Shakespeare and classic works of literature, but films and television sitcoms and even the most ephemeral magazine advertisement — as if it were a kind of secular scripture whose every word demands deep interpretation? Why must students become analysts of texts, instead of simply enjoying them?

We believe that this objection is crucial and needs to be addressed at some length. We note, first, that like the objection from some teachers, it is based on an underlying opposition between reading for pleasure and reading for analysis and criticism. Again we believe that under careful scrutiny the distinction is hard to maintain. If you reflect on your life outside of formal classes, we believe you will find that you are always doing criticism of a kind, and that you assume it is better to do it well than poorly. In other words, you are already doing criticism the moment you begin to talk about a newspaper article, a TV show, a sports event, or a friend's behavior on a given occasion, as well as about a book, play, or film. After all, even the most modest assertions about a text or an event carry implied claims about its meaning, value, or consequences in the world. Merely in saying to a classmate that a book "is a great read" or that "it's so boring" or that the person who interviewed you for a part-time job was "a jerk," you are performing a rudimentary act of criticism. If you go on to give a reason or two for your judgment —"*Farewell, My Lovely* makes me long for the kind of mastery in my life that Marlowe has in his"; "the interviewer was far more interested in himself than in my qualifications for the job"— you are moving toward a more sophisticated critical act.

Furthermore, in making such critical judgments, you are also implicitly beginning to practice what has come to be called "theory." When you describe someone as "a jerk" or judge a television show as "boring," you are operating with a theory or set of principles about what qualities in a person or a show are acceptable or unacceptable and why. In a similar way, when you say you like *Farewell, My Lovely* because its main character's mastery is so appealing, you are suggesting that, for you, a novel is good if it holds out a convincing ideal that you can imagine guiding your life. Of course, articulating the theories behind your likes and dislikes in this way risks adding another layer of abstraction to literary discussion and so may further deepen the "hidden meaning" problem. The advantage of being theoretically explicit in this way, however, is that it enables you to compare and discuss the often very different reasons people have for liking and disliking books — including reasons that may be different for students and teachers.

Of course we recognize that there is a difference between your declaration that you find a book boring and the complicated and often obscure cogitations of sophisticated literary critics and theorists. Because of this very difference, however, and the intimidating effect that published criticism and theory may have on you, we think it is important to remember that even these sophisticated discourses often have their roots in the kind of responses you yourself have. Some of the issues in the debate between TRADITIONALIST PROFESSOR and POSTCOLONIALIST PROFESSOR arise out of their different answers to such basic questions as "Whom do I like in this play, Prospero or Caliban?" and "Which character am I supposed to like, and how do I know?" Academic criticism and theory, in other words, are formalized book-talk, book-talk elevated to the level of rigorous argumentation.

We suspect that when students (and sometimes teachers) are turned off by published literary criticism and resist the idea of bringing such criticism directly into class discussion, they are reacting — understandably enough — to an encounter with instances of overly abstruse, arid, or jargon-ridden forms of theory or textual explication. Or they may be reacting to works of criticism and theory that are written in a clear enough style, but fail to address what might be called the "So-What Question"— that is, that fail to make clear to the reader why their analysis is useful or worthwhile. As we hope our selections in this volume will show, the most useful critics do not hesitate to spell out their main point clearly, even bluntly, and to indicate why the point needs to be made in the first place, though they may go on to complicate that point at some length.

Another reason there is finally no choice about whether to do criticism and theory is that practical decisions arise all the time about what to publish, what to teach, and what to read and what to write about in a course, and these decisions require us to make evaluative judgments about texts. You may be tempted, when faced with the question of, say, whether Shakespeare is really a better writer than Stephen King, to reply that any answer will inevitably be subjective. Some of us admire and enjoy the work of Shakespeare, even if we prefer to relax with a book by the modern master of horror — but who is to say, finally, which writer is ultimately better or best? What sense does it make to debate these subjective evaluations, as academics seem endlessly to do?

There is a long history of philosophic attempts, going back at least to Plato, to address this question of whether value judgments can ever be more than subjective. But without plunging into those interesting chapters in the history of philosophy, we can provide another kind of answer. We need to debate questions of value (and therefore examine our theories of value) because in making decisions we inevitably need to make value judgments, to persuade others to accept them, and to listen to their arguments in turn. You are studying Shakespeare (and other British writers) today because, around the turn of the previous century, a debate among educators about what should be taught was won by the partisans of English and European "modern" literatures (including especially French, German, and Spanish), who were more persuasive than those who insisted that only Greek and Latin texts were worthy of study. A variety of self-interested prejudices and biases certainly played a crucial role in this victory for the moderns over the ancients, but these interests had to be established and buttressed through reasons and arguments.

Our point here is that when your community has to decide on a policy — over what texts to study in school, for instance, or if tax money should be invested in schools or a new sports arena — you and your fellow citizens do not have the luxury of saying, "It's all a matter of subjective opinion." The community has to make a value judgment that one choice is better than the other, and if you want your choice to be accepted, you need to be able to make persuasive arguments in favor of it. Simply to opt out of the debate is to surrender one of the most important forms of action available to a citizen of a democracy. In short, value judgments and debates about values are both inescapable and important.

Typically, we become aware of the inescapable intervention of critical decision making when somebody comes along and questions a book's generally accepted value and meaning, something that has been happening more frequently lately as the literary canon traditionally taught in schools and colleges has come to seem more open to controversy and less self-evident. Our student's POSTCOLONIALIST PROFESSOR is doing this kind of questioning, and her TRADITIONALIST PROFESSOR in his turn is clearly challenging her questioning. Our edition highlights this process of questioning and counterquestioning and seeks to draw you into its pleasures.

LEARNING BY CONTROVERSY — AND OTHER WAYS OF LEARNING

The mixed messages you are likely to receive from different teachers go beyond the subject matter of courses to styles of teaching, learning, and classroom authority. You have probably already discovered that certain codes and buzzwords, such as "empowerment," "excellence," "dialogue," often betray a given teacher's allegiance to one or another theory of pedagogy — and that failing to decode the signals can cause you problems. For some professors, your role as a student is to master the knowledge they present and to reproduce that knowledge in examinations. For other professors, who reject this "banking" model of education (as they call it), with its assumption that knowledge is a substance to be deposited in and then withdrawn from your brain, your role is to be an active constructor of knowledge. In class, these teachers may try to get out of your way, intervening little in the discussion in order to "empower" you and your classmates to take control over your own learning. For still other professors, the best teacher is a passionate activist who tries to transform your not yet enlightened consciousness, turning you against the patriarchal, racist, and homophobic attitudes that you presumably brought to the classroom, and converting you into an agent of social change. For yet another set of professors, this last group in turn may be viewed as an unprofessional and intolerant cadre of ideologues bent on coercing you into political correctness.

Learning by controversy assumes that just as a diversity of interpretations of *The Tempest* is a good thing for education, so too is a diversity of teaching theories and styles. In our view, there is no magic formula for teaching, no single right way for all teachers and all students to follow, and we know of good and bad teachers who represent each of the modes of teaching and learning described above. We also believe, however, that just as you should be part of the controversies over subject matters and interpretations, you should also be brought into the controversies about authority and pedagogy.

Learning by controversy also provides you with a set of issues and reference points that should help you to focus your reading as well as some terms and concepts that will help you articulate your responses.

We recognize that not everyone would choose the issues we have selected for this edition of *The Tempest*. While we believe that these issues are central to reading the play at the beginning of the new millennium, we also acknowledge that it is in the nature of controversy itself that some readers of this edition will object that certain issues have been excluded or marginalized while others have been unduly privileged. We welcome this kind of criticism — and invite those who want to make it to tell us which controversies they think should take precedence over the ones we have chosen or which contributions to our controversies they would like to see added or deleted.

We also recognize that conflict and controversy are not themselves neutral terms. "Learning by controversy" may strike some of you — and some of your teachers — as a symptom of a masculinist professional and cultural ethic, one that rewards critical John Waynes who excel in shootouts with rival critics and critical schools. Others may be put off by the aridly legalistic feel of an approach to literature that may seem to treat authors as accused parties facing trial, with their fates in the hands of critical prosecuting attorneys and defense lawyers. We want to be clear that for us the aim of literary education is not to determine who is the best critical prosecuting attorney or fastest critical gunslinger (or, for that matter, bullslinger). The reason for introducing you to critical conflicts is not to encourage you to unleash your aggressions but to help you excel in the kind of analysis and reasoned argument that will make you an effective citizen as well as a good student. If our approach runs the risk of turning classroom discussions into the academic equivalent of Western shoot-outs or bad prosecutorial bullying, it also has the potential to generate significant breakthroughs in teaching and learning. The first key is to distinguish between productive and unproductive critical controversies; the second is to engage with these controversies in ways that open up insights into texts rather than merely lock us into frustrating oppositions or elevate winning over understanding.

You be the judge. "Why study critical controversies?" See how you might answer our initial question after you've worked through the texts in the rest of this book.

Literary Study, Politics,
and Shakespeare: A Debate

These two brief essays suggest how the battle lines have typically been drawn (and perhaps overdrawn) in recent debates over the new emphasis on politics and ideology in the academic study of literature and of Shakespeare in particular. *Newsweek* columnist George Will and Renaissance scholar Stephen Greenblatt disagree sharply over the appropriateness of interpretations that see the politics of imperialism in classics like *The Tempest*.

Will's piece was immediately occasioned by a controversy that erupted in 1991 when Lynne V. Cheney, who had been appointed by President Ronald Reagan as chairman of the National Endowment for the Humanities, nominated Carol Iannone to be a member of the NEH advisory board. Iannone's nomination was opposed by the Executive Council of the Modern Language Association, the nation's largest organization of humanities professors. The MLA claimed to oppose the nomination because Iannone lacked scholarly credentials, but critics charged that its real objection was to Iannone's conservative political leanings. Since the NEH is one of the leading sources of funds for academic humanities research, the struggle between NEH and MLA represented a larger conflict over the kinds of academic work that merit public support and the place of politics in relation to such decisions. Similar conflicts have arisen over the funding of controversial or offensive art by the National Endowment for the Arts.

Though Will and Greenblatt claim to speak for no one but themselves, it seems significant that it is the journalist who attacks political
readings and the academic scholar who defends them. Will's argument implicitly speaks for the nonacademic common reader against
the academic expert, suggesting that the academics who reinterpret
Shakespeare in the light of colonialism, feminism, and other current
preoccupations are rendering the plays unrecognizable to the ordinary
reader and playgoer. Greenblatt replies by arguing that these preoccupations with political power were not at all unfamiliar to Shakespeare
and his audience, and that recognizing the presence of issues of colonialism and slavery in Shakespeare should deepen the ordinary reader's
pleasure rather than undermine it.

GEORGE WILL

Literary Politics

George Will (b. 1941) is a Pulitzer Prize–winning political
commentator who writes a widely syndicated newspaper column
and a biweekly column for *Newsweek,* and appears regularly
on the ABC television network. Before embarking on his career
in journalism, Will taught political philosophy at Michigan
State University and the University of Toronto. Before joining
the staff of *Newsweek,* Will served as Washington editor of the
conservative *National Review.* The following selection is a column that appeared in the April 22, 1991, issue of *Newsweek.*

The Modern Language Association's opposition to the nomination of Carol Iannone to the National Council on the Humanities is not
quite sufficient reason for supporting her. But MLA hostility is nearly
necessary for creating confidence in anyone proposed for a position of
cultural importance. The president nominated Iannone at the behest of
the chairman of the National Endowment for the Humanities, Lynne
Cheney, to whom the council tenders advice. The MLA, composed
mostly of professors of literature and languages, is shocked —
shocked! — that people suspect it of political motives. Oh? The MLA is
saturated with the ideology that politics permeates everything. The

unvarnished truth is that the MLA's sniffy complaint amounts to this: Iannone is not "one of us." Her writings confirm that virtue.

She teaches at NYU and is vice president of the National Association of Scholars, a burgeoning organization resisting the politicization of higher education. She is a trenchant critic of the watery Marxism that has gone to earth in the MLA and elsewhere on campuses. Academic Marxists deny the autonomy of culture, explaining it as a "reflection" of other forces, thereby draining culture of its dignity. The reduction of the study of literature to sociology, and of sociology to mere ideological assertion, has a central tenet: All literature is, whether writers are conscious of it or not, political.

Writers, say the academics Iannone refutes, are captives of the conditioning of their class, sex, race. All literature on which canonical status is conferred represents the disguised or unexamined assumptions and interests of the dominant class, sex, race. Hence culture is oppressive and a literary canon is an instrument of domination. This ideology radically devalues authors and elevates the ideologists — the critics — as indispensable decoders of literature, all of which is, by definition, irreducibly political.

Shakespeare's "Tempest" reflects the imperialist rape of the Third World. Emily Dickinson's poetic references to peas and flower buds are encoded messages of feminist rage, exulting clitoral masturbation to protest the prison of patriarchal sex roles. Jane Austen's supposed serenity masks boiling fury about male domination, expressed in the nastiness of minor characters who are "really" not minor. In "Wuthering Heights," Emily Brontë, a subtle subversive, has Catherine bitten by a *male* bulldog. Melville's white whale? Probably a penis. Grab a harpoon!

The supplanting of esthetic by political responses to literature makes literature primarily interesting as a mere index of who had power and whom the powerful victimized. For example, feminist literary criticism is presented as a political act, liberating women writers from the oppression of "patriarchal literary standards." Thus does criticism dovetail with the political agenda of victimology. The agenda is the proliferation of groups nursing grievances and demanding entitlements. The multiplication of grievances is (if radicals will pardon the expression) the core curriculum of universities that are transformed into political instruments. That curriculum aims at delegitimizing Western civilization by discrediting the books and ideas that gave birth to it.

Iannone tartly criticizes the "eruption of group politics in literature," noting that many scholarly activities, from the shaping of curriculums to the bestowing of academic awards, have become instruments of racial, ethnic, and sexual reparations for Western civilization's sins. The left's agenda does liberate, in this perverse way: it emancipates literature from the burden of esthetic standards. All such standards are defined as merely sublimated assertions of power by society's dominant group. So all critics and authors from particular victim groups should be held only to the political standards of their group. Administration of these, and of the resulting racial and sexual spoils system in the academy, "requires" group politics: Under the spreading chestnut tree, I tenure you and you tenure me.

As esthetic judgments are politicized, political judgments are estheticized: the striking of poses and the enjoyment of catharsis are central in the theater of victimization in academic life. All this, although infantile, is not trivial. By "deconstructing," or politically decoding, or otherwise attacking the meaning of literary works, critics strip literature of its authority. Criticism displaces literature and critics displace authors as bestowers of meaning.

It might seem odd, even quixotic, that today's tenured radicals have congregated in literature departments, where the practical consequences of theory are obscure. Obscure, but not negligible. As James Atlas writes, the transmission of the culture that unites, even defines America — transmission through knowledge of literature and history — is faltering. The result is collective amnesia and deculturation. That prefigures social disintegration, which is the political goal of the victim revolution that is sweeping campuses.

HIGH-INTENSITY WAR

The fight over Iannone's nomination is particularly important precisely because you have not hitherto heard of it or her. The fight is paradigmatic of the many small skirmishes that rarely rise to public attention but cumulatively condition the nation's cultural, and then political, life. In this low-visibility, high-intensity war, Lynne Cheney is secretary of domestic defense. The foreign adversaries her husband, Dick, must keep at bay are less dangerous, in the long run, than the domestic forces with which she must deal. Those forces are fighting against the conservation of the common culture that is the nation's social cement. She, even more than a Supreme Court justice, deals with constitutional things. The real Constitution, which truly constitutes America, is the national mind as shaped by the intellectual legacy that gave rise to the Constitution and all the habits, mores, customs, and ideas that sustain it.

There has been a historic reversal: Many of the most enlightened defenders of our cultural patrimony are now out in the "practical" world, including government, and many philistines are in the academies shaping tomorrow's elites, and hence tomorrow's governance. That is why Lynne Cheney and Carol Iannone matter more than do most of the things that get the public's attention.

STEPHEN GREENBLATT

The Best Way to Kill Our Literary Inheritance Is to Turn It into a Decorous Celebration of the New World Order

Stephen Greenblatt (b. 1943) is the Cogan University Professor of the Humanities at Harvard University. One of the most influential contemporary critics of Renaissance literature and culture, Greenblatt has been, since the 1970s, instrumental in the rise and development of the critical movement known as New Historicism. Greenblatt's many influential books include *Renaissance Self-Fashioning* (1980), *Shakespearean Negotiations* (1988), *Learning to Curse* (1990), *Marvelous Possessions* (1991), *Hamlet in Purgatory* (2001), and *Will in the World* (2004). He is also the general editor of *The Norton Shakespeare* and co–general editor of *The Norton Anthology of English Literature*. This essay originally appeared in response to George Will's article, on June 12, 1991, in *The Chronicle of Higher Education*.

The columnist George F. Will recently declared that Lynne V. Cheney, the chairman of the National Endowment for the Humanities, is "secretary of domestic defense."

"The foreign adversaries her husband, Dick, must keep at bay," Mr. Will wrote, "are less dangerous, in the long run, than the domestic forces with which she must deal." Who are these homegrown enemies, more dangerous even than Saddam Hussein with his arsenal of chemical weapons? The answer: professors of literature. You know, the kind of people who belong to that noted terrorist organization, the Modern Language Association.

Mr. Will, who made these allegations in *Newsweek* (April 22), doesn't name names — I suppose the brandishing of a list of the insidious fifth column's members is yet to come — but he does mention, as typical of the disease afflicting Western civilization, the professor who suggests that Shakespeare's *Tempest* is somehow about imperialism.

This a curious example — since it is very difficult to argue that *The Tempest* is *not* about imperialism. (It is, of course, about many other things, as well, including the magical power of the theater.) The play — set on a mysterious island over whose inhabitants a European prince has assumed absolute control — is full of conspicuous allusions to contemporary debates over the project of colonization: The Virginia Company's official report on the state of its New World colony and the account by William Strachey, secretary of the settlement at Jamestown, of a violent storm and shipwreck off the coast of Bermuda, are examples.

Colonialism was not simply a given of the period. The great Spanish Dominican, Bartolomé de Las Casas, argued that his countrymen should leave the New World, since they were bringing only exploitation and violence. Spanish jurists like Francisco de Vitoria presented cases against the enslavement of the Indians and against the claim to imperial possession of the Americas. The most searing attack on colonialism in the sixteenth century was written by the French essayist Montaigne, who in "Of Cannibals" wrote admiringly of the Indians and in "Of Coaches" lamented the whole European enterprise: "So many cities razed, so many nations exterminated, so many millions of people put to the sword, and the richest and most beautiful part of the world turned upside down, for the traffic in pearls and pepper!" We know that Shakespeare read Montaigne; one of the characters in *The Tempest* quotes from "Of Cannibals."

Shakespeare's imagination was clearly gripped by the conflict between the prince and the "savage" Caliban (is it too obvious to note the anagrammatic play on "cannibal"?). Caliban, enslaved by Prospero, bitterly challenges the European's right to sovereignty. The island was his birthright, he claims, and was unjustly taken from him. Caliban's claim is not upheld in *The Tempest,* but neither is it simply dismissed, and at the enigmatic close of the play all of the Europeans — every one of them — leave the island.

These are among the issues that literary scholars investigate and encourage their students to consider, and I would think that the columnists who currently profess an ardent interest in our cultural heritage would approve.

But for some of them such an investigation is an instance of what is intolerable — a wicked plot by renegade professors bent on sabotaging Western civilization by delegitimizing its founding texts and ideas. Such critics want a tame and orderly canon. The painful, messy struggles over rights and values, the political and sexual and ethical dilemmas that great art has taken upon itself to articulate and to grapple with, have no place in their curriculum. For them, what is at stake is the staunch reaffirmation of a shared and stable culture that is, as Mr. Will puts it, "the nation's social cement." Also at stake is the transmission of that culture to passive students.

But art, the art that matters, is not cement. It is mobile, complex, elusive, disturbing. A love of literature may help to forge community, but it is a community founded on imaginative freedom, the play of language, and scholarly honesty, and not on flag waving, boosterism, and conformity.

The best way to kill our literary inheritance is to turn it into a decorous liturgical celebration of the new world order. Poets cannot soar when their feet are stuck in social cement.

The student of Shakespeare who asks about racism, misogyny, or anti-Semitism is not on the slippery slope toward what George Will calls "collective amnesia and deculturation." He or she is on the way to understanding something about *Othello*, *The Taming of the Shrew*, and *The Merchant of Venice*. It is, I believe, all but impossible to understand these plays without grappling with the dark energies upon which Shakespeare's art so powerfully draws.

And it is similarly difficult to come to terms with what *The Tempest* has to teach us about forgiveness, wisdom, and social atonement if we do not also come to terms with its relations to colonialism.

If we allow ourselves to think about the extent to which our magnificent cultural tradition — like that of every civilization we know of — is intertwined with cruelty, injustice, and pain, do we not, in fact, run the risk of "deculturation"? Not if our culture includes a regard for truth. Does this truth mean that we should despise or abandon great art?

Of course not.

Like most teachers, I am deeply committed to passing on the precious heritage of our language, and I take seriously the risk of collective amnesia. Yet there seems to me a far greater risk if professors of literature, frightened by intemperate attacks upon them in the press, refuse to ask the most difficult questions about the past — the risk that we might turn our artistic inheritance into a simple, reassuring, soporific lie.

Sources and Contexts

Unlike most of Shakespeare's plays, *The Tempest* was not based on any earlier story or work. The play does, however, reflect the influence of several contemporary documents that suggested situations, ideas, and language that Shakespeare borrowed and adapted to his purposes. We hope that reading these materials on the sources of *The Tempest* alongside the play itself will help you see how history — and historical conflict — can enter into the form and content of a major literary work.

The most famous of these sources is an essay "Of the Cannibals," by the French writer Michel de Montaigne, which in 1603 appeared in an English translation by John Florio, a translation that Shakespeare is believed to have read. Montaigne's argument that the natural state in which cannibals live is superior in virtue and innocence to the condition of civilization is echoed in Gonzalo's speech on the innocence of nature in *The Tempest*, 2.1. Montaigne's meditation on cannibals may have also suggested the name "Caliban" to Shakespeare.

The other major source reflected in the play is a set of written accounts that reached England in 1610 of a shipwreck near the Bermuda islands in the summer of 1609. These so-called Bermuda pamphlets describe a storm encountered by a fleet of nine English ships, one of which was given up for lost but whose survivors sailed almost a year later into the port of Jamestown, Virginia. We include here two excerpts from these accounts, one by William Strachey, the other by Sylvester Jourdain.

Interestingly for readers of *The Tempest,* these accounts present sharply contrasting images of nature. On the one hand, there is the "dreadful storm and hideous" described by Strachey (p. 122 in this volume) and "the dangerous and dreaded" Bermuda islands the sailors expect —"the Devil's islands . . . feared and avoided of all sea travelers alive above any other place in the world" (p. 123). On the other hand, there is the paradise the sailors do find, described succinctly by Jourdain as a "country so abundantly fruitful of all fit necessaries for the sustenation and preservation of man's life" (p. 125). These clashing views of nature — is it the opposite of civilization or the harmonious complement to it? — become a central theme of *The Tempest.*

The question of whether nature is good or evil is at the heart of the problem of Caliban, insofar as he resembles the "natives" who were being encountered by European travelers and adventurers. Were such native "Others" human and worthy of respect, or were they "natural" in the worst sense, subhuman savages who could be conquered, enslaved, or slaughtered with impunity? The sharply clashing views of Shakespeare's contemporaries over this question of the natural man are dramatized by Richard Hakluyt's "Reasons for Colonization" (1585) and Bartolomé de Las Casas's "Letter to Philip, Great Prince of Spain" (1550).

Hakluyt's "Reasons for Colonization" reveals that supposedly enlightened Englishmen had few scruples about conquering and dominating the Indians of the New World. In his enumeration of the various justifications for colonizing the New World, Hakluyt takes for granted a kind of entitlement on the part of English (p. 130):

> The ends of this voyage are these:
> 1. To plant Christian religion. ⎫
> 2. To traffic [i.e., trade]. ⎬ Or, to do all three.
> 3. To conquer. ⎭

From Hakluyt's perspective, the desires of the natives themselves were obviously not worth mentioning.

In view of documents like Hakluyt's, it is tempting to assume that the emergence of humane attitudes toward distant peoples had to wait till the advent of modern democratic times. Nor is it surprising that readers often find hopelessly improbable and anachronistic the suggestion that Shakespeare conveys some partial sympathy for Caliban. It is noteworthy, however, that even Hakluyt defines limits beyond which the colonizers must not go:

> But if, seeking revenge on every injury of the savages, we seek blood and raise war, our vines, our olives, our fig trees, our sugar-canes,

our oranges and lemons, corn, cattle, etc., will be destroyed and trade of merchandise in all things overthrown. (p. 134)

Such passages indicate that the colonizers did at times have misgivings about the consequences of militaristic colonization, even if those misgivings were predominantly about economic consequences.

These misgivings rise to the level of articulate moral protest in Las Casas's powerful letter of 1550 to the king of Spain, which demonstrates that some Europeans of this period did regard the conquest of the New World as a serious violation of Christian principles. Protesting that "the Indians are being brought to the point of extermination," Las Casas invokes the principle that "seizing what belongs to others and increasing one's property by shedding human blood" (p. 139) is indefensible for any nation that claims to be Christian.

With the essays by Daniel Wilson and E. M. W. Tillyard, we move to two very different contexts for understanding the play. Writing in the wake of Charles Darwin's *Origin of Species* (1859), the work in which Darwin first proposed the theory of evolution, Wilson argues that Caliban is a possible "missing link" between higher order mammals and humans. Wilson does not fully endorse either Prospero's view of Caliban or Caliban's view of himself, but, by looking at Caliban through a Darwinian lens, Wilson offers a fresh analysis of Caliban's character and an equally fresh take on his relations with Prospero and with Stephano and Trinculo.

Tillyard, writing in 1944, also places Caliban in a hierarchy of biological species, but Tillyard is concerned not with the theory of evolution but with what he calls the Elizabethan world picture, the view of the universe that Shakespeare and his contemporaries presumably so took for granted that they rarely even needed to assert it. In this picture, the cosmos is seen as a well-ordered and hierarchical "chain of being" with God at the top, angels just below God, then humans, animals, plants, and inanimate things. At every level of this hierarchy one creature occupies a higher place than the others: the eagle is first among birds; the lion is first among beasts; the emperor or king is chief among humans; the husband and father has justifiable sovereignty over the wife and the family; the master over the servant; and so on. Tillyard also contends that the Elizabethans, though unified in their belief in this ordered system, were very worried that possible disruptions to it — for example, the usurpation of a dukedom like that of Prospero or the rebellion of a lower creature like Caliban — would result in the spread of chaos to all other levels. Tillyard regards *The Tempest* as Shakespeare's most direct commentary on the chain of being. Like Wilson, he places Caliban closer to the beasts than to other humans, but Tillyard also reads Prospero's acknowledgment of Caliban as evidence that Shakespeare endorses the view that even the most exalted human must recognize that he cannot escape the bestial element within himself.

Tillyard's approach of contextualizing Shakespeare within the cultural beliefs of his age, though now regarded as an outdated "old historicism," was widely influential in its day and informed much of the teaching of Shakespeare. Indeed, throughout the 1940s and 1950s his approach was the main rival to the New Critical approach to interpretation represented most clearly in this volume by Reuben A. Brower (see p. 224). Two of Tillyard's assumptions are particularly challenged by today's postcolonial and feminist critics: that the worldview of Shakespeare's time was so widely shared that there were few cultural conflicts; and that readers and critics of Shakespeare's plays should not just understand this worldview in its own terms but accept it as a great intellectual system rather than criticize it in light of modern ideas of justice and equality.

Both Wilson and Tillyard provide suggestive frames within which to view the portfolio of images of Caliban that follow Wilson's essay. After those images we have suggested a couple of exercises that we believe will further stimulate your thinking about Caliban.

Finally, the chapter we have included on the historical context of *The Tempest* by current historian Ronald Takaki from his *A Different Mirror* (1993) provides further evidence of the tensions felt by Shakespeare's contemporaries in their attitudes toward New World Indians. For the most part, these attitudes assumed the unquestioned superiority of European culture, which at the time the play was written, according to Takaki, had begun to use such native peoples to delineate "the border, the hierarchical division between civilization and wildness" (p. 189). The supposed laziness and "savagery" of the Indians justified the English in dispossessing them (p. 198), just as similar beliefs about the Irish, Takaki notes, justified English rule over Ireland. *The Tempest*, according to Takaki, can be approached "as a defining moment in the making of an English-American identity based on race" (p. 182). The only issue in dispute seems to have been whether the Indians were unregenerate devils or capable of being "civilized." Yet despite this dominant attitude, Takaki points out that counterviews did exist: for example, Pope Paul III had proclaimed that Indians "should not be deprived of their liberty and property" despite being outside the Christian faith (pp. 190–91). "Clearly," Takaki argues, "Caliban was no mere victim: capable of acculturation, he could express his anger" (p. 191).

MICHEL DE MONTAIGNE
From Of the Cannibals

Michel de Montaigne (1533–1592) was a French courtier and author of *Essais,* the extensive collection of philosophical writings that was instrumental in establishing the essay as a literary form. Educated at the Collège de Guyenne at Bordeaux and then as a lawyer, probably at Toulouse, Montaigne spent the early years of his adult life in the public realm. Though he would always remain engaged in public life (serving as the mayor of Bordeaux from 1581 to 1585, for example), in 1571, he sold his seat in Parliament and began work on the *Essais,* a project that would occupy him for the rest of his life. The first two volumes of *Essais* were published in 1580; "Of the Cannibals," which appears here, was one of those in the first volume. This excerpt, translated by John Florio, is reprinted from the Signet Classic paperback edition of *The Tempest,* edited by Robert Langbaum (New York: Penguin, 1998).

. . . I find (as far as I have been informed) there is nothing in that nation [the American Indians], that is either barbarous or savage, unless men call that barbarism which is not common to them. As indeed, we have no other aim of truth and reason than the example and idea of the opinions and customs of the country we live in. There is ever perfect religion, perfect policy, perfect and complete use of all things. They are even savage, as we call those fruits wild which nature of herself and of her ordinary progress hath produced; whereas indeed, they are those which ourselves have altered by our artificial devices, and diverted from their common order, we should rather term savage. In those are the true and most profitable virtues and natural properties most lively and vigorous, which in these we have bastardized, applying them to the pleasure of our corrupted taste. And if notwithstanding, in divers fruits of those countries that were never tilled, we shall find that, in respect of ours, they are most excellent and as delicate unto our taste, there is no reason art should gain the point of honor of our great and puissant mother Nature. We have so much by our inventions surcharged the beauties and riches of her works that we have altogether overchoked her; yet wherever her purity shineth, she makes our vain and frivolous enterprises wonderfully ashamed. . . .

All our endeavor or wit cannot so much as reach to represent the nest of the last birdlet, its contexture, beauty, profit and use, no nor the web of a seely[1] spider. "All things," saith Plato, "are produced either by nature, by fortune, or by art. The greatest and fairest by one or other of the two first, the least and imperfect by the last." Those nations seem therefore so barbarous unto me, because they have received very little fashion from human wit and are yet near their original naturality. The laws of nature do yet command them, which are but little bastardized by ours, and that with such purity, as I am sometimes grieved the knowledge of it came no sooner to light, at what time there were men that better than we could have judged of it. I am sorry Lycurgus and Plato had it not; for me seemeth that what in those nations we see by experience, doth not only exceed all the pictures wherewith licentious Poesy hath proudly embellished the golden age, and all her quaint inventions to fain a happy condition of man, but also the conception and desire of Philosophy. They could not imagine a genuity so pure and simple as we see it by experience; nor ever believe our society might be maintained with so little art and humane combination. It is a nation, would I answer Plato, that hath no kind of traffic, no knowledge of letters, no intelligence of numbers, no name of magistrate, nor of politic superiority; no use of service, of riches, or of poverty; no contracts, no successions, no partitions, no occupation but idle; no respect of kindred but common, no apparel but natural, no manuring of lands, no use of wine, corn, or metal. The very words that import lying, falsehood, treason, dissimulations, covetousness, envy, detraction, and pardon, were never heard of amongst them. How dissonant would he find his imaginary commonwealth from this perfection? . . .

Furthermore, they live in a country of so exceeding pleasant and temperate situation that, as my testimonies have told me, it is very rare to see a sick body amongst them; and they have further assured me they never saw any man there either shaking with the palsy, toothless, with eyes dropping, or crooked and stooping through age.

I am not sorry we note the barbarous horror of such an action, but grieved that, prying so narrowly into their faults, we are so blinded in ours. I think there is more barbarism in eating men alive than to feed upon them being dead; to mangle by tortures and torments a body full of lively sense, to roast him in pieces, to make dogs and swine to gnaw and tear him in mammocks (as we have not only read but seen very lately, yea and in our own memory, not amongst ancient enemies but our neighbors and fellow citizens; and which is worse, under pretense of piety and religion) than to roast and eat him after he is dead.

[1]**seely:** fortunate, happy.

WILLIAM STRACHEY

From True Repertory of the Wrack

William Strachey (1572–1621), a Cambridge-educated historian, sailed to Virginia in 1609 with the appointed governor of the colony of Virginia, Sir Thomas Gates. On the journey, their ship encountered a storm and wrecked in the Bermudas, where Strachey and the other passengers remained for almost a year before building two new ships and continuing their trip to Virginia. "True Repertory of the Wrack," a letter written by Strachey to an unidentified woman, is one of several accounts of the shipwreck Shakespeare is believed to have read before composing *The Tempest*. Strachey is also known for his writing about Virginia, published as *Historie of Travaille into Virginia Britannia*, written after the group finally reached their destination. This excerpt from "True Repertory" comes from the Signet Classic paperback edition of *The Tempest*, edited by Robert Langbaum (New York: Penguin, 1998).

A dreadful storm and hideous began to blow from out the northeast, which swelling and roaring as it were by fits, some hours with more violence than others, at length did beat all light from heaven; which like an hell of darkness turned black upon us, so much the more fuller of horror, as in such cases horror and fear use to overrun the troubled and overmastered senses of all, which (taken up with amazement) the ears lay so sensible to the terrible cries and murmurs of the winds, and distraction of our company, as who was most armed and best prepared was not a little shaken.

For four and twenty hours the storm in a restless tumult had blown so exceedingly, as we could not apprehend in our imaginations any possibility of greater violence, yet did we still find it, not only more terrible, but more constant, fury added to fury, and one storm urging a second more outrageous than the former; whether it so wrought upon our fears or indeed met with new forces. Sometimes strikes [shrieks?] in our ship amongst women and passengers not used to such hurly and discomforts made us look one upon the other with troubled hearts and panting bosoms; our clamors drowned in the winds, and the winds in thunder. Prayers might well be in the heart and lips, but drowned in the outcries of the officers. Nothing heard that could give comfort, nothing seen that might encourage hope. . . . It could not be said to rain, the waters like whole rivers did flood in the air. . . . Here the glut of water (as if throttling the wind erewhile) was no sooner a little emptied and qualified, but instantly the winds (as having gotten their mouths now free and at liberty) spake more loud and grew tumultuous and malignant. . . . There was not a moment in which the sudden splitting or instant oversetting of the ship was not expected.

Howbeit this was not all. It pleased God to bring a greater affliction yet upon us; for in the beginning of the storm we had received likewise a mighty leak. And the ship . . . was grown five foot suddenly deep with water above her ballast, and we almost drowned within whilst we sat looking when to perish from above. This, imparting no less terror than danger, ran through the whole ship with much fright and amazement, startled and turned the blood, and took down the braves of the most hardy mariner of them all, insomuch as he that before happily felt not the sorrow of others, now began to sorrow for himself when he saw such a pond of water so suddenly broken in, and which he knew could not (without present avoiding) but instantly sink him. . . .

Once, so huge a sea brake upon the poop[1] and quarter[2] upon us, as it covered our ship from stern to stem, like a garment or a vast cloud, it filled her brim full for a while within, from the hatches up to the spar deck.[3] . . . with much clamor encouraged and called upon others; who gave her now up, rent in pieces and absolutely lost.

. . . Sir George Sommers, when no man dreamed of such happiness, had discovered and cried land. . . . We were enforced to run her ashore as near the land as we could, which brought us within three-quarters of a mile of shore. . . .

We found it to be the dangerous and dreaded island, or rather islands of the Bermuda; whereof let me give your Ladyship a brief description before I proceed to my narration. And that the rather, because they be so terrible to all that ever touched on them, and such tempests, thunders, and other fearful objects are seen and heard about them, that they be called commonly the Devil's Islands, and are feared and avoided of all sea travelers alive above any other place in the world. Yet it pleased our merciful God to make even this hideous and hated place both the place of our safety and means of our deliverance.

[1]**poop:** the aftermost part of a ship; the stern.
[2]**quarter:** part of the ship where the sailors lodged.
[3]**spar deck:** a roof-like covering over one part of a ship.

And hereby also, I hope to deliver the world from a foul and general error: it being counted of most that they can be no habitation for men, but rather given over to devils and wicked spirits. Whereas indeed we find them now by experience to be as habitable and commodious as most countries of the same climate and situation; insomuch as if the entrance into them were as easy as the place itself is contenting, it had long ere this been inhabited as well as other islands. Thus shall we make it appear that Truth is the daughter of Time, and that men ought not to deny everything which is not subject to their own sense.

SYLVESTER JOURDAIN

From A Discovery of the Barmudas

Sylvester Jourdain (?–1650?), like William Strachey, was a passenger on the *Sea Venture,* the ship that wrecked in the Bermudas in 1609 before reaching its destination of Virginia; he also wrote an account of the wreck, one that presents a slightly more jovial image of the survivors' encounter with the Bermudas. Little is known of Jourdain's life; he was a resident of Lyme Regis in Dorsetshire and had a wealthy brother, who worked as a merchant and was a member of Parliament. Jourdain himself may have been a merchant; a shipper by the same name is listed in the Port Book of Poole in 1603. This excerpt from *A Discovery of the Barmudas* is reprinted from the Signet Classic paperback edition of *The Tempest,* edited by Robert Langbaum (New York: Penguin, 1998).

. . . All our men, being utterly spent, tired, and disabled for longer labor, were even resolved, without any hope of their lives, to shut up the hatches and to have committed themselves to the mercy of the sea (which is said to be merciless) or rather to the mercy of their mighty God and redeemer. . . . So that some of them, having some good and comfortable waters in the ship, fetched them and drunk the one to the other, taking their last leave one of the other, until their more joyful and happy meeting in a more blessed world; when it pleased God out of His most gracious and merciful providence, so to direct and guide our ship (being left to the mercy of the sea) for her most advantage; that Sir George Somers . . . most wishedly happily descried land; whereupon he most comfortably encouraged the company to follow their pumping, and by no means to cease bailing out of the water. . . . Through which weak means it pleased God to work so strongly as the water was stayed for that little time (which, as we all much feared, was the last period of our breathing) and the ship kept from present sinking, when it pleased God to send her within half an English mile of that land that Sir George Somers had not long before descried — which were the islands of the Barmudas. And there neither did our ship sink, but more fortunately in so great a misfortune fell in between two rocks, where she was fast lodged and locked for further budging.

But our delivery was not more strange in falling so opportunely and happily upon the land, as our feeding and preservation was beyond our hopes and all men's expectations most admirable. For the islands of the Barmudas, as every man knoweth that hath heard or read of them, were never inhabited by any Christian or heathen people, but ever esteemed and reputed a most prodigious and enchanted place affording nothing but gusts, storms, and foul weather; which made every navigator and mariner to avoid them, as Scylla and Charybdis, or as they would shun the Devil himself; and no man was ever heard to make for the place, but as against their wills, they have by storms and dangerousness of the rocks, lying seven leagues into the sea, suffered shipwrack. Yet did we find there the air so temperate and the country so abundantly fruitful of all fit necessaries for the sustenation and preservation of man's life, that most in a manner of all our provisions of bread, beer, and victual being quite spoiled in lying long drowned in salt water, notwithstanding we were there for the space of nine months (few days over or under) not only well refreshed, comforted, and with good satiety contented but, out of the abundance thereof, provided us some reasonable quantity and proportion of provision to carry us for Virginia and to maintain ourselves and that company we found there, to the great relief of them, as it fell out in their so great extremities . . . until it pleased God . . . that their store was better supplied. And greater and better provisions we might have had, if we had had better means for the storing and transportation thereof. Wherefore my opinion sincerely of this island is, that whereas it hath been and is full accounted the most dangerous, unfortunate, and most forlorn place of the world, it is in truth the richest, healthfulest, and pleasing land (the quantity and bigness thereof considered) and merely natural, as ever man set foot upon.

RICHARD HAKLUYT

Reasons for Colonization

Richard Hakluyt (1552?–1616), born to a family with connections among merchants, geographers, and explorers, was the first professor of modern geography at Oxford. He wrote at length about the topic of English colonization and was an especially strong advocate for colonizing North America, in the hopes of establishing northern passages to the Orient. His interest in such a venture is documented in various writings, including early works such as *Divers Voyages Touching the Discovery of America* (1582) and *The Discourse on the Western Planting* (a report on the Virginia colonial project written in 1584 but not published until 1877). His colonial interests can also be seen in his major work, *The Principal Navigations, Voyages, Traffics, and Discoveries of the English Nation* (1598–1600). This piece, "Reasons for Colonization" (1585), is reprinted from *The Elizabethans' America: A Collection of Early Reports by Englishmen on the New World,* edited by Louis B. Wright (Cambridge: Harvard University Press, 1966).

---

1. The glory of God by planting of religion among those infidels.

2. The increase of the force of the Christians.

3. The possibility of the enlarging of the dominions of the Queen's Most Excellent Majesty, and consequently of her honor, revenues, and of her power by this enterprise.

4. An ample vent in time to come of the woollen cloths of England, especially those of the coarsest sorts, to the maintenance of our poor, that else starve or become burdensome to the realm; and vent also of sundry our commodities upon the tract of that firm land, and possibly in other regions from the northern side of that main.

5. A great possibility of further discoveries of other regions from the north part of the same land by sea, and of unspeakable honor and benefit that may rise upon the same by the trades to ensue in Japan, China, and Cathay, etc.

6. By return thence, this realm shall receive woad, oil, wines, hops, salt, and most or all the commodities that we receive from the best parts of Europe, and we shall receive the same better cheap than now we receive them, as we may use the matter.

7. Receiving the same thence, the navy, the human strength of this realm, our merchants and their goods, shall not be subject to arrest of ancient enemies and doubtful friends as of late years they have been.

8. If our nation do not make any conquest there but only use traffic and change of commodities, yet, by means the country is not very mighty but divided into petty kingdoms, they shall not dare to offer us any great annoy but such as we may easily revenge with sufficient chastisement to the unarmed people there.

9. Whatsoever commodities we receive by the Steelyard Merchants, or by our own merchants from Eastland, be it flax, hemp, pitch, tar, masts, clapboard, wainscot, or such-like; the like good[s] may we receive from the north and north-east part of that country near unto Cape Breton, in return for our coarse woollen cloths, flannels, and rugs fit for those colder regions.

10. The passage to and fro is through the main ocean sea, so as we are not in danger of any enemy's coast.

11. In the voyage we are not to cross the burnt zone, nor to pass through frozen seas encumbered with ice and fogs, but in temperate climate at all times of the year; and it requireth not, as the East Indies voyage doth, the taking in of water in divers places, by reason that it is to be sailed in five or six weeks; and by the shortness the merchant may yearly make two returns (a factory once being erected there), a matter in trade of great moment.

12. In this trade by the way, in our pass to and fro, we have in tempests and other haps all the ports of Ireland to our aid and no near coast of any enemy.

13. By this ordinary trade we may annoy the enemies to Ireland and succour the Queen's Majesty's friends there, and in time we may from Virginia yield them whatsoever commodity they now receive from the Spaniard; and so the Spaniards shall want the ordinary victual that heretofore they received yearly from thence, and so they shall not continue trade, nor fall so aptly in practice against this government as now by their trade thither they may.

14. We shall, as it is thought, enjoy in this voyage either some small islands to settle on or some one place or other on the firm land to fortify for the safety of our ships, our men, and our goods, the like whereof we have not in any foreign place of our traffic, in which respect we may be in degree of more safety and more quiet.

15. The great plenty of buff hides and of many other sundry kinds of hides there now presently to be had, the trade of whale and seal fishing and of divers other fishings in the great rivers, great bays, and seas

there, shall presently defray the charge in good part or in all of the first enterprise, and so we shall be in better case than our men were in Russia, where many years were spent and great sums of money consumed before gain was found.

16. The great broad rivers of that main that we are to enter into, so many leagues navigable or portable into the mainland, lying so long a tract with so excellent and so fertile a soil on both sides, do seem to promise all things that the life of man doth require and whatsoever men may wish that are to plant upon the same or to traffic in the same.

17. And whatsoever notable commodity the soil within or without doth yield in so long a tract, that is to be carried out from thence to England, the same rivers so great and deep do yield no small benefit for the sure, safe, easy, and cheap carriage of the same to shipboard, be it of great bulk or of great weight.

18. And in like sort whatsoever commodity of England the inland people there shall need, the same rivers do work the like effect in benefit for the incarriage of the same aptly, easily, and cheaply.

19. If we find the country populous and desirous to expel us and injuriously to offend us, that seek but just and lawful traffic, then, by reason that we are lords of navigation and they not so, we are the better able to defend ourselves by reason of those great rivers and to annoy them in many places.

20. Where there be many petty kings or lords planted on the rivers' sides, and [who] by all likelihood maintain the frontiers of their several territories by wars, we may by the aid of this river join with this king here, or with that king there, at our pleasure, and may so with a few men be revenged of any wrong offered by any of them; or may, if we will proceed with extremity, conquer, fortify, and plant in soils most sweet, most pleasant, most strong, and most fertile, and in the end bring them all in subjection and to civility.

21. The known abundance of fresh fish in the rivers, and the known plenty of fish on the sea-coast there, may assure us of sufficient victual in spite of the people, if we will use salt and industry.

22. The known plenty and variety of flesh of divers kinds of beasts at land there may seem to say to us that we may cheaply victual our navies to England for our returns, which benefit everywhere is not found of merchants.

23. The practice of the people of the East Indies, when the Portugals came thither first, was to cut from the Portugals their lading of spice; and hereby they thought to overthrow their purposed trade. If these people shall practice the like, by not suffering us to have any

commodity of theirs without conquest (which requireth some time), yet may we maintain our first voyage thither till our purpose come to effect by the sea-fishing on the coasts there and by dragging for pearls, which are said to be on those parts; and by return of those commodities the charges in part shall be defrayed: which is a matter of consideration in enterprises of charge.

24. If this realm shall abound too too much with youth, in the mines there of gold (as that of Chisca and Saguenay), of silver, copper, iron, etc., may be an employment to the benefit of this realm; in tilling of the rich soil there for grain and in planting of vines there for wine or dressing of those vines which grow there naturally in great abundance; olives for oil; orange trees, lemons, figs and almonds for fruit; woad, saffron, and madder[1] for dyers; hops for brewers; hemp, flax; and in many such other things, by employment of the soil, our people void of sufficient trades may be honestly employed, that else may become hurtful at home.

25. The navigating of the seas in the voyage, and of the great rivers there, will breed many mariners for service and maintain much navigation.

26. The number of raw hides there of divers kinds of beasts, if we shall possess some island there or settle on the firm, may presently employ many of our idle people in divers several dressings of the same, and so we may return them to the people that cannot dress them so well, or into this realm, where the same are good merchandise, or to Flanders, etc., which present gain at the first raiseth great encouragement presently to the enterprise.

27. Since great waste woods be there of oak, cedar, pine, walnuts, and sundry other sorts, many of our waste people may be employed in making of ships, hoys,[2] busses,[3] and boats, and in making of rosin, pitch, and tar, the trees natural for the same being certainly known to be near Cape Breton[4] and the Bay of Menan,[5] and in many other places thereabout.

28. If mines of white or grey marble, jet, or other rich stone be found there, our idle people may be employed in the mines of the same and in preparing the same to shape, and, so shaped, they may be carried

---

[1]**woad, saffron, and madder:** dyes derived from different plants; woad is a blue dye; saffron is orange; madder is reddish-purple.

[2]**hoys:** small boats similar to sloops which have only one mast; used for short trips.

[3]**busses:** boats larger than hoys; typically having two or three masts.

[4]**Cape Breton:** Cape Breton Island is just off the coast of Nova Scotia, Canada.

[5]**Bay of Menan:** located off the coast of what is now Maine, near the Menan Islands.

into this realm as good ballast for our ships and after serve for noble buildings.

29. Sugar-canes may be planted as well as they are now in the South of Spain, and besides the employment of our idle people, we may receive the commodity cheaper and not enrich infidels or our doubtful friends, of whom now we receive that commodity.

30. The daily great increase of wools in Spain, and the like in the West Indies, and the great employment of the same into cloth in both places, may move us to endeavour, for vent of our cloth, new discoveries of peopled regions where hope of sale may arise; otherwise in short time many inconveniences may possibly ensue.

31. This land that we purpose to direct our course to, lying in part in the 40th degree of latitude, being in like heat as Lisbon in Portugal doth, and in the more southerly part, as the most southerly coast of Spain doth, may by our diligence yield unto us, besides wines and oils and sugars, oranges, lemons, figs, raisins, almonds, pomegranates, rice, raw silks such as come from Granada, and divers commodities for dyers, as anil[6] and cochineal,[7] and sundry other colours and materials. Moreover, we shall not only receive many precious commodities besides from thence, but also shall in time find ample vent of the labor of our poor people at home, by sale of hats, bonnets, knives, fish-hooks, copper kettles, beads, looking-glasses, bugles, and a thousand kinds of other wrought wares that in short time may be brought in use among the people of that country, to the great relief of the multitude of our poor people and to the wonderful enriching of this realm. And in time, such league and intercourse may arise between our stapling seats[8] there, and other ports of our Northern America, and of the islands of the same, that incredible things, and by few as yet dreamed of, may speedily follow, tending to the impeachment of our mighty enemies and to the common good of this noble government.

The ends of this voyage are these:
1. To plant Christian religion. ⎫
2. To traffic.   ⎬ Or, to do all three.
3. To conquer.   ⎭

To plant Christian religion without conquest will be hard. Traffic easily followeth conquest; conquest is not easy. Traffic without conquest seemeth possible and not uneasy. What is to be done is the question.

[6]**anil:** indigo dye derived from the Indigo shrub.
[7]**cochineal:** scarlet dye derived from cacti.
[8]**stapling seats:** sites where wool and other trading materials were gathered.

If the people be content to live naked and to content themselves with few things of mere necessity, then traffic is not. So then in vain seemeth our voyage, unless this nature may be altered, as by conquest and other good means it may be, but not on a sudden. The like whereof appeared in the East Indies, upon the Portugals seating there.

If the people in the inland be clothed, and desire to live in the abundance of all such things as Europe doth, and have at home all the same in plenty, yet we cannot have traffic with them, by means they want not anything that we can yield them.

Admit that they have desire to your commodities, and as yet have neither gold, silver, copper, iron, nor sufficient quantity of other present commodity to maintain the yearly trade, what is then to be done?

The soil and climate first is to be considered, and you are with Argus eyes[9] to see what commodity by industry of man you are able to make it to yield that England doth want or both desire: as for the purpose, if you can make it to yield good wine or good oil, as it is like you may by the climate (where wild vines of sundry sorts do naturally grow already in great abundance), then your trade may be maintained. But admit the soil were in our disposition (as yet it is not), in what time may this be brought about?

For wine this is to be affirmed, that, first, the soil lying in 36 or 37 degrees, in the temperature of South Spain, in setting your vine plants this year you may have wine within three years. And it may be that the wild vines growing there already, by orderly pruning and dressing at your first arrival, may come to profit in shorter time.

And planting your olive trees this year, you may have oil within three years.

And if the sea-shores be flat and fit for receipt of salt water and for salt making, without any annoy of near freshes, then the trade of salt only may maintain a yearly navigation (as our men now trade to the isle of Maio[10] and the Hollanders to *terra firma* near the west end of the Isle of Margarita[11]).

But how the natural people of the country may be made skillful to plant vines and to know the use, or to set olive trees and to know the making of oil, and withal to use both the trades, that is a matter of small consideration; but to conquer a country or province in climate and soil of Italy, Spain, or the islands from whence we receive our wines and

[9]**Argus eyes:** Argus was a giant with a hundred eyes.

[10]**Maio:** small island off the west coast of Africa, part of the Cape Verde archipelago.

[11]**Margarita:** island located in the Caribbean Sea, twenty-three miles northeast of Venezuela.

oils, and to man it, to plant it, and to keep it, and to continue the making of wines and oils able to serve England, were a matter of great
importance both in respect of the saving at home of our great treasure
now yearly going away, and in respect of the annoyance thereby growing to our enemies. The like consideration would be had touching a
place for the making of salt, of temperature like those of France, not too
cold, as the salts of the northern regions be, nor too too fiery, as those
be that be made more southerly than France. In regard whereof, many
circumstances are to be considered, and, principally, by what means the
people of those parties may be drawn by all courtesy into love with our
nation, that we become not hateful unto them as the Spaniard is in Italy
and in the West Indies and elsewhere by their manner of usage: for a
gentle course without cruelty and tyranny best answereth the profession of a Christian, best planteth Christian religion, maketh our seating
most void of blood, most profitable in trade of merchandise, most firm
and stable, and least subject to remove by practice of enemies. But that
we may in seating there not be subject wholly to the malice of enemies,
and may be more able to preserve our bodies, ships, and goods in more
safety, and to be known to be more able to scourge the people there,
civil or savage, than willing to offer any violence, and for the more quiet
exercise of our manurance of the soils where we shall seat and of our
manual occupations, it is to be wished that some ancient captains of mild
disposition and great judgment be sent thither with men most skilful in
the art of fortification, and that direction be taken that the mouths of
great rivers and the islands in the same (as things of great moment) be
taken, manned, and fortified, and that havens be cut out for safety of the
navy, that we may be lords of the gates and entries to go out and come in
at pleasure, and to lie in safety and be able to command and to control
all within, and to force all foreign navigation to lie out in open road subject to all weathers, to be dispersed by tempests and flaws, if the force
within be not able to give them the encounter abroad.

1. The red muscatel grape that Bishop Grindal procured out of
Germany, the great white muscatel, the yellow grape: the cuts of these
were wont yearly to be set at Fulham and after one year's rooting to be
given by the Bishop and to be sold by his gardener. These presently
provided and placed in earth, and many of these so rooted, with store
of cuts unrooted besides, placed in tubs of earth shipped at the next
voyage, to be planted in Virginia, may begin vineyards and bring wines
out of hand.

2. Provision of great wild olive trees may be made out of this city so
then to be carried to increase great store of stocks to graft the best olive

on; and Virginia standing in the same degree that the Shroff, the olive place, doth in Spain, we may win that merchandise, grafting the wild.

3. Sugar-canes, if you cannot procure them from the Spanish islands, yet may you by your Barbary merchants procure them.

4. There is an herb in Persia whereof anil is made, and it is also in Barbary; to procure that by seed or root were of importance for a trade of merchandise for our clothing country.

5. Woad by the seeds you may have, for you may have hundreds of bushels in England, as it is multiplied; and having soil and labor in Virginia cheap, and the woad in great value, lying in small room, it will be a trade of great gain to this clothing realm, and the thing cannot be destroyed by savages. The roots of this you may have in plenty and number coming in the trade; so this may grow in trade within a year ready for the merchant.

6. Fig trees of many good kinds may be had hence in barrel, if now presently they be provided; and they in that climate will yield noble fruit and feed your people presently, and will be brought in frails home as merchandise, or in barrel, as raisins also may be.

7. Sawed boards of sassafras and cedar, to be turned into small boxes for ladies and gentlewomen, would become a present trade.

8. To the infinite natural increase of hogs, to add a device how the same may be fed by roots, acorns, etc., without spoiling your corn, would be of great effect to feed the multitude continually employed in labor; and the same, cheaply bred and salted, and barrelled there and brought home, will be well sold for a good merchandise; and the barrels after will serve for our home herring fishing; and so you sell your woods and the labor of your cooper.

9. Receiving the savage women and their children of both sexes by courtesy into your protection, and employing the Englishwomen and the others in making of linen, you shall raise a wonderful trade of benefit, both to carry into England and also into the islands and into the main of the West Indies, victual and labor being so cheap there.

10. The trade of making cables and cordage there will be of great importance, in respect of a cheap maintenance of the navy that shall pass to and fro and in respect of such navy as may in those parties be used for the venting of the commodities of England to be brought thither. And poldavies,[12] etc., made for sails of the poor savages, yield to the navy a great help and a great gain in the traffic.

---

[12]**poldavies:** coarse canvas used to make sails.

But if, seeking revenge on every injury of the savages, we seek blood and raise war, our vines, our olives, our fig trees, our sugar-canes, our oranges and lemons, corn, cattle, etc., will be destroyed and trade of merchandise in all things overthrown; and so the English nation there planted and to be planted shall be rooted out with sword and hunger.

Sorts of men which are to be passed in this voyage

1. Men skilful in all mineral causes.

2. Men skilful in all kind of drugs.

3. Fishermen, to consider of the sea-fishings there on the coasts, to be reduced to trade hereafter: and others for the freshwater fishings.

4. Salt-makers, to view the coast and to make trial how rich the sea-water there is, to advise for the trade.

5. Husbandmen, to view the soil, to resolve for tillage in all sorts.

6. Vineyard men bred, to see how the soil may serve for the planting of vines.

7. Men bred in the Shroff in South Spain, for discerning how olive trees may be planted there.

8. Others for planting of orange trees, fig trees, lemon trees, and almond trees, for judging how the soil may serve for the same.

9. Gardeners, to prove the several soils of the islands and of our settling places, to see how the same may serve for all herbs and roots for our victualling, since by rough seas sometimes we may want fish, and since we may want flesh to victual us, by the malice of the natural people there; and the gardeners for planting of our common trees of fruit, as pears, apples, plums, peaches, medlars,[13] apricots, quinces for conserves, etc.

10. Lime-makers, to make lime for buildings.

11. Masons, carpenters, etc., for buildings there.

12. Brickmakers and tile-makers.

13. Men cunning in the art of fortification, that may choose out places strong by nature to be fortified, and that can plot out and direct workmen.

14. Choice spade-men, to trench cunningly and to raise bulwarks[14] and rampires[15] of earth for defense and offense.

15. Spade-makers that may out of the woods there make spades like those of Devonshire, and of other sorts, and shovels from time to time for common use.

[13]**medlar:** fruit resembling a small brown-skinned apple.

[14]**bulwark:** substantial defensive work of earth or other material; a rampart or fortification.

[15]**rampire:** synonym for bulwark, though it may also include a low wall at the top and a walkway behind a wall.

16. Smiths, to forge the irons of the shovels and spades, and to make black bills and other weapons, and to mend many things.

17. Men that use to break ash trees for pikestaves, to be employed in the woods there.

18. Others, that finish up the same so rough hewed, such as in London are to be had.

19. Coopers, to make casks of all sorts.

20. Forgers of pikes'-heads and of arrow-heads, with forges, with Spanish iron, and with all manner of tools to be carried with them.

21. Fletchers, to renew arrows, since archery prevaileth much against unarmed people and gunpowder may soon perish by setting on fire.

22. Bowyers also, to make bows there for need.

23. Makers of oars, since for service upon those rivers it is to great purpose for the boats and barges they are to pass and enter with.

24. Shipwrights, to make barges and boats, and bigger vessels, if need be, to run along the coast and to pierce the great bays and inlets.

25. Turners, to turn targets of elm and tough wood for use against the darts and arrows of savages.

26. Such also as have knowledge to make targets of horn.

27. Such also as can make armour of hides upon moulds, such as were wont to be made in this realm about an hundred years since and were called Scottish Jacks: such armour is light and defensive enough against the force of savages.

28. Tanners, to tan hides of buffs, oxen, etc., in the isles where you shall plant.

29. Whittawers[16] of all other skins there.

30. Men skilful in burning of soap-ashes and in making of pitch and tar and rosin to be fetched out of Prussia and Poland, which are thence to be had for small wages, being there in manner of slavers.

The several sorts of trees, as pines, firs, spruces, birch and others, are to be bored with great augers a foot or half a yard above the ground, as they use in Vézelay towards Languedoc and near Bayonne in Gascony; and so you shall easily and quickly see what gums, rosin, turpentine, tar, or liquor is in them, which will quickly distil out clearly without any filthy mixture and will show what commodity may be made of them; their goodness and greatness for masts is also to be considered.

31. A skilful painter is also to be carried with you, which the Spaniards used commonly in all their discoveries to bring the descriptions of all beasts, birds, fishes, trees, towns, etc.

---

[16]**Whittawer:** a tanner, especially one who work in leather.

BARTOLOMÉ DE LAS CASAS

From Letter to Philip, Great Prince of Spain

Bartolomé de Las Casas (1474–1566) was a Spanish historian and Dominican missionary to the Americas, whose experience led him to oppose the oppression of the Indians of North America by European colonizers. First a soldier and then a member of expeditions to the West Indies, Las Casas learned of the oppression of Indians firsthand when he received, for his involvement in expeditions, land grants containing Indian inhabitants. At first, he concentrated on evangelizing the Indians, but he soon returned them to the governor and began to work for their cause. The letter included here is one of a number Las Casas wrote over the course of his life in which he urged specific people and institutions to adopt a less brutal method of colonization. This letter is reprinted from *In Defense of the Indians: The Defense of the Most Reverend Lord, Don Fray Bartolomé de Las Casas . . .*, translated, edited, and annotated by Stafford Poole (1974).

Illustrious Prince:

It is right that matters which concern the safety and peace of the great empire placed in your keeping by the divine goodness be reported to you, for you rule Spain and that marvelous New World in the name of the great Charles, your father, and you strive for immortal glory, not just with the imperial power but especially with the generous spirit and with the wisdom implanted in you by Christ. Therefore I have thought it advisable to bring to the attention of Your Highness that there has come into my hands a certain brief synopsis in Spanish of a work that Ginés de Sepúlveda is reported to have written in Latin. In it he gives four reasons, each of which, in his opinion, proves beyond refutation that war against the Indians is justified, provided that it be waged properly and the laws of war be observed, just as, up to the present, the kings of Spain have commanded that it be waged and carried out.

I hear that it is this man's intention to demonstrate the title by which the Kings of Spain possess the empire of the Indies and to bolster his position with arguments and laws, so that from now on no one will be able to slander you even tacitly on this point. I have read and reread this work carefully. And it is said that Sepúlveda drives home various other points at greater length in his Latin work (which I have not yet had the chance to see). What impression it has made on others I do not know. I certainly have detected in it poisons disguised with honey. Under pretext of pleasing his prince, a man who is a theologian offers honey-coated poison. In place of bread, he offers a stone. Great Prince, unless this deadly poison is stopped by your wisdom, so that it will not become widespread, it will infect the minds of readers, deceive the unwary, and arm and incite tyrants to injustice. Believe me, that little book will bring ruin to the minds of many.

In the first place, while claiming that he wants to vindicate your jurisdiction over the Indies, he tears to pieces and reduces your rights by presenting arguments that are partly foolish, partly false, partly of the kind that have the least force. Furthermore, if this man's judgment in this matter should be printed, [and] sanctioned with the royal license and privilege, there can be no doubt that within a short time the empire of the Indies will be entirely overthrown and destroyed.

Indeed, if so many laws already issued, so many decrees, so many harsh threats, and so many statutes conscientiously enacted by the Emperor Charles and his predecessors have been ineffective in preventing so many thousands of innocent men from perishing by sword, hunger, and all the misfortunes of total war, and extensive areas of their highly civilized kingdoms and most fertile provinces from being savagely devastated; if the fear of God and the dread of hell have not even moderated (I shall not say curbed) the utterly ruthless and cruel spirits of the Spaniards; if the outcries of preachers and holy men that they were barred from the sacraments of the Church and were not forgiven in sacramental confession were of no avail, what will happen when evil men (for whom, according to the old proverb, nothing is wanting except the opportunity) read that a scholar, a doctor of theology, and the royal historian has published books approving those criminal wars and hellish campaigns and, by supporting arguments, confirms and defends the unheard-of crime whereby Christian men, forgetting Christian virtue, hold in slavery those people, the most unfortunate of all, who appear to have escaped the ferocity of that most cruel race by chance rather than by the mercy of the Spaniards? Furthermore, [what will happen when they read] that he teaches that soldiers may lawfully keep everything they take in these wars, even though they undertook the campaign with the evil intention of looting, that is, of pillaging by fire, sword, murder, plunder and violence, upsetting, overturning, and throwing into confusion all laws, divine and human, and that they are not bound to restore such goods because the Spaniards who do these things and shed the blood of the innocent consecrate their hands to God (as I hear Sepúlveda has written) and merit Christ's grace because they prevent the worship of idols?

Whom will they spare? What blood will they not shed? What cruelty will they not commit, these brutal men who are hardened to seeing fields bathed in human blood, who make no distinction of sex or age, who do not spare infants at their mothers' breasts, pregnant women, the great, the lowly, or even men of feeble and gray old age for whom the weight of years usually awakens reverence or mercy? What will they not do if they hear that there is a man teaching that they are consecrating their hands to God when they crush the Indians with massacres, pillaging, and tyranny — that they are doing the same as those who killed the Children of Israel who were adoring the calf? They will give more trust to him, as to someone who tells them what they want to hear, than they would to the son of God himself if he were face to face before us and teaching something different.

If, then, the Indians are being brought to the point of extermination, if as many peoples are being destroyed as widespread kingdoms are being overthrown, what sane man would doubt that the most flourishing empire of the New World, once its native inhabitants have been destroyed, will become a wilderness, and nothing but dominion over tigers, lions, and wild beasts for the Kings of Spain? When the all-wise God commanded certain nations to be overthrown, he did not want them completely destroyed at once, lest the empty lands without human beings become the lair of wild animals which might harm the few Jews who were the new inhabitants.[1]

Therefore when Sepúlveda, by word or in his published works, teaches that campaigns against the Indians are lawful, what does he do except encourage oppressors and provide an opportunity for as many crimes and lamentable evils as these [men] commit, more than anyone would find it possible to believe? In the meantime, with most certain harm to his own soul, he is the reason why countless human beings, suffering brutal massacres, perish forever, that is, men who, through the inhuman brutality of the Spaniards, breathe their last before they hear the word of God, [or] are fed by Christ's gentle doctrine, [or] are

[1]So we read in the seventh chapter of Deuteronomy.

strengthened by the Christian sacraments. What more horrible or unjust occurrence can be imagined than this?

Therefore, if Sepúlveda's opinion (that campaigns against the Indians are lawful) is approved, the most holy faith of Christ, to the reproach of the name Christian, will be hateful and detestable to all the peoples of that world to whom the word will come of the inhuman crimes that the Spaniards inflict on that unhappy race, so that neither in our lifetime nor in the future will they want to accept our faith under any condition, for they see that its first heralds are not pastors but plunderers, not fathers but tyrants, and that those who profess it are ungodly, cruel, and without pity in their merciless savagery.

Furthermore, since Sepúlveda's book is polished, painstaking, persuasive, and carefully built up throughout with many tricky kinds of argument, it will permanently deceive these thieves, these enemies of the human race, so that they will never come to their senses nor, admitting their crimes, flee to the mercy of God, who, in his unutterable love, is perhaps calling them to penance, nor will they implore his help. Under the pretext of religion, [Sepúlveda] excuses the criminal wickedness of these men, which carries with it all the evils to be found anywhere in the lives of mortal men. He praises with lofty language these plunderers who loot with utmost savagery, and he commends their warlike virtue.

Finally, it is intolerable that a man to whom has been entrusted the duty of writing the imperial history should publish a destructive error that is in total disagreement with the words of the gospel and the meekness and kindness of which all Christ's teaching is redolent and which the Church, imitating its master, exercises toward those who do not know Christ. For men of the future will, with good reason, decide that a man who has gone wrong so disgracefully in a matter so clear has taken no account of the truth when writing history, a fact that, no matter how learnedly and gracefully that history will have been written, will tarnish the most celebrated victories of the Emperor.

Therefore I considered the many misfortunes, the great harvest of evils so deserving of rebuke, and the severest punishment which will arise from his teaching: offense against God, ill repute and hatred for our most holy religion, irreparable damage, the loss of so many believing souls, and the loss of the right of the Kings of Spain to the empire of the New World. I considered also that these opinions of his will spread through all the nations of the world the savage and firmly rooted practice of seizing what belongs to others and increasing one's property by shedding human blood (an evil reproach under which the Spanish people have labored for so long), which, Sepúlveda claims, are for the power and glory of Spain.

I could not contain myself. Mindful that I am a Christian, a religious, a bishop, a Spaniard, and a subject of the King of Spain, I cannot but unsheathe the sword of my pen for the defense of the truth, the honor of God's house, and the spreading of the revered gospel of Our Lord Jesus Christ so that, according to the measure of the grace given to me, I might wipe the stain from the Christian name, take away the obstacles and stumbling blocks hindering the spread of belief in the gospel, and proclaim the truth which I have vowed in baptism, have learned in the religious life, and finally, however unworthy, have professed when consecrated bishop. For by all these titles I am bound to set myself up as a wall against the wicked for the defense of a completely innocent people, soon to be grafted onto the true house of Israel, whom the ravening wolves unceasingly pursue. I am also obliged to block the road along which so many thousands of men are lured to their eternal destruction and to defend with my life my sheep, whom I promised by a solemn oath to protect against every wolf, ecclesiastical or lay, who breaks into my sheepfold.

Finally, I want to set forth the true right of my prince, that is, the title by which he may possess the New World, and to hide [*sic*] the frightful and disgraceful crimes that my own people, the Spaniards, have inflicted in violation of justice and right during these last few years on the Indians, who have been ruined by terrible butchery, and to wash away the shame brought upon that name among all the nations.

Four things, therefore, that I must give a full account of are to be treated here.

First, I shall refute Sepúlveda's opinion claiming that war against the Indians is justified because they are barbarous, uncivilized, unteachable, and lacking civil government.

Second, I shall show that, to the most definite ruin of his own soul, Sepúlveda is wrong when he teaches that war against the Indians is justified as punishment for their crimes against the natural law, especially the crimes of idolatry and human sacrifice.

Third, we shall attack his third argument, on the basis of which Sepúlveda teaches that war can be waged unconditionally and indiscriminately against those peoples in order to free the innocent.

Fourth, I shall discuss how foreign to the teaching of the gospel and Christian mercy is his fourth proposition, maintaining that war against the Indians is justified as a means of extending the boundaries of the

Christian religion and of opening the way for those who proclaim and preach the gospel.

When I have finished, the truth of this case and the magnitude of the crime committed by those who have maltreated the Indians by robberies, massacres, and other incredible misfortunes of war, and continue to do so, will be clear; and at the same time how groundless are the arguments of a man who is wrong both in law and in fact, by what design he was led to write that dangerous book, in what way he has distorted the teachings of philosophers and theologians, falsified the words of Sacred Scripture, of divine and human laws, and how no less destructively he has quoted statements of Pope Alexander VI to favor the success of his wicked cause. Finally, the true title by which the Kings of Spain hold their rule over the New World will be shown.

For this reason, Most Excellent Prince, I beg Your Highness to order this work, which I have written at the cost of much sweat and [many] sleepless nights, to be weighed and examined by learned men. If anything is found to be stated improperly or badly, I shall be most pleased to have my sleepless nights perfected by their charity. If, however, anything is found to be expressed well, I look for no other human reward except that Your Highness command Sepúlveda to give me a copy of the Latin work he wrote on this subject so that, when I have refuted his falsehoods more completely, the truth may shine forth and rule the consciences of all men.

Farewell!

DANIEL WILSON

The Monster Caliban

Sir Daniel Wilson (1816–1892) was born in Edinburgh, Scotland, and became an artist, a writer, and an archaeologist interested in the prehistory of Scotland. His first book, *The Archeology and Prehistory of the Annals of Scotland* (1851), helped establish prehistory as an important area of study. In 1853, he moved to Toronto to become a professor of history and English literature at the University of Toronto, and he served as president of the university from 1887 to 1892. Among his many books are *Prehistoric Man: Researches into the Origin of Civilisation in the Old and the New World* (1862), *The Lost Atlantis and Other Ethnographic Studies* (1892), and *Caliban: the Missing Link* (1873). The following piece is a chapter from that book.

The Monster Caliban

> "Arise, and fly
> The reeling Faun, the sensual feast;
> Move upward, working out the beast,
> And let the ape and tiger die."
>
> *In Memoriam.*

The innate and seemingly instinctive aptitude of the human mind to conceive of the supernatural is so universal, and so intimately interwoven with that other conception of a spiritual life, the successor of this present corporeal existence, — which, far more than any supposed belief in a Supreme Being, seems the universal attribute of man, — that Shakespeare's whole conception of the supernatural may fitly come under review as a sequel to the more limited subject specially occupying our consideration. But it is sufficient for the present to bear in mind the originality and prolific powers revealed in his supernatural imaginings, in order the more clearly to appreciate the one portraiture of a being which, though in no sense spiritual, is so far as all experience goes, thoroughly supra-natural.

" 'Tis strange, my Theseus," says Hippolyta to her ducal lover, as the fifth act of "A Midsummer Night's Dream" opens in a hall of his palace at Athens, where they hold discourse on the themes that lovers speak of. The previous scenes have been ripe with the sportive creations of the poet's fancy, with his Oberon, Titania, and all their fairy train; and now, in true dramatic fashion, he claims the shadowy beings as his own. "More strange than true," Theseus replies: —

> "I never may believe
> These antique fables, nor these fairy toys.
> Lovers and madmen have such seething brains,

Such shaping fantasies, that apprehend
More than cool reason ever comprehends;"

and then, after quaintly coupling the lover and the lunatic as beings "of imagination all compact," he adds this other picture of the poet's fantasies: —

"The poet's eye, in a fine frenzy rolling,
    Doth glance from heaven to earth, from earth to heaven;
    And as imagination bodies forth
    The forms of things unknown, the poet's pen
Turns them to shapes, and gives to airy nothing
A local habitation and a name.
Such tricks hath strong imagination."

As to the actual belief in the beings so dealt with, among the men of that generation, it was vague and indeterminate as themselves. When, indeed, the poet glanced to earth, and called up on the blasted heath, near by the scene of Macbeth's great victory over the Norweyan host, those wild and withered hags, that "looked not like the inhabitants o' the earth, and yet were on't," he idealized a very harsh and deep-rooted belief of his age. When again he glanced from earth, not to heaven, but to that intermediate spirit-world, with all the ghostly or airy habitants with which fancy or superstition had favored it, he wrought with materials that had fashioned the creed of many generations. He had, himself, believed in fairies; and doubtless still regarded ghosts with becoming awe. They had held mastery over his youthful imagination; constituted the fancies and the terror of his childhood; and were in his maturer years translated into those supernatural beings which have proved so substantial to other generations.

But the poet's own age had been familiarized with ideal beings of a wholly different kind, the reality of which seemed scarcely to admit of question. Of the new world of the West which Columbus had revealed, there was, at any rate, no room for doubt; and yet when, nearly a century after its discovery, Spenser refers, in his "Faerie Queen," not only to the Indian Peru and the Amazon, but to that "fruitfullest Virginia" of which his friend Raleigh[1] had told him many a wondrous tale, it is obvious that to his fancy America was still almost as much a world apart as if his "Shepherd of the Ocean" had sailed up the blue vault of

[1]**Raleigh:** Sir Walter Raleigh, explorer and courtier during the reign of Queen Elizabeth I.

heaven, and told of the dwellers in another planet on which it had been his fortune to alight. He is defending the verisimilitude of that Fairyland in which Una and the Red Cross Knight, Duessa, Belphœbe, Orgoglio, Malecastaes[2] and so many more fanciful impersonations disport themselves, with King Arthur and the Faerie Queen herself: and he argues that since Peru, Virginia, and all the wonders of that new-found hemisphere prove to be real, what marvel if this Fairyland of his fancy be no less substantial a verity. For even now, of the world the least part is known to us; and daily through hardy enterprise new regions are discovered, as unheard-of as were the huge Amazon, the Indian Peru, or other strange lands now found true: —

> "Yet all these were, when no man did them know,
> Yet have from wisest ages hidden been;
> And later times things more unknown shall show:
> Why then should witless man so much misween,[3]
> That nothing is but that which he hath seen?
> What if, within the moon's fair shining sphere,
> What if, in every other star unseen
> Of other worlds he happily should hear?
> He wonder would much more; yet such to some appear."

For voyagers to return from that new world with stories of its being peopled with human beings like themselves, was a kind of blasphemy intolerable to all honest Christians. The council of clerical sages which assembled in the Dominican Convent of St. Stephen, at Salamanca, in 1486, to take into consideration the theory of Columbus as to a Cathaya,[4] or other world of humanity lying beyond the Atlantic, after bringing all the science and philosophy of the age to bear on the subject, pronounced the idea of the earth's spherical form heterodox, and a belief in antipodes incompatible with the historical traditions of our faith: since to assert that there were inhabited lands on the opposite side of the globe, would be to maintain that there were nations not descended from Adam, it being impossible for them to have passed the intervening ocean. This would be, therefore, to discredit the Bible, which expressly declares that all men are descendants of one common pair.

It is amusing, but also instructive, thus to find an ethnological problem of our own day adduced by the orthodox sages of Salamanca[5]

---

[2]**Una . . . Malecastaes:** all characters in Spencer's *The Faerie Queene.*
[3]**misween:** to misconceive; to believe or suppose incorrectly.
[4]**Cathaya:** (aka Cathay) China.
[5]**Salamanca:** city in western Spain.

in the fifteenth century to prove that America could not exist. It is obvious enough, that with such Dominican philosophers in the councils of science, it was safer for their orthodoxy as well as their credibility, for travellers to tell of "anthropophagi, and men whose heads do grow beneath their shoulders," than to hint of a race of ordinary men and women. This kind of union of scepticism and credulity belongs exclusively to no special epoch. A story is told of a Scottish sailor returning to his old mother, and greeting her with an account of the wonders he had seen in far-away lands and seas. But his most guarded narrations conflicted so entirely with her personal experience that they were repelled as wholly incredible. "Weel, mother," said the baffled traveller, "what will ye say when I tell you that, in sailing up the Red Sea, on pulling up our anchor, we fand ane o' Pharaoh's chariot-wheels on the fluke?" "Ay, ay! Sandy, that I can weel believe," responded the old dame; "there's Scripture for that!" It was in a like critical spirit that the men of the fifteenth and sixteenth centuries refused all belief in the humanity of the antipodes, while they welcomed the most monstrous exaggerations for the very air of truthfulness they bore, when tried by their own canons of credibility.

The reasoning of that age arranged itself in a very simple syllogism. All men were descended from Adam; the beings inhabiting the worlds beyond the ocean could not possibly be descended from Adam; therefore they were not human beings. Yet as truth slowly dawned through a whole century, it became more and more obvious that, whatever their pedigree might be, they had many points in common with humanity. They had a kind of speech of their own; and could be taught with no great difficulty that of their discoverers. They had arts, arms, architecture and sculpture, and even religious rites, though of a very horrible kind. So the Spanish Dominicans pronounced them to be devils; and yet did not wholly abandon the hope of converting them, and making them Christians after a sort. The English adventurers, having no love for the Spaniards of the New World, and a very special aversion to their priests, were the less likely to be guided by their estimation of the Carib or Mexican; and hence there grew up a vague idea of inhabitants of the strange islands reported from time to time by returned voyagers, who, though they could not possibly be of the race of Adam, had yet a far nearer resemblance, in many ways, to our perfected humanity than any ape, baboon, or other anthropomorphous being with which older travellers had made them familiar.

On this ideal Shakespeare unquestionably wrought in the creation of that "freckled whelp," as disproportioned in manners as in shape, whom Prospero found sole habitant of the lonely island on which he and Miranda were cast. As to Caliban's maternity, the theories of man's descent, and the consequent transitional stages of an unperfected humanity, with which we are now familiar, are of very modern date, and did not at all lie in Shakespeare's vein, whatever Bacon might have said of them. Unless the poet had contented himself with simply letting Prospero find the strange monster on the island, he had, like more modern philosophers, to account in some way for his being; and so he vaguely hints at supernatural conception, known to Prospero only at second-hand. For the witch Sycorax had died, and Ariel had writhed and groaned for years, imprisoned in the rifted pine where she had left him, till Prospero arrived and set him free. "As thou report'st thyself," is accordingly the form in which Prospero alludes to Sycorax and all else that pertained to those prehistoric island-times before he set foot there. Sufficient for us, therefore, is it, that the Duke of Milan found on that strange island just such a monstrous being as travellers' tales had already made familiar to all men as natives of such regions. The terms Carib and Cannibal were synonymous. The edicts of Isabella expressly excluded the Carribeans from all the ordinary rights of humanity on this very ground. They therefore were the anthropophagi of travellers' tales; and Caliban is but an anagram of the significant name.

"Do you put tricks upon us with savages and men of Ind?" says Stephano; while the drunken Trinculo, puzzling, in his besotted fashion, over Caliban, who has fallen flat at his approach in the hope of escaping notice, exclaims: "What have we here? a man or a fish? A strange fish! Were I in England now, as once I was, and had but this fish painted, not a holiday fool there but would give a piece of silver; there would this monster make a man; any strange beast there makes a man; when they will not give a doit to relieve a lame beggar, they will lay out ten to see a dead Indian. Legged like a man! and his fins like arms! Warm, o' my troth! I do now let loose my opinion; hold it no longer: this is no fish, but an islander, that hath lately suffered by a thunderbolt." It would be curious to recover an exact delineation of the Caliban of the Elizabethan stage. "This is a strange thing as e'er I looked on," is the exclamation of the King of Naples, when Caliban is driven in, along with the revellers who have been plotting who should "be king o' the isle;" and on his brother, Sebastian, asking, "What things are these, my Lord Antonio?" he replies: "One of them is a plain fish, and no doubt marketable." There was obviously something marine, or fish-like, in the aspect of the island monster. "In the dim obscurity of the past," says Darwin, "we can see that the early progenitor of all the vertebræ must have been an aquatic animal;" in its earliest stages "more like the larvæ of our existing marine Ascidians than any other known form," but destined in process of time, through lancelot, ganoid, and other kindred transitions, to —

> "Suffer a sea change
> Into something rich and strange."

In Caliban there was undesignedly embodied, seemingly, an ideal of the latest stages of such an evolution. Mr. Joseph Hunter in dealing with this, as with other details, in his "Disquisition on Shakespeare's Tempest," lets his learning come into needless conflict with the idealization of the poet. He will by no means admit of so simple a solution of the name of Caliban as the mere metathesis of *cannibal*, but goes in search for it among the many names by which Gaspar, Melchior, and Balthazar, the three magi, were known throughout medieval Europe. In like fashion he finds his form to be of Hebraistic origin, and not at all "a pure creation of Shakespeare's own mind." He accordingly proceeds to "compare him with the fish-idol of Ashdod, the Dagon of the Philistines: —

> 'Sea-monster! upward man,
> And downward fish.' — P. L.,[6] Bk. i.

"Here we have also a figure half-fish, half-man;" and so the learned commentator proceeds to questions of Rabbinical literature; discusses how the two elements of fish and man coalesced in the form of Dagon; quotes Abarbinel and Kimchi; and finally arrives at this conclusion: "The true form of Dagon was a figure shaped like a fish, only with feet and hands like a man. Now this is precisely the form of Shakespeare's Caliban, 'a fish legged like a man, and his fins like arms.' Nothing can be more precise than the resemblance. The two are in fact one, as to form. Caliban is therefore a kind of tortoise, the paddles expanding in arms and hands, legs and feet. And accordingly, before he appears upon the stage, the audience are prepared for the strange figure by the words of Prospero: —

> "Come forth, thou tortoise!"

[6]**P. L.:** Paradise Lost.

"How he became changed into a monkey, while the play is full of allusions to his fish-like form," the learned critic leaves to others to explain.

There is an amusing literalness in this application alike of the confused ideas of the drunken Trinculo, and of the invective of Prospero. The wrathful magician calls to the creature whom Miranda has been denouncing as a villain, — "What ho! slave! Caliban! Thou earth, thou!" and as he still lingers, muttering his refusal, Prospero shouts, "Come forth, I say; come, thou tortoise! when?" In a milder mood he might have said, "Come, thou snail!" expressing thereby the same idea of tardy reluctant obedience, with equally little reference to his form.

In reality, though by some scaly or fin-like appendages, the idea of a fish or sea-monster, is suggested to all, the form of Caliban is, nevertheless, essentially human. In a fashion more characteristic of Milton's than of Shakespeare's wonted figure of speech, this is affirmed in language that no doubt purposely suggests the opposite idea to the mind, where Prospero says: —

> "Then was this island —
> Save for the son that she did litter here,
> A freckled whelp, hag-born, — not honoured with
> A human shape."

The double bearing of this is singularly expressive: — save for this son of Sycorax, the island was not honoured with a human shape. And, having thus indicated that his shape was human, by the use of the terms "whelp" and "littered" the brutish ideal is strongly impressed on the mind. But his strictly anthropomorphic character is delicately suggested in other ways. When Miranda says of Ferdinand —

> "This
> Is the third man that e'er I saw, the first
> That e'er I sigh'd for,"

she can only refer to her father and Caliban. In this the poet purposely glances at the simplicity of the inexperienced maiden, to whom the repulsive monster had hitherto been the sole ideal of manhood presented to her mind, apart from the venerable Prospero. How far he falls short of all manly perfections is indicated immediately afterwards in the contrast instituted between him and Ferdinand: —

"Thou think'st there are no more such shapes as he,
 Having seen but him and Caliban. Foolish wench!
 To the most of men this is a Caliban,
 And they to him are angels."

This is, of course, the purposed exaggeration of Prospero, in his fear "lest
too light winning make the prize light." But so soon as Miranda has
become thoroughly impressed with the image of her new-found lover,
with "no ambition to see a goodlier man," she ceases to think of Caliban
as a being to be associated with him in common manhood. When,
accordingly, she responds to Ferdinand's admiring exclamation —

"But you, O you,
 So perfect and so peerless, are created
 Of every creature's best,"

it is by a declaration which wholly ignores Caliban's claims to rank in
the same order of beings with those among whom she had so recently
classed him.

"I do not know
 One of my sex; no woman's face remember,
 Save, from my glass, mine own; nor have I seen
 More that I may call men, than you, good friend,
 And my dear father."

In this way the gradual expansion of the ideas of this innocent maiden
are traced by the most delicate indications; until at length, when
Alonzo and his company are introduced into Prospero's cell, where
Ferdinand and Miranda are seated, playing at chess, she exclaims —

"Oh! wonder!
 How many goodly creatures are there here!
 How beauteous mankind is! O brave new world
 That has such people in't!"

The development being thus completed, and the perfection of true
manhood fairly presented to her eye and mind, Caliban is then introduced, with the awe-struck exclamation —

"O Setebos, these be brave spirits indeed!"

and immediately thereafter we have the remark of Antonio — "One of them is a plain fish, and no doubt marketable." He is a "thing of darkness," as Prospero calls him; a being "as disproportioned in his manners as in his shape;" yet nevertheless so closely approximating, in the main, to ordinary humanity, that Miranda had associated him in her own mind, along with her father, as "honoured with a human shape."

Again, we are furnished with a tolerably definite clue to the age which Caliban has attained at the date of his introduction to our notice. Littered on the island soon after the reputed arrival of Sycorax, we learn that that malignant hag, unable to subdue the delicate Ariel to the execution of her abhorred commands, imprisoned him in the cloven pine, where he groaned out twelve wretched years, till relieved from his torments by the art of Prospero. Next, it appears from the discourse of her father to Miranda that she has grown up on that lonely island for a like period. "Twelve years since, Miranda, thy father was the Duke of Milan, and a prince of power." But she was not then three years old, and so the memory of that former state, and of the maidens who tended her in her father's palace, has faded away, "far off, and like a dream;" while the banished Duke, "rapt in secret studies," his library "a dukedom large enough," had more and more perfected himself in occult science, until he learns by its aid that now the very crisis of their fates has come. Caliban is, therefore, to all appearance in his twenty-fifth year, as we catch a first glimpse of this pre-Darwinian realization of the intermediate link between brute and man. It seems moreover to be implied that he has already passed his maturity. At an earlier age than that at which man is capable of self-support, the creature had been abandoned to the solitude of his island-home, and learned with his long claws to dig for pig-nuts; and now, says Prospero, "as with age his body uglier grows, so his mind cankers." We may conceive of the huge canine teeth and prognathous jaws which in old age assume such prominence in the higher quadrumana.[7] Darwin claims for the bonnet-monkey "the forehead which gives to man his noble and intellectual appearance;" and it is obvious that it was not wanting in Caliban: for when he discovers the true quality of the drunken fools he has mistaken for gods, his remonstrance is, "we shall all be turned to apes with foreheads villainous low." Here then is the highest developement of "the beast that wants discourse of reason." He has attained to all the maturity his nature admits of, and so is perfect as the study of a living creature distinct from, yet next in order below the level of humanity.

---

[7]**quadrumana:** four-footed primate in which all four feet resemble hands in having an opposable digit.

The being thus called into existence for the purposes of dramatic art is a creation well meriting the thoughtful study of the modern philosopher, whatever deductions he may have based on the hypotheses of recent speculation. Caliban's is not a brutalized, but a natural brute mind. He is a being in whom the moral instincts of man have no part; but also in whom the degradation of savage humanity is equally wanting. He is a novel anthropoid of a high type — such as on the hypothesis of evolution must have existed intermediately between the ape and man, — in whom some spark of rational intelligence has been enkindled, under the tutorship of one who has already mastered the secrets of nature. We must not be betrayed into a too literal interpretation of the hyperboles of the wrathful Duke of Milan. He is truly enough the "freckled whelp" whom Prospero has subdued to useful services, as he might break in a wild colt, or rear a young wolf to do his bidding, though in token of higher capacity he has specially trained him to menial duties peculiar to man. For not only does he "fetch in our wood," as Prospero reminds his daughter, "and serves in offices that profit us," but "he does make our fire."

No incident attending the discovery of the New World is more significant than that of Columbus stationed on the poop of the Santa Maria, his eye ranging along the darkened horizon, when the sun had once more gone down on the disappointed hopes of the voyagers. Suddenly a light glimmered in the distance, once and again reappeared to the eyes of Pedro Gutierrez and others whom the great admiral summoned to catch this gleam of realized hopes; and then darkness and doubt resumed their reign. But to Columbus all was light. That feeble ray had told of the presence of the fire-maker, man. The natural habits of Caliban, however, are those of the denizen of the woods. We may conceive of him like the pongoes of Mayombe, described by Purchas, who would come and sit by the travellers' deserted camp-fire, but had not sense enough to replenish it with fuel. We have no reason to think of him as naturally a cooking or fire-using animal; though, under the training of Prospero, he proves to be so far in advance of the most highly developed anthropoid as to be capable of learning the art of fire-making.

"We'll visit Caliban, my slave, who never yields us kind answers," Duke Prospero says to his daughter in the second scene of "The Tempest," where they first appear, and Caliban is introduced; but the gentle Miranda recalls with shuddering revulsion the brutal violence of their strange servitor, and exclaims with unwonted vehemence: " 'Tis a villain, sir, I do not love to look on." But repulsive as he is, his services cannot be dispensed with. "As 'tis, we cannot miss him," is Prospero's reply; and then, irritated alike by the sense of his obnoxious instincts and reluctant service, he heaps opprobrious epithets upon him: "What, ho! slave! Caliban! thou earth, thou! Come forth, I say, thou tortoise!" and at length, as he still lingers, muttering in his den, Prospero breaks out in wrath — "Thou poisonous slave, got by the devil himself upon thy wicked dam, come forth!" Schlegel[8] and Hazlitt[9] accordingly speak in nearly the same terms of "the savage Caliban, half brute, half demon;" while Gervinus[10] — although elsewhere characterizing him with more appreciative acumen as "an embryonic being defiled as it were by his earthly origin from the womb of savage nature," — does, with prosaic literalness, assume that his mother was the witch Sycorax, and the devil his father. Shakespeare assuredly aimed at the depiction of no such foul ideal. It is the recluse student of nature's mysteries, and not the poor island monster that is characteristically revealed in such harsh vituperations. Prospero habitually accomplishes his projects through the agency of enforced service. He has usurped a power over the spirits of air, as well as over this earth-born slave; and both are constrained to unwilling obedience. Hence he has learned to exact and compel service to the utmost; to count only on the agency of enslaved power: until an imperious habit disguises the promptings of a generous and kindly nature. With all his tenderness towards the daughter whose presence alone has made life endurable to him, he flashes up in sudden ire at the slightest interference with his plans for her; as when she interposes on behalf of Ferdinand, he exclaims — "Silence! One word more shall make me chide thee, if not hate thee." He is indeed acting an assumed part, "lest too light winning" should make the lover undervalue his prize; but it is done in the imperious tone with which habit has taught him to respond to the slightest thwarting of his commands. This is still more apparent in his dealings with the gentle Ariel, who owes to him delivery from cruellest bondage. The relations subsisting between them are indicated with rare art, and are as tender as is compatible with beings of different elements. The sylph is generally addressed in kindly admiring terms, as "my brave spirit," "my tricksy spirit," "my delicate, my dainty Ariel." Yet on the slightest questioning of Prospero's orders, he is told: "Thou

[8]**Schlegel:** Karl Wilhelm Friederich von Schlegel (1772–1829), German critic and poet, a leader of German Romanticism.

[9]**Hazlitt:** William Hazlitt (1778–1830), English critic.

[10]**Gervinus:** George Gottfried Gervinus (1805–1871), German literary and political historian.

liest, malignant thing!" and on the mere show of murmuring is threatened with durance more terrible than that from which he has been set free.

In all this the characteristics of the magician are consistently wrought out. According to the ideas of an age which still believed in magic, he has usurped the lordship of nature, and subdued to his will the spirits of the elements, by presumptuous, if not altogether sinful arts. They are retained in subjection by the constant exercise of this supernatural power, and yield him only the reluctant obedience of slaves. This has to be borne in remembrance, if we would not misinterpret the ebullitions of imperious harshness on the part of Prospero towards beings who can only be retained in subjection by such enforced mastery. That Caliban regards him with as malignant a hatred as the caged and muzzled bear may be supposed to entertain towards his keeper, is set forth with clear consistency. Nor is it without abundant reason. He is dealt with not merely as a "lying slave, whom stripes may move, not kindness;" but by his master's magical art, the most familiar objects of nature are made instruments of torture. They pinch, affright him, pitch him into the mire, as deceptive fire-brands mislead him in the dark, grind his joints with convulsions, contort his sinews with cramp, and, as he says,

> "For every trifle are they set upon me:
> Sometimes like apes, that mow and chatter at me,
> And after bite me: then like hedgehogs, which
> Lie tumbling in my barefoot way, and mount
> Their pricks at my footfall; sometimes am I
> All wound with adders, who with cloven tongues
> Do hiss me into madness."

To reconcile such harsh violence with the merciful forgiving character of Prospero in his dealings with those who, after having done him the cruellest wrongs, are placed in his power, we have to conceive of the outcast father and child compelled in their island solitude to subdue a gorilla, or other brute menial, to their service; and, after in vain trying kindness, driven in self-defense to protect themselves from its brutal violence. The provocation which had roused the unappeasable wrath of Miranda's father was indeed great; but recognizing the "most poor credulous monster" as the mere brute that he is, it involved no moral delinquency; and therefore he is not to be regarded as devilish in origin and inclinations, because he tells Stephano what is literally true — "I am subject to a tyrant, a sorcerer, that by his cunning hath cheated me of the island." He accordingly invites the drunken butler to be his supplanter: —

> "If thy greatness will
> Revenge it on him, — for I know thou darest, —
> Thou shalt be lord of it, and I'll serve thee."

He gloats on the idea of braining the tyrant, just as an abused human slave might, and indeed many a time has done.

> "Why, as I told thee, 'tis a custom with him
> I' the afternoon to sleep: there thou mayst brain him,
> Having first seized his books; or with a log
> Batter his skull, or paunch him with a stake,
> Or cut his weazand[11] with thy knife. Remember
> First to possess his books; for without them
> He's but a sot, as I am, nor hath not
> One spirit to command: they all do hate him
> As rootedly as I."

All this would be hateful enough in a human being; but before we pronounce Caliban a "demi-devil," we must place alongside of him the butler Stephano, who, with no other provocation than that of a base nature, and with no wrongs whatever to avenge, is ready with the response — "Monster, I will kill this man; his daughter and I will be king and queen, and Trinculo and thyself shall be viceroys;" and so the poor servant monster already fancies his slavery at an end and exclaims, "Freedom, hey-day! hey-day, freedom!"

He who undertakes to subdue the wild nature of ape, leopard, wolf, or tiger, must not charge it with moral delinquency when it yields to its native instincts. It maybe, as modern science would teach us, that our most human characteristics are but developed instincts of the brute; for the churl

> "Will let his coltish nature break
> At seasons through the gilded pale."

The savage, though familiarized with habits of civilization, reverts with easy recoil to his barbarian license; and the highest happiness which the tamed monster of the island could conceive of, was once more to range

---

[11]**weazand:** windpipe or throat.

in unrestrained liberty, digging up the pig-nuts with his long nails, or following the jay and the nimble marmoset over rock and tree. But there is nothing malignant in this; and that nothing essentially repulsive is to be assumed as natural to him is apparent from the very invectives of Prospero: —

> "Thou most lying slave,
> Whom stripes may move, not kindness: I have used thee,
> Filth as thou art, with human care; and lodged thee
> In mine own cell, till thou didst seek to violate
> The honour of my child."

Leaving aside, then, the exaggerations of the incensed Prospero, which have their legitimate place in the development of the drama, let us study, as far as may be, the actual characteristics of the strange islander. His story is told, briefly indeed, yet with adequate minuteness. Prospero retorts on him the recapitulation of kindnesses which had been repaid with outrage never to be forgiven: —

> "Abhorred slave,
> Which any print of goodness will not take,
> Being capable of all ill! I pitied thee,
> Took pains to make thee speak, taught thee each hour
> One thing or other: when thou didst not, savage,
> Know thine own meaning, but wouldst gabble like
> A thing most brutish, I endowed thy purposes
> With words that made them known. But thy vile race,
> Though thou didst learn, had that in't which good natures
> Could not abide to be with."

In other words, he proved to be simply an animal, actuated by the ordinary unrestrained passions and desires which in the brute involve no moral evil, and but for the presence of Miranda would have attracted no special notice. Situated as he actually is, he is not to be judged of wholly from the invectives of his master. With brute instincts which have brought on him the condign punishment of Prospero, and a savage nature which watches, like any wild creature under harsh restraint, for escape and revenge, his feelings are nevertheless rather those of the captive bear than of "one who treasures up a wrong." There is in him still a dog-like aptitude for attachment, a craving even for the mastership of some higher nature, and an appreciation of kindness not unlike that of the domesticated dog, though conjoined with faculties of intelligent enjoyment more nearly approximating to humanity. When compelled reluctantly to emerge from his den, he enters muttering curses; yet even they have a smack of nature in them. They are in no ways devilish, but such as the wild creature exposed to the elements may be supposed to recognize as the blight and mildew with which Nature gratifies her ill-will. He imprecates on his enslaver —

> "As wicked dew as e'er my mother brushed
> With raven's feather from unwholesome fen
> Drop on you both! A south-west blow on ye
> And blister you all o'er!"

Prospero threatens him with cramps, side-stitches that shall pen his breath up, urchins to prick him, and pinching pains more stinging than the bees; but his answer has no smack of fiendishness, though he does retort with bootless imprecations. He stolidly replies —

> "I must eat my dinner.
> This island's mine, by Sycorax my mother,
> Which thou takest from me. When thou camest first,
> Thou strokedst me, and madest much of me; wouldst give me
> Water with berries in't; and teach me how
> To name the bigger light, and how the less,
> That burn by day and night; and then I loved thee,
> And shew'd thee all the qualities o' the isle,
> The fresh springs, brine-pits, barren place and fertile;
> Cursed be I that did so! All the charms
> Of Sycorax, toads, beetles, bats, light on you!
> For I am all the subjects that you have,
> Which first was mine own king; and here you sty me
> In this hard rock, whiles you do keep from me
> The rest o' the island."

Prospero replies to him as a creature "whom stripes may move, not kindness," who had been treated companionably, with human care, till his brute instincts compelled the subjection of him to such restraint. He describes the pity with which he at first regarded the poor monster, whose brutish gabble he had trained to the intelligent speech which is now used for curses. In all this do we not realize the ideal anthropoid in the highest stage of Simian evolution, stroked and made much of like a favorite dog, fed with dainties, and at length taught to frame his brute cries into words by which his wishes could find intelligible utterance. The bigger and the lesser light receive names, and are even traced, as we may presume, to their origin. But the intellectual development compasses, at the utmost, a very narrow range; and when the drunken Stephano plies him with his bottle of sack, the dialogue runs in this characteristic fashion: —

> "STEPH. How now, moon-calf? how does thine ague?
> CAL. Hast thou not dropt from heaven?
> STEPH. Out o' the moon, I do assure thee: I was the man in the
> moon, when time was.
> CAL. I have seen thee in her, and I do adore thee. My mistress
> shewed me thee, and thy dog, and thy bush.
> STEPH. Come, swear to that; kiss the book: I will furnish it anon
> with new contents: swear.
> TRIN. By this good light, this is a very shallow monster! I am afeard
> of him! A very weak monster! The man i' the moon! A most
> poor credulous monster! Well drawn, monster, in good sooth!
> CAL. I'll shew thee every fertile inch o' the island: And I will kiss
> thy foot: I pr'ythee, be my god."

But we presently see Caliban in another and wholly different aspect. Like the domesticated animal, which he really is, he has certain artificial habits and tastes superinduced in him; but whenever his natural instincts reveal themselves we see neither a born devil, nor a being bearing any likeness to degraded savage humanity. He is an animal at home among the sounds and scenes of living nature. "Pray you, tread softly, that the blind mole may not hear a footfall," is his exhortation to his drunken companions as they approach the entrance of Prospero's cell. When Trinculo frets him, his threatened revenge is, "He shall drink nought but brine; for I'll not show him where the quick freshes are;" and he encourages his equally rude companion with the assurance —

> "Be not afeard; the isle is full of noises,
> Sounds, and sweet airs, that give delight and hurt not.
> Sometimes a thousand twangling instruments
> Will hum about mine ears; and sometimes voices,
> That, if I then had waked after long sleep,
> Will make me sleep again: and then, in dreaming.
> The clouds, methought, would open, and shew riches
> Ready to drop upon me; that, when I waked,
> I cried to dream again."

To the drunken butler and his comrade, Caliban is "a most poor credulous monster! a puppy-headed, scurvy, abominable monster! a most ridiculous monster!" and when, by their aid, he has drowned his tongue in sack, he is no more to them than a debauched fish. But Shakespeare has purposely placed the true anthropomorphoid alongside of these types of degraded humanity, to shew the contrast between them. He is careful to draw a wide and strongly-marked distinction between the coarse prosaic brutality of debased human nature, and the inferior, but in no ways degraded, brute nature of Caliban. "He is," says Prospero, "as disproportioned in his manners as in his shape," He had associated for years in friendly dependence, lodged with Prospero in his own cell; for we have to remember that Miranda was but three years old when her father took in hand the taming of the poor monster, and used him with human care, until compelled to drive him forth to his rocky prison. His narrow faculties have thus been forced into strange development; but though the wrathful Prospero pronounces him a creature "which any print of goodness will not take, being capable of all ill," that is by no means the impression which the poet designs to convey. Man, by reason of his higher nature which invites him to aspire, and his moral sense which clearly presents to him the choice between good and evil, is capable of a degradation beyond reach of the brute. The very criminality which has so hardened Prospero's heart against his poor slave, involves to himself no sense of moral wrong. "O ho! O ho! would it had been done!" is his retort to Prospero; "thou didst prevent me; I had peopled else this isle with Calibans."

The distinction between the coarse sensuality of degraded humanity, and this most original creation of poetic fancy, with its gross brute-mind, its limited faculties, its purely animal cravings and impulses, is maintained throughout. The first scene opens with the sailors, released from all ordinary deference and restraint by the perils of the storm, shouting and blaspheming in reckless desperation; and no sooner are they ashore than Caliban is brought into closest relations with the still more worthless topers who win his admiration, till experience teaches him —

> "What a thrice-double ass
> Was I, to take this drunkard for a god,
> And worship this dull fool!"

The dog-like attachment which had drawn him to Prospero, till harsh treatment and restraint eradicated this feeling, and utterly alienated him

from his first master, is transferred to the next being who treats him
with any appearance of kindness. "I'll shew thee every fertile inch o' the
island," is the first form in which his gratitude finds utterance;

> "I'll shew thee the best springs; I'll pluck thee berries;
> I'll fish for thee, and get thee wood enough.
> A plague upon the tyrant that I serve!
> I'll bear him no more sticks, but follow thee,
> Thou wondrous man."

The drunken butler, with his bottle of sack, seems to the poor monster to have dropped from heaven, or rather from the moon, where
once his mistress showed him that favorite myth of old popular folklore, the man-in-the-moon, with his dog and bush: and so he fawns
on him as a dog might on an old acquaintance. "A most ridiculous
monster," thinks Trinculo, "to make a wonder of a poor drunkard;"
but Caliban is ready to lavish all his dog-like fidelity on his new-found
master.

> "I prithee, let me bring thee where crabs grow;
> And I, with my long nails, will dig thee pig-nuts;
> Shew thee a jay's nest, and instruct thee how
> To snare the nimble marmoset; I'll bring thee
> To clustering filberts; and sometimes I'll get thee
> Young scamels[12] from the rock. Wilt thou go with me?"

If we can conceive of a baboon endowed with speech, and moved
by gratitude, have we not here the very ideas to which its nature would
prompt it. It is a creature native to the rocks and the woods, at home in
the haunts of the jay and marmoset: a fellow-creature of like nature and
sympathies with themselves. The talk of the ship's crew is not only
coarse, but even what it is customary to call brutal; while that of
Stephano and Trinculo accords with their debased and besotted
humanity. Their language never assumes a rhythmical structure, or rises
to poetic thought. But Caliban is in perfect harmony with the rhythm
of the breezes and the tides. His thoughts are essentially poetical,
within the range of his lower nature; and so his speech is, for the most
part, in verse. He has that poetry of the senses which seems natural to
his companionship with the creatures of the forest and the seashore.

---

[12]**scamels:** meaning uncertain, but the reference here seems to be to some kind of
delicacy.

Even his growl, as he retorts impotent curses on the power that has enslaved him, is rhythmical. Bogs, fens, and the infectious exhalations that the sun sucks up, embody his ideas of evil; and his acute senses are chiefly at home with the dew, and the fresh springs, the clustering filberts, the jay in his leafy nest, or the blind mole in its burrow.

No being of all that people the Shakespearean drama more thoroughly suggests the idea of a pure creation of the poetic fancy than Caliban. He has a nature of his own essentially distinct from the human beings with whom he is brought in contact. He seems indeed the half-human link between the brute and man; and realizes, as no degraded Bushman or Australian savage can do, a conceivable intermediate stage of the anthropomorphous existence, as far above the most highly organized ape as it falls short of rational humanity. He excites a sympathy such as no degraded savage could. We feel for the poor monster, so helplessly in the power of the stern Prospero, as for some caged wild beast pining in cruel captivity, and rejoice to think of him at last free to range in harmless mastery over his island solitude. He provokes no more jealousy as the inheritor of Prospero's usurped lordship over his island home than the caged bird which has escaped to the free forest again. His is a type of development essentially non-human, — though, for the purposes of the drama, endued to an extent altogether beyond the highest attainments of the civilized, domesticated animal, with the exercise of reason and the use of language; — a conceivable civilization such as would, to a certain extent, run parallel to that of man, but could never converge to a common center.

A Portfolio of Images of Caliban

We have selected these seven images of Caliban because they represent a range of interpretations of his character: as more beast than man; as a figure on the border between human and animal; as a man but a brutish one; as a sympathetic victim; and as a man who is the equal of Prospero. A worthwhile exercise is to match the images to these categories and to corresponding interpretations of *The Tempest* by the critics in this book, noting where the fit is easy and where it is more difficult. With the more difficult cases, try to identify the elements of the image that resist the categorization and then come up with categories that would better account for these elements. You can then compare the results with your classmates and even write an essay about the debates that ensue.

Another worthwhile exercise is to match each image with that part of Shakespeare's text that best supports the image's interpretation of Caliban. After you have done that with each image, collate all the textual passages and discuss whether it is possible to find a coherent vision of Caliban that cuts across them all. You can then discuss the consequences of concluding either that the play contains a coherent view of Caliban or that it ultimately offers conflicting views of him.

A lithograph of Caliban *(Shakespeare Visionen)* by Alfred Kubin (1877–1959) made in 1917.

Sprite and Monster, an illustration by Arthur Rackham (1867–1939) made in 1909, found in *Tales from Shakespeare* by Charles and Mary Lamb.

Sprite and Monster, an illustration from *Tales from Shakespeare* by Charles (1775–1834) and Mary Lamb (1764–1847) 1909 (pen and ink, w/c) by Arthur Rackham (1867–1939). Copyright © Private Collection/© Chris Beetles, London, U.K./ The Bridgeman Art Library.

An etching by John Hamilton Mortimer (1740–1779) from the 1770s, commonly titled *Monstrous Male Figure, Caliban*? This image bears resemblance to other drawings that Mortimer created, and is presumed to be an unfinished character study of Caliban.

John Hamilton Mortimer, *Monstrous Male Figure, Caliban*? Copyright © Tate, London 2008.

Photograph of Sir Frank Benson as Caliban in a 1900 production of *The Tempest*, Lyceum Theatre, London.

Image of David Suchet as Caliban, in the 1978 production of *The Tempest* directed by Clifford Williams, Royal Shakespeare Theatre, Stratford-upon-Avon.

CALIBAN · MR. TREE.

Charles Buchel's depiction of Caliban, as portrayed in the 1904 Beerbohm Tree's production of *The Tempest*, His Majesty's Theatre, Australia.

Illustration of Herbert Beerbohm Tree as Caliban from a 1904 edition of *The Tempest*, illustrated by Charles Buchel (PR 2833 1904-1 Sh.Col.). By permission of The Folger Shakespeare Library.

Photograph of Alec Clunes as Caliban in a 1957 production of *The Tempest*, directed by Peter Brook, Royal Shakespeare Theatre, Stratford-upon-Avon.

Angus McBean. Copyright © Royal Shakespeare Company.

E. M. W. TILLYARD

From The Elizabethan World Picture

Eustace Mandeville Wetenhall Tillyard (1889–1962) was an eminent scholar of the English Renaissance who taught for many years at Cambridge University. Although most famous for his book *The Elizabethan World Picture* (1944), from which the following essay is taken, he wrote and edited many books, including *The English Renaissance, Fact or Fiction* (1952), *The English Epic and Its Background* (1954), and *The Metaphysicals and Milton* (1956).

People still think of the Age of Elizabeth as a secular period between two outbreaks of Protestantism: a period in which religious enthusiasm was sufficiently dormant to allow the new humanism to shape our literature. They admit indeed that the quiet was precarious and that the Puritans were ever on the alert. But they allow the emphasis to be on the Queen's political intuitions, the voyages of discovery, and the brilliant externals of Elizabethan life. The first pages of Virginia Woolf's *Orlando* are in these matters typical. They do not tell us that Queen Elizabeth translated Boethius, that Raleigh was a theologian as well as a discoverer, and that sermons were as much a part of an ordinary Elizabethan's life as bear-baiting. The way Hamlet's words on man are often taken will illustrate this habit of mind.

> What a piece of work is a man: how noble in reason; how infinite in faculty; in form and moving how express and admirable; in action how like an angel; in apprehension how like a god; the beauty of the world, the paragon of animals.

This has been taken as one of the great English versions of Renaissance humanism, an assertion of the dignity of man against the asceticisms of medieval misanthropy. Actually it is in the purest medieval tradition: Shakespeare's version of the orthodox encomia[1] of what man, created in God's image, was like in his prelapsarian[2] state and of what ideally he is still capable of being. It also shows Shakespeare placing man in the traditional cosmic setting between the angels and the beasts. It was what the theologians had been saying for centuries. Here is a typical version, by Nemesius, a Syrian bishop of the fourth century, in George Wither's translation:

> No eloquence may worthily publish forth the manifold preeminences and advantages which are bestowed on this creature. He passeth over the vast seas; he rangeth about the wide heavens by his contemplation and conceives the motions and magnitudes of the stars. . . . He is learned in every science and skilful in artificial workings. . . . He talketh with angels yea with God himself. He hath all the creatures within his dominion.

What is true of Hamlet on man is in the main true of Elizabethan modes of thought in general.

The thing that *Orlando* (and for that matter *Shakespeare's England* taken all in all) misses is that the Puritans and the courtiers were more united by a common theological bond than they were divided by ethical disagreements. They had in common a mass of basic assumptions

---

[1] **orthodox encomia:** standard praises.
[2] **prelapsarian:** man's (and woman's) condition before Adam and Eve's fall in Eden.

about the world, which they never disputed and whose importance varied inversely with this very meagerness of controversy. . . .

Those (and they are at present the majority) who take their notion
of the Elizabethan age principally from the drama will find it difficult to
agree that its world picture was ruled by a general conception of order,
for at first sight that drama is anything but orderly. However, people are
beginning to perceive that this drama was highly stylized and conventional, that its technical licenses are of certain kinds and fall into a pattern, that its extravagant sentiments are repetitions and not novelties;
that it may after all have its own, if queer, regulation. Actually . . . the
conception of order is so taken for granted, so much part of the collective mind of the people, that it is hardly mentioned except in explicitly
didactic passages. It is not absent from non-didactic writing, for it
appears in Spenser's *Hymn of Love* and in Ulysses's speech on "degree"
in Shakespeare's *Troilus and Cressida.* It occurs frequently in didactic
prose: in Elyot's *Governor,* the Church Homily *Of Obedience,* the first
book of Hooker's *Laws of Ecclesiastical Polity,* and the preface to
Raleigh's *History of the World.* Shakespeare's version is the best known.
For this reason and because its full scope is not always perceived I begin
with it.

> The heavens themselves, the planets, and this centre
> Observe degree priority and place
> Insisture course proportion season form
> Office and custom, in all line of order;
> And therefore is the glorious planet Sol
> In noble eminence enthron'd and spher'd
> Amidst the other, whose med'cinable eye
> Corrects the ill aspects of planets evil
> And posts like the commandment of a king,
> Sans check, to good and bad. But when the planets
> In evil mixture to disorder wander,
> What plagues and what portents, what mutiny,
> What raging of the sea, shaking of earth,
> Commotion in the winds, frights changes horrors,
> Divert and crack, rend and deracinate
> The unity and married calm of states
> Quite from their fixure. Oh, when degree is shak'd,
> Which is the ladder to all high designs,
> The enterprise is sick. How could communities,
> Degrees in schools and brotherhoods in cities,
> Peaceful commerce from dividable shores,
> The primogenitive and due of birth,

Prerogative of age, crowns sceptres laurels,
But by degree stand in authentic place?
Take but degree away, untune that string,
And hark, what discord follows. Each thing meets
In mere oppugnancy.[3] The bounded waters
Should lift their bosoms higher than the shores
And make a sop of all this solid globe.
Strength should be lord to imbecility,
And the rude son should strike his father dead.
This chaos, when degree is suffocate,
Follows the choking.

Much of what I have to expound is contained in this passage, and I shall revert to its details later. The point here is that so many things are included simultaneously within this "degree" or order, and so strong a sense is given of their interconnections. The passage is at once cosmic and domestic. The sun, the king, primogeniture hang together; the war of the planets is echoed by the war of the elements and by civil war on earth; the homely brotherhoods or guilds in cities are found along with an oblique reference to creation out of the confusion of chaos. Here is a picture of immense and varied activity, constantly threatened with dissolution, and yet preserved from it by a superior unifying power. The picture, however, though so rich, is not complete. There is nothing about God and the angels, nothing about animals, vegetables, and minerals. For Shakespeare's dramatic purposes he brought in quite enough, but it would be wrong to think that he did not mean to imply the two extremes of creation also or that he would have disclaimed the following account of "degree": Raleigh, after enlarging on the joys of heaven, which will make any earthly joy negligible, continues,

> Shall we therefore value honour and riches at nothing and neglect them as unnecessary and vain? Certainly no. For that infinite wisdom of God, which hath distinguished his angels by degrees, which hath given greater and less light and beauty to heavenly bodies, which hath made differences between beasts and birds, created the eagle and the fly, the cedar and the shrub, and among stones given the fairest tincture to the ruby and the quickest light to the diamond, hath also ordained kings, dukes or leaders of the people, magistrates, judges, and other degrees among men.

[3]**oppugnancy:** antagonism, opposition.

One of the clearest expositions of order (and close to Shakespeare's though a good deal earlier in date) is Elyot's in the first chapter of the *Governor.* It has this prominent place because order is the condition of all that follows; for of what use to educate the magistrate without the assurance of a coherent universe in which he can do his proper work?

> Take away order from all things, what should then remain? Certes[4] nothing finally, except some man would imagine eftsoons[5] chaos. Also where there is any lack of order needs must be perpetual conflict. And in things subject to nature nothing of himself only may be nourished; but, when he hath destroyed that wherewith he doth participate by the order of his creation, he himself of necessity must then perish; whereof ensueth universal dissolution.
>
> Hath not God set degrees and estates in all his glorious works? First in his heavenly ministers, whom he hath constituted in divers degrees called hierarchies. Behold the four elements, whereof the body of man is compact, how they be set in their places called spheres, higher or lower according to the sovereignty of their natures. Behold also the order that God hath put generally in all his creatures, beginning at the most inferior or base and ascending upward. He made not only herbs to garnish the earth but also trees of a more eminent stature than herbs. Semblably[6] in birds beasts and fishes some be good for the sustenance of man, some bear things profitable to sundry uses, other be apt to occupation and labour. Every kind of trees, herbs, birds, beasts, and fishes have a peculiar disposition appropered[7] unto them by God their creator; so that in everything is order, and without order may be nothing stable or permanent. And it may not be called order except it do contain in it degrees, high and base, according to the merit or estimation of the thing that is ordered.

This is all very explicit and prosaic. It is what everyone believed in Elizabeth's days and it is *all* there behind such poetic statements of order as the following from Spenser's *Hymn of Love* describing creation:

> The earth the air the water and the fire
> Then gan to range themselves in huge array
> And with contrary forces to conspire

---

[4]**Certes:** certainly.
[5]**eftsoons:** again.
[6]**Semblably:** similarly.
[7]**appropered:** to set aside for special purpose.

Each against other by all means they may,
Threat'ning their own confusion and decay:
Air hated earth and water hated fire,
Till Love relented their rebellious ire.

He then them took and, tempering goodly well
Their contrary dislikes with loved means,
Did place them all in order and compel
To keep themselves within their sundry reigns
Together linkt with adamantine[8] chains;
Yet so as that in every living wight
They mix themselves and show their kindly might.

So ever since they firmly have remained
And duly well observed his behest,
Through which now all these things that are contained
Within this goodly cope, both most and least,
Their being have.

The conception of order described above must have been common to all Elizabethans of even modest intelligence. Hooker's elaborated account must have stated pretty fairly the preponderating conception among the educated. Hooker is not easy reading to a modern but would have been much less difficult to a contemporary used to his kind of prose. He writes not for the technical theologian but mediates theology to the general educated public of his day. He is master of the sort of summary which, though it avoids irksome and controversial detail, presents the general and the simplified with consummate force and freshness. He has the acutest sense of what the ordinary educated man can grasp and having grasped ratify. It is this tact that assures us that he speaks for the educated nucleus that dictated the current beliefs of the Elizabethan Age. He represents far more truly the background of Elizabethan literature than do the coney-catching pamphlets[9] or the novel of low life.

Hooker's version is of course avowedly theological and it is more explicit, but the order it describes is Elyot's and Shakespeare's. His name for it is law, law in its general sense. Above all cosmic or earthly orders or laws there is Law in general, "that Law which giveth life unto all the rest

---

[8]**adamantine:** here, impregnable.
[9]**coney-catching pamphlets:** a "coney" is a gullible person, someone who is easily duped; during Elizabethan England, the clever used pamphlets of various kinds to scam the gullible.

which are commendable just and good, namely the Law whereby the Eternal himself doth work." By a masterly ambiguity he avoids the great traditional dispute whether a thing is right because God wills it, or God wills it because it is right. God created his own law both because he willed it and because it was right. Though voluntary it was not arbitrary, but based on reason. That divine reason is beyond our understanding; yet we know it is there. God's law is eternal, "being that order which God before all ages hath set down with himself, for himself to do all things by." God chose to work in finitude in some sort to show his glory; and having so chosen he expressed the abundance of his glory in variety. The sense of full life given by Shakespeare's "degree" speech is a close poetical parallel to this theological doctrine of variety. From this single generating law of God Hooker goes on to describe the subordinate and separate laws; for law too must become multiple when it is applied to an abundantly diversified creation. God, as well as creating his own eternal law, issued his command in accordance with it:

> That part of it which ordereth natural agents we call usually
> nature's law; that which angels do clearly behold and without
> any swerving observe is a law celestial and heavenly; the law of
> reason, that which bindeth creatures reasonable in this world and
> with which by reason they may most plainly perceive themselves
> bound; that which bindeth them and is not known but by special
> revelation from God, divine law; human law, that which out of
> the law either of reason or of God men probably gathering to be
> expedient, they make it a law.

Hooker's first book comes to rest in a final summary, which includes the notion of law or order as harmony ("Take but degree away, untune that string, And hark what discord follows."):

> Wherefore that here we may briefly end: of law there can be no
> less acknowledged than that her seat is the bosom of God, her
> voice the harmony of the world: all things in heaven and earth do
> her homage, the very least as feeling her care and the greatest not
> exempted from her power; both angels and men and creatures of
> what condition soever, though each in different sort and manner
> yet all with uniform consent, admiring her as the mother of their
> peace and joy.

Though little enlarged on by the poets, cosmic order was yet one of the master-themes of Elizabethan poetry. It has its positive and its negative expressions. First there is an occasional full statement, as in

Spenser's *Hymns*. Then there are the partial statements or the hints. Ulysses's "degree" speech is a partial statement. The long scene between Malcolm and Macduff at the English court and the reference to the healing power of the English king draw their strength from the idea. There is a short passage in the first part of *Henry VI* whose pivotal meaning any other than a contemporary reader might easily miss. It shows Talbot during a truce with the French doing homage to Henry VI, who has arrived at Paris to be crowned, and Henry rewarding him with the earldom of Shrewsbury. The scene is an example of the sort of thing that ought to happen in an orderly kingdom and it serves as a norm by which the many disorders in the same play are judged. Talbot's speech in its references to the places of God, the king, and himself in their due degrees carries with it the whole context of Hooker and the great Homily of obedience:

> My gracious prince and honorable peers,
> Hearing of your arrival in this realm,
> I have awhile given truce unto my wars,
> To do my duty to my sovereign.
> In sign whereof this arm, that hath reclaim'd
> To your obedience fifty fortresses
> Twelve cities and seven walled towns of strength,
> Beside five hundred prisoners of esteem,
> Lets fall his sword before your highness' feet
> And with submissive loyalty of heart
> Ascribes the glory of his conquest got
> First to my God and next unto your grace.

The gorgeous emblematical figure of Ceremony coming to rebuke the lawless loves of Hero and Leander in Chapmans' continuation of Marlowe's poem is yet another, and far more explicit and academic, version:

> The goddess Ceremony, with a crown
> Of all the stars . . .
> Her flaming hair to her bright feet descended,
> By which hung all the bench of deities.
> And in a chain, compact of ears and eyes,
> She led Religion. All her body was
> Clear and transparent as the purest glass,
> For she was all presented to the sense.
> Devotion Order State and Reverence
> Her shadows were.

The notion of cosmic order pervades the entire *Fairy Queen* and prompts such a detail as Spenser's iteration of the phrase "in comely rew [row]" or "on a row." The arrangement is comely not just because it is pretty and seemly but because it harmonizes with a universal order.

But the negative implication was even more frequent and emphatic. If the Elizabethans believed in an ideal order animating earthly order, they were terrified lest it should be upset, and appalled by the visible tokens of disorder that suggested its upsetting. They were obsessed by the fear of chaos and the fact of mutability; and the obsession was powerful in proportion as their faith in the cosmic order was strong. To us *chaos* means hardly more than confusion on a large scale; to an Elizabethan it meant the cosmic anarchy before creation and the wholesale dissolution that would result if the pressure of Providence relaxed and allowed the law of nature to cease functioning. Othello's "chaos is come again" or Ulysses's "this chaos, when degree is suffocate," cannot be fully felt apart from orthodox theology. Hooker's own description of chaos gives the proper context:

> Now if nature should intermit her course and leave altogether, though it were but for a while, the observation of her own laws; if those principal and mother elements of the world, whereof all things in this lower world are made, should lose the qualities which now they have; if the frame of that heavenly arch erected over our heads should loosen and dissolve itself; if celestial spheres should forget their wonted motions and by irregular volubility turn themselves any way as it might happen; if the prince of the lights of heaven, which now as a giant doth run his unwearied course, should as it were through a languishing faintness begin to stand and to rest himself; if the moon should wander from her beaten way, the times and seasons of the year blend themselves by disordered and confused mixture, the winds breathe out their last gasp, the clouds yield no rain, the earth be defeated of heavenly influence, the fruits of the earth pine away as children at the withered breasts of their mother no longer able to yield them relief: what would become of man himself, whom these things now do all serve? See we not plainly that obedience of creatures unto the law of nature is the stay of the whole world?

If Shakespeare in *Henry VI*, *Troilus and Cressida*, and *Macbeth* gives us his version of order, it bulks small compared with the different kinds of chaos that reign or threaten in all these plays. Yet Shakespeare's chaos is without meaning apart from the proper background of cosmic order by which to judge it.

While Shakespeare puts the opposition to order and his desire for it in terms of chaos mainly, Spenser (and above all in the *Fairy Queen*) does so in terms of mutability. In the Garden of Adonis, the generative workshop of nature, time, which works changes, is the great enemy; and in the last stanzas of the poem the goddess Mutability claims sway in the world. Like Boethius at the beginning of his second book of the *Consolation of Philosophy* Spenser concludes that Mutability is part of a larger stability, just as the wind shows its constancy in never failing to be changeable; but it is through the poignancy of his regrets for earthly instability that he so wonderfully expresses his overmastering passion for order and the old double pull to relish the world and to despise it:

When I bethink me on that speech whilere[10]
Of Mutability and well it weigh,
Me seems that though she all unworthy were
Of the heav'n's rule, yet, very sooth[11] to say,
In all things else she bears the greatest sway:
Which makes me loathe this state of life so tickle
And love of things so vain to cast away;
Whose flow'ring pride, so fading and so fickle,
Short time shall soon cut down with his consuming sickle.

Then gin I think on that which Nature said
Of that same time when no more change shall be.
But stedfast rest of all things, firmly stay'd
Upon the pillars of eternity,
That is contrare to mutability:
For all that moveth doth in change delight:
But henceforth all shall rest eternally
With him that is the God of Sabaoth[12] hight.
O, that great Sabaoth God, grant me that Sabbath's sight.
. . . .

. . . A charming attribute of the chain of being is that it allowed every class to excel in a single particular. The idea is Pythagorean or Platonic and it finds noble expression in the sixth chapter of the first book of Hooker's *Laws of Ecclesiastical Polity.* Stones may be lowly but they exceed the class above them, plants, in strength and durability. Plants, though without sense, excel in the faculty of assimilating nourishment. The beasts are stronger than man in physical energy and

---

[10]**whilere:** a while before; some time ago.
[11]**sooth:** here, true.
[12]**Sabaoth:** Hebrew word that means *armies* or *hosts.*

desires. Man excels the angels in his power of learning, for his very imperfection calls forth that power, while the angels as perfect beings have already acquired all the knowledge they are capable of holding. Only the angels, through their peculiar gift, the faculty of adoration, cannot claim to go beyond the class of being above them.

Another form of excellence, found in most accounts of the chain of being and certainly to be connected with it, is that within every class there was a primate. An example occurred in Gelli's exaltation of the elephant. Sebonde speaks of the dolphin among the fishes, the eagle among birds, the lion among the beasts, the emperor among men. One of the most elaborate of these lists of primacy is in Peacham's *Complete Gentleman,* almost at the beginning. (It will be seen that opinion sometimes varied, the lion competing with the elephant, the whale with the dolphin, for primacy among beasts and fishes.)

> If we consider arightly the frame of the whole universe and method of the all-excellent wisdom in her work as creating the forms of things infinitely divers, so according to dignity of essence and virtue in effect, we must acknowledge the same to hold a sovereignty and transcendent predominance as well of rule as place each over either. Among the heavenly bodies we see the nobler orbs and of greatest influence to be raised aloft, the less effectual depressed. Of elements the fire, the most pure and operative, to hold the highest place. The lion we say is king of beasts, the eagle chief of birds, the whale and whirlpool among fishes, Jupiter's oak the forest's king. Among flowers we most admire and esteem the rose, among fruit the pomeroy and queen-apple; among stones we value above all the diamond, metals gold and silver. And since we know to transfer their inward excellence and virtues to their species successively, shall we not acknowledge a nobility in man of greater perfection, of nobler form, and prince of these?

Other primacies were God among the angels, the sun among the stars, justice among the virtues, and the head among the body's members.

References to these primacies abound in literature but they lose greatly if it is not known that they are all part of a greater whole and that a reference to two or three implies both the rest of them and the ordered universe, in the background. For instance in *Richard II* III 3 Bolingbroke before Flint Castle says

Be he the fire, I'll be the yielding water,

and a few lines later

> See, see King Richard doth himself appear,
> As doth the blushing discontented sun
> From out the fiery portal of the east,
> When he perceives the envious clouds are bent
> To dim his glory and to stain the track
> Of his bright passage to the occident.

To which York adds,

> Yet looks he like a king: behold, his eye,
> As bright as is the eagle's, lightens forth
> Controlling majesty.

There in short space we have four of the traditional primacies: fire among the elements, the sun among the planets, the king among men, the eagle among the birds. Again at the beginning of act five Richard is first a rose and then a lion. . . .

The other major work that demands mention here is the *Tempest*. With the general notion of order Shakespeare was always concerned, with man's position on the chain of being between beast and angel acutely during his tragic period; but only in the *Tempest* does he seem to consider the chain itself. Here indeed man is distanced into a more generally cosmic setting. The heavens are actively alive. It was by Providence divine that Prospero and Miranda survived in the boat. Destiny has this lower world as its instrument. The thunder proclaims Alonso's guilt. Ariel and the other angelic powers, elves and demi-puppets, are all, according to W. C. Curry, in the orthodox tradition of the Renaissance Neo-Platonists, who were the great exponents of the chain of being. Prospero is at the apex of humanity with his magic power and his decision to spend what remains of his life in contemplation. Trinculo and Stephano are low in the scale of humanity. Caliban is largely bestial, a better log-carrier than a man and perhaps of cruder appetites, strong too in fancy in which according to one Renaissance theory beast excelled man. Nor are the beasts forgotten. Prospero tells Ariel that his groans from the pine-tree prison

> Did make wolves howl and penetrate the breasts
> Of ever angry bears.
>
> (1.2.289–90)

The whole play is alive with the sense of creation's flux and not blind to creation's limit. Caliban may hover between man and beast, yet in the end he shows himself incapable of the human power of education. Prospero too learns his own lesson. He cannot transcend the terms of his humanity. In the end he acknowledges Caliban, "this thing of darkness, mine" (5.1.275–76): man for all his striving towards the angels can never be quit utterly of the bestial, of the Caliban, within him.

RONALD TAKAKI

The "Tempest" in the Wilderness

Ronald Takaki (b. 1939) is professor emeritus of ethnic studies at the University of California, Berkeley. A nationally recognized scholar of multicultural studies, he is the author of several books, including *Strangers from a Different Shore: A History of Asian Americans* (1989), *A Different Mirror: A History of Multicultural America* (1993), and *Hiroshima: Why America Dropped the Atomic Bomb* (1995). The following is a chapter from *A Different Mirror*.

In their first encounters with Europeans, the Indians tried to relate the strangers to what was familiar in their world. Traditional Penobscot accounts had described the earth as flat and surrounded by ocean, the "great salt water," *ktci-sobe-k*. Beyond this body of water, there were other islands and countries inhabited by "tribes of strangers." The Indians of Massachusetts Bay, according to early reports by the English, "took the first ship they saw for a walking island, the mast to be a tree, the sail white clouds, and the discharging of ordnance for lightning and thunder. . . ." They were seized by curiosity. By word of mouth, the fantastic news spread, and the "shores for many miles were filled with this naked Nation, gazing at this wonder." Armed with bows and arrows, some of them approached the ship in their canoes, and "let fly their long shafts at her . . . some stuck fast, and others dropped into the water." They wondered why "it did not cry." The native people were struck by the "ugliness" and "deformity" of the strangers — their "white" complexions, hair around their mouths, the eyes with "the color of the blue sky." They tried to identify the visitors. According to Roger Williams, the Indians in Rhode Island used the term *Manittoo,* meaning "god," to describe excellence in human beings and animals. When they saw the English arriving on their ships, they exclaimed: "*Mannittowock.* They are Gods."[1]

Indian dreams had anticipated the coming of the strangers. In New England an old Wampanoag story told about a wise chief foretelling the arrival of Europeans: "On his death-bed he said that a strange white people would come to crowd out the red men, and that for a sign, after his death a great white whale would rise out of the witch pond below. That night he died . . . and the great white whale rose from the witch pond." Another version of this story recounted how the old man was describing his approaching death when suddenly "a white whale arose from the water off Witch Pond." The chief said: "That's a sign that another new people the color of the whale [would arrive], but don't let them have all the land because if you do the Indians will disappear." In Virginia, a Powhatan shaman predicted that "bearded men should come & take away their Country & that there should be none of the original Indians be left, within an hundred & fifty years." Similarly, an Ojibwa prophet had a dream many years before actual contact between the two peoples: "Men of strange appearance have come across the great water. Their skins are white like snow, and on their faces long hair grows. [They came here] in wonderfully large canoes which have great white wings like those of a giant bird. The men have long and sharp knives, and they have long black tubes which they point at birds and animals. The tubes make a smoke that rises into the air just like the smoke from our pipes. From them come fire and such terrific noise that I was frightened, even in my dream."[2]

[1]Frank G. Speck, "Penobscot Tales and Religious Beliefs," *Journal of American Folklore,* vol. 48, no. 187 (January–March 1915), p. 19; William Wood, quoted in William S. Simmons, *Spirit of New England Tribes: Indian History and Folklore, 1620–1984* (Hanover, N.H., 1986), p. 66; Edward Johnson, *Wonder-working Providence, 1628–1651,* edited by F. Franklin Jameson (New York, 1910; originally published in 1654), p. 39; Colin G. Calloway (ed.), *Dawnland Encounters: Indians and Europeans in Northern New England* (Hanover, N.H., 1991), pp. 30, 50; Roger Williams, *A Key into the Language of America* (Detroit, 1973), p. 191. See also James Axtell, "Through Another Glass Darkly: Early Indian Views of Europeans," in Axtell, *After Columbus: Essays in the Ethnohistory of Colonial North America* (New York, 1988), pp. 125–43.

[2]Simmons, *Spirit of New England Tribes,* pp. 71, 72; Axtell, *After Columbus,* p. 129; James Axtell, *The Invasion Within: The Contest of Cultures in Colonial North America* (New York, 1985), p. 8.

SHAKESPEARE'S DREAM
ABOUT AMERICA

"O brave new world that has such people in't!" they heard Miranda exclaim. The theatergoers were attending the first performance of William Shakespeare's *Tempest*. This play was first presented in London in 1611, a time when the English were encountering what they viewed as strange inhabitants in new lands. The circumstances surrounding the play determined the meaning of the utterances they heard. A perspicacious few in the audience could have seen that this play was more than a mere story about how Prospero was sent into exile with his daughter, took possession of an island inhabited by Caliban, and redeemed himself by marrying Miranda to the king's son.[3]

Indeed, *The Tempest* can be approached as a fascinating tale that served as a masquerade for the creation of a new society in America. Seen in this light, the play invites us to view English expansion not only as imperialism, but also as a defining moment in the making of an English-American identity based on race. For the first time in the English theater, an Indian character was being presented. What did Shakespeare and his audience know about the native peoples of America, and what choices were they making in the ways they characterized Caliban? Although they saw him as "savage," did they racialize savagery? Was the play a prologue for America?

The Tempest, studied in relationship to its historical context, can help us answer these questions. While *Othello* also offers us an opportunity to analyze English racial attitudes, as Winthrop Jordan has demonstrated so brilliantly, our play is a more important window for understanding American history, for its story is set in the New World.

---

[3]William Shakespeare, *The Tempest*, Act V, sc. i, 183–84. *The Tempest* has recently been swept into the storm over "political correctness." In 1991, George Will issued a scathing attack on "left" scholars and their "perverse" "liberation" of literature, especially their interpretation of this play as a reflection of "the imperialist rape of the Third World." Shakespeare specialist Stephen Greenblatt responded: "This is a curious example — since it is very difficult to argue that *The Tempest* is *not* about imperialism." Such an authoritative counterstatement clears the way for a study of this story in relationship to its historical setting. See George Will, "Literary Politics: 'The Tempest'? It's 'really' about imperialism. Emily Dickinson's poetry? Masturbation," *Newsweek*, April 22, 1991, p. 72 [reprinted in this volume, p. 110]; and Stephen Greenblatt, "The Best Way to Kill Our Literary Inheritance Is to Turn It into a Decorous Celebration of the New World Order," *Chronicle of Higher Education,* vol. 37, no. 39 (June 12, 1991), pp. B1, 3 [reprinted in this volume, p. 113]. As Adam Begley has recently noted, literary critic Stanley Fish reminds us that "the circumstances of an utterance determine its meaning." See Begley, "Souped-up Scholar," *New York Times Magazine,* May 3, 1992, p. 52. My appreciation to Frederick E. Hoxkie and David Thelen for helping me develop the critical contours of my analysis.

Moreover, the timing of *The Tempest* was crucial: it was first performed after the English invasion of Ireland but before the colonization of New England, after John Smith's arrival in Virginia but before the beginning of the tobacco economy, and after the first contacts with Indians but before full-scale warfare against them. This was an era when the English were encountering "other" peoples and delineating the boundary between "civilization" and "savagery." The social constructions of both these terms were dynamically developing in three sites — Ireland, Virginia, and New England.[4]

One of the places the English were colonizing at the time was Ireland, and Caliban seemed to resemble the Irish. Theatergoers were familiar with the "wild Irish" onstage, for such images had been presented in plays like *Sir John Oldcastle* (1599) and *Honest Whore* (1605). Seeking to conquer the Irish in 1395, Richard II had condemned them as "savage Irish, our enemies." In the mid-sixteenth century, shortly before the beginning of the English migrations to America, the government had decided to bring all of Ireland under its rule and encouraged private colonization projects.[5]

Like Caliban, the Irish were viewed as "savages," a people living outside of "civilization." They had tribal organizations, and their practice of herding seemed nomadic. Even their Christianity was said to be merely the exterior of strongly rooted paganism. "They are all Papists by their profession," claimed Edmund Spenser in 1596, "but in the same so blindly and brutishly informed for the most part as that you would rather think them atheists or infidels." To the colonists, the Irish lacked "knowledge of God or good manners." They had no sense of private property and did not "plant any Gardens or Orchards, Inclose or improve their lands, live together in setled Villages or Townes." The Irish were described as lazy, "naturally" given to "idleness" and unwilling to work for "their own bread." Dominated by "innate sloth," "loose, barbarous and most wicked," and living "like beasts," they were

---

[4]Winthrop Jordan, *White over Black: American Attitudes toward the Negro, 1550–1812* (Chapel Hill, N.C., 1968), pp. 37–40. *Othello* was first performed in 1604, before the founding of Jamestown. Jordan overlooked the rich possibility of studying *The Tempest*.

[5]Nicholas P. Canny, "The Idology of English Colonization: From Ireland to America," *William and Mary Quarterly*, 3rd series, vol. 30, no. 4 (October 1973), p. 585; David B. Quinn, *The Elizabethans and the Irish* (Ithaca, N.Y., 1966), p. 161; Francis Jennings, *The Invasion of America: Indians, Colonialism, and the Cant of Conquest* (New York, 1976), p. 7. In *White Supremacy: A Comparative Study in American & South African History* (New York, 1971), George Frederickson describes the conquest of Ireland as a "rehearsal" (p. 13).

also thought to be criminals, an underclass inclined to steal from the English. The colonists complained that the Irish savages were not satisfied with the "fruit of the natural unlaboured earth" and therefore continually "invaded the fertile possessions" of the "English Pale."[6]

The English colonizers established a two-tiered social structure: "Every Irishman shall be forbidden to wear English apparel or weapon upon pain of death. That no Irishman, born of Irish race and brought up Irish, shall purchase land, bear office, be chosen of any jury or admitted witness in any real or personal action." To reinforce this social separation, British laws prohibited marriages between the Irish and the colonizers. The new world order was to be one of English over Irish.[7]

The Irish also became targets of English violence. "Nothing but fear and force can teach duty and obedience" to this "rebellious people," the invaders insisted. While the English were generally brutal in their warfare practices at that time, they seemed to have been particularly cruel toward the Irish. The colonizers burned the villages and crops of the inhabitants and relocated them on reservations. They slaughtered families, "man, woman and child," justifying their atrocities by arguing that families provided support for the rebels. After four years of bloody warfare in Munster, according to Edmund Spenser, the Irish had been reduced to wretchedness. "Out of every corner of the woods and glens they came creeping forth upon their hands, for their legs would not bear them. They looked anatomies of death; they spake like ghosts crying out of their graves." The death toll was so high that "in short space there were none almost left and a most populous and plentiful country suddenly left void of man and beast." The "void" meant vacant lands for English resettlement.[8]

The invaders took the heads of the slain Irish as trophies. Sir Humphrey Gilbert pursued a campaign of terror: he ordered that "the heads of all those . . . killed in the day, should be cut off from their bodies and brought to the place where he encamped at night, and should there be laid on the ground by each side of the way leading into his own tent so that none could come into his tent for any cause but commonly

[6]Canny, "Idology," pp. 585, 588; Howard Mumford Jones, *O Strange New World: American Culture, the Formative Years* (New York, 1965), p. 169; Keith Thomas, *Man and the Natural World: A History of the Modern Sensibility* (New York, 1983), p. 42; Jennings, *Invasion of America*, pp. 46, 49; James Muldoon, "The Indian as Irishman," *Essex Institute Historical Collections,* vol. III (October 1975), p. 269; Quinn, *Elizabethans and Irish,* p. 76.

[7]Muldoon, "Indian as Irishman," p. 284; Quinn, *Elizabethans and Irish,* p. 108.

[8]Canny, "Ideology," pp. 593, 582; Jennings, *Invasion of America,* p. 153; Frederickson, *White Supremacy,* p. 15; Quinn, *Elizabethans and Irish,* pp. 132–33.

he must pass through a lane of heads. . . . [It brought] great terror to the people when they saw the heads of their dead fathers, brothers, children, kinsfolk, and friends. . . ." After seeing the head of his lord impaled on the walls of Dublin, Irish poet Angus O'Daly cried out:

O body which I see without a head,
It is the sight of thee which has withered up my strength.
Divided and impaled in Ath-cliath,
The learned of Banba will feel its loss.
Who will relieve the wants of the poor?
Who will bestow cattle on the learned?
O Body, since thou art without a head,
It is not life which we care to choose after thee.[9]

The English claimed that they had a God-given responsibility to "inhabit and reform so barbarous a nation" and to educate the Irish "brutes." They would teach them to obey English laws and stop "robbing and stealing and killing" one another. They would uplift this "most filthy people, utterly enveloped in vices, most untutored of all peoples in the rudiments of faith." Thus, although they saw the Irish as savages and although they sometimes described this savagery as "natural" and "innate," the English believed that the Irish could be civilized, improved through what Shakespeare called "nurture." In short, the difference between the Irish and the English was a matter of culture.[10]

As their frontier advanced from Ireland to America, the English began making comparisons between the Irish and Indian "savages" and wondering whether there might be different kinds of "savagery."

The parallels between English expansionism in Ireland and America were apparent. Sir Humphrey Gilbert, Lord De La Warr, Sir Francis Drake, and Sir Walter Raleigh participated in both the invasion of Ireland and the colonization of the New World. The conquest of Ireland and the settlement of Virginia were bound so closely together that one correspondence, dated March 8, 1610, stated: "It is hoped the plantation of Ireland may shortly be settled. The Lord Delaware [Lord De La Warr] is preparing to depart for the plantation of Virginia." Commander John Mason conducted military campaigns against the Irish before he sailed to New England, where he led troops against the Pequots

[9]Canny, "Ideology," p. 582; Jennings, *Invasion of America,* p. 168; Douglas Hyde, *Literary History of Ireland* (London, 1894), p. 473.
[10]Canny, "Ideology," p. 588; Jennings, *Invasion of America,* pp. 46, 49; Quinn, *Elizabethans and Irish,* p. 76; Shakespeare, *Tempest,* Act IV, sc. i, 188–89.

of Connecticut. Samuel Gorton wrote a letter to John Winthrop, Jr., connecting the two frontiers: "I remember the time of the wars in Ireland (when I was young, in Queen Elizabeth's days of famous memory) where much English blood was spilt by a people much like unto these [Indians]. . . . And after these Irish were subdued by force, what treacherous and bloody massacres have they attempted is well known."[11]

The first English colonizers in the New World found that the Indians reminded them of the Irish. In Virginia, Captain John Smith observed that the deerskin robes worn by the Indians did not differ much "in fashion from the Irish mantels." Thomas Morton noticed that the "Natives of New England [were] accustomed to build themselves houses much like the wild Irish." Roger Williams reported that the thick woods and swamps of New England gave refuge to the Indians engaged in warfare, "like the bogs to the wild Irish." Thus, in their early encounters, the English projected the familiar onto the strange, their images of the Irish onto the native people of America. Initially, "savagery" was defined in relationship to the Irish, and the Indians were incorporated into this definition.[12]

The Tempest, the London audience knew, was not about Ireland but about the New World, for the reference to the "Bermoothes" (Bermuda) revealed the location of the island. What was happening onstage was a metaphor for English expansion into America. The play's title was inspired by a recent incident: caught in a violent storm in 1609, the *Sea Adventure* had been separated from a fleet of ships bound for Virginia and had run aground in the Bermudas. Shakespeare knew many of the colonizers, including Sir Humphrey Gilbert and Lord De La Warr. One of his personal friends was geographer Richard Hakluyt, author of widely read books about the New World. The future of Englishmen lay in America, proclaimed Hakluyt, as he urged them to "conquer a country" and "to man it, to plant it, and to keep it, and to continue the making of Wines and Oils able to serve England."[13]

[11]Quinn, *Elizabethans and Irish*, p. 121; William Christie MacLeod, "Celt and Indian: Britain's Old World Frontier in Relation to the New," in Paul Bohannan and Fred Plog (eds.), *Beyond the Frontier: Social Process and Cultural Change* (Garden City, N.Y., 1967), pp. 38–39; Jennings, *Invasion of America*, p. 312.

[12]Quinn, *Elizabethans and Irish*, p. 121; Muldoon, "Indian as Irishman," p. 270; MacLeod, "Celt and Indian," p. 26; see also Canny, "Ideology," p. 576.

[13]Shakespeare, *Tempest*, Act I, sc. ii, 229; Frank Kermode, "Introduction," *The Tempest*, The Arden Edition of the Works of William Shakespeare (London, 1969), p. xxvii;

The scene of the play was actually the mainland near the "Bermoothes"— Virginia. "The air breathes upon us here most sweetly," the theatergoers were told. "Here is everything advantageous to life." "How lush and lusty the grass looks! how green!" Impressed by the land's innocence, Gonzalo of *The Tempest* depicted it as an ideal commonwealth where everything was as yet unformed and unbounded, where letters, laws, metals, and occupations were yet unknown. Both the imagery and the language revealed America as the site of Prospero's landing: it was almost as if Shakespeare had lifted the material from contemporary documents about the New World. Tracts on Virginia had described the air as "most sweet" and as "virgin and temperate," and its soil *"lusty"* with meadows "full of *green grass.*" In *A True Reportory of the Wracke,* published in 1609, William Strachey depicted Virginia's abundance: "no Country yieldeth goodlier *Corn,* nor more manifold increase. . . . [W]e have thousands of goodly *Vines.*" Here was an opportunity for colonists to enhance the "fertility and pleasure" of Virginia by "cleansing away her woods" and converting her into "goodly meadow."[14]

Moreover, the play provided a clever clue that the story was indeed about America: Caliban, one of the principal characters, was a New World inhabitant. "Carib," the name of an Indian tribe, came to mean a savage of America, and the term *cannibal* was a derivative. Shakespeare sometimes rearranged letters in words ("Amleth," the name of a prince in a Viking era tale, for example, became "Hamlet"), and here he had created another anagram in "Caliban."[15]

The English had seen or read reports about Indians who had been captured and brought to London. Indians had been displayed in Europe by Christopher Columbus. During his first voyage, he wrote: "Yesterday came [to] the ship a dugout with six young men, and five

Robert R. Cawley, "Shakespeare's Use of the Voyagers in *The Tempest,*" *Publications of the Modern Language Association of America,* vol. 41, no. 3 (September 1926), pp. 699–700, 689; Frederickson, *White Supremacy,* p. 22. See also Leo Marx, *The Machine in the Garden: Technology and the Pastoral Ideal in America* (New York, 1964), pp. 34–75.

[14]Shakespeare, *Tempest,* Act II, sc. i, 45–53, 148–53; Cawley, "Shakespeare's Use," pp. 702, 703, 704; Kirkpatrick Sale, *The Conquest of Paradise: Christopher Columbus and the Columbian Legacy* (New York, 1990), p. 102. For analysis of America imaged as a woman, see Carolyn Merchant, *Ecological Revolutions: Nature, Gender, and Science in New England* (Chapel Hill, N.C., 1989), p. 101; Annette Kolodny, *The Lay of the Land: Metaphor as Experience and History in American Life and Letters* (Chapel Hill, N.C., 1975).

[15]Kermode (ed.), introduction, *Tempest,* p. xxiv. For anagram of Hamlet, see dedication to William Shakespeare at Kronborg Castle, Denmark.

came on board; these I ordered to be detained and I am bringing them." When Columbus was received by the Spanish court after his triumphal return, he presented a collection of things he had brought back, including some gold nuggets, parrots in cages, and six Indians. During his second voyage in 1493, Columbus again sent his men to kidnap Indians. On one occasion, a captive had been "wounded seven times and his entrails were hanging out," reported Guillermo Coma of Aragon. "Since it was thought that he could not be cured, he was cast into the sea. But keeping above water and raising one foot, he held on to his intestines with his left hand and swam courageously to the shore. . . . The wounded Carib was caught again on shore. His hands and feet were bound more tightly and he was once again thrown headlong. But this resolute savage swam more furiously, until he was struck several times by arrows and perished." When Columbus set sail with his fleet to return to Spain, he took 550 Indian captives. "When we reached the waters around Spain," Michele de Cuneo wrote matter-of-factly, "about 200 of those Indians died, I believe because of the unaccustomed air, colder than theirs. We cast them into the sea."[16]

Similarly, English explorers engaged in this practice of kidnapping Indians. When Captain George Waymouth visited New England in 1605, he lured some Abenakis to his ship; taking three of them hostage, he sailed back to England to display them. An early seventeenth-century pamphlet stated that a voyage to Virginia was expected to bring back its quota of captured Indians: "Thus we shipped five savages, two canoes, with all their bows and arrows." In 1614, the men on one of Captain John Smith's ships captured several Indians on Cape Cod. "Thomas Hunt," Smith wrote, ". . . betrayed four and twenty of these poor savages aboard this ship, and most dishonestly and inhumanely . . . carried them with him to Maligo [Málaga] and there for a little private gain sold . . . those savages for Rials of eight."[17] In 1611, according to a biographer of William Shakespeare, "a native of New England called Epnew was brought to England . . . and 'being a man of so great a stature' was showed up and down London for money as a monster." In the play, Stephano considered capturing Caliban: "If I can recover him, and keep him tame, and get to Naples with him, he's a

---

[16]Christopher Columbus, Journal, November 12, 1492, in Samuel Eliot Morison (ed.), *Journals and Other Documents on the Life and Voyages of Christopher Columbus* (New York, 1963), p. 126; Sale, *Conquest of Paradise*, p. 126; Guillermo Coma to the Duke of Milan, December 13, 1494, in Morison (ed.), *Journals of Columbus*, p. 238; Cuneo to Lord Hieronymo Annari, October 15, 1495, in Morison (ed.), *Journals of Columbus*, pp. 226–27.

[17]**Rials of eight:** (aka pieces of eight) a rial is a Spanish coin made of silver.

present for any emperor. . . . ." Such exhibitions of Indians were "profitable investments," literary scholar Frank Kermode noted, and were "a regular feature of colonial policy under James I. The exhibits rarely survived the experience."[18]

To the spectators of these "exhibits," Indians personified "savagery." They were depicted as "cruel, barbarous and most treacherous." They were thought to be cannibals, "being most furious in their rage and merciless . . . not being content only to kill and take away life, but delight to torment men in the most bloody manner . . . flaying some alive with the shells of fishes, cutting off the members and joints of others by piecemeal and broiling on the coals, eating the collops of their flesh in their sight whilst they live." According to Sir Walter Raleigh, Indians had "their eyes in their shoulders, and their mouths in the middle of their breasts." In *Nova Brittania,* published in 1609, Richard Johnson described the Indians in Virginia as "wild and savage people," living "like herds of deer in a forest." One of their striking physical characteristics was their skin color. John Brereton described the New England Indians as "of tall stature, broad and grim visage, of a blacke swart complexion."[19]

Indians seemed to lack everything the English identified as civilized — Christianity, cities, letters, clothing, and swords. "They do not bear arms or know them, for I showed to them swords and they took them by the blade and cut themselves through ignorance," wrote Columbus in his journal, noting that the Indians did not have iron. George Waymouth tried to impress the Abenakis: he magnetized a sword "to cause them to imagine some great power in us; and for that to love and fear us."[20]

Like Caliban, the native people of America were viewed as the "other." European culture was delineating the border, the hierarchical division between civilization and wildness. Unlike Europeans, Indians

[18]Kenneth M. Morrison, *The Embattled Northeast: The Elusive Ideal of Alliance in Abenaki-Euramerican Relations* (Berkeley, Calif., 1984), pp. 22–23; Leonard A. Adolf, "Squanto's Role in Pilgrim Diplomacy," *Ethnohistory,* vol. II, no. 4 (fall 1964), pp. 247–48; Cawley, "Shakespeare's Use," pp. 720, 721; Shakespeare, *Tempest,* Act, II, sc. ii, 72–74; Kermode (ed.), text explanation, *Tempest,* p. 62.

[19]William Bradford, *Of Plymouth Plantation: 1620–1647* (New York, 1967), p. 26; Frederickson, *White Supremacy,* p. 11; Roy Harvey Pearce, *Savagism and Civilization: A Study of the Indian and the American Mind* (Baltimore, 1967), p. 12; Calloway (ed.), *Dawnland Encounters,* p. 33.

[20]Wilcomb Washburn (ed.), *Indian and White Man* (New York, 1964), pp. 4–5; Morrison, *Embattled Northeast,* pp. 22–23; see Riane Eisler, *The Chalice and the Blade: Our History, Our Future* (New York, 1988), for the significance of "the sword."

were allegedly dominated by their passions, especially their sexuality. Amerigo Vespucci was struck by how the natives embraced and enjoyed the pleasures of their bodies: "They . . . are libidinous beyond measure, and the women far more than the men. . . . When they had the opportunity of copulating with Christians, urged by excessive lust, they defiled and prostituted themselves." Caliban personified such passions. Prospero saw him as a sexual threat to the nubile Miranda, her "virgin-knot" yet untied. "I have used thee (filth as thou art) with humane care," Prospero scolded Caliban, "and lodged thee in mine own cell till thou didst seek to violate the honor of my child." And the unruly native snapped: "O ho, O ho! Would't had been done! Thou didst prevent me; I had peopled else this isle with Calibans."[21]

To the theatergoers, Caliban represented what Europeans had been when they were lower on the scale of development. To be civilized, they believed, required denial of wholeness — the repression of the instinctual forces of human nature. A personification of civilized man, Prospero identified himself as mind rather than body. His epistemology was reliant on the visual rather than the tactile and on the linear knowledge of books rather than the polymorphous knowledge of experience. With the self fragmented, Prospero was able to split off his rationality and raise it to authority over the "other"— the sensuous part of himself and everything Caliban represented.

But could Caliban, the audience wondered, ever become Christian and civilized? The Spanish lawyer Juan Gines de Sepúlveda had justified the Spanish conquest of Indians by invoking Aristotle's doctrine that some people were "natural slaves." The condition of slavery, Sepúlveda argued, was natural for "persons of both inborn rudeness and of inhuman and barbarous customs." Thus what counted was an ascriptive quality based on a group's nature, or "descent."[22]

On the other hand, Pope Paul III had proclaimed that Indians, as well as "all other people" who might later be "discovered" by "Christians," should not be deprived of their liberty and property, even

[21]Shakespeare, *Tempest*, Act IV, sc. i, 15; Act I, sc. ii, 348–54; Washburn (ed.), *Indian and White Man*, pp. 4, 5, 7.

[22]Frederickson, *White Supremacy*, p. 9; the terms "descent" and "consent" are from Werner Sollors, *Beyond Ethnicity: Consent and Descent in American Culture* (New York, 1986), p. 6. Sollors minimizes the significance of race, arguing that it is "merely one aspect of ethnicity" (p. 36). I take the opposite position here as well as in Takaki, "Reflections on Racial Patterns in America," in Takaki (ed.), *From Different Shores: Perspectives on Race and Ethnicity in America* (New York, 1987), pp. 26–38; and Takaki, *Iron Cages: Race and Culture in Nineteenth-Century America* (New York, 1979).

though they were outside the Christian faith. Christopher Columbus had reported that Indians were "very gentle and without knowledge of . . . evil." He added: "They love their neighbors as themselves, and have the sweetest talk in the world, and gentle, and always with a smile." In *The Tempest,* Gonzalo told theatergoers: "I saw such islanders . . . who, though they are of monstrous shape, yet, note, their manners are more gentle, kind, than of our human generation you shall find many — nay, almost any." Thus, Indians were not always viewed as brutish by nature: they could be acculturated, become civilized through "consent."[23]

Indeed, Caliban seemed educable. Prospero had taught him a European language: "I . . . took pains to make thee speak, taught thee each hour one thing or other. When thou didst not, savage, know thine own meaning, but wouldst gabble like a thing most brutish." Defiantly, the native retorted: "You taught me language, and my profit on't is, I know how to curse. The red plague rid you for learning me your language." Clearly, Caliban was no mere victim: capable of acculturation, he could express his anger. A Virginia tract stated that the colonists should take Indian children and "train them up with gentleness, teach them our English tongue." In the contract establishing the Virginia Company in 1606, the king endorsed a plan to propagate the "Christian Religion to such people" who as yet lived in "darkness and miserable ignorance of the true knowledge and worship of God." Three years later, the Virginia Company instructed the colony's governor to encourage missionaries to convert Indian children. They should be taken from their parents if necessary, since they were "so wrapped up in the fog and misery of their iniquity." A Virginia promotional tract stated that it was "not the nature of men, but the education of men" that made them "barbarous and uncivil." Every man in the new colony had a duty to bring the savage Indians to "civil and Christian" government.[24]

All of these cultural constructs of Indians at this point in time were either the fantasy of Shakespeare or the impressions of policymakers

[23]Sollors, *Beyond Ethnicity,* pp. 36–37; Frederickson, *White Supremacy,* p. 8; Columbus, Journal, November 12 and December 25, 1492, in Morison (ed.), *Journals of Columbus,* pp. 92, 136; Shakespeare, *Tempest,* Act III, sc. iii, 29–34.

[24]Shakespeare, *Tempest,* Act I, sc. ii, 356–68; Cawley, "Shakespeare's Use," p. 715; Frederickson, *White Supremacy,* p. 12; Pearce, *Savagism and Civilization,* pp. 9, 10. Aimé Césaire also recognized this angry and articulate Caliban and moved him from margin to center. See his *Tempest* (New York, 1969). [Reprinted in part in this volume, p. 309.]

and tract writers in London. What would happen to these images on the stage of history?

The first English settlement in the New World was in Virginia, the home of fourteen thousand Powhatans. An agricultural people, they cultivated corn — the mainstay of their subsistence. Their cleared fields were as large as one hundred acres, and they lived in palisaded towns, with forts, storehouses, temples, and framed houses covered with bark and reed mats. They cooked their food in ceramic pots and used woven baskets for storing corn: some of their baskets were constructed so skillfully they could carry water in them. The Powhatans had a sophisticated numbering system for evaluating their harvests. According to John Smith, they had numbers from one to ten, after which counting was done by tens to one hundred. There was also a word for "one thousand." The Powhatan calendar had five seasons: "Their winter some call *Popanow*, the spring *Cattaapeuk*, the sommer *Cohattayough*, the earing of their Corne *Nepinough*, the harvest and fall of the leafe *Taquitock*. From September until the midst of November are the chief Feasts and sacrifice."[25]

In Virginia, the initial encounters between the English and the Indians opened possibilities for friendship and interdependency. After arriving in 1607, the first one hundred and twenty colonists set up camp. Then, John Smith reported, came "the starving time." A year later, only thirty-eight of them were still alive, hanging precariously on the very edge of survival. The reality of America did not match the imagery of the New World as a garden; the descriptions of its natural abundance turned out to be exaggerated. Many of the English were not prepared for survival in the wilderness. "Now was all our provision spent . . . all help abandoned, each hour expecting the fury of the savages," Smith wrote. Fortunately, in that "desperate extremity," the Powhatans brought food and rescued the starving strangers.[26]

A year later, several hundred more colonists arrived, and again they quickly ran out of provisions. They were forced to eat "dogs, cats, rats, and mice," even "corpses" dug from graves. "Some have licked up the blood which hath fallen from their weak fellows," a survivor reported. "One [member] of our colony murdered his wife, ripped the child out

[25]Axtell, *After Columbus,* p. 190; Helen C. Rountree, *The Powhatan Indians of Virginia: Their Traditional Culture* (Norman, Okla., 1990), pp. 44, 45, 46, 49, 60, 63.
[26]Mortimer J. Adler (ed.), *The Annals of America,* vol. 1, *Discovering a New World* (Chicago, 1968), pp. 21, 26, 22.

of her womb and threw it into the river, and after chopped the mother in pieces and salted her for his food, the same not being discovered before he had eaten part thereof." "So great was our famine," John Smith stated, "that a savage we slew and buried, the poorer sort took him up again and ate him; and so did diverse one another boiled and stewed with roots and herbs."[27]

Hostilities soon broke out as the English tried to extort food supplies by attacking the Indians and destroying their villages. In 1608, an Indian declared: *"We hear you are come from under the World to take our World from us."* A year later, Governor Thomas Gates arrived in Virginia with instructions that the Indians should be forced to labor for the colonists and also make annual payments of corn and skins. The orders were brutally carried out. During one of the raids, the English soldiers attacked an Indian town, killing fifteen people and forcing many others to flee. Then they burned the houses and destroyed the cornfields. According to a report by commander George Percy, they marched the captured queen and her children to the river where they "put the Children to death . . . by throwing them overboard and shooting out their brains in the water."[28]

Indians began to doubt that the two peoples could live together in peace. One young Indian told Captain John Smith: "[We] are here to intreat and desire your friendship and to enjoy our houses and plant our fields, of whose fruits you shall participate." But he did not trust the strangers: "We perceive and well know you intend to destroy us." Chief Powhatan had come to the same conclusion, and he told Smith that the English were not in Virginia to trade but to "invade" and "possess" Indian lands.[29]

Indeed, Smith and his fellow colonists were encouraged by their culture of expansionism to claim entitlement to the land. In *The Tempest,* the theatergoers were told: "I think he will carry this island home in his pocket and give it his son for an apple." Prospero declared that he had been thrust forth from Milan and "most strangely" landed on this shore "to be the lord on't." Projecting his personal plans and dreams onto the wilderness, he colonized the island and dispossessed Caliban. Feeling robbed, Caliban protested: "As I told thee before, I am subject to a tyrant, a sorcerer, that by his cunning hath cheated me of the

[27]Gary Nash, *Red, White, and Black: The Peoples of Early America* (Englewood Cliffs, N.J., 1974), p. 58; Adler (ed.), *Annals of America,* vol. 1, p. 26.
[28]Cotton Mather, *Magnalia Christi Americana,* books 1 and 2 (Cambridge, Mass., 1977), p. 116; Frederickson, *White Supremacy,* p. 24; Sale, *Conquest of Paradise,* p. 277.
[29]Jennings, *Invasion of America,* p. 66; Nash, *Red, White, and Black,* p. 57.

island." But the English did not see their taking of land as robbery. In *Utopia*, Sir Thomas More justified the appropriation of Indian lands: since the natives did not "use" the soil but left it "idle and waste," the English had "just cause" to drive them from the territory by force. In 1609, Robert Gray declared that "the greater part" of the earth was "possessed and wrongfully usurped by wild beasts . . . or by brutish savages." A Virginia pamphlet argued that it was "not unlawful" for the English to possess "part" of the Indians' land.[30]

But the English soon wanted more than just a "part" of Indian territory. Their need for land was suddenly intensified by a new development — the cultivation of tobacco as an export crop. In 1613, the colony sent its first shipment of tobacco to London, a small but significant four barrels' worth. The exports grew dramatically from 2,300 pounds in 1616 to 19,000 the following year, and to 60,000 by 1620. The colonists increasingly coveted Indian lands, especially the already cleared fields. Tobacco agriculture stimulated not only territorial expansion but also immigration. During the "Great Migration" of 1618–1623, the colony grew from four hundred to forty-five hundred people.

In 1622, the natives tried to drive out the intruders, killing some three hundred colonists. John Smith denounced the "massacre" and described the "savages" as "cruel beasts," who possessed "a more unnatural brutishness" than wild animals. The English deaths, Samuel Purchas argued, established the colonists' right to the land: "Their carcasses, the dispersed bones of their countrymen . . . speak, proclaim and cry, This our earth is truly English, and therefore this Land is justly yours O English." Their blood had watered the soil, entitling them to the land. "We, who hitherto have had possession of no more ground than their [Indian] waste, and our purchase . . . may now by right of War, and law of Nations," the colonists declared, "invade the Country, and destroy them who sought to destroy us." They felt they could morally sweep away their enemies and even take their developed lands. *"We shall enjoy their cultivated places. . . . Now their cleared grounds in all their villages (which are situated in the fruitfulest places of the land) shall be inhabited by us."*[31]

In their fierce counterattack, the English waged total war. "Victory may be gained in many ways," a colonist declared: "by force, by surprise,

[30]Merchant, *Ecological Revolutions,* p. 22; Shakespeare, *Tempest,* Act II, sc. i, 87–88; Act V, sc. i, 160–62; Act III, sc. ii, 40–42; Thomas More, *Utopia* (New Haven, Conn., 1964), p. 76; Thomas, *Man and the Natural World,* p. 42; Cawley, "Shakespeare's Use," p. 715.

[31]Jennings, *Invasion of America,* pp. 78, 80; Sale, *Conquest of Paradise,* p. 295.

by famine in burning their Corn, by destroying and burning their Boats, Canoes, and Houses . . . by pursuing and chasing them with our horses, and blood-hounds to draw after them, and mastives to tear them." In 1623, Captain William Tucker led his soldiers to a Powhatan village, presumably to negotiate a peace treaty. After he concluded the treaty, he persuaded the Indians to drink a toast, but he served them poisoned wine. An estimated two hundred Indians died instantly, and Tucker's soldiers then killed another fifty and "brought home part of their heads." In 1629, a colonist reported, the English forced a hostile Indian leader to seek peace by "continual incursions" and by "yearly cutting down, and spoiling their corn." The goal of the war was to "root out [the Indians] from being any longer a people."[32]

What happened in Virginia, while terrible and brutal, was still based largely on the view that Indian "savagery" was cultural. Like the Irish, Indians were identified as brutal and backward, but they were not yet seen as incapable of becoming civilized because of their race, or "descent." Their heathenism had not yet been indelibly attached to distinctive physical characteristics such as their skin color. So far at least, "consent" was possible for Indians. What occurred in New England was a different story, however, and here again, the play was preview.[33]

Although the theatergoers were given the impression that Caliban could be acculturated, they also received a diametrically opposite construction of his racial character. They were told that Caliban was "a devil, a born devil" and that he belonged to a "vile race." "Descent" was determinative: his "race" signified an inherent moral defect. On the stage, they saw Caliban, with long shaggy hair, personifying the Indian. He had distinct racial markers. "Freckled," covered with brown spots, he was "not honored with human shape." Called a "fish," he was mockingly told: "Thy eyes are almost set in thy head." "Where should they be set else? He were a brave monster indeed if they were set in his tail." More important, his distinctive physical characteristics signified intellectual incapacity. Caliban was "a thing of darkness" whose "nature nurture [could] never stick." In other words, he had natural qualities that precluded the possibility of becoming civilized through "nurture," or education. The racial distance between Caliban and Prospero was inscribed geographically. The native was forced to live on a reservation located in a barren region. "Here you sty [to lodge, to place in a pig

---

[32]Nash, *Red, White, and Black,* pp. 62, 63; Sale, *Conquest of Paradise,* pp. 293, 294; Jennings, *Invasion of America,* p. 153.

[33]Sollors, *Beyond Ethnicity,* pp. 6, 36, 37.

pen or sty] me in this hard rock," he complained, "whiles you do keep from me the rest o' the island." Prospero justified this segregation, charging that the "savage" possessed distasteful qualities, "which good natures could not abide to be with. Therefore wast thou deservedly confined into this rock, who hadst deserved more than a prison." The theatergoers saw Caliban's "sty" located emblematically at the back of the stage, behind Prospero's "study," signifying a hierarchy of white over dark and cerebral over carnal.[34]

This deterministic view of Caliban's racial character would be forged in the crucible of New England. Five years after the first performance of *The Tempest,* Captain John Smith sailed north from Virginia to explore the New England coast, where again he found not wild men but farmers. The "paradise" of Massachusetts, he reported, was "all planted with corn, groves, mulberries, savage gardens." "The sea Coast as you pass shews you all along large Corne fields." Indeed, while the Abenakis of Maine were mainly hunters and food gatherers dependent on the natural abundance of the land, the tribes in southern New England were horticultural. For example, the Wampanoags, whom the Pilgrims encountered in 1620, were a farming people, with a representative political system as well as a division of labor, with workers specializing in arrowmaking, woodwork, and leathercrafts.[35]

The Wampanoags as well as the Pequots, Massachusetts, Nausets, Nipmucks, and Narragansets cultivated corn. As the main source of life for these tribes, corn was the focus of many legends. A Narraganset belief told how a crow had brought this grain to New England: "These Birds, although they do the corn also some hurt, yet scarce one *Native* amongst a hundred will kill them, because they have a tradition, that the Crow brought them at first an *Indian* Grain of Corn in one Ear, and an *Indian* or French bean in another, from the Great God *Kautantouwits* field in the Southwest from whence . . . came all their Corn and Beans." A Penobscot account celebrated the gift of Corn Mother: during a time of famine, an Indian woman fell in love with a snake in the forest. Her secret was discovered one day by her husband, and she told him that she had been chosen to save the tribe. She instructed him to kill her with a stone ax and then drag her body through a clearing.

[34]Shakespeare, *Tempest,* Act IV, sc. i, 188–89; Act I, sc. ii, 283–84; Act II, sc. ii, 25; Act III, sc. ii, 7–8; Act I, sc. ii, 345–47; Act I, sc. ii, 354–65; Kermode (ed.), text explanation, *Tempest,* p. 63.

[35]Howard S. Russell, *Indian New England Before the Mayflower* (Hanover, N.H., 1980), p. 11; John Smith, "A Description of New England," in Adler (ed.), *Annals of America,* vol. 1, p. 39.

"After seven days he went to the clearing and found the corn plant rising above the ground. . . . When the corn had born fruit and the silk of the corn ear had turned yellow he recognized in it the resemblance of his dead wife. Thus originated the cultivation of corn."[36]

These Indians had a highly developed agricultural system. Samuel de Champlain found that "all along the shore" there was "a great deal of land cleared up and planted with Indian corn." Describing their agricultural practices, he wrote: "They put in each hill three or four Brazilian beans [kidney beans]. . . . When they grow up, they interlace with the corn . . . and they keep the ground very free from weeds. We saw there many squashes, and pumkins, and tobacco, which they likewise cultivate." According to Thomas Morton, Indians "dung[ed] their ground" with fish to fertilize the soil and increase the harvest. After visiting the Narragansets in Rhode Island, John Winthrop, Jr., noted that although the soil in that region was "sandy & rocky," the people were able to raise "good corn without fish" by rotating their crops. "They have every one 2 fields," he observed, "which after the first 2 years they let one field rest each year, & that keeps their ground continually [productive]." According to Roger Williams, when the Indians were ready to harvest the corn, "all the neighbours men and women, forty, fifty, a hundred," joined in the work and came "to help freely." During their green corn festival, the Narragansets erected a long house, "sometimes a hundred, sometimes two hundred feet long upon a plain near the Court . . . where many thousands, men and women," gathered. Inside, dancers gave money, coats, and knives to the poor. After the harvest, the Indians stored their corn for the winter. "In the sand on the slope of hills," according to Champlain, "they dig holes, some five or six feet, more or less, and place their corn and other grains in large grass sacks, which they throw into the said holes, and cover them with sand to a depth of three or four feet above the surface of the ground. They take away their grain according to their need, and it is preserved as well as it be in our granaries." Contrary to the stereotype of Indians as hunters and therefore savages, these Indians were farmers.[37]

[36]Eva L. Butler, "Algonkian Culture and the Use of Maize in Southern New England," *Bulletin of the Archeological Society of Connecticut*, no. 22 (December 1948), p. 6; Speck, "Penobscot Tales," p. 75; Merchant, *Ecological Revolutions*, p. 72.

[37]Russell, *Indian New England*, pp. 10, 11, 166; Merchant, *Ecological Revolutions*, p. 80; Peter A. Thomas, "Contrastive Subsistence Strategies and Land Use as Factors for Understanding Indian-White Relations in New England," *Ethnohistory*, vol. 23, no. 1 (winter 1976), p. 10; Williams, *A Key into the Language of America*, p. 170; Butler, "Algonkian Culture," pp. 15, 17. For a study of the Abenakis as hunters, see Merchant, *Ecological Revolutions*, pp. 29–68.

However, many colonists in New England disregarded this reality and invented their own representations of Indians. What emerged to justify dispossessing them was the racialization of Indian "savagery." Indian heathenism and alleged laziness came to be viewed as inborn group traits that rendered them naturally incapable of civilization. This process of Indian dehumanization developed a peculiarly New England dimension as the colonists associated Indians with the Devil. Indian identity became a matter of "descent": their racial markers indicated inerasable qualities of savagery.

This social construction of race occurred within the economic context of competition over land. The colonists argued that entitlement to land required its utilization. Native men, they claimed, pursued "no kind of labour but hunting, fishing and fowling." Indians were not producers. "The *Indians* are not able to make use of the one fourth part of the Land," argued Reverend Francis Higginson in 1630, "neither have they any settled places, as Towns to dwell in, nor any ground as they challenge for their owne possession, but change their habitation from place to place." In the Puritan view, Indians were lazy. "Fettered in the chains of idleness," they would rather starve than work, William Wood of Boston complained in 1634. Indians were sinfully squandering America's resources. Under their irresponsible guardianship, the land had become "all spoils, rots," and was "marred for want of manuring, gathering, ordering, etc." Like the "foxes and wild beasts," Indians did nothing "but run over the grass."[38]

The Puritan possession of Indian lands was facilitated by the invasion of unseen pathogens. When the colonists began arriving in New England, they found that the Indian population was already being reduced by European diseases. Two significant events had occurred in the early seventeenth century: infected rats swam to shore from Samuel de Champlain's ships, and some sick French sailors were shipwrecked on the beaches of New England. By 1616, epidemics were ravaging Indian villages. Victims of "virgin soil epidemics," the Indians lacked immunological defenses against the newly introduced diseases. Between 1610 and 1675, the Indian population declined sharply — from 12,000 to a mere 3,000 for the Abenakis and from 65,000 to 10,000 for the southern New England tribes.[39]

[38]Johnson, *Wonder-working Providence*, p. 262; William Cronon, *Changes in the Land: Indians, Colonists, and the Ecology of New England* (New York, 1983), pp. 55, 56; William Wood, *New England's Prospect*, edited by Alden T. Vaughn (Amherst, Mass., 1977), p. 96.

[39]Alfred W. Crosby, "Virgin Soil Epidemics as a Factor in the Aboriginal Depopulation in America," *William and Mary Quarterly*, vol. 33, no. 2 (April 1976), p. 289; Dean

Describing the sweep of deadly diseases among the Indians, William Bradford reported that the Indians living near the trading house outside of Plymouth "fell sick of the smallpox, and died most miserably." The condition of those still alive was "lamentable." Their bodies were covered with "the pox breaking and mattering and running one into another, their skin cleaving" to the mats beneath them. When they turned their bodies, they found "whole sides" of their skin flaying off. In this terrible way, they died "like rotten sheep." After one epidemic, William Bradford recorded in his diary: "For it pleased God to visit these Indians with a great sickness and such a mortality that of a thousand, above nine and a half hundred of them died, and many of them did rot above ground for want of burial."[40]

The colonists interpreted these Indian deaths as divinely sanctioned opportunities to take the land. John Winthrop declared that the decimation of Indians by smallpox manifested a Puritan destiny: God was "making room" for the colonists and "hath hereby cleared our title to this place." After an epidemic had swept through Indian villages, John Cotton claimed that the destruction was a sign from God: when the Lord decided to transplant His people, He made the country vacant for them to settle. Edward Johnson pointed out that epidemics had desolated "those places, where the English afterward planted."[41]

Indeed, many New England towns were founded on the very lands the Indians had been living on before the epidemics. The Plymouth colony itself was located on the site of the Wampanoag village of Pawtuxet. The Pilgrims had noticed the village was empty and the cornfields overgrown with weeds. "There is a great deal of Land cleared," one of them reported, "and hath beene planted with Corne three or foure yeares agoe." The original inhabitants had been decimated by the epidemic of 1616. "Thousands of men have lived there, which died in a great plague not long since," another Pilgrim wrote; "and pity it was and is to see so many goodly fields, and so well seated, without men to dress and manure the same." During their first spring, the Pilgrims went out into those fields to weed and manure them. Fortunately, they had some corn seed to plant. Earlier, when they landed on Cape Cod,

R. Snow, "Abenaki Fur Trade in the Sixteenth Century," *Western Canadian Journal of Anthropology,* vol. 6, no. 1 (1976), p. 8; Merchant, *Ecological Revolutions,* p. 90.

[40]Bradford, *Of Plymouth Plantation,* pp. 270–71.

[41]Roy Harvey Pearce, "The 'Ruines of Mankind': The Indian and Puritan Mind," *Journal of the History of Ideas,* vol. 13 (1952), p. 201; Peter Carroll, *Puritanism and the Wilderness: The Intellectual Significance of the Frontier, 1629–1700* (New York, 1969), p. 13; Johnson, *Wonder-working Providence,* p. 40.

they had come across some Indian graves and found caches of corn. They considered this find, wrote Bradford, as "a special providence of God, and a great mercy to this poor people, that here they got seed to plant them corn the next year, or else they might have starved." The survival of these pallid strangers was so precarious that they probably would have perished had it not been for the seeds they found stored in the Indian burial grounds. Ironically, Indian death came to mean life for the Pilgrims.[42]

However, the Puritans did not see it as irony but as the destruction of devils. They had demonized the native peoples, condemning Indian religious beliefs as "diabolical, and so uncouth, as if . . . framed and devised by the devil himself." The Wampanoags of Martha's Vineyard, wrote Reverend Thomas Mayhew in 1652, were "mighty zealous and earnest in the Worship of False gods and Devils." They were under the influence of "a multitude of Heathen Traditions of their gods . . . and abounding with sins."[43]

To the colonists, the Indians were not merely a wayward people: they personified something fearful within Puritan society itself. Like Caliban, a "born devil," Indians failed to control their appetites, to create boundaries separating mind from body. They represented what English men and women in America thought they were not — and, more important, what they must not become. As exiles living in the wilderness far from "civilization," the English used their negative images of Indians to delineate the moral requirements they had set up for themselves. As sociologist Kai Erikson explained, "deviant forms of behavior, by marking the outer edges of group life, give the inner structure its special character and thus supply the framework within which the people of the group develop an orderly sense of their own cultural identity. . . . One of the surest ways to confirm an identity, for communities as well as for individuals, is to find some way of measuring what one is *not*." By depicting Indians as demonic and savage, the colonists, like Prospero, were able to define more precisely what they perceived as the danger of becoming Calibanized.[44]

---

[42]Cronon, *Changes in the Land*, p. 90; Alfred W. Crosby, "God . . . Would Destroy Them, and Give Their Country to Another People," *American Heritage*, vol. 29, no. 6 (October/November 1978), p. 40; Bradford, *Of Plymouth Plantation*, pp. 65–66.

[43]William S. Simmons, "Cultural Bias in the New England Puritans' Perception of Indians," *William and Mary Quarterly*, 3rd series, vol. 38 (January 1981), pp. 70, 62.

[44]Kai Erikson, *Wayward Puritans: A Study in the Sociology of Deviance* (New York, 1966), pp. 13, 64; see also Pearce, *Savagism and Civilization*, p. 8.

The Indians presented a frightening threat to the Puritan errand in America. "The wilderness through which we are passing to the Promised Land is all over fill'd with fiery flying serpents," warned Reverend Cotton Mather. "Our Indian wars are not over yet." The wars were now within Puritan society and the self: the dangers were internal. Self-vigilance against sin was required, or else the English would become like Indians. "We have too far degenerated into Indian vices. The vices of the Indians are these: They are very lying wretches, and they are very lazy wretches; and they are out of measure indulgent unto their children; there is no family government among them. We have [become] shamefully Indianized in all those abominable things."[45]

To be "Indianized" meant to serve the Devil. Cotton Mather thought this was what had happened to Mercy Short, a young girl who had been a captive of the Indians and who was suffering from tormenting fits. According to Mather, Short had seen the Devil. "Hee was not of a Negro, but of a Tawney, or an Indian colour," she said; "he wore an high-crowned Hat, with straight Hair; and had one Cloven-foot." During a witchcraft trial, Mather reported, George Burroughs had lifted an extremely heavy object with the help of the Devil, who resembled an Indian. Puritan authorities hanged an English woman for worshiping Indian "gods" and for taking the Indian devil-god Hobbamock for a husband. Significantly the Devil was portrayed as dark complected and Indian.[46]

For the Puritans, to become Indian was the ultimate horror, for they believed Indians were "in very great subjection" of the Devil, who "kept them in a continual slavish fear of him." Governor Bradford harshly condemned Thomas Morton and his fellow prodigals of the Merrymount settlement for their promiscuous partying with Indians: "They also set up a maypole, drinking and dancing about it many days together, inviting the Indian women for their consorts, dancing and frisking together like so many fairies." Interracial cavorting threatened to fracture a cultural and moral border — the frontier of Puritan identity. Congress of bodies, white and "tawney," signified defilement, a frightful boundlessness. If the Puritans were to become wayward like the Indians, it would mean that they had succumbed to savagery and

[45]Cotton Mather, *On Witchcraft: Being, The Wonders of the Invisible World* (New York, n.d.; originally published in 1692), p. 53; Simmons, "Cultural Bias," p. 71.
[46]Richard Slotkin, *Regeneration through Violence: The Mythology of the American Frontier, 1600–1860* (Middetown, Conn., 1973), pp. 132, 142, 65.

failed to shrivel the sensuous parts of the self. To be "Indianized" meant to be decivilized, to become wild men.[47]

But they could not allow this to happen, for they were embarking on an errand to transform the wilderness into civilization. "The whole earth is the Lord's garden and he hath given it to the sons of men [to] increase and multiply and replentish the earth and subdue it," asserted John Winthrop in 1629 as he prepared to sail for New England. "Why then should we stand starving here for the places of habitation . . . and in the meantime suffer a whole Continent as fruitful and convenient for the use of man to lie waste without any improvement."[48]

Actually, Indians had been farming the land, and this reality led to conflicts over resources. Within ten years after the arrival of Winthrop's group, twenty thousand more colonists came to New England. This growing English population had to be squeezed into a limited area of arable land. Less than 20 percent of the region was useful for agriculture, and the Indians had already established themselves on the prime lands. Consequently, the colonists often settled on or directly next to Indian communities. In the Connecticut Valley, for example, they erected towns like Springfield (1636), Northampton (1654), Hadley (1661), Deerfield (1673), and Northfield (1673) adjacent to Indian agricultural clearings at Agawam, Norwottuck, Pocumtuck, and Squakheag.[49]

Over the years, the expansion of English settlement sometimes led to wars that literally made the land "vacant." During the Pequot War of 1637, some seven hundred Pequots were killed by the colonists and their Indian allies. Describing the massacre at Fort Mystic, an English officer wrote: "Many were burnt in the fort, both men, women, and children. . . . There were about four hundred souls in this fort, and not above five of them escaped out of our hands. Great and doleful was the bloody sight." Commander John Mason explained that God had pushed the Pequots into a "fiery oven," "filling the place with dead bodies." By explaining their atrocities as divinely driven, the English were sharply inscribing the Indians as a race of devils. This was what happened during King Philip's War of 1675–76. While one thousand English were killed during this conflict, over six thousand Indians died

[47]Johnson, *Wonder-working Providence,* p. 263; Bradford, *Of Plymouth Plantation,* p. 205.

[48]John Winthrop, *Winthrop Papers,* vol. 2 (1623–1630), Massachusetts Historical Society (1931), p. 139.

[49]Thomas, "Contrastive Subsistence Strategies and Land Use," p. 4.

from combat and disease. Altogether, about half of the total Indian population was destroyed in southern New England. Again, the colonists quickly justified their violence by demonizing their enemies. The Indians, Increase Mather observed, were "so *Devil driven* as to begin an unjust and bloody war upon the English, which issued in their speedy and utter extirpation from the face of God's earth." Cotton Mather explained that the war was a conflict between the Devil and God: "The Devil decoyed those miserable savages [to New England] in hopes that the Gospel of the Lord Jesus Christ would never come here to destroy or disturb His *absolute empire* over them."[50]

Indians, "such people" of this "brave new world," to use Shakespeare's words, personified the Devil and everything the Puritans feared — the body, sexuality, laziness, sin, and the loss of self-control. They had no place in a "new England." This was the view trumpeted by Edward Johnson in his *Wonder-working Providence.* Where there had originally been "hideous Thickets" for wolves and bears, he proudly exclaimed in 1654, there were now streets "full of Girls and Boys sporting up and down, with a continued concourse of people." Initially, the colonists themselves had lived in "wigwams" like Indians, but now they had "orderly, fair, and well-built houses . . . together with Orchards filled with goodly fruit trees, and gardens with variety of flowers." The settlers had fought against the Devil, who had inhabited the bodies of the Indians, Johnson observed, and made it impossible for the soldiers to pierce them with their swords. But the English had violently triumphed. They had also expanded the market, making New England a center of production and trade. The settlers had turned "this Wilderness" into "a mart." Merchants from Holland, France, Spain, and Portugal were coming here. "Thus," proclaimed Johnson, "hath the Lord been pleased to turn one of the most hideous, boundless, and unknown Wildernesses in the world in an instant . . . to a well-ordered Commonwealth."[51]

But, in a sense, all of these developments had already been acted out in *The Tempest*. Like Prospero, the English colonists had sailed to a

[50]Charles M. Segal and David C. Stineback (eds.), *Puritans, Indians & Manifest Destiny* (New York, 1977), pp. 136–37, 111; Sherburne F. Cook, "Interracial Warfare and Population Decline among the New England Indians," *Ethnohistory*, vol. 20 (winter 1973), pp. 19–21; Simmons, "Cultural bias," p. 67; Segal and Stineback (eds.), *Puritans, Indians & Manifest Destiny*, p. 182.

[51]Johnson, *Wonder-working Providence*, pp. 71, 168, 211, 247–48; see Cronon, *Changes in the Land*, pp. 166–67.

new land, and many of them also felt they were exiles. They viewed the native peoples as savages, as Calibans. The strangers occupied the land, believing they were entitled to be "the lord on't."[52]

Still, in Shakespeare's fantasy, race as a social construction had not yet been firmly formed, and Caliban's qualities as "other" not yet definitely fixed by race. What happened in history, however, was a different story.

The English possessed tremendous power to define the places and peoples they were conquering. As they made their way westward, they developed an ideology of "savagery," which was given form and content by the political and economic circumstances of the specific sites of colonization. Initially, in Ireland, the English had viewed savagery as something cultural, or a matter of "consent": they assumed that the distance between themselves and the Irish, or between civilization and savagery, was quantitative rather than qualitative. The Irish as "other" was educable: they were capable of acquiring the traits of civilization. But later, as colonization reached across the Atlantic and as the English encountered a new group of people, many of them believed that savagery for the Indians might be inherent. Perhaps the Indians might be different from the English in kind rather than degree; if so, then the native people of America would be incapable of improvement because of their race. To use Shakespeare's language, they might have a "nature" that "nurture" would never be able to "stick" to or change. Race or "descent" might be destiny.[53]

What happened in America in the actual encounters between the Indians and the English strangers was not uniform. In Virginia, Indian savagery was viewed largely as cultural: Indians were ignorant heathens. In New England, on the other hand, Indian savagery was racialized: Indians had come to be condemned as a demonic race, their dark complexions signifying an indelible and inherent evil. Why was there such a difference between the two regions? Possibly the competition between the English and the Indians over resources was more intense in New England than in Virginia, where there was more arable land. More important, the colonists in New England had brought with them a greater sense of religious mission than the Virginia settlers. For the Puritans, theirs was an "errand into the wilderness"— a mission to create what John Winthrop had proclaimed as "a city upon a hill" with the eyes of

[52]Shakespeare, *Tempest,* Act V, sc. i, 162.
[53]Shakespeare, *Tempest,* Act IV, sc. i, 188–89; Sollors, *Beyond Ethnicity,* pp. 6–7, 36–37.

the world upon them. Within this economic and cultural framework, a "discovery" occurred: the Indian "other" became a manifest devil. Thus savagery was racialized as the Indians were demonized, doomed to what Increase Mather called "utter extirpation." Once the process of this cultural construction was under way, it set a course for the making of a national identity in America for centuries to come.[54]

A WORLD TURNED UPSIDE DOWN

Indians viewed these developments very differently. One of their legends told about a creature named Ki-wa-kwe-skwe, "woman wandering in the woods." She was a cannibal, and a boy whom she called her brother lived with her. She always kept her back turned toward him to hide her face. She also taught him to hunt rabbits and offered him frequent meals in order to fatten him. Once a rabbit came to the boy and said: "You have already killed a great many of us. That is enough; don't hunt us too persistently or you will exterminate us. Henceforth do not obey that woman who is ordering you. She is not your sister. On the contrary, she is a bad magician who is only lying to you and just fattening you up until you are prime, when she will kill and eat you. For her food is human beings." That night the boy pretended to fall asleep, and he had a chance to see the woman's face, her true cannibalistic self. The next morning he ran away, with the evil spirit woman in pursuit. A heron and a porcupine tried to protect the boy and killed the woman repeatedly, but she kept returning to life. Finally, an old man came to his rescue and ordered his dog to tear the evil woman to shreds. The old man then took the boy to the village where his father and mother lived. "And when the people saw that the boy who had been stolen was still alive, lo, there was great rejoicing and feasting." What happened in history, however, had a much different ending.[55]

Like the rabbit of this story, a Narraganset leader tried to warn his fellow Indians about the English invaders. "You know our fathers had plenty of deer and skins, our plains were full of deer, as also our woods, and of turkeys, and our coves full of fish and fowl," Miantonomo told

[54]Perry Miller, "Errand into the Wilderness," in Miller, *Errand into the Wilderness* (New York, 1964), pp. 1–15; Miller's metaphor and theme originally came from Samuel Danforth's sermon, delivered on May 11, 1670, entitled "A Brief Recognition of New England's Errand into the Wilderness"; John Winthrop, "A Model of Christian Charity," in Perry Miller (ed.), *The American Puritans: Their Prose and Poetry* (New York, 1956), pp. 79–84; Simmons, "Cultural Bias," p. 67.

[55]Speck, "Penobscot Tales," pp. 66–70.

the Montauks of Long Island in 1642. "But these English having gotten our land, they with scythes cut down the grass, and with axes fell the trees; their cows and horses eat the grass, and their hogs spoil our clam banks, and we shall all be starved." Miantonomo called for pan-Indian unity to resist the strangers: "For so are we all Indians as the English are, and say brother to one another; so must we be one as they are, otherwise we shall all be gone shortly." They should attack the colonists, and "kill men, women and children, but no cows." They should raise the cattle for food "till our deer be increased again."[56]

In 1735, twenty-seven Pequots complained to the governor of Connecticut that the English settlers had encroached on their lands, planting wheat fields and allowing their cattle to roam into Indian cornfields. The Pequots protested: "We see plainly that their chiefest desire is to deprive us of the privilege of our land, and drive us off to our utter ruin." The native people of America were finding that the white strangers from across the ocean were threatening their way of life. In a 1789 petition to the Assembly of Connecticut, the Mohegans lamented that "the times" had been "Exceedingly alter'd":

> Yea the Times have turn'd everything Upside down, or rather we
> have Chang'd the good Times, Chiefly by the help of the White
> People. For in Times past our Fore-Fathers live in Peace, Love and
> great harmony, and had everything in Great plenty. When they
> Wanted meat they would just run into the Bush a little ways
> with their Weapons and would Soon bring home good venison,
> Racoon, Bear and Fowl. If they Choose to have Fish, they Wo'd
> only go to the River or along the Sea Shore and they wou'd
> presently fill their Cannous With Veriety of Fish, both Scaled and
> shell Fish, and they had abundance of Nuts, Wild Fruit, Ground
> Nuts and Ground Beans, and they planted but little Corn and
> Beans and they kept no Cattle or Horses for they needed none —
> And they had no Contention about their Lands, it lay in Common
> to them all, and they had but one large Dish and they Cou'd all
> eat together in Peace and Love — But alas, it is not so now, all our
> Fishing, Hunting and Fowling is entirely gone, And we have now
> begun to Work on our Land, keep Cattle, Horses and Hogs And
> We Build Houses and fence in Lots, And now we plainly See that
> one Dish and one Fire will not do any longer for us — Some few
> there are Stronger than others and they will keep off the poor,

---

[56]Cronon, *Changes in the Land*, pp. 162–63.

weak, the halt and the Blind, And Will take the Dish to themselves. Yea, they will rather Call White People and Molattoes to eat
With them out of our Dish, and poor Widows and Orphans Must
be pushed one side and there they Must Set a Crying, Starving
and die.[57]

Aware of these changing times, Delaware leader Neolin warned
Indians in the 1760s that they must either return to their original state
before the arrival of white people or face slow extinction at the hands of
the settlers.

What is to be done, and what remedy is to be applied? I will tell
you, my friends. Hear what the Great Spirit has ordered me to tell
you! You are to make sacrifices, in the manner that I shall direct;
to put off entirely from yourselves the customs which you have
adopted since the white people came among us; you are to return
to that former happy state, in which we live in peace and plenty,
before these strangers came to disturb us, and above all, you must
abstain from drinking their deadly beson [liquor] which they have
forced upon us for the sake of increasing their gains and diminish-
ing our numbers. . . . Wherefore do you suffer the whites to dwell
upon your lands? Drive them away; wage war against them.[58]

But by the 1760s, the strangers and their descendants had established colonies and had also begun a movement that would lead to the
creation of a new nation. An emerging question was: What would be
the Indians' future in the republic? One of the Founding Fathers who
addressed this issue was a young lawyer and planter who would later
become president of the United States. In 1781, as governor of Virginia, Thomas Jefferson declared to the Kaskaskias that whites and
Indians were both "Americans, born in the same land," and that he
hoped the two peoples would "long continue to smoke in friendship
together." At the same time, Jefferson advocated the removal and even
the destruction of hostile Indians. "Nothing will reduce those wretches
so soon as pushing the war into the heart of their country," he wrote to
a colleague in 1776. "But I would not stop there. I would never cease
pursuing them while one of them remained on this side [of] the Mississippi. . . . We would never cease pursuing them with war while one

[57]Merchant, *Ecological Revolutions,* p. 93; Axtell, *Invasion Within,* p. 167.
[58]Nash, *Red, White, and Black,* pp. 302–03.

remained on the face of the earth." In his view, Indians were to be civilized or exterminated.[59]

To civilize Indians meant, for Jefferson, to take them from their hunting way of life and convert them into farmers. President Jefferson explained to the Shawnees why they had no choice but to accept civilization: "When the white people first came to this land, they were few, and you were many; now we are many, and you few; and why? because, by cultivating the earth, we produce plenty to raise our children, while yours . . . suffer for want of food . . . are exposed to weather in your hunting camps, get diseases and die. Hence it is that your numbers lessen." They were, in other words, victims of their own culture, not the decimation of their game to satisfy the voracious fur trade, the introduction of unfamiliar diseases, the appropriation of their lands, and the brutal warfare waged against them.[60]

In blaming the Indians for their own decline, Jefferson insisted that the transfer of Indian lands to whites had been done fairly and legally. "That the lands of this country were taken from them by conquest," he argued in *Notes on the State of Virginia,* "is not so general a truth as is supposed. I find in our historians and records, repeated proofs of purchase. . . ." If Jefferson's denial of guilt contained a quality of defensiveness, there was a reason for it. In the original manuscript, he had written and then crossed out: "It is true that these purchases were sometimes made with the price in one hand and the sword in the other."[61]

In order to survive, Jefferson declared, Indians must adopt the culture of the white man. They must no longer live so boundlessly; instead, they must enclose farms as private property and learn arithmetic so they would be able to keep accounts of their production. "My children," Jefferson told the Cherokees, "I shall rejoice to see the day when the red man, our neighbors, become truly one people with us, enjoying all the rights and privileges we do, and living in peace and plenty as we do. . . . But are you prepared for this? Have you the resolution to leave off hunting for your living, to lay off a farm for each family to itself, to live by industry, the men working that farm with their

---

[59]Thomas Jefferson to Brother John Baptist de Coigne, chief of Kaskaskia, June 1781, and to John Page, August 5, 1776, in Andrew A. Lipscomb and Albert E. Bergh (eds.), *Writings of Thomas Jefferson,* 20 vols. (Washington, D.C., 1904), vol. 16, p. 372; vol. 4, pp. 270–71.

[60]Jefferson to chiefs of the Shawnee Nation, February 19, 1807, in Lipscomb and Bergh (eds.), *Writings of Jefferson,* vol. 16, p. 424.

[61]Thomas Jefferson, *Notes on the State of Virginia* (New York, 1861), p. 91.

hands . . . ?" "Indians must learn how," Jefferson explained, "a little land, well cultivated, was superior in value to a great deal, unimproved." He offered a grisly analogy to illustrate his point: "The wisdom of the animal which amputates and abandons to the hunter the parts for which he is pursued should be theirs, with this difference, that the former sacrifices what is useful, the latter what is not." Possibly Jefferson did not fully realize the implications of this metaphor. Likened to "animals," Indians could survive by "amputating" their lands and leaving them behind for whites, the "hunters."[62]

Jefferson, however, was actually more concerned about white expansion than Indian survival. Civilizing the Indians was a strategy designed to acquire land for white settlement. As president, he assured the Indians that whites would respect their territorial possessions. "We take from no nation what belongs to it," he told them. "Our growing numbers make us always willing to buy lands from our red brethren, when they are willing to sell." He elaborated: "Your lands are your own; your right to them shall never be violated by us; they are yours to keep or to sell as you please. . . . When a want of land in a particular place induces us to ask you to sell, still you are always free to say 'No'. . . ."[63]

However, while he offered these assurances, Jefferson worked to create conditions that would make Indians "willing to sell." In an 1803 "Confidential Message" to Congress, he explained how this could be done. First, encourage them to abandon hunting and turn to agriculture. "The extensive forests necessary in the hunting life will then become useless." Second, sell more manufactured goods to Indians by multiplying the trading houses and bring them into the market. This policy, Jefferson predicted, would lead the Indians to transfer their lands to whites. On February 27, 1803, in an "unofficial and private" letter to Indiana governor William Henry Harrison, Jefferson recommended: "To promote this disposition to exchange lands, which they have to spare and we want, we shall push our trading houses, and be glad to see the good and influential individuals among them run in

[62] Jefferson to chiefs of the Upper Cherokees, May 4, 1808, in Lipscomb and Berg (eds.), *Writings of Jefferson*, vol. 16, p. 434; Jefferson to John Baptist de Coigne, June 1781, in Julian Boyd (ed.), *The Papers of Thomas Jefferson*, 18 vols. (Princeton, N.J., 1950–1965), vol. 6, pp. 60–63; Jefferson to Delawares, Mohicans, and Munries, December 21, 1808, in Lipscomb and Bergh (eds.), *Writings of Jefferson*, vol. 16, p. 452.

[63] Jefferson to Choctaw Nation, December 17, 1803, and to chiefs of the Ottawas, Chippewas, Powtewatamies, Wyandots, and Senecas of Sandusky, April 22, 1808, in Lipscomb and Bergh (eds.), *Writings of Jefferson*, vol. 16, pp. 401, 429.

debt, because we observe that when these debts get beyond what the individuals can pay, they become willing to lop them off by a cession of lands." To destroy Indians financially, Jefferson favored federal over private trading houses. While private business had to make profits, government enterprise could sell goods to Indians at prices "so low as merely to repay us cost and charges." By this process, he continued, white settlements would gradually "circumscribe" the Indians, and in time they would either "incorporate" with whites as "citizens" or retreat westward beyond civilization.[64]

All Indians, regardless of whether they were farmers or hunters, were subject to removal, even extermination, if they continued in their "barbarism." Should any tribe be foolhardy enough to take up the hatchet against the United States, the president wrote Governor Harrison, the federal government should seize the whole country of that tribe and drive them across the Mississippi as the only condition of peace. During a conflict between the United States and England in 1809, President Jefferson warned his Indian "children": "If you love the land in which you were born, if you wish to inhabit the earth which covers the bones of your fathers, take no part in the war between the English and us. . . . [T]he tribe which shall begin an unprovoked war against us, we will extirpate from the earth, or drive to such a distance as they shall never again be able to strike us."[65]

But Jefferson's feelings toward Indians were complex. In a letter to John Adams, he described childhood memories of Indian chiefs visiting his home. "They were in the habit of coming often. . . . I knew much the great Outasette, the warrior and orator of the Cherokees. He was always the guest of my father, on his journeys to and from Williamsburg. I was in camp when he made his great farewell oration to his people, the evening before his departure for England. . . . His sounding

[64]Jefferson, "Confidential Message Recommending a Western Exploring Expedition," January 18, 1803, in Lipscomb and Bergh (eds.), *Writings of Jefferson*, vol. 3, pp. 489–90; Jefferson to Governor William H. Harrison, February 27, 1803, in Lipscomb and Bergh (eds.), *Writings of Jefferson*, vol. 10, pp. 370–73; Jefferson to Horatio Gates, July 11, 1803, in Paul L. Ford (ed.), *The Works of Thomas Jefferson*, 20 vols. (New York, 1892–1899), vol. 10, p. 13; Jefferson, draft of an amendment to the Constitution, July 1803, in Ford (ed.), *Works of Jefferson*, vol. 8, pp. 241–48; Jefferson to Cherokees, January 9, 1809, in Lipscomb and Bergh (ed.), *Writings of Jefferson*, vol. 16, pp. 458–59.
[65]Jefferson to John Adams, June 11, 1812, in Lester J. Cappon (ed.), *The Adams-Jefferson Letters*, 2 vols. (Chapel Hill, N.C., 1959), vol. 2, pp. 307–08; Jefferson to Governor William H. Harrison, February 27, 1803; to chiefs of the Ottawas, Chippewas, Powtewatamies, and Senecas, April 22, 1808; and to chiefs of the Wyandots, Ottawas, Chippewas, Powtewatamies, and Shawnees, January 10, 1809, in Lipscomb and Bergh (eds.), *Writings of Thomas Jefferson*, vol. 10, pp. 370–73; vol. 16, pp. 431–32, 463.

voice, distinct articulation, animated action, and the solemn silence of
his people at their several fires, filled me with awe and veneration, altho'
I did not understand a word he uttered." Jefferson explained to Adams
that these early "impressions" had created "attachment and commisera-
tion" for the Indians which had "never been obliterated."[66]

Jefferson's hope was to save the Indians. In this letter to Adams, he
noted how the Cherokees had "enclosed fields" as well as livestock and
had chosen to advance themselves "in civilization." But any Indians
who rejected assimilation would face a different future. "These will
relapse into barbarism and misery, lose numbers by war and want, and
we shall be obliged to drive them, with the beasts of the forest into the
Stony mountains." Ultimately, for Jefferson, Indians as Indians would
not be allowed to remain within the borders of civilized society. A century or so earlier, Puritans had celebrated the disappearance of wolves
and bears in "new" England; now Jefferson and men like him were
clearing more wilderness for a new nation. The very transformation of
the land emblematized progress, the distance whites in America had
come from the time when barbarism had been dominant:

> Let a philosophic observer commence a journey from the savages
> of the Rocky Mountains, eastwardly towards our sea-coast. There
> he would observe in the earliest stage of association living under
> no law but that of nature, subsisting and covering themselves with
> flesh and skins of wild beasts. He would next find those on our
> frontiers in the pastoral state, raising domestic animals to supply
> the defects of hunting. Then succeed our own semi-barbarous
> citizens, the pioneers of the advance of civilization, and so in
> progress he would meet the gradual shades of improving man
> until he would reach his, as yet, most improved state in our
> seaport towns. This, in fact, is equivalent to a survey, in time,
> of the progress of man from infancy to the present day.[67]

Here was a vision of progress — a Jeffersonian version of John
Winthrop's "city upon a hill" and Edward Johnson's New England of
the "wonder-working Providence." The land was not to be allowed
to "lie waste without any improvement," the early forefathers had
commanded, and now the republican "errand into the wilderness" was

---

[66]Jefferson to John Adams, June 11, 1812, in Cappon (ed.), *The Adams-Jefferson Letters*, vol. 2, pp. 307–08.

[67]Jefferson to Adams, June 11, 1812, in Cappon (ed.), *The Adams-Jefferson Letters*, vol. 2, pp. 307–08; Jefferson to William Ludlow, September 6, 1824, in Lipscomb and Bergh (eds.), *Writings of Jefferson*, vol. 16, pp. 74–75.

requiring the citizens of the new nation to subdue the land and advance their frontier westward. Such a view carried dire consequences for the Calibans of America called Indians. Jefferson, like Prospero before him, saw the triumph over the continent and the Indians as the movement from "savagery" to "civilization."

Shakespeare and
the Power of Order

The selections in this chapter represent three different approaches to Shakespeare, two that celebrate his plays as unified works of art, and one that sees them as bound up in conflicting cultural discourses of their time. The first, by historical critic Frank Kermode, from his *Shakespeare: The Final Plays* (1963), finds the unity of *The Tempest* in its expression of an intricate vision of cosmic order that was widely held in the Renaissance. In this respect, Kermode's approach resembles the one advocated by E. M. W. Tillyard (see p. 168 in this volume), who called this vision "the Elizabethan world picture." In Kermode's account of this vision, the arts represent a triumph of civilized control over the untamed wilderness of external nature and the rebellious impulses in the human self and the social order. For Kermode, Prospero, who tames the disorderly tempests of nature with his book-derived magic, emerges as the clear hero of the play, whereas Caliban represents the lower bestial impulses that must be mastered by civilization, "the wild man by whom civility is estimated" (p. 219).

The second approach is represented by a chapter from Reuben A. Brower's *Fields of Light* (1951). Brower, too, finds a pattern of order and unity in the play, but he parts company with Tillyard and Kermode in his method of finding that pattern in literary works. For Brower the play's order and unity are internal features of its linguistic structure rather than a reflection of the culture outside it. Brower's treatment of the play as a self-contained formal entity bound together by elaborately linked "analogies" is a good illustration of the New Criticism, an approach founded on the principle that literature employs a special kind of language whose unity resides in linguistic patterns and the themes those patterns suggest. Brower identifies six strands of metaphor in the play and then relates them to the overarching theme of metamorphosis.

The third approach is represented by an excerpt from Leah Marcus's introduction to *Unediting the Renaissance: Shakespeare, Marlowe, Milton* (1996), a collection of essays examining the ways in which standard editions of Renaissance texts have closed off rather than opened up interpretive possibilities. Marcus focuses on Prospero's reference to Caliban's mother, Sycorax, as a "blue-eyed hag" (1.2.270). Marcus first traces the cultural assumptions by nineteenth- and twentieth-century editors that led most of them to annotate the phrase as David Bevington does in this edition: "with dark circles under the eyes or with blue eyelids, implying pregnancy" (p. 23). These assumptions dictate that Sycorax could not have literally had blue eyes because such an appearance would have made her less alien to an English sensibility, and, indeed, more of Prospero's cultural equal. "The witch cannot have blue eyes, because the cultural image of blue eyes [in the nineteenth and twentieth centuries] is overwhelmingly positive and Sycorax has to be understood as negative" (p. 256). Marcus then "unedits" the phrase by showing the variety of meanings it could have had in Shakespeare's time, including both the one given to Bevington and most other editors, and the one most modern readers would give it without such editing: a description of the color of Sycorax's irises. Marcus discusses the various implications of the different meanings, noting that they lead to different and conflicting interpretations of Sycorax and by extension Caliban and Prospero. "The eyes of Sycorax, like the charms of Prospero, eerily reverberate with their supposed moral opposites" (p. 263).

Marcus argues that it is a better editorial choice to uncover these multiple meanings, and, thus, possible conflicting attitudes in the play, than to let modern assumptions about the meaning of blue eyes determine our understanding of Shakespeare's line. Marcus's larger point is that unediting the phrase unsettles the kind of assumptions about the unity of the play and about the relation between Shakespeare and order that we find in Kermode's historical approach and Brower's New Critical approach. As she puts it, "[t]o unedit the phrase 'blue-eyed hag' is. . . . to open the play once more to an unsettling, polysemous menace that Prospero and modern editors have worked very hard to contain" (p. 264). In this respect, Marcus's essay provides a good launching pad for the move from considering Shakespeare and the power of order to considering the challenge to readings such as Kermode's and Brower's posed by the postcolonial critics whom we'll meet in the next section. Like Marcus, these critics reject Kermode's and Brower's founding assumption that any legitimate interpretation of the play will demonstrate its ultimate unity and coherence.

FRANK KERMODE

From Shakespeare: The Final Plays

Sir Frank Kermode (b. 1919), now professor emeritus at Columbia University, also taught at Cambridge University, England, at the University of Manchester, at Bristol University, and at University College, London. One of the most prolific and influential critics of the latter half of the twentieth century, Kermode has written on a wide range of literary and theoretical subjects. His many books include *The Sense of an Ending* (1966), *Shakespeare* (1968), *The Classic* (1975), *The Genesis of Secrecy* (1979), *The Art of Telling* (1983), *Forms of Attention* (1985), and *Not Entitled: A Memoir* (1995). He was knighted in 1991. The following essay comes from *Shakespeare: The Final Plays* (1963).

Much criticism of *The Tempest* stems directly from the fact that it is, in all probability, the last play Shakespeare wrote without a collaborator, so that it can be the focus of liberal speculation on the pattern of the poet's entire career. Indeed *The Tempest* does touch upon matters Shakespeare had treated earlier, and it has in particular much in common with the other Romances. But it remains a very puzzling work.

Once more recognition is the heart of the piece; and once more Time is the unfolder of error and the servant of eternity, as chance is the servant of providence. The sea may appear to be random and cruel to these castaways, but it is the agent of purgation and reunion:

> Though the seas threaten, they are merciful;
> I have curs'd them without cause,
>
> (5.1.178–79)

says Ferdinand on regaining his father. The sense of a mysterious movement of providence, which achieves its ends in spite of, and even through the agency of, human wickedness and the chances of life, is very strong in Gonzalo's rejoicing at the end. He thanks the gods, saying it is they "that have chalk'd forth the way / Which brought us hither," and goes on:

> Was Milan thrust from Milan, that his issue
> Should become kings of Naples? O, rejoice
> Beyond a common joy, and set it down
> With gold on lasting pillars: In one voyage
> Did Claribel her husband find at Tunis,
> And Ferdinand, her brother, found a wife
> Where he himself was lost; Prospero his dukedom
> In a poor isle; and all of us ourselves
> When no man was his own.
>
> (5.1.205–13)

Here is that unmistakable flavor of Christian joy at the "high miracle" which turns the discord of human tragedy into the harmony of divine comedy, at the renewal of the world after penitence and expiation.

If this was familiar ground to Shakespeare, so it was to the company of the *Sea Adventure,* which in 1609 ran aground off the Bermudas in circumstances of great danger; but they came out of the storm into what seemed an earthly paradise —"these infortunate (yet fortunate) Ilands," as Strachey, their spokesman, called the Bermudas. "It pleased our mercifull God, to make even this hideous and hated place [the Bermudas had a reputation for fairies and devils] both the place of our safetie, and the meanes of our deliverance" (p. 123 in this volume). Shakespeare's indebtedness to Strachey and the other so-called "Bermuda pamphlets" is clear. There is external evidence that he had more than a casual interest in the Virginian voyages, and he was well-read in travel literature. And his interest in the New World must have refreshed his interest in old problems. Although he knew not only the topical works of Strachey and others but Eden's *History of Travaile* (1577), he places his enchanted island in the Mediterranean, somewhere on the way from Tunis to Naples; and his Caliban is partly the savage of the New World, partly the wild man of European pageant, church-architecture, and poem. Some thought of the Indian as natural and therefore unspoilt; so Montaigne in the essay "Of Cannibals" to which Shakespeare probably alludes in Gonzalo's speech on the commonwealth (2.1.144–53) (p. 120). Others, and Shakespeare among them, thought him natural and therefore base, degenerate, lacking in cultivation and "better nature." Caliban is by no means the first wild man in drama, but he is the first to be affected by reports from America of natives who, though they "knew no use of riches" and possessed useful mechanic arts such as building dams for fish, proved treacherous to the European who arrived in Virginia "to be the lord on't." Naturally, this information from the New World was made as far as possible to fit older preconceptions, and Caliban is basically the *homo salvaticus,* the savage man, of tradition; as Malone remarked he ought to be dressed conventionally in skins, and not got up to look like a fish. Such a being, man without grace or civility, makes an interesting measure for art and cultivation, and he is the measure Miranda uses.

Apart from the travel literature, Montaigne, and Ovid (who is the source of Prospero's speech abjuring magic [5.1.33ff.]) there is no known source for *The Tempest.* That the plot has strong affinities with known romance themes is not in doubt; recently it has been shown how close is the resemblance between some elements of *The Tempest* and the *Daphnis and Chloe* of Longus. It is often argued, though it cannot be demonstrated, that Shakespeare borrowed the plot from the scenario of some *commedia dell'arte;* later examples are extant which have some points of resemblance, and Shakespeare shows elsewhere that he knew something of these unscripted plays. One branch of the *commedia dell'arte* was called "pastoral tragicomedy," and that is a genre to which in some ways *The Tempest* belongs. To academic pastoral tragicomedy there is, whether or no through Fletcher, some indebtedness in all these plays; it was very fashionable on the continent, and there were some English examples, though the pervasive influence of Sidney and Spenser is really much more important.

Of the form of the play there are two obvious things to be said. First, in sharp contrast with the errant narrative of *Pericles,* the multiple plots of *Cymbeline,* and the unique design of *The Winter's Tale* (two counter-balancing masses and a final act), *The Tempest* confines its action to one place, to three hours, and to a closely related group of characters. It could be said to observe all the neo-Aristotelian unities. Secondly, it is much the most spectacular of all the plays, and includes a storm, a courtly entertainment, and a magic banquet interrupted by the apparition of a Harpy.

The obvious result of the choice of this very intensive form is to throw the whole weight of the play on to the recognition, for the preliminary disaster can only be talked about, not represented. To begin at the end, when Prospero can say "lies at my mercy all mine enemies," is to change the role of Time in the play; there can be no pause at a seemingly tragic conclusion, no vivid contrast between the past and the present, to emphasize its destructive and redemptive power. It is as if *The Winter's Tale* had begun with the arrival of Perdita in Sicily. Furthermore, Prospero is clearly in charge of the whole action, so that there is no genuine uncertainty, little sense that Providence is wearing the mask of Chance. All the interest is in bringing together rather than in tearing apart. This is, in some ways, impoverishing. Prospero's account of his brother's treachery has none of the savage actuality of Leontes' outburst; all those events in Milan — except in so far as the plot of Antonio and Sebastian recapitulate them — remain in "the dark backward and abysm of time"; and it is worth noting that whereas Shakespeare could not risk sending Perdita to sea in a leaky fairy-tale cockboat, he could use the idea for Prospero and Miranda. As to the final recognition, there can be little of that sense of the marvellous — the drifting together through time, wind and weather — that impregnates the climactic scene of *Pericles;* and the omnipotence and omniscience of Prospero even preclude the excited dénouement of *Cymbeline.*

Yet Shakespeare is clearly just as interested as before in the Romance themes — guilt and repentance, the finding of the lost, forgiveness, the renewal of the world, the benevolence of the unseen powers. Only this time he gave them treatment at once more philosophical and more spectacular; he blends with the neoclassic design of his plot elements undoubtedly borrowed from the court masque.

This form had recently, as we have seen, reached new heights of allegorical spectacle in the hands of Ben Jonson. The main roles were played by courtiers, but professional actors often appeared in them, and dances, music, and costumes borrowed from masques were sometimes used in public performances. Indeed, a new fashion followed; and the Blackfriars was capable of elaborate scenic and musical effects. *The Tempest* has much spectacle and music; it has also a more general resemblance to the masque. Prospero is like a masque-presenter, and the castaways wander helpless in an enchanted scene under his spell, until he chooses to release them, drawing back a curtain to display a symbol of aristocratic concord, Ferdinand and Miranda at chess. At the climax of each subplot there is a spectacular contrivance that owes something to masque: the rapacity of the "three men of sin" is confronted with its own image in the allegorical figure of the Harpy; the disorderly desires of Caliban and his confederates are chastised, Actaeon-like, by hounds; and the betrothal of Ferdinand and Miranda is marked by a courtly mythological entertainment (not strictly a masque, because it lacks an indispensable element, the dance of the masquers with the onlookers; Shakespeare probably ended this scene so abruptly because it could not be played out). Prospero's famous lament, "Our revels now are ended," echoes the regret conventionally expressed at the ephemeral nature of the incredibly costly furnishings of court masques. If we take all this together with the close adherence to traditional five-act structure, we may conclude that Shakespeare was deliberately blending these "tricks" with a conventional form that lent itself well to a necessarily intensive presentation of the material.

As in the other plays of the group, the focusing of attention on the moment of recognition, here carried a stage further, involves the illumination also of related ideas — the supernatural beauty of the princess, the contrast between the noble and the natural. *The Tempest* describes the healing of a political wound and the forgiveness of enemies; but it takes this theme of art and nature further than the other plays. It includes a "natural" man, and an "artist" who controls by super-natural means; and it conscientiously elaborates the parallel between Miranda and Caliban in respect of their "nurture" or education. Hers is the good seed which benefits by nurture; he is the "born devil on whose nature / Nurture can never stick." That they were at first brought up together and educated alike by Prospero merely emphasizes this difference. She is astonished by the beauty of the brave new world; he comes to terms at once with new cruelty and foolishness. She is the cultivated plant, he the wild which rejects cultivation. Caliban is thus a central figure in the play, the wild man by whom civility is estimated; a "saluage and deformed slaue" as the original "Names of the Actors" in the Folio calls him. We know why he is called "salvage"; he is deformed, like his mother Sycorax, because in romance ugliness within is platonically represented as ugliness without, just as the virtue of the heroines shine through their bodies; he is a slave because naturally inferior to European nobility. He is also the offspring of a witch by a devil, and so associated with a base natural magic, the antithesis of Prospero's "Art," the product of virtue and learning.

This contrast Shakespeare develops in other ways. To bring off his experiment, Prospero must control his passions, and that is proof of civility and grace. Caliban attempts the virtue of Miranda; Ferdinand on the other hand can say, in response to Prospero's stern injunction:

> As I hope
> For quiet days, fair issue, and long life,
> With such love as 'tis now, the murkiest den,

The most opportune place, the strong'st suggestion
Our worser genius can, shall never melt
Mine honor into lust . . .

(4.1.23–28)

And so forth. Caliban is not, as this might suggest, a walking abstraction; Shakespeare cunningly varies the type of the lustful, angry wild
man with material from the New World. He begins amiably, like the
native Indians, but turns to treachery; like those "wild men without
any certaine language" reported by Peter Martyr, he is "wonderfully
astonied at the sweete harmony" of music. But so, according to Horace,
were the beasts of the field. Caliban is not a diagrammatic character, but
for all his unexpectedness he serves very faithfully the elaborate ethical
scheme of *The Tempest*.

The design of the play — Prospero's experiment in Art — is the
recognition, acceptance, and continuance of nobility, together, necessarily, with the exposure of baseness and the righting of political wrongs.
Prospero makes the storm; the vivid opening scene does the work of
acts, and precipitates the characters at once into the final crisis. But
exposition is necessary, and the long second scene, in which Prospero
impatiently tells Miranda of the past she has forgotten, is somewhat
clumsy, though the nervous energy of Prospero's utterance sustains it:

He being thus lorded,
Not only with what my revenue yielded
But what my power might else exact, like one
Who, having into truth by telling of it,
Made such a sinner of his memory
To credit his own lie, he did believe
He was indeed the Duke, out o' the substitution,
And executing th' outward face of royalty
With all prerogative.

(1.2.97–105)

And whatever else may be said about this scene, Shakespeare has certainly not lost his power to dispose of a great quantity of business of all
kinds very rapidly. We learn of the past, discover Prospero's magical
powers, learn of Ariel's services past and his release to come; we not
only meet Caliban but hear of his parentage and his ugliness before
he comes in and starts his flyting with Prospero (Nature against Art);
and before the end of the scene Ferdinand has arrived. In Ariel's songs
and in Ferdinand's first words we catch a new note in Shakespeare; the

sea-music we know from earlier verse, but this is the final rather faint, exotic development of it:

> Sitting on a bank,
> Weeping again the King my father's wreck,
> This music crept by me upon the waters . . .
> (1.2.393–95)

Turning to Ferdinand after her recent encounter with the deformed Caliban, Miranda says: "There's nothing ill can dwell in such a temple"; and, "nothing natural / I ever saw so noble." She may, as Prospero later suggests, have to modify this platonic certainty; but it is appropriate to the making of a brave new world. Ferdinand is likewise certain that Miranda is more than natural, and retires to his patient log-bearing.

The other castaways appear in the second act, and are soon under Prospero's close management. First the royal party, in a strange, desultory conversation, remind us that this is not an ordinary shipwreck; the talk underlines the similarity of their voyage to that of Aeneas, who sailed from Carthage to Cumae, as they from Tunis to Naples; and according to their characters they comment upon the utopian view of a natural commonwealth, such as Montaigne found among savages. The plot against Alonso, invented by Antonio and Sebastian, recapitulates the old usurpation, and although we are aware of Ariel's presence, and the absolute control of Prospero, this is a fine, tensely written scene, economically suggesting the depth of Antonio's baseness, and the feeble but perhaps not irredeemable conscience of Sebastian. The plebeian castaways Stephano and Trinculo join forces with Caliban in 2.2; Caliban thinks they must be spirits, so grand are they, and, like the Indians described by voyagers, supposes them to have dropped from the moon. This scene is also recapitulatory, for Caliban offers the newcomers the same service he had twelve years before given Prospero:

> I prithee, let me bring thee where crabs grow,
> And I with my long nails will dig thee pignuts,
> Show thee a jay's nest, and instruct thee how
> To snare the nimble marmoset. I'll bring thee
> To clustering filberts, and sometimes I'll get thee
> Young scamels from the rock. Wilt thou go with me?
> (2.2.160–65)

With these groups moving about under Prospero's control, Shakespeare turns to Ferdinand and Miranda, and what Prospero calls the "fair encounter / Of two most rare affections." But Caliban and his friends, a miniature of any Shakespearean mob, go on with their plot to kill Prospero and burn his books, and the third act ends with the spectacular frustration of the plot against Alonso. The three guilty men "stand to and feed"; but the banquet vanishes, and they are confronted by their own guilt and the threat of retribution:

> You are three men of sin, whom Destiny —
> That hath to instrument this lower world
> And what is in 't — the never-surfeited sea
> Hath caused to belch up you and on this island
> Where man doth not inhabit, you 'mongst men
> Being most unfit to live . . .
>
> (3.3.53–58)

At this relatively early moment Prospero has already all his enemies "knit up / In their distractions," and the fourth act is devoted — most unusually — to the entertainment celebrating the betrothal of the young lovers, with its insistence on prenuptial chastity (another mark of civility). The show does not reach its conclusion because Prospero is, he says, much disturbed at the thought of Caliban's conspiracy; not a very plausible reason for a necessary intervention, but it enables Shakespeare to pass on to the beginning of the end, *via* Prospero's famous speech, "Our revels now are ended." Next we see the hunting of Caliban and his bedraggled friends.

There remains the last movement, of recognition and forgiveness. First, Prospero, having used his art for the last time and brought his great experiment to a head, abjures magic in a great speech drawn from Ovid:

> this rough magic
> I here abjure, and when I have required
> Some heavenly music — which even now I do —
> To work mine end upon their senses that
> This airy charm is for, I'll break my staff,
> Bury it certain fathoms in the earth,
> And deeper than did ever plummet sound
> I'll drown my book.
>
> (5.1.50–57)

Prospero's forgiveness of his enemies certainly lacks that generosity which is prescribed as a part of courtesy in *Faerie Queene* 6, and which is exhibited to some extent in *Cymbeline* and *The Winter's Tale:*

For you, most wicked sir, whom to call brother
Would even infect my mouth, I do forgive
Thy rankest fault. . . .

(5.1.130–32)

he says to the unnatural Antonio. The discovery of Ferdinand and Miranda at chess is a blessing to Alonso, and converts even Sebastian: "A most high miracle!" But Antonio seems to stand unmoved outside the circle of the reconciled. Shakespeare is not here interested in a high harmony such as he renders in *Pericles*, though the happiness of the moment is registered by Gonzalo's awed rejoicing, and Miranda's cry of pleasure at the beauty of the more than natural world to which she is henceforth to belong gives the scene its difference from the corresponding moments in other Romances. It is hard to forget Prospero's sardonic qualification of Miranda's rapture at the "brave new world": " 'Tis new to thee."

The Epilogue, focus of much allegorizing, alludes to the parallel between Prospero's abandonment of his art, and the actor's abandonment of his role when he steps forward to ask for applause. But Shakespeare will not often allow such things to be as simple as they might, and the sense of the lines is altered and deepened by the final allusion to the Lord's Prayer.

The Tempest is in some ways the strangest of all Shakespeare's plays; to return to it after a lapse of a year or two is to receive with new force the impression that it has always eluded, and may continue to elude, relevant comment. It deals in illusions — not in theatrical illusions of reality, but in the reality of theatrical illusions; as if Prospero in charge of the plot, spirits and machines, were after all a figure of the playwright himself, showing what depths may be found in traps and flying-machines and music in the right places. Though its whole dramatic force is devoted to the arrangement of the romance-recognition, it has a coldness of tone not to be found in *The Winter's Tale,* and deliberately avoids a sustained employment of that note of solemn joy sounded in the closing scenes of *Pericles.* In a sense it is perhaps, a self-indulgence on the part of Shakespeare, a play for the theater of his own mind; but if the mass of puzzled, barrenly ingenious commentary does nothing else, it shows that the world is in no danger of under-estimating the value of such self-indulgence when the talent exercised is Shakespeare's.

REUBEN A. BROWER

The Mirror of Analogy: *The Tempest*

Reuben Arthur Brower (1908–1975) was professor of English and American literature at Harvard University, and an especially influential critic of English poetry during the 1950s and 1960s. His books include *Alexander Pope: The Poetry of Allusion* (1959), *On Translation* (1959), *Fields of Light* (1951), and *The Poetry of Robert Frost* (1963). The following piece is from *The Fields of Light*.

The Mind, that Ocean where each kind
Does streight its own resemblance find;
Yet it creates, transcending these,
Far other Worlds, and other Seas . . .
                    Andrew Marvell

Of *The Tempest,* we may say what Ferdinand said of the masque,

This is a most majestic vision, and
Harmonious charmingly.
                    (4.1.18–19)

The harmony of the play lies in its metaphorical design, in the closeness and completeness with which its rich and varied elements are linked through almost inexhaustible analogies. It is hard to pick a speech at random without coming on an expression that brings us by analogy into direct contact with elements that seem remote because of their place in the action or because of the type of experience they symbolize. Opening the play at the second act we read,

Four legs and two voices; a most delicate monster!
                    (2.2.85–86)

The last phrase is comic enough as used of Caliban and as issuing from the lips of Stephano, a "most foul" speaker. But "delicate" evokes a more subtle incongruity by recalling characters and a world we might suppose were forgotten. Stephano is parodying Prospero when he rebukes Ariel as "a spirit too delicate / To act her [Sycorax's] earthy and abhorr'd commands" and when he says,

> Delicate Ariel,
> I'll set thee free for this!
>   (1.2.145–46)

We have in Stephano's words not only the familiar Shakespearean balancing of comic and serious, but a counterpointing of analogies that run throughout the play. "Delicate" as the antithesis of "earth" points to the opposition of Ariel and Caliban and to the often recurring earth-air symbolism of *The Tempest*. "Delicate" used of this remarkable island creature echoes also the "delicate temperance" of which the courtiers spoke and "the air" that "breathes . . . here most sweetly." "Monster"— almost another name for Caliban — balances these airy suggestions with an allusion to "the people of the island . . . of monstrous shape" and thereby to the strain of fantastic sea lore in *The Tempest,* which is being parodied in this scene.

So viewed, Shakespeare's analogies may perhaps seem too much like exploding nebulae in an expanding though hardly ordered universe. But Shakespeare does not "multiply variety in a wilderness of mirrors"; he makes use of a few fairly constant analogies that can be traced through expressions sometimes the same and sometimes extraordinarily varied. And the recurrent analogies (or continuities) are linked through a key metaphor into a single metaphorical design. Shakespeare is continually prodding us — often in ways of which we are barely conscious — to relate the passing dialogue with other dialogues into and through a super-design of metaphor.

In concentrating on how the design is built up, I am not forgetting that it is a metaphorical design in a *drama,* that we are interested in how Shakespeare has linked stages in a presentation of changing human relationships. Toward the end of the chapter I hope to show how wonderfully the metaphorical design is related to the main dramatic sequence of *The Tempest,* especially in the climactic speeches of Acts 4 and 5.

The play moves forward, we should remember, from a scene of tempest to a final promise of "calm seas, auspicious gales," and through a series of punishments or trials to a series of reconciliations and restorations. Although, as Dr. Johnson might say, there is a "concatenation of events" running through Prospero's "project" and though the play has a curiously exact time schedule, there is often little chronological or logical connection between successive dialogues or bits of action. To be sure Shakespeare has the Elizabethan conventions on his side, but the freedom of his dramatic composition in *The Tempest* never seems merely conventional or capricious because the linkage of analogy is so varied and so pervasive.

The surest proof of the pervasiveness of Shakespeare's design lies in the mere number of continuities that can be discovered in the play. But some are more important than others because they can be traced through more expressions or in more scenes and because they express analogies more closely related to the key metaphor. The six main continuities, roughly labeled to indicate their character, are: "strange-wondrous," "sleep-and-dream," "sea-tempest," "music-and-noise," "earth-air," "slavery-freedom," and "sovereignty-conspiracy."

All of these continuities appear during the second scene of Act 1, which is an exposition of Shakespeare's metaphorical and dramatic designs for the entire play. Near the close of the scene, Ariel's two songs offer wonderfully concentrated expressions of both designs. "Come unto these yellow sands" calms the "fury" of the waves and Ferdinand's "passion," thus charting in brief the course of the action. "Full fathom five" is anticipatory in a very different fashion. It presents in miniature the main lines of the metaphorical design and sounds they key note of "sea change," Shakespeare's most direct expression of the key metaphor of *The Tempest*. (See 1.2.1–178.)

As we trace the first two continuities ("strange-wondrous," "sleep-and-dream"), the reader can appreciate how unobtrusively they emerge from the developing dramatic pattern. Prospero's narrative, with which the scene opens, tells us of the past and describes the present situation while symbolizing the quality of *The Tempest* world. Prospero explains that his enemies have come to this shore "by accident most strange," and Miranda, who falls to sleep at the end of his tale, accounts for her lapse by saying,

> The strangeness of your story put
> Heaviness in me.
>
> (1.2.309–10)

Prospero's tale was strange indeed: it included a ruler "rapt in secret studies," a "false uncle" who "new created / The creatures" of the state, the miraculous voyage of Prospero and Miranda (who was "a cherubin") and their safe arrival "by Providence divine." This "strangeness" is best defined by Alonso's remarks near the end of the play:

These are not natural events; they strengthen
From strange to stranger . . .
This is as strange a maze as e'er men trod;
And there is in this business more than nature
Was ever conduct of . . .
                              (5.1.227–28, 242–44)

They are "unnatural" in a broad seventeenth-century sense of the term;
that is, outside the order which includes all created things. The theme is
almost constantly being played on: "strange," "strangely," or "strangeness" occur altogether some seventeen times, and similar meanings are
echoed in "wondrous," "monstrous," "divine."

Of all the analogies of the play this is probably the vaguest, the near-
est in effect to the atmospheric unity of nineteenth-century Romantic
poetry. But a more precise metaphor of strangeness appears, the
"strangeness" of "new created creatures." From the "accident most
strange" of the shipwreck we come to Alonso's ponderous woe:

              O thou, mine heir
Of Naples and of Milan! what strange fish
Hath made his meal on thee?
                              (2.1.108–10)

and then to Trinculo's discovery of Caliban —"A strange fish!" With a
similar comic antiphony, Miranda finds Ferdinand "a thing divine," and
Ferdinand replies, "O you wonder"; while a little later Caliban hails
Trinculo as his god and cries, "Thou wondrous man." The full significance of these strange births will appear later.

The vague "strangeness" of the island world is closely allied to a
state of sleep, both continuities appearing in Miranda's remark about
the "heaviness" that came over her while listening to Prospero's story.
The feeling that we are entering on an experience of sleep-and-dream
arises beautifully out of the dramatic and rhythmic texture of the
opening dialogue between father and daughter. The movement of
these speeches with their oddly rocking repetitions is in key with the
sleepy incredibility of the events about to be described: "Canst
thou remember . . . thou canst . . . I can . . . thy remembrance . . . my
remembrance . . . thou remember'st . . . Twelve year since, Miranda,
twelve year since . . ." Throughout the story Prospero is continually
reminding Miranda to "attend" to the telling, and it seems perfectly
natural that at the end she should be "inclin'd to sleep." (Note in passing how neatly Shakespeare has broken a long narrative into dialogue

and also given a distinct impression of Prospero's firmness and of Miranda's innocent dependence.) Miranda's images of the past come back to her "rather like a dream," and Prospero seems to be drawing their story from a world of sleep, "the dark backward and abysm of time."

With the next scene (the mourning King and his courtiers) we meet one of Shakespeare's typical analogical progressions. The sleep which affects the courtiers is, like Miranda's, a strange "heaviness." Their dialogue runs down, psychologically and rhythmically, through three echoes of Miranda's words:

> GONZALO: Will you laugh me asleep, for I am very heavy? . . .
> SEBASTIAN: Do not omit the heavy offer of it . . .
> ALONSO: Thank you. Wondrous heavy.
> SEBASTIAN: What a strange drowsiness possesses them!
> (2.1.182–83, 188, 192–93)

The conversation that follows between the conspirators shows how Shakespeare uses an analogy to move to a new level of action and experience and to make them harmonious with what precedes and follows. Sebastian and Antonio begin by talking about actual sleep and waking: why are they not drowsy like the others? Then Antonio shifts to talking of sleepiness and alertness of mind, and from that to imagining that he sees "a crown dropping" upon Sebastian's head. The wit becomes more complex as Sebastian describes Antonio's talk as "sleepy language"— without meaning — though indicating that it does have meaning, "There's meaning in thy snores." This dialogue, which readers are liable to dismiss as so much Elizabethan wit, has its place within the play's metaphorical pattern. The plotting takes on a preposterous dreamy-sleepy character like that of Prospero's narrative and Miranda's recollections. Through such verbal trifling Shakespeare maintains the continuous quality of his imagined world.

References to similar wakings and sleepings, to dreams and dreamlike states, abound from here to the end of the play, where the sailors are "brought moping . . . even in a dream," and the grand awakening of all the characters is completed. But up to that point confusion between waking and sleep is the rule, being awake is never far from sleep or dream. In *The Tempest* sleep is always imminent, and more than once action ends in sleep or trance.

The witty talk of the conspirators glides from conceits of "sleep" to conceits of "the sea," to talk of "standing water" and "flowing" and

"ebbing." The "good Gonzalo," in consoling the King, speaks in similar figures:

> It is foul weather in us all, good sir,
> When you are cloudy.
>
> (2.1.138–39)

Recurrent expressions of "sea and tempest," like those of "sleep and
dream," are numerous and have a similar atmospheric value of not letting us forget the special quality of life on Prospero's island. But they
also have far more important effects, for many of them become
metaphors which are more precisely and more variously symbolic and
which link more kinds of experience together.

By tracing two groups of "tempest" expressions, metaphors of
"sea-swallowing" and images of "clouds," we may understand how
these more complex analogies are built up. We may also see how
Shakespeare moves from narrative fact to metaphor, from image or
metaphor referring only to narrative fact to metaphor rich in moral and
psychological implications. As in creating the analogies of "strangeness" and "sleep," Shakespeare starts from a dramatic necessity: the
audience must be told what the situation was in the storm scene with
which the play opens, and they must learn through an actor (Miranda)
how they are to take it. (See 1.2.1–178.) Although there is a hint of
magic in Miranda's vision of the tempest, she pictures it as a violent
actuality:

> Had I been any god of power, I would
> Have sunk the sea within the earth, or e'er
> It should the good ship so have swallowed and
> The freighting souls within her.
>
> (1.2.10–13)

As if there were an inner rhythm in these responses, this metaphor, like
others we have been tracing, recurs in the plotting episode. Antonio is
speaking of his sister Claribel, left behind in Tunis:

> she that from whom
> We all were sea-swallowed, though some cast again,
> And by that destiny to perform an act
> Whereof what's past is prologue, what to come
> In yours and my discharge.
>
> (2.1.244–48)

In this new context "sea-swallowed" does several things at once. It brings back Miranda's horrified impression; but the magical nature of the storm now being known, the phrase reminds us that there was no "sea-swallowing," no actual sinking of "fraughting souls." Next, with a curiously Shakespearean "glide and a jump" via the pun on "cast," "sea-swallowed" merges into another metaphor (they are now "cast" as actors in destiny's drama). "Sea-swallowing" has become a metaphor that expresses destiny's extraordinary way of bringing Sebastian to the throne.

The irony of Antonio's words, which is clear to the audience, is made explicit later in the solemn speech in which Ariel explains the purpose of the tempest:

> You are three men of sin, whom Destiny —
> That hath to instrument this lower world
> And what is in 't — the never-surfeited sea
> Hath caused to belch up you . . .
> (3.3.53–56)

Few passages could show better how Shakespeare carries his analogies along and at the same time completely renews them. The "belching up" recalls the wreck and the casting ashore and the earlier connection with destiny. But the sea's action is now described in much grosser terms and with grim sarcasm, while the oddly compact grammar makes "the never-surfeited sea" very nearly a synonym for "Destiny." The violence though increased is now religious and moral; the imagery has become expressive of the strenuous punishment and purification of "three men of sin."[1] So by the continuity of his varying metaphor Shakespeare has expressed an unbroken transition from actual storm to the storm of the soul. This sequence, which expresses both physical and metaphysical transformations, points very clearly to the key metaphor of *The Tempest*.

The recurrent cloud images present a similar sequence as they take on various symbolic meanings in the course of the play. "Cloud" does not actually occur in the opening storm scene, but when Trinculo sees "another storm brewing" and speaks of a "black cloud," we are reminded of the original tempest. The cloud undergoes an appropriate change in Trinculo's speech; it "looks like a foul bombard that would shed his liquor." This comic cloud is very different from "the curl'd

---

[1] Alonso, Antonio, Sebastian.

clouds" on which Ariel rides, though they too are associated with storms. The clouds of Caliban's exquisite speech are those of Ariel and the deities of the masque:

> and then, in dreaming,
> The clouds methought would open and show riches
> Ready to drop upon me . . .
>
> (3.3.135–37)

Clouds — here linked with magical riches — become in Prospero's "cloud-capp'd towers" speech a symbol for the unsubstantial splendor of the world. One of the subordinate metaphors there, the "melting into air" and the "dissolving" of the clouds, is picked up in Prospero's later words about the courtiers:

> The charm dissolves apace;
> And as the morning steals upon the night,
> Melting the darkness, so their rising senses
> Begin to chase the ignorant fumes that mantle
> Their clearer reason.
>
> (5.1.64–68)

This dissolution of night clouds (suggested also by "fumes") is a figure for the change from madness to sanity, from evil ignorance to the clear perceptions of reason. Although the cloud images of the play are so varied, they have a common symbolic value, for whether they are clouds of tempest or of visionary riches or of the soul, they are always magically unsubstantial. The reader is led to feel some touch of likeness among experiences as different as a storm at sea, a bit of drunken whimsy, a vision of heavenly and earthly beauty, and a spiritual regeneration. The cloud sequence, as an arc of metaphor, is in perfect relation to the gradual dramatic movement from tempest and punishment to fair weather and reconciliation, the images having meanings more and more remote from any actual storm.

The "cloudlike" change in the distracted souls of the guilty nobles was induced (as if in reminiscence of Plato) by *Solemn music* —

> A solemn air and the best comforter
> To an unsettled fancy.
>
> (5.1.58–59)

Many of the expressions referring to music, like the stage direction above, are not explicitly metaphorical, but along with the continuities of "sleep" and "strangeness" they help maintain the magical character of the action. The music is always the music of spirits and always a sign of more than natural events.

The one fairly constant musical metaphor[2] in *The Tempest* is the symbolic opposition of confused noises, especially storm sounds, and harmonious music. The key word and the central impression of the opening scene is certainly "noise"[3] in the modern sense. The impression is carried over in the first words of the next scene:

> If by your art, my dearest father, you have
> Put the wild waters in this roar, allay them.
> (1.2.1–2)

Miranda's request is soon answered by Ariel's first song, "the wild waves" are "whist." The *solemn and strange music* heard when the *strange Shapes* bring a banquet to the courtiers makes Alonso say, "What harmony is this? my good friends, hark!" Gonzalo replies: "Marvelous sweet music!" By contrast, when Ariel enters shortly after, in order to inform the "three men of sin" of their punishment by the storm, there is an offstage sound of *Thunder and lightning.* The masque vision which Ferdinand finds "harmonious charmingly" is rudely interrupted by *a strange, hollow, and confused noise* which symbolizes the stormy anger expressed by Prospero in the speeches that follow. When in the next scene he prepares to forgive his enemies, he abjures the "rough magic" by which he

> call'd forth the mutinous winds,
> And 'twixt the green sea and the azur'd vault
> Set roaring war . . .
> (5.1.42–44)

As the *solemn music* is played the clouds of ignorance "dissolve," and so the musical metaphor, like the sea metaphor, has moved from outer to inner weather.

---

[2]The music and tempest metaphors have been traced in a very different fashion and with quite different aims by G. Wilson Knight in *The Shakespearian Tempest*. My analysis (which I had worked out before reading Professor Knight's essay) has a more limited purpose: to show a continuity of analogy and a development of metaphor parallel to that of the other continuities I have traced.

[3]The scene is full of expressions such as: *A tempestuous noise of thunder and lightning heard,* "roarers," "command these elements to silence," *A cry within,* "A plague upon this howling! they are louder than the weather, or our office," "insolent noisemaker," *A confused noise within,* et cetera.

The music analogy has some close links with the earth-air continuity which we glanced at in the introductory chapter of the book. Ferdinand, following Ariel's "yellow sands" song, asks, "Where should this music be? i' th' air, or th' earth?" And a little later:

> This is no mortal business, nor no sound
> That the earth owes: I hear it now above me.
>   (1.2.410–11)

The connection of air and music can never be long forgotten: Ariel and his spirits of "thin air" are the musicians of the island.

The earth-air, Caliban-Ariel antithesis coincides at points with what we might call a slavery-freedom continuity, for Caliban is in Prospero's words both "slave" and "earth." Ariel too is called a "slave"[4] by Prospero, and for the time of the play he is as much a slave as Caliban. He is always asking for his freedom, which is at last granted, his release being symbolically expressed in the airy rovings of his final song. He flies into perpetual summer and, like air, becomes merged with the elements. By contrast, the "high-day, freedom!" of which Caliban sings is ironically enough simply a change of masters.

The "slaves" and "servants" of the play suffer various kinds of imprisonment, from Ariel in his "cloven pine" to Ferdinand's mild confinement, and before the end of Act 4 everyone except Prospero and Miranda has been imprisoned in one way or another. During the course of Act 5 all the prisoners except Ferdinand (who has already been released) are set free, each of them by Prospero's special command.

A sovereignty-conspiracy analogy parallels very closely the slavery-freedom analogy, some of the same persons, e.g., Ferdinand and Caliban, appearing as both slaves and conspirators. "That foul conspiracy / Of the beast Caliban, and his confederates" is of course a parody version of the "Open-ey'd Conspiracy" of Sebastian and Antonio. Ferdinand, too, is charged fantastically by Prospero with plotting against his island rule. Talk of kings and royalty turns up in many scenes, being connected usually with the denial of kingship, as in "good Gonzalo's" speech on his golden-age commonwealth where "he would be king" and yet have "no sovereignty." Though no single explicit metaphor for conspiracy or usurpation is often repeated, Shakespeare rings many changes on the theme as he moves from plot to plot. Prospero's brother, we recall, is said to have "new created the creatures" of state. Alonso's seizure of power is called a "substitution": "crediting his own

---

[4]Both are called "slaves" in Act 1.2, the scene of metaphorical exposition.

lies," he began to believe "he was indeed the duke," and from merely playing a part he went on to become "absolute Milan." The figure is picked up in the somnolent dialogue of Sebastian and Antonio:

> I remember
> You did supplant your brother Prospero.
> (2.1.265–66)

In the second of the scenes in which Caliban and his fellows plot to overthrow the island "tyrant," Sebastian's "supplant" is recalled with a difference:

> CALIBAN: I would my valiant master would destroy thee. I do not
>   lie.
> STEPHANO: Trinculo, if you trouble him any more in his tale, by this
>   hand, I will supplant some of your teeth.
>   (3.2.44–47)

The figure recurs a little later in a more serious context:

> . . . you three
> From Milan did supplant good Prospero.
> (3.3.69–70)

In Act 5 after various supplantings, serious and comic, accomplished or merely projected, all true kings are restored and all false ones dethroned.

The two continuities, sovereignty-conspiracy and slavery-freedom, are also alike in the fact that their metaphorical force is expressed through scenes that are just one step removed from allegory. The more serious of the restorations and releases convey similar kinds of moral meaning. Ferdinand's release from "wooden slavery" signifies that he is a true lover and a true prince. In being freed from madness Alonso has escaped from "heart-sorrow" and regained his rightful rank and a "clear life ensuing." Both continuities convey an impression of topsy-turvydom in the order of things, an unnatural interchange of status among creatures of every kind. Both express a return to stability after a disturbance of degree.

What then is the key metaphor through which the various continuities are linked, and how are they connected through it? Shakespeare's most direct expression of his key metaphor is "sea change," the key phrase of Ariel's song. But what does Shakespeare mean by "sea change"?

Ariel sings of "bones" being made into "coral" and of "eyes" becoming "pearls." "A change into something rich and strange," we now understand, is a change "out of nature." "Sea change" is a metaphor for "magical transformation," for metamorphosis. The key metaphor of the play is "change" in this special sense, and "change" is the analogy common to all of the continuities we have been tracing. (I am not forgetting that they are also expressive of many other relationships, or that Shakespeare is often playing with two or three metaphors at once, as in the various figures of "sea-swallowing." But all are at least expressive of change, or changeableness.)

Through the first rather vague analogies we traced, of "strangeness" and "sleep-and-dream," numerous events and persons in the play are qualified as belonging to a realm where anything may happen. Expressions of "strangeness" and "sleep," like many of the references to sea and music, suggest "far other Worlds and other Seas," where magical change is to be expected. A more particular metaphor of change is expressed through the stress on the "strangeness" of "new creations" and on the confusion between sleep and dream and waking. The island is a world of fluid, merging states of being and forms of life. This lack of dependable boundaries between states is also expressed by the many instances of confusion between natural and divine. Miranda says that she might call Ferdinand

> A thing divine; for nothing natural
> I ever saw so noble.
>   (1.2.422–23)

Ferdinand cannot be sure whether she is a goddess or a maid, and Caliban takes Trinculo for a "brave god." There is a further comic variation on this theme in Trinculo's difficulty in deciding whether to classify Caliban as fish or man, monster or devil.

But "change" is most clearly and richly expressed through the sequence of tempest images (especially "cloud" and "sea-swallowed") and through the noise-music antithesis. All kinds of sounds, harmonious and ugly, like the manifestations of sea and storm, are expressive of magical transformation. "The fire and cracks / Of sulfurous roaring" (imagery in which both storm and sound analogies are blended) "infects" the courtiers' "reason," and *solemn music* induces the "clearing" of their understanding. The "music" and the "tempest" continuities, taken together as metaphors of "sea change," are perhaps the most extensive of all the analogies in their organizing power. They recur often, they connect a wide diversity of experiences, and they express in symbolic form some of the main steps in the drama, in particular, the climactic moments of inner change: Ariel's revelation to the courtiers of their guilt, Alonso's first show of remorse, and the final purification.

The earth-air or Caliban-Ariel antithesis may seem to have very little to do with metamorphosis. But the relation of this theme to the key metaphor is clear and important. Air, Ariel, and his music are a blended symbol of change as against the unchanging Caliban, "the thing of darkness." He can be punished, but hardly humanized; he is, says Prospero,

> A devil, a born devil, on whose nature
> Nurture can never stick; on whom my pains,
> Humanely taken, are all lost, quite lost.
> (4.1.188–90)

The other continuities parallel to earth-air, of slavery-freedom and conspiracy-sovereignty, are frequently expressive of major and minor changes of status among the inhabitants and temporary visitors on Prospero's island.

But the interconnection of Shakespeare's analogies through the key metaphor cannot be adequately described, since we are able to speak of only one point of relationship at a time. We can get a better sense of the felt union of various lines of analogy in *The Tempest* by looking at the two passages where Shakespeare expresses his key metaphor most completely, the "Full fathom five" song and Prospero's "cloud-capp'd towers" speech.

Rereading Ariel's song at this point, we can see how many of the main continuities are alluded to and related in the description of "sea change" and how the song anticipates the metaphorical design that emerges through the dialogue of the whole play. The total metaphorical pattern is to an amazing degree an efflorescence from this single crystal:

> Full fathom five thy father lies;
> Of his bones are coral made:
> Those are pearls that were his eyes:
> Nothing of him that doth fade,
> But doth suffer a sea change
> Into something rich and strange.
> Sea nymphs hourly ring his knell:
> *Burthen:* "Ding-dong!"
> Hark! now I hear them — Ding-dong, bell.
> (1.2.400–8)

In addition to the more obvious references to the deep sea and its powers and to the "strangeness" of this drowning, there are indirect anticipations of other analogies. "Fade" prefigures the "dissolving cloud" metaphor and the theme of tempest changes, outer and inner. "Rich," along with "coral" and "pearls," anticipates the opulent imagery of the dream-world passages and scenes, the "riches ready to drop" on Caliban and the expressions of wealth[5] and plenty in the masque. The song closes with the nymphs tolling the bell, the transformation and the "sea sorrow" are expressed through sea music. Ferdinand's comment reminds us that the song has connections with two other lines of analogy:

> The ditty does remember my drown'd father.
> This is no mortal business, nor no sound
> That the earth owes: — I hear it now above me.
> (1.2.409–11)

The song convinces Ferdinand that he is now King of Naples (the first of the interchanges of sovereignty), and it is a "ditty" belonging not to the "earth," but to the "air."

The sense of relationship between the many continuities is still more vividly felt in the lines of Prospero's most memorable speech:

> You do look, my son, in a mov'd sort,
> As if you were dismay'd: be cheerful, sir:
> Our revels now are ended. These our actors,
> As I foretold you, were all spirits and
> Are melted into air, into thin air:
> And, like the baseless fabric of this vision,
> The cloud-capp'd towers, the gorgeous palaces,
> The solemn temples, the great globe itself,
> Yea, all which it inherit, shall dissolve
> And, like this insubstantial pageant faded,
> Leave not a rack behind. We are such stuff
> As dreams are made on, and our little life
> Is rounded with a sleep.
>
> (4.1.146–58)

In Prospero's words Shakespeare has gathered all the lights of analogy into a single metaphor which sums up the metaphorical design and the essential meaning of *The Tempest*. The language evokes nearly every

---

[5]"Rich" and "riches" occur no less than five times in the masque.

continuity that we have traced. "Melted into air," "dissolve," "cloud," and "rack" bring us immediately to Ariel and tempest changes, while "vision," "dream," and "sleep" recall other familiar continuities. "Revels," "gorgeous palaces," and "pageant" (for Elizabethans closely associated with royalty) are echoes of the kingly theme; and "solemn" is associated particularly with the soft music of change. The "stuff" of dreams is at once cloud-stuff (air) and cloth, both images being finely compressed in "baseless fabric." Taken with "faded" these images refer obliquely to the garments so miraculously "new-dyed . . . with salt water," one of the first signs of "sea change" noted by Gonzalo. Within the metaphor of tempest-clearing and of cloudlike transformation, Shakespeare has included allusions to every important analogy of change in the play.

But it is through the twofold progress of the whole figure that the change metaphor is experienced and its most general meaning fully understood. We read first: that like the actors and scenery of the vision, earth's glories and man shall vanish into nothingness. Through a happy mistake we also read otherwise. By the time we have passed through "dissolve," "insubstantial," and "faded," and reached "leave not a rack behind," we are reading "cloudcapped towers" in reverse as a metaphor of towerlike clouds. "Towers," "palaces," "temples," "the great globe," "all which it inherit" are now taken for cloud forms. Through a sort of Proustian[6] merging of icon and subject, we experience the blending of states of being, of substantial and unsubstantial, or real and unreal, which is the essence of *The Tempest* metamorphosis.

Similar meanings are expressed through the closing dream figure, which grows equally out of the metaphorical context of the speech and the play. "Rounded," we should take with Kittredge as "surrounded," but without losing the force of round, as in Donne's "surrounded with tears." "Our little life" is more than sentimental, it is our little life (microcosm) in contrast with "the great globe" (macrocosm). There may also be an over-image in "surrounded" of the world in classical myth and geography with its encircling ocean, sleep being the stream that "rounds" the lesser world. In relation to the metaphorical design of the play, "rounded with a sleep" and the notion of life ending in dreams express again the sense of confusion between sleep and dream and waking. This metaphor which completes the figure of cloud-change is Shakespeare's most perfect symbol for the closeness of states

---

[6]This merging in Proust was brought to my attention by J. I. Merrill in [an unpublished honors thesis done at Amherst].

that to our daylight sense are easily separable. Although the vision here expressed goes far beyond the play, it is still a natural extension of the dramatic moment and a fulfillment of the metaphor that has been implicit since the noisy opening lines of *The Tempest*.

But if Shakespeare's total metaphor is in a sense present everywhere, it is also a design that develops in close relation to the main dramatic movement of the play. As we have noted more than once, a particular metaphor will be varied to fit a new dramatic situation and so serve to express the situation more fully and to anticipate the next step in the development of the drama. The best example of this adaptation of metaphor comes in a speech in which Shakespeare seems to be playing capriciously with his noise-music theme. At first sight the passage seems inconsistent with the symbolic contrast between storm noise and music:

> ALONSO: O, it is monstrous! monstrous!
> Methought the billows spoke and told me of it;
> The winds did sing it to me; and the thunder,
> That deep and dreadful organ pipe, pronounc'd
> The name of Prosper: it did bass my trespass.
>   (3.3.95–99)

It is admittedly odd that the confused noise of the tempest should, in Alonso's soul, compose a harmony — however gloomy — but the paradox fits in perfectly with the developing structure of the play. Alonso has just been told by Ariel that the storm had a purpose as an instrument of Destiny. Since at this moment remorse first appears in the play and the inner clearing begins, it is exactly right that the storm sounds should seem harmonious and so point forward to the events of the fourth and fifth acts. No use of metaphor in *The Tempest* reveals more clearly Shakespeare's exact sense of the movement of his drama, of the changing human relations and feelings he is presenting.

In building up his metaphorical design, Shakespeare prepares us for the moment in *The Tempest* when the major shift in dramatic relationships takes place. The moment comes in the speech in which Prospero describes the behavior of the King and the courtiers as they slowly return from madness to sanity. The first important step toward this climax, Alonso's acknowledgment of his guilt, was expressed through a metaphor combining both sea and musical changes. The next step, Ferdinand's release from his tempest-trials and from dreamlike enchantment, is expressed through the masque, which is an elaborate dramatization of metamorphosis, Ariel's "meaner fellows," "the rabble," being now transformed into majestic Olympian goddesses. Once again, familiar continuities appear, and again they are transformed to fit a new occasion. "Earth," for example, is no longer "barren place and fertile," but the earth enriched by human cultivation and symbolized now by Ceres — not by Caliban, who is "nature resisting nurture." Iris summons this new Earth in the gorgeous speech beginning "Ceres, most bounteous lady, thy rich leas . . . ," lines in which we hear a quite new majesty of tone and movement. The couplet form sets the dialogue apart from human speech, while the longer periods, the added stresses, the phrasal balancings are especially appropriate to "that large utterance of the early gods." (Here is one of many instances of how Shakespeare adapts his sound patterns to his metaphorical and dramatic designs.) Prospero's visionary speech that ends "the revels" is not simply a concentration of metaphor without reference to the dramatic development. It announces the changes to come, it gives a rich expression of their meaning, and it anticipates the dreamlike flux of the psychological events of the last act.

If we now read Prospero's words in Act 5, in which he describes the great changes as they take place, we see many references back to Shakespeare's metaphorical preparation for this moment. We also realize that various lines of action and various lines of analogy are converging almost simultaneously. The speech opens with Prospero's farewell to his art, after which he turns his thoughts to "restoring the senses" of the courtiers, whom Ariel has just gone to release:

A solemn air and the best comforter
To an unsettled fancy, cure thy brains,
Now useless, boil'd within thy skull! There stand,
For you are spell-stopp'd.
Holy Gonzalo, honorable man,
Mine eyes, even sociable to the show of thine,
Fall fellowly drops. The charm dissolves space;
And as the morning steals upon the night,
Melting the darkness, so their rising senses
Begin to chase the ignorant fumes that mantle
Their clearer reason. O good Gonzalo!
My true preserver, and a loyal sir
To him thou follow'st, I will pay thy graces
Home, both in word and deed. Most cruelly
Didst thou, Alonso, use me and my daughter:
Thy brother was a furtherer in the act;

Thou'rt pinch'd for 't now, Sebastian. Flesh and blood,
You, brother mine, that entertain'd ambition,
Expell'd remorse and nature; who, with Sebastian —
Whose inward pinches therefore are most strong —
Would here have kill'd your king; I do forgive thee,
Unnatural though thou art! Their understanding
Begins to swell, and the approaching tide
Will shortly fill the reasonable shores
That now lie foul and muddy. Not one of them
That yet looks on me, or would know me. Ariel,
Fetch me the hat and rapier in my cell: [*Exit Ariel.*]
I will discase me, and myself present,
As I was sometime Milan. Quickly, spirit;
Thou shalt ere long be free.

                                        (5.1.58–87)

If this is a climactic moment, what changes in dramatic relationships
are taking place, what is happening dramatically? The "men of sin," like
Ferdinand, have come to the end of the trials which began with the
storm and continued through various "distractions." Now, as Prospero
explains, they are undergoing a moral as well as a mental regeneration,
they are "pinch'd" with remorse and are being forgiven. The twofold
regeneration is further dramatized in the speeches that follow: "th'
affliction of Alonso's mind amends," he resigns Prospero's dukedom
and "entreats" him to pardon his "wrongs."

But these are the prose facts, the bare bones of the changes in dramatic relationships. We cannot feel the peculiar quality of what is taking
place or grasp its meaning apart from the metaphorical language
through which it is being expressed. And the expressions acquire their
force and precision from the whole metaphorical preparation we have
been tracing. The courtiers' senses are restored by "an airy charm," by
magic similar to that which was worked by Ariel and his spirits. The
allusions to "heavenly music" and "a solemn air," in contrast to the
"rough magic" that Prospero has abjured, remind us that these changes
will be musically harmonious, like the songs of Ariel, and not noisy and
confused like the storm sent to punish these men and reveal their
"monstrous" guilt. Toward the end of the speech, the imagery recalls
the tempest metaphor, but it is altered so as to express the mental and
moral change that is taking place. The return of understanding is like an
approaching tide that covers the evidence of a storm (both "foul" and
"muddy" have storm associations from earlier occurrences).

But the metaphor that best expresses this clearing is the one for which the preparation has been most complete:

> The charm dissolves apace;
> And as the morning steals upon the night,
> Melting the darkness, so their rising senses
> Begin to chase the ignorant fumes that mantle
> Their clearer reason.
>
> (5.1.64–68)

"Dissolving" and "melting" and "fumes" take us back at once to the grand transformations of the masque speech, to the earlier cloud transformations both serious and comic; and they take us back further to the association of clouds with magical tempests, inner storms, and clearing weather. We read of the moral and psychological transformations with a present sense of these analogies. They are qualified for us as a dreamlike dissolution of tempest clouds, as events in the "insubstantial" region where reality and unreality merge.

It is through such links that Shakespeare concentrates at this climactic moment the fullest meaning of his key metaphor. There is of course no separation in the reader's experience between the dramatic fact and the metaphorical qualification. The images that recur in Prospero's speech take us back to felt qualities, but to felt qualities embedded in particular dramatic contexts. "Melting," for example, carries us to the spiritlike dissolution of "spirits . . . melted into air, into thin air"; but it also reminds us of the masque pageantry and of Prospero's calming of Ferdinand's fears. We hear Prospero's soothing and mysterious tone in both the earlier and later uses of the word. The dramatic links and the analogical links are experienced at once, which is to say that metaphorical design and dramatic design are perfectly integrated.

We can now realize that metamorphosis is truly the key metaphor to the *drama*, and not the key metaphor to a detachable design of decorative analogies. Through the echoes in Prospero's speech of various lines of analogy, Shakespeare makes us feel each shift in dramatic relationships as a magical transformation, whether it is the courtiers' return to sanity, or Prospero's restoration to his dukedom, or Ariel's flight into perpetual summer. While all of the "slaves" and "prisoners" are being freed, and while all of the "sovereigns" are being restored, the sense of magical change is never wholly lost. The union of drama and metaphor in *The Tempest* is nowhere more complete than in the last act of the play.

The larger meaning of Shakespeare's total design, which was anticipated in the cloud and dream metaphor of Prospero's visionary speech, is most clearly and fully expressed in these final transformations. In a world where everything may become something else, doubts naturally arise, and in the swift flow of change the confusion about what is and what is not becomes fairly acute. When Prospero "discases" himself and appears as Duke of Milan, Gonzalo says with understandable caution:

> Whether this be,
> Or be not, I'll not swear.
> (5.1.122–23)

And Prospero answers:

> You do yet taste
> Some subtilties o' the isle, that will not let you
> Believe things certain.
> (5.1.123–25)

Whereas in the earlier acts the characters had often accepted the unreal as real (spirits, shipwrecks, drownings, visions), they now find it difficult to accept the real as truly real. The play concludes with their acceptance of the unexpected change to reality. But for the spectator there remains the heightened sense of the "thin partitions" that "do divide" these states. The world that common sense regards as real, of order in nature and society and of sanity in the individual, is a shimmering transformation of disorder. "We shall all be changed, in a moment, in the twinkling of an eye." (This or something like it is as near as we can come to describing the total attitude conveyed by *The Tempest*.)

Thus *The Tempest* is, like Marvell's "Garden," a Metaphysical poem of metamorphosis,[7] though the meaning of change is quite different for the two writers. It is worth noting too that Shakespeare "had Ovid in his eye," a fact that is obvious from the echoes of Golding's famous translation. There could be no better proof of Shakespeare's maturity than the contrast between the "sweet witty" Ovidianism of "Venus and Adonis" and the metaphorical design of *The Tempest*, which gives philosophic meaning to a drama of Ovidian metamorphosis. We remember "a lily prison'd in a jail of snow" as an isolated "beauty," but hardly as an apt symbol of the amorous relations of Venus and Adonis, or as symbolic of some larger meaning in their story. (Indeed a "jail of snow" is rather inept for the fervid goddess of the poem.) "Those were pearls

---

[7]See the excellent analysis of the poem in M. C. Bradbrook and M. G. Lloyd Thomas, *Andrew Marvell* (Cambridge, 1940), pp. 59–64.

that were his eyes" revives Ariel's sea music, Ferdinand's melancholy, and a world of fantasy and transshifting states of being. The increased concentration in meaning of the image from *The Tempest* is a sign of a growth in the command of language which is command of life for a poet. As Arnold said of Wordsworth, Shakespeare now "deals with more of *life*" and "he deals with *life*, as a whole, more powerfully." His maturity and power appear in the variety of experience so perfectly harmonized through the imaginative design of *The Tempest*.

LEAH MARCUS

The Blue-Eyed Witch

Leah Marcus (b. 1945) is the Edwin Mims Professor of English at Vanderbilt University, a position she has held since 1998. She is the author of *Childhood and Cultural Despair* (1978), *The Politics of Mirth: Jonson, Herrick, Milton, Marvell, and the Defense of Old Holiday Pastimes* (1986), *Puzzling Shakespeare: Local Reading and Its Discontents* (1988), and *Unediting the Renaissance: Shakespeare, Marlowe, Milton* (1996). She has also coedited two volumes of the writings of Elizabeth I: *Elizabeth I: Autograph Compositions and Foreign Language Originals* (2003) and *Elizabeth I: Collected Works* (2000), which won the Prize for the Outstanding Professional and Scholarly Publication in Language and Literature from the Association of American Publishers. The following piece is excerpted from her introductory essay to *Unediting the Renaissance*.

What is it that we hope to experience when we read a literary text from an earlier era? Are we looking for unimpeded access to a culture far removed from our own, for contact with the mind of a writer far distant in time? Are we looking for amusement or instruction or moral elevation or escape? For an encounter with transcendence, for visceral engagement with past conflicts, for a glimpse of something alien, or for some or all of the above, mutually exclusive though they may appear to be? What we want out of our reading will depend greatly on the genre, type, and specific subject matter of the work we happen to choose: most of us would not go to the poetry of the Earl of Rochester for moral elevation, nor to the *Enneads* of Plotinus for light entertainment. But what we want from a given text will also depend on the social and intellectual baggage we ourselves bring to it, on the specific coordinates of our individual lives, on the shared assumptions that characterize our particular cultural affiliations and our broader historical situation.

As readers most of us have become quite comfortable with at least some of these forms of relativism. Yet unless we are trained textual scholars or bibliographers, we probably do not occupy ourselves unduly with another form of relativism at least as significant as those listed above — the variability over time and space of any given work itself. The work's material history since its inception, the vast and largely uncharted alterations imposed by that history and by the mediation of generation upon generation of printers, editors, publishers — this is a relativism we are prone to ignore, but ignore at our peril. The approach and critical interests we wish to bring to a given piece of writing may be facilitated, discouraged, or even blocked altogether by the specific version in which we receive it.

The present study is designed with at least two audiences in mind. It is aimed first at readers who already have an active interest in textual studies, in the myriad subtle ways in which literary works are altered by their histories, and by the shaping hands of scholars who transform them in the very act of editing them to make them accessible to a broader community of readers. From at least the 1950s until the mid- to late 1970s, scholarly editors and literary critics lived for the most part in divided and distinguished worlds. There was a fruitful division of labor between them: scholars who identified themselves primarily as editors and bibliographers worked to produce authoritative critical editions of the standard authors; serious lay readers and scholars who identified themselves primarily as literary critics made use of these authoritative editions as a reliable basis for interpretation. Some editors and bibliographers looked with mingled amusement and scorn upon the ephemeral pursuits of the madding crowd of literary critics, who could be relied upon year after year to produce new "definitive" readings of the symbolism of the white whale in *Moby Dick* or the madness of King Lear. By contrast, their own bibliographical efforts — the establishing of a given author's canon, the compilation of a definitive descriptive bibliography, the creation of a standard edition — would endure over time because such work was scientifically based.

On the other side of the divide, literary critics sometimes looked ruefully upon the embarrassing plenitude of their own interpretive efforts, but tended to view them as incremental steps toward some definitive conclusion or larger synthesis: at some point, the "truth" about Melville's novel or Shakespeare's play would finally be attained. Literary critics and lay readers tended to look with considerable scorn upon the "dry as dust" labors of the editors and bibliographers, even while relying heavily upon their work. When I was in graduate school at Columbia University in the late 1960s, most students avoided the bibliography courses like a plague: to specialize in such mechanical matters, we felt in what then passed for wisdom, was to give evidence of some grave defect of personality or imagination. The stereotyped image of the bibliographer among literary critics in the late 1960s is nicely captured in Frederick Crews' caricature, Smedley Force, the impossibly pompous editor of *The Watermark* and Professor of English at the University of Texas. Mr. Force insists that criticism cannot possibly begin until he and his ilk have established sufficient appendices, concordances, and (in the case of Shakespeare) accurate scale models of the Blackfriars Theater.[1] And yet, we felt obliged to heed Mr. Force and use the "correct" edition — which was, for my period, usually bound in dark blue and labelled "Clarendon" — or risk the solecism of an interpretation based on a non-authoritative text.

More recently, however, the division of labor between critics and bibliographers has broken down, as has some of the mutual distrust that kept the two groups divided. Bibliographers with the profound scholarship, daring, and imagination of D. F. McKenzie have challenged their own discipline's positivist underpinnings by demonstrating the degree to which, for example, the investigation of seventeenth- and eighteenth-century printinghouse practices has been skewed by our twentieth-century author-bound presuppositions about how printed books must have been put together. Scholars like McKenzie, Philip Gaskell, and Jerome J. McGann, among many others, have chipped away at some of the insufficiently historicized assumptions behind the "New Bibliography" (as represented in the work of Alfred Pollard, W. W. Greg, Fredson Bowers, and others) and its standardization of editorial practice. Textual critics like McGann and D. C. Greetham have sought for a rapprochement between the field of textual studies and recent critical theory, so that editors and their readers alike would become more aware of the constructed nature of even the most "definitive" edition. The area of Renaissance literature has been at the

---

[1]Frederick C. Crews, *The Pooh Perplex* (1963; reprinted New York: E. P. Dutton, 1965).

forefront of this vital revisionism. In arguing for two texts of *King Lear* rather than a single conflated text, Steven Urkowitz, Gary Taylor, Michael Warren, and others have unleashed a torrent of questions about the reliability of all twentieth-century editions of Renaissance authors. From a different angle of vision, Elizabeth Eisenstein has reinterpreted the meaning of the set of historical shifts we call the "Renaissance" in terms of the development of print culture. And all the while, the vast interdisciplinary project entitled "The History of the Book," under the international leadership of scholars like Henri-Jean Martin, Robert Darnton, Roger Chartier, McKenzie, Ian Willison, David McKitterick, and Asa Briggs, has gathered its energies toward the task of discovering how material texts of all kinds have been conceptualized, produced, marketed, and consumed at specific moments in history.[2]

[2]For work representative of the new currents mentioned here, see D. F. McKenzie, "Printers of the Mind: Some Notes on Bibliographical Theories and Printing-House Practices," *Studies in Bibliography* 22 (1969): 1–75; and his *Panizzi Lectures 1985: Bibliography and the Sociology of Texts* (London: British Library, 1986); Philip Gaskell, *From Writer to Reader: Studies in Editorial Method* (Oxford: Clarendon Press, 1978); Jerome J. McGann, *A Critique of Modern Textual Criticism* (1983; paperback edition Chicago and London: University of Chicago Press, 1985); his *The Beauty of Inflections: Literary Investigations in Historical Method and Theory* (1985; reprinted Oxford: Clarendon Press, 1988); and his *Black Riders: The Visible Language of Modernism* (Princeton: Princeton University Press, 1993); D. C. Greetham, *Textual Scholarship: An Introduction* (New York and London: Garland, 1992); his *Theories of the Text* (Oxford: Oxford University Press, 1999); and Robert Darnton, "What Is the History of Books?" *Daedalus* 111 (1982): 65–83, and reprinted in his *The Kiss of Lamourette* (New York: W. W. Norton, 1990), pp. 107–35.

For the new work specifically in the field of Renaissance/early modern studies, see, for example, the Shakespearean studies by Steven Urkowitz, *Shakespeare's Revision of King Lear* (Princeton: Princeton University Press, 1980); Gary Taylor and Michael Warren, eds. *The Division of the Kingdoms: Shakespeare's Two Versions of King Lear* (Oxford: Clarendon Press, 1983); Stanley Wells, "The Unstable Image of Shakespeare's Text," in *Images of Shakespeare: Proceedings of the Third Congress of the International Shakespeare Association, 1986,* ed. Werner Habicht, D. J. Palmer, and Roger Pringle (Newark: University of Delaware Press; London and Toronto: Associated University Presses, 1988), pp. 305–13; Random Cloud [Randall McLeod], "The Marriage of Good and Bad Quartos," *Shakespeare Quarterly* 33 (1982): 421–31; Michael D. Bristol, *Shakespeare's America, America's Shakespeare* (London and New York: Routledge, 1990), especially chap. 4, "Editing the Text: The Deuteronomic Reconstruction of Authority," pp. 91–119; and the witty summation in Margreta de Grazia and Peter Stallybrass, "The Materiality of the Shakespearean Text," *Shakespeare Quarterly* 44 (1993): 255–83, which appeared after most of the present study was written but clearly anticipates a number of my arguments. For more general studies focused on the period, see, for example, Elizabeth L. Eisenstein, *The Printing Press as an Agent of Change,* 2 vols (Cambridge: Cambridge University Press, 1979); Roger Chartier, ed., *The Culture of Print: Power and the Uses of Print in Early Modern Europe,* trans. Lydia G. Cochrane (Princeton: Princeton University Press, 1989); and his very recent *The Order of Books,* trans. Lydia G. Cochrane (1992; English translation Cambridge: Polity Press; and Stanford: Stanford University Press, 1994).

The present study is designed as a contribution to the newly active field of textual studies, but I also have a second audience in mind — those readers and critics who are as yet unconverted, who are either unaware of the new developments or consider them a tempest in a teapot that can be safely overlooked. As part of our interpretive activity, those of us who read or "profess" literature need to consider the subtle, pervasive rhetorical power exerted by the editions we use. From among the many forces and institutions that may shape a given work, the present study will concentrate on printed books in the Renaissance (as opposed to manuscripts and other materials) and on ways in which their texts are transformed, often disfigured, by the twentieth-century editorial processes to which they have been subjected. No single version of a literary work, whether Renaissance or modern, can offer us the fond dream of unmediated access to an author or to his or her era; the more aware we are of the processes of mediation to which a given edition has been subject, the less likely we are to be caught up in a constricting hermeneutic knot by which the shaping hand of the editor is mistaken for the intent of the author, or for some lost, "perfect" version of the author's creation.

Until recently, of course, it has been the business of editors to accomplish those very things: to give us the work insofar as possible as the author intended it, or at least in its "original" written form. Editors usually do, and should, strive for objectivity in their labors, but they are, as we all are, creatures of their times: what looks like objectivity to one generation may well look like distortion to another. The present study is dependent on recent critiques of scientific method that demonstrate the rhetorical and socio-political nature of scientific explanation. What we consider the factual basis for our conclusions may well alter its truth-bearing status over time: the human power to elucidate or otherwise account for a phenomenon is always limited by the local parameters of the man or woman doing the elucidation.

Until recently, the successful edition of a literary work was one that created for its readers an aura of near transparency, or unmediated access to the author and his or her achievement. From our present relativist point of view, such an edition was successful not because it had uncovered the "true" version of the literary work (although it might well be based on brilliant scholarship and meticulous analysis of the requisite historical materials), but because it successfully met reader expectations about the author and work in question. The editor's own taste and sensibility were sufficiently at one with that of his audience for his edition to achieve the illusion of transparency. In very recent editions influenced by poststructuralist theory and by the new textual studies, the editor's shaping hand is likely to be much more obvious — we may think, for example, of Hans Gabler's controversial version of *Ulysses* or of the almost equally controversial new single-volume Oxford Shakespeare. Whether we like it or not, scholarly editing is becoming a very different activity than it was even two decades ago: it is revealing, even flaunting, its own plastic energies rather than striving to conceal them; it is coming to be understood as a form of cultural practice. What, then, might be the specific cultural practice behind the standard editions many of us still accept unquestioningly?

We have much to lose by "Unediting the Renaissance." If modern scholars, students, and general readers were suddenly deprived of all the historical, linguistic, and literary investigation that lies behind the average standard edition, we would find ourselves crippled and disoriented. We might well find ourselves repeating the past — assembing new standard editions if only to have a stable reference point for future departures from them. Despite the agenda encapsulated in its title, the present study will by no means contend that editing has become unnecessary. Our discussion here will regularly depend on edited versions of works that are not at the forefront of our analysis. *Ars longa, vita brevis*: there is only so much primary textual investigation that any given scholar can be expected to accomplish. Adopting the purist position that all previous editions must be avoided would bring scholarly writing and research to a halt. It would also have a devastating effect on our ability to teach literature from past centuries or, indeed, to read such literature at all. To call for an investigation of past editorial practice is by no means to throw its achievements out the window — only to suggest that we need to be aware of its dynamics and limitations in the same way that we train ourselves to be attentive to the other implements available to us in the jumbled toolbox we bring to the activity of textual interpretation.

If there is much to be lost by "Unediting the Renaissance," there is also much to be gained. Because of the sheer weight of erudition involved, if for no other reason (and I will suggest a few more later on), editing has tended to be a profoundly conservative activity. To an extent that few of us recognize, our standard editions are shaped by nineteenth-century or even earlier assumptions and ideologies. Even the new, more experimental editions sometimes collapse back into received orthodoxy at moments that are crucial for interpretation. "Unediting the Renaissance" is proposed not as a permanent condition, but as an activity that all editors should engage in as part of their own revisionary efforts, that all readers should practice mentally even as they make use of edited texts. It requires a temporary abandonment of modern editions in favor of Renaissance editions that have not gathered centuries of editorial accretion around them. It requires a questioning of the origins of even the most standard glosses and emendations. To illustrate the value of this process for the benefit of the unconverted, I offer as an example the mysterious case from *The Tempest* of the blue-eyed witch, a crone whose physical demeanor has altered curiously over the centuries along with prevailing attitudes toward women, sexuality, and race.

GRAY EYES, BLACK EYES, BLUE EYES

In Act 1, scene 2 of *The Tempest,* Prospero describes Caliban's mother Sycorax as a "damn'd Witch" condemned to death in "*Argier*" on account of her "mischiefes manifold" and "sorceries terrible." I quote here from the First Folio, the only early text of the play, although most modern edited versions introduce only minor changes to the lines in question.[3] Because of "one thing" Sycorax "did / They wold not take her life" but banished her instead: "This blew ey'd hag, was hither brought with child" — her child being Caliban, born somewhat later on the island where he, Prospero, Miranda, and the others presently reside (TLN 391–96).

Our discussion will focus on the witch's blue eyes, but we may wish to pause briefly over her crime. What was it that Sycorax did to avoid execution? Until the second half of the nineteenth century, readers and editors were in a quandary over this matter. Charles Lamb found the passage puzzling "beyond measure." It aroused "infinite hopeless curiosity" in him until he read of the infamous career of an actual Algerian witch (unnamed in his source) who had earned a reprieve from death by delivering Algiers from the siege of Emperor Charles V.[4] Staid

---

[3]Here and throughout, my quotations from the First Folio will be to Charlton Hinman's Norton Facsimile edition (London and New York: Paul Hamlyn, 1968), and indicated by Through Line Number in the text. Given that Hinman's facsimile combines "best" versions of each page of the First Folio rather than reproducing any single printed copy, it is, ironically from the point of view of the present study, far from being an "unedited" version of the Folio. As I will argue later on, the heuristic need to make use of an accessible standardized exemplar frequently overrides the need for absolute fidelity to any single printed text.

[4]"Nugae Criticae," *London Magazine*, November, 1823; as cited in *Charles Lamb on Shakespeare*, ed. Joan Coldwell (London: Colin Smythe; New York: Barnes & Noble, 1978), pp. 62–64.

Victorian editions tended to avoid what now appears the obvious explanation, while displaying unease over the passage's sexual innuendo. The
matter remained in debate until the early twentieth century; since then,
editors have regularly noted that the "one thing" Sycorax did to avoid
execution was become pregnant, as actual female convicts sometimes
did in early modern England to postpone execution.

This is an example of a genuinely helpful editorial intervention, but
it leaves open the question of Caliban's parentage. Was Sycorax pregnant by the devil, as Prospero repeatedly asserts, or by some other
father? At some point in her history, Sycorax "with Age and Envy / Was
growne into a hoope" (TLN 384–5), and she died sometime before
Prospero's and Miranda's arrival on the island. But that deformity was
the effect of age and malice: what was she like before that? In this passage and throughout the play, Sycorax is a shadowy figure, and even
here, the seemingly specific information we are offered is Prospero's
recounting of a story Ariel had apparently told him previously, a narration of events even Ariel had in all likelihood not witnessed himself.
Nearly everything we know about Sycorax we know only through Prospero's secondhand information, which may or may not be accurate but
is certainly not without prejudice: he has supplanted her son on the
island and his magic has rivalled and exceeded hers. To what degree
might he, or even Ariel, have "edited" her story? To what extent, if we
were editing *The Tempest,* would we want to align ourselves with his
perceptions?

Let us return to Sycorax's blue eyes — "blew" in the First Folio,
but regularly modernized to "blue" in recent editions. Why has so little
been made of their color in recent critical studies of the play? The mention of eye color in Shakespeare is rare, and blue eyes are particularly
rare. Why are the witch's eyes blue? Much of the interpretive energy
surrounding *The Tempest* in the late twentieth century has gone toward
the deconstruction of the play's apparent opposition between the properly European (Prospero, Miranda, Ferdinand) and the colonial or otherwise alien stranger (Caliban, Sycorax). We might have supposed that
Sycorax's eye color would be a prominent piece of evidence in such critical revisionism, since blue eyes, in our culture at least, are associated
with the Anglo-American imperialist and with the "self," rather than
with the colonized peoples and with the "other." As a blue-eyed Algerian, Sycorax would fail to fit our racial stereotypes in a number of interesting ways. We tend not to think of Africans as blue eyed, even though
North Africans of "Argier" and elsewhere sometimes are. But the
witch's blue eyes scarcely surface in the critical discussions I have

read: the critics have dutifully read the explanatory notes to the play in the editions they have used, and modern editions overwhelmingly reject the possibility that "blue-eyed" in this instance can possibly mean blue eyed.

In nearly all modern editions, "blew ey'd," "blue-ey'd," or "blue-eyed" is glossed in a way that cancels out its potential for disrupting the self/other binary that has characterized most readings of the play. Among popular teaching editions of the complete works of Shakespeare, the Riverside glosses "blue-ey'd" as "with dark circles around the eyes"; the Bevington fourth edition suggests, "with dark circles under the eyes or with blue eyelids, implying pregnancy," the Signet edition offers, "referring to the livid color of the eyelid, a sign of pregnancy."[5]

Standard single-play editions are only slightly more informative. Frank Kermode's Arden edition glosses "blue-ey'd" as "Alluding to the eyelid; blueness there was regarded as a sign of pregnancy." G. L. Kittredge suggests, somewhat more creatively, "with blueish settled streaks (often called *circles*) under and partly surrounding her eyes — a sign of exhaustion or debility" and follows the suggested reading with a long list of analogues from other Renaissance texts. John Dover Wilson's notes to the New Shakespeare offer paleographical evidence for a possible emendation of "blew-ey'd" to "blear-ey'd": in the passage of *Sir Thomas More* which had been suggested only a few years before Dover's edition as a sample of Shakespeare's handwriting, final *r* and final *w* are almost indistinguishable. Wilson suggests that Shakespeare may have written "bler-ey'd" and been misread by the compositor.[6] In the hand of the *Sir Thomas More* passage, the two letters are indeed easily confused, but we have no conclusive evidence that the hand in *Sir Thomas More* is Shakespeare's. As Paul Werstine has pointed out, a recent volume of essays on the subject succeeds in

---

[5]Cited respectively from *The Riverside Shakespeare*, ed. G. Blakemore Evans (Boston: Houghton Mifflin, 1974), p. 1615; *The Complete Works of Shakespeare*, ed. David Bevington, 4th edition (New York: HarperCollins, 1992), p. 1534; and *The Complete Signet Classic Shakespeare*, ed. Sylvan Barnet (New York and Chicago: Harcourt Brace Jovanovich, 1972), p. 1547.

[6]See Frank Kermode, ed., *The Tempest*, The Arden Shakespeare, 6th edition (London: Methuen, 1958), p. 27 n.; George Lyman Kittredge, ed., *The Tempest* (Boston: Ginn, 1939), pp. 96–97; and Sir Arthur Quiller-Couch and John Dover Wilson, eds, *The Tempest* (Cambridge: Cambridge University Press; New York: Macmillan, 1921), p. 93. Most other twentieth-century single-play editions follow the standard formula, with Alfred Harbage and Northrop Frye's Pelican editions of *The Tempest* (Baltimore: Penguin, 1959; reprinted 1970) representing a prominent exception: the Pelican editors leave the line unglossed.

demonstrating only that none of the contributors is willing to rule out Shakespeare as possible author of the *More* passage.[7] In most Renaissance hands, final *r* and final *w* are quite easy to distinguish. Wilson's argument is cogent only if we have already accepted his assumption that Sycorax could not possibly be blue eyed. Only a few twentieth-century single-volume editors of *The Tempest* have left the line unannotated: most notably, Northrop Frye and Alfred Harbage in the Pelican Shakespeare. Most editions that do not annotate the line supply the requisite information in a glossary: "blue-eyed" in Shakespeare means with "a dark circle round the eye" or "with blueness about the eyes."[8]

Why are twentieth-century editors so relatively uniform in their interpretation of the line, which would seem, on the face of it, to be receptive to a wide range of explications? In this, as in many other editorial matters, they have followed the lead of William Aldis Wright's prestigious Clarendon edition of *The Tempest* (1874), which contended that " 'blue-eyed' does not describe the colour of the pupil of the eye, but the livid colour of the eyelid, and a blue eye in this sense was a sign of pregnancy. See Webster, *Duchess of Malfi;* ii, I, 'The fins of her eyelids look most teeming blue.' "[9] But nineteenth-century editors were by no means so formulaic as their successors have been in their interpretation of the witch's startling blue eyes. In fact, the idea that Sycorax could not possibly be blue eyed in our usual sense of the term seems to have been hatched around mid-century along with the dissemination of Charles Darwin's theory of evolution.

Surprisingly enough, the phrase "blue-eyed hag" went unannotated in editions of Shakespeare from the early folios (which were, of course, not annotated), through all of the eighteenth- and early nineteenth-century annotated editions, until the late 1850s. Even Thomas Bowdler's *Family Shakespeare* (1818) left the description of the pregnant, blue-eyed Sycorax intact, despite his resolve to remove words and

[7]Paul Werstine, review of T. H. Howard-Hill, ed., *Shakespeare and Sir Thomas More: Essays on the Play and its Shakespearian Interest* (Cambridge: Cambridge University Press, 1989), in *Essays in Theatre* 9 (1990): 91–94.

[8]Cited from the glossaries to *The Comedies of Shakespeare,* ed. W. J. Craig and Edward Dowden (London: Oxford University Press, 1932); and *The Temple Shakespeare: The Tempest,* ed. Israel Gollancz (London: J. M. Dent, 1910). Interestingly, Peter Alexander's editions, which do not have notes but do include a glossary, do not gloss the phrase.

[9]William Aldis Wright, ed., *The Tempest,* The Clarendon Shakespeare (Oxford: Clarendon Press, 1874), pp. 91–92; see also Alexander Schmidt's supporting definition in his authoritative *Shakespeare-Lexicon: A Complete Dictionary of All the English Words. Phrases and Constructions in the Works of the Poet,* 2 vols (Berlin: Georg Reimer; London: Williams & Norgate, 1874–75), 1: 123.

expressions "which cannot with propriety be read aloud in a family."[10]
The first edition of *The Tempest* to take issue with Sycorax's eye color
was the Gilbert Shakespeare (1858–60), edited by Howard Staunton.
Staunton suggested emendation of "blew-ey'd" to "blear-ey'd" as a
more appropriate epithet for the "damn'd witch." His edition also happened to anticipate Darwin's *Descent of Man* by depicting Caliban as a
"missing link" between primate and human. In one of Sir John Gilbert's
illustrations, a simian Caliban is attended by his close cousin, the monkey. The page on which Sycorax is described is adorned with a portrait
of her in standard witch-like garb. She is apparently on the point of
imprisoning Ariel, who recoils from the hunched forms of the witch
and her half-human son.[11] A decade and a half later, Daniel Wilson's
Caliban: The Missing Link (1873) accepted the emendation as settled,
referring several times to the "blear-eyed" Sycorax as part of his discussion of Caliban's borderline status between the animal and the human.
Wilson contended:

> Sycorax is spoken of with every term of loathing: as a "foul witch,"
> a "hag," a "damned witch," &c. There seems no propriety in cou-
> pling with these the term *blue-eyed* — one of the tokens, according
> to Rosalind, in "As You Like It," whereby to know a man in love.

Some Victorian stage Calibans followed Gilbert and Wilson, modelling
their portrayals of the savage on the behavior patterns of great apes.[12]

Although Staunton's and Wilson's textual emendation was not followed by later editors, who at most admitted it into their notes as con-
jectural, the rationale behind the suggested emendation was generally
accepted. In nineteenth-century literature and culture, blue eyes were
commonly associated with beauty, innocence, and transcendence, as in
Keats' "beauteous woman's large blue eyes" or Shelley's eyes "like the
deep, blue, boundless heaven" or Arnold's "eyes, so blue, so kind."[13]

[10]Thomas Bowdler, ed., *The Family Shakespeare, in Ten Volumes* (London: Longman,
1818), title page.
[11]See the survey of visual depictions of Caliban in Alden T. Vaughan and Virginia
Mason Vaughan, *Shakespeare's Caliban: A Cultural History* (Cambridge: Cambridge
University Press, 1991), pp. 215–51; and Howard Staunton, ed., *The Plays of Shakespeare*,
vol. 3 (London and New York: Routledge, Warne & Routledge, 1860), pp. 12 and 23.
[12]Daniel Wilson, *Caliban: The Missing Link* (London: Macmillan & Co., 1873),
p. 227. For a history of nineteenth-century stage Calibans, see Stephen Orgel, ed., *The
Tempest*, The Oxford Shakespeare (Oxford and New York: Oxford University Press,
1987; paperback reprint, 1991), pp. 71–75.
[13]Cited respectively from "To J. H. Reynolds, Esq.," line 53, in *The Poetical Works
of John Keats*, ed. H. W. Garrod, 2nd edition (Oxford: Clarendon Press, 1958), p. 485;

Blue eyes were also associated, at a time of expanding colonization and racial consciousness, with British culture and national heritage, with the "white man's burden," and with the superior moral elevation attained by English-speaking peoples. To imagine Sycorax as "blue-eyed" in any positive sense of the term was to violate deeply engrained cultural assumptions.

Some nineteenth-century editors searched for ways of associating "blue" with malevolence: Sycorax's eyes might be a blue like that "cold, startling blue which suggests malignity so strongly," or like the "pale-blue, fish-like, malignant eye, which is often seen in hag-like women."[14] As Charles and Mary Cowden Clarke explained in their popular edition designed to elevate Shakespeare for families and purge his texts of phrases "coarse and unfit for modern utterance," the "epithet [blue-eyed], as applied by Shakespeare; is far from being commendatory, as at present. He uses it here to describe the dull, bleared, neutral colour seen in the eyes of old crones."[15] Charles Cowden Clarke was a noted lecturer on literary subjects; he had been intimate with several of the Romantics and had tutored John Keats. He, as much as any other single person, helped to popularize the strict separation in late nineteenth-century editions of *The Tempest* between the heavenly blue eyes of the English cultural ideal and the malignant eyes of the she-demon Sycorax.

The main piece of cultural business performed by annotations of "This blue-eyed hag" in nineteenth-century editions was the policing of boundaries between the acceptably civilized and the loathsomely, dangerously alien. But the range of suggested interpretations during that period was free and wide-ranging by comparison with that of twentieth-century editions, which have frozen earlier editorial speculation into dogma. The only annotated edition since the Pelican to depart from reigning orthodoxy on the subject of the "blue-eyed" witch (at least among the editions that I have encountered) is Stephen Orgel's

---

Prometheus Unbound 2.1.114, in *Shelley's* Prometheus Unbound, *A Variorum Edition*, ed. Lawrence John Zillman (Seattle: University of Washington Press, 1959), p. 187; and "A Memory Picture," line 41, in *The Poems of Matthew Arnold*, ed. Kenneth Allott, 2nd edition, ed. Miriam Allott (London and New York: Longman, 1979), p. 115.

[14]See J. Surtees Phillpotts, ed., *The Tempest*, The Rugby Edition (London: Rivington's, 1876), as cited in Horace Howard Furness, ed., *A New Variorum Edition of Shakespeare*, vol. 9 *The Tempest* (Philadelphia and London: J. B. Lippincott, 1892), p. 61 n.; and Richard Grant White, *Studies in Shakespeare* (Boston and New York: Houghton Mifflin; Cambridge, Massachusetts: The Riverside Press, 1885), p. 324.

[15]Charles and Mary Cowden Clarke, eds., *The Plays of William Shakespeare* (London, Paris, and New York: Cassell, Petter & Galpin, [1864–68]), vol. 3, *The Tragedies*, Preface, p. vii, and vol. 1, *The Comedies*, p. 10 n.

recent Oxford edition (1987), which repeats the usual explanations but offers them more as hypothesis than as self-evident truth.

Having indicated some of the cultural pressures underlying the typical annotation of "blue-eyed hag," however, we have by no means completed our task. Editors have not only registered discomfort with the idea of a witch who is blue eyed, they have also done exhaustive historical research into the meaning of "blue-eyed" in the Renaissance to support their annotation of the line. They have, in fact, uncovered considerable evidence that the phrase in English Renaissance culture could be used in senses very different from our own. If twentieth-century editions may be said to be impoverished in terms of their interpretation of the line, they are often copious in providing historical evidence to support the reigning dogma. And indeed, if they are correct in concluding, as they have, that "blue-eyed" could not possibly refer simply to eye color in Shakespeare's culture, then perhaps their intervention is helpful rather than obfuscating.

We in the twentieth century have inherited the nineteenth century's marked cultural emphasis on blue eyes, particularly insofar as they are found in young women and accompanied by the requisite blond hair and an aura of combined innocence and sexual availability, as in Marilyn Monroe, blond-haired Barbie dolls, and so on. If Shakespeare's "blew-ey'd" did not resonate for his culture in the ways that "blue-eyed" tends to resonate in ours, then perhaps the editorial intervention is justified. We will note, however, that twentieth-century explications of the line, like their forebears from the previous century, serve to smooth out an apparent incongruity. The witch cannot have blue eyes, because the cultural image of blue eyes is overwhelmingly positive and Sycorax has to be understood as negative.

Part of the purpose of a good edition has traditionally been to bridge historical distance — to make a text and its cultural milieu accessible to people with different practices and assumptions. But that process always involves the risk of over-normalization, of making the past over to accommodate one's own, and one's readers', sense of what constitutes acceptable meaning. Particularly in our own poststructural critical climate, an edition allowing for cultural dissonance and distance might well be more desirable than one that consistently irons out interpretive difficulties. At what point does editorial assistance become unwanted intrusion? We plunge to the heart of the matter when we investigate the range of signification carried by blue eyes in the Renaissance. No doubt many of the unfortunates hanged as witches in early seventeenth-century England had eyes of a color that we would now describe as blue, but the naming of eye colors, then as now, was as much cultural construction as perception. What perceptions matched the phrase "blue-eyed" in England of the early modern era?

According to Wright and most subsequent editors, "blue-eyed" refers not to the iris of the eye, but to the area around the eye. And there are indeed many instances of such usage in the Renaissance. Kittredge cites Shakespeare's *Lucrece* (1587): "And round about her tear-distained eye / Blue circles stream'd" and Davenant's *The Cruel Brother.* "His eyes . . . Encircled with the weakly colour blue" (Kittredge 96; see n. 6). But much more commonly cited is the example from *The Duchess of Malfi,* already quoted above from Wright's edition, which brings in the association with pregnancy: "The fins of her eyelids look most teeming blue." Although each of these examples refers explicitly to the area around the eye while the Shakespearean passage does not, there are other contemporary instances in which the phrase "blue eyes" seems clearly to mean what we would call "black and blue eyes" or "eyes with dark circles around them." Kittredge cites Dekker's *Honest Whore,* Part II, "Out, you blue-eyed Rogue" and, following Wright, Davenant's *The Playhouse to be Let;* "Her eyes look blue; pray heav'n she be not breeding!" (96–97). The examples do not all support the same precise reading of the origin of Sycorax's "blue-eyed" demeanor: some imply pregnancy, while others suggest grief or physical bruising. But all of them together demonstrate fairly conclusively that in late sixteenth- and early seventeenth-century England, "blue-eyed" did not necessarily mean what we mean by blue eyed.

The case against the standard emendation is not yet lost, however. To pursue it further, we need to probe into the cultural construction of eye color. For if editors are to be allowed to annotate the line with the interpretive assurance conveyed by most twentieth-century editions, they need to demonstrate not only that "blue-eyed" *could* mean "blue circled" as a result of pregnancy or some other debility; they should be willing to demonstrate an overwhelming likelihood that it meant "blue circled" as opposed to "blue." As we have noted, by no means did all nineteenth-century editors agree about the eyes of Sycorax — some of them opted for eyes of a baleful or malignant blue. Horace Howard Furness queried in his *New Variorum Edition of The Tempest* (1892):

> Is it not possible to accept the blueness as referring not only to the dark eyelids and circles round the eyes, but also to the pupil itself, where the *arcus senilis,* as the ophthalmologists call it, is wont to give the baleful expression which we associate with witches?

Following an earlier hint by Edmund Malone, Furness made the interesting suggestion that some of the positive connotations associated with blue eyes in recent Anglo-American culture were in Shakespeare attached to gray eyes:

> Instances are as plenty as blackberries where what we now call blue eyes were by Shakespeare called grey eyes. There are two in *Rom. & Jul.*, where the Friar speaks of "The grey-ey'd morn," and Mercutio of "Thisbe, a grey eye or so." Since, then, our "blue eyes" and Shakespeare's "blue eyes" are not the same, I think we are at liberty to include, in the present phrase, whatsoever tends to add abhorrence to the repulsive witch.[16]

If we combine all of these suggestions about historical differences in meaning, a Shakespearean taxonomy of eye color would run something like this: his blue eyes = our dark circled eyes, his gray eyes = our blue eyes. And in fact, in pre-Shakespearean literature the eyes of the desired woman are often gray rather than blue. In Chaucer, for example, the desirable woman typically has "eyen greye as glas" or at least "greye." John Skelton gives her "eyen grey and steep."[17] "The phrase "grey as glasse" occurs in *Two Gentlemen of Verona* 4.4.196 (F TLN 2010), Olivia has grey eyes in *Twelfth Night* 1.5.256 (F TLN 538), and there are similar references in *Romeo and Juliet* 2.4.45 and 3.5.19. The *OED* confirms that "blue eye" gradually migrated in signification from what we would term a "black eye" in the sense of black-and-blue to "blue eye" in our sense of blue, but the precise chronology of the change is left unclear. Unlike most eye colors, "blue eye" receives its own entry in the *OED*. The first cited usage of "blue eyes" in the nineteenth- and twentieth-century sense appears to be to 1735 (Alexander Pope's *Moral Essay* 2.284.[18] The *OED* glosses our specific crux — Shakespeare's description of Sycorax — to mean black or blue around the eyes rather than blue-eyed in the more recent sense of the term.

At this point, as Smedley Force would be happy to inform us, our potential case against the standard annotation of "blue-eyed hag"

---

[16]Furness, ed. (n. 14) 9: 62 n.

[17]See *The Works of Geoffrey Chaucer,* ed. F. N. Robinson, 2nd edition (Boston: Houghton Mifflin, 1961), p. 18 (*General Prologue,* 152), p. 56 (*Reeve's Tale,* 3974); and John Skelton, *Philip Sparrow,* line 1014, in *The Complete Poems of John Skelton, Laureate,* ed. Philip Henderson 1931, revised edition (London and Toronto: J. M. Dent and Sons, 1948), p. 89.

[18]Alexander Pope, *Epistles to Several Persons,* ed. F. W. Bateson, The Twickenham Edition of the Poems of Alexander Pope (London: Methuen; New Haven: Yale University Press, 1951; 2nd edition, 1961), vol. 3 part ii, p. 73.

appears lost. If the *OED* and standard editions confirm each other, we are confronted with a powerful array of authority. We need to remind ourselves, however, that the *OED* however invaluable, is not without its biases: it is a product of the same late nineteenth-century codifying impulse that has given us our standard editions of Shakespeare and many other writers. Some of the same minds who prepared the Shakespearean editions also participated in the monumental cultural enterprise of the *OED*, and a similar cultural agenda is to be expected in both. Indeed, a major purpose of the *OED* entry on "blue eyes" may have been to help solidify the post-Wrightian interpretation of the Shakespearean line, rather than vice versa. We need to go beyond the *OED* itself if we are to determine whether Sycorax's eyes could have been blue.

In English Renaissance literature, there are hordes of golden-tressed women — particularly in blazons *à la* Petrarch of an idealized beloved — but there are precious few blue eyes. As we have already seen, the traditional eye color for the beautiful woman in earlier literature appears to have been gray. This does not necessarily mean, of course, that people in early modern England favored gray eyes over blue eyes; they may simply have perceived the blue-gray that we call blue as gray. In literature of the late sixteenth and seventeenth centuries, however, black eyes come strongly into favor: Philoclea in the *Old Arcadia* is black-eyed, and so, famously, is Sidney's Stella in *Astrophil and Stella*, Shakespeare's dark lady is also described in Sonnet 127 as having eyes of "raven black," and there are numerous other examples from the period.[19] Part of this preference may relate to the eye color of actual women celebrated in the verse, as in the case of Shakespeare's dark lady and Sidney's Stella: other poets also celebrated Penelope Devereux Rich's "black sparckling eyes."[20]

On stage or in verse celebrating a generic mistress, such specificity might have been a drawback, limiting the range of actors who could play a given part, or the range of women who could be wooed with the aid of a given poem. English Petrarchan poetry is strongly fixated on the beautiful woman's eyes, but more for their power than for their color. Most frequently, the woman's eyes are likened to stars, suns, or some other emitter of celestial light, without their color being specified. Often they are crystal, which may or may not connote a color like our

---

[19]See Stephen Booth, ed., *Shakespeare's Sonnets* (New Haven and London: Yale University Press, 1977), p. 111; and for other examples from among many, James Shirley's "To Odelia" and Sir John Suckling's Sonnet II as printed in *Ben Jonson and the Cavalier Poets,* ed. Hugh Maclean (New York: W. W. Norton, 1974), pp. 188 and 258.

[20]See, for example, *The Poems of Henry Constable,* ed. Joan Grundy (Liverpool: Liverpool University Press, 1960), Sonnet Seven, p. 158.

blue: it tends to be associated in verse of the period with the heavens and with "crystal streams" (both of which we might be more inclined to think of as blue) but sometimes it seems to suggest a translucent paleness. Often the eyes are diamonds, or other precious stones. Following Petrarch, whose Laura was clearly what we would call blond-haired and blue-eyed, English poets sometimes described their mistress's eyes as "sapphire," as in Spenser's *Amoretti* and the famous blazon from the *Epithalamion:* "Her goodly eyes lyke Saphyres shining bright."[21]

In Spenser, as in the case of Sidney's Stella, we may be dealing with the perceived eye color of an actual woman, except that Spenser's beloved, unlike Sidney's, happens to conform to the Petrarchan ideal. But only rarely in the English Renaissance verse that has survived are the beautiful woman's "sapphire" eyes explicitly associated with the word "blue." One popular and widely anthologized exception is Sidney's *contreblason* of Mopsa the Shepherdess from the *Arcadia;* it mocks the Petrarchan ideal by interchanging the conventionalized colors of Mopsa's physical attributes. She is as fair as Saturn and as chaste as Venus, "Her forhead jacinth like, her cheekes of opall hue, / Her twinkling eies bedeckt with pearle, her lips of Saphir blew:"[22] The pearls that in the usual Petrarchan blazon would represent teeth here suggest a dropping rheum about the eyes; the sapphire blue that should shine from the eyes is instead the color of her lips. The joke depends on a conventionalized expectation that eyes will be blue and teeth pearly white, rather than vice versa. Obviously, at least some members of a cultural elite in the sixteenth century were able to imagine eyes that were "blue" in our sense rather than in the commoner Renaissance meaning.

The evidence I have collected suggests that the Shakespearean taxonomy of eye color accepted by earlier editors may be too simple. In Renaissance culture, "blue eyes" sometimes suggested black-and-blue eyes, or eyes rimmed with black as a result of pregnancy or fatigue, but, *pace* the *OED,* "blue eyes" sometimes meant what we mean by blue eyes

---

[21] *The Poetical Works of Edmund Spenser,* ed. J. C. Smith and E. de Selincourt (London and New York: Oxford University Press, 1929), pp. 565 (Sonnet XV) and 581 (*Epithalamion,* line 171). For another example, see the poem attributed to Thomas Lodge in *The Phoenix Nest 1593,* ed. Hyder Edward Rollins (Cambridge: Harvard University Press, 1931), p. 58. On the Petrarchan construction of beauty more generally, see Elizabeth Cropper, "The Beauty of Woman: Problems in the Rhetoric of Renaissance Portraiture," in *Rewriting the Renaissance: The Discourses of Sexual Difference in Early Modern Europe,* ed. Margaret W. Ferguson, Maureen Quilligan, and Nancy J. Vickers (Chicago and London: University of Chicago Press, 1986), pp. 175–90.

[22] Cited from *The Poems of Sir Phillip Sidney,* ed. William A. Ringler, Jr (Oxford: Clarendon Press, 1962), p. 12.

today. The phrase "blue eye" seems to have carried then some of the ambiguity that "black eye" carries in our own culture, where the phrase can be used for an eye with a dark brown or black iris, or for an eye that is black and blue. We can speculate that "blue eyes" in the twentieth-century sense may have been a recent import in early modern England, associated with foreign models and with elite culture rather than with the native English tradition of gray-eyed beauty. Within Shakespeare's own corpus, the color blue is at least once associated with the heavens, but the reference appears in one of his last plays: in a famous textual crux, *Cymbeline* describes Imogen's closed eyes and/or eyelids as "White and Azure lac'd / With Blew of Heauens owne tinct" (F TLN 929–30). A little after Shakespeare, blue eyes become more common in poetry, but may still have been regarded as exotic. Charles Cotton wrote a blazon of his sister's beauty in which he praised her black eyes above "English grey, or French blue eyes," seeming to suggest an equivalence between the two colors: what the French (and Italians?) conventionally termed blue or sapphire eyes the English traditionally called gray.[23]

And indeed, if we move outside the realm of lyric poetry, we find a similar equivalence. In the standard modern translations of Homer, Athena's most customary epithet is "gray-eyed." In Chapman's Homer, however, composed about the same time as Shakespeare's *Tempest*, Athena is regularly described as either "blue-eyed" or "gray-eyed." In translating Athena's Homeric epithet γλαυκῶπις, Chapman uses "blue" and "gray" indifferently: there is no clear contextual reason for the choice of one color over the other, Athena in her irenic, as opposed to her martial, demeanor, is repeatedly called "blue eyed," and her eyes are also associated with things we think of as blue, such as the sky. By the time Dryden translated Homer, Virgil, and Ovid toward the end of the century, Athena was regularly described as "blue-eyed" in our sense of the term.[24] We can safely assume that for neither Chapman nor

[23]See *Poems of Charles Cotton 1630–1687,* ed. John Beresford (New York: Boni & Liveright, n.d.), p. 124.

[24]See George Chapman, trans., *The Iliads of Homer Prince of Poets* (London: for Nathaniell Butter [1612]), p. 20, line 24; p. 64, line 4; p. 66, line 18; p. 71, line 44; p. 96, line 17; p. 106, line 1, etc.; and Chapman, trans., *Homer's Odysses* (London: for Nathaniell Butter [1614]), p. 4, line 31; p. 7, line 28; p. 83, line 48; p. 209, line 7, etc. Since Dryden never translated a Homeric epic in full, the examples are more scattered, and sometimes from Latin rather than Greek. But see his "Last Parting of Hector and Andromache," (*Examen Poeticum,* 1693), line 19 "blue-ey'd progeny of Jove"; *The Second Book of the Aeneis,* line 243 "blue-ey'd maid"; and *The Twelfth Book of Ovid His Metamorphoses,* line 208 "blue-ey'd maid"; all cited from *The Poetical Works of Dryden,* ed. George R. Noyes, new revised and enlarged edition (Cambridge, Massachusetts: The Riverside Press, 1950).

Dryden did calling the virgin goddess "blue-eyed" connote that she had bleary eyes "ringed in blue, as in pregnancy."

We have turned up a number of alternative possibilities for reading Shakespeare's description of Sycorax. Her eyes may have been "blue" in the popular sense of rimmed with blue or black, but there is at least the possibility that Prospero's brief and fragmentary description of the witch can be read in terms of the Petrarchanists' mock blazon: at the time that she was exiled to the island, she had the blue eyes of a Petrarchan heroine but was (monstrously) pregnant. Can we imagine that at the time of her exile, as opposed to the time of her death, she may have been physically attractive rather than repulsive, that she may have radiated an aura of eroticism? Interestingly enough, eighteenth- and nineteenth-century adaptations of the play regularly retain the description of Sycorax as "blue-eyed," even though by those periods the phrase had lost the ambiguity of its earlier meaning. In Restoration adaptations of *The Tempest,* one of which survived on stage until the early nineteenth century, Sycorax is regularly brought to life as a character on stage — Caliban's sister, daughter of his blue-eyed mother. The Restoration stage Sycorax is comically loathsome but sexually available — perhaps like her mother?[25] The witch's sexuality seems to have been a more acceptable subject for Restoration and eighteenth-century audiences than for their Victorian descendants. At least one adaptation makes Sycorax the subject of a mock blazon like Sidney's on Mopsa.[26] In such an eroticized conceptualization of the witch, "blue-eyed" might well mean "blue-eyed."

Or, alternatively, the "blue-eyed" Sycorax could be associated through her exotic eye color with the blue-eyed Athena as popularized by Chapman, much in the way that the play appropriates for Prospero's own magic spells some of the incantatory language of the Ovidian witch Medea. As Orgel's edition has recently emphasized, Prospero's magic has not always been envisioned as benign before our own century: on the eighteenth-century stage, in particular, it carried sinister overtones of black magic, and Prospero's spirits were sometimes

---

[25]See in particular John Dryden, *The Tempest, or The Enchanted Island. A Comedy* (London: for Henry Herringman, 1670), available in George Robert Guffey's collection of facsimile editions, *After* The Tempest (Los Angeles: William Andrews Clark Memorial Library, 1969).

[26]See T[homas] Duffett, *The Mock-Tempest or The Enchanted Castle* (London: for William Cademan, 1675), p. 52. This play is also available in the Guffey facsimile edition.

referred to as "devils."[27] For both Prospero and Sycorax, the play's surface moral valuation of an enchanter is complicated by resonances that contradict the superficial impression. The eyes of Sycorax, like the charms of Prospero, eerily reverberate with their supposed moral opposites, and the play's many Virgilian echoes facilitate a contextualization of "blue eyes" in terms of classical epic tradition rather than in terms of the native English tradition. To associate Sycorax's mysterious eye color with the uncanny power and attributes of a goddess rather than with the debility of pregnancy is to achieve rather a different perspective on her nature and activities, and on those of her inheritor, Caliban. It is also to adopt a reading of the "hag" that is far from the one promulgated by Prospero.

All of Shakespeare's linkings of "blue" with eyes are difficult cruxes, and we will never know certainly what he "meant." Nor, if we wish to operate within a traditional intentionalist scheme of explanation, can we expect that Shakespeare was utterly consistent in his conceptualization of "blue eyes." But even if we were able (by some miracle) to establish that chimerical entity, the meaning of the passage as the author intended it, we would still be left with the strong likelihood that in Shakespeare's culture, the phrase "blue-eyed" was highly ambiguous and likely to be understood differently by different segments of his audience, depending on their social class, education, and life experience. *The Tempest* is a play that dramatizes a series of encounters between Europeans and denizens of a strange island that appears alien to the Europeans. It was written at a time when similar Europeans were embarked on actual voyages of discovery, and beginning to confront racial and cultural difference in an unprecedentedly radical form through their encounters with natives of the New World. What greater likelihood than that the play itself should record a sense of dissonance, even shock, over the difficulty of using physical characteristics to separate the cultural "self" from the "other"?

How, then, should the "blue-eyed hag" be explicated in our modern editions? Our investigation has been inconclusive in that it has not allowed us to settle on any single eye color or condition as properly glossing the phrase, but it has been highly conclusive about the suspect origins of the standard emendation. If the edition's format

---

[27]Orgel (n. 12), pp. 72, 189–90. On the play's classical echoes, see also Donna B. Hamilton, *Virgil and* The Tempest: *The Politics of Imitation* (Columbus: Ohio State University Press, 1990).

allows only very brief indications of meaning, I would suggest that the phrase is best left unglossed, rather than glossed in a way that replicates nineteenth-century cultural assumptions and removes too much of its Renaissance range of signification. In an edition permitting more copious annotation, however, the phrase should be annotated with due respect to the broad perspective of meanings "blue-eyed" could have carried in early modern culture; the highly restrictive interpretation of "with dark circles about the eyes as a result of pregnancy" should be offered to readers only as one possibility among others. In thinking about Shakespeare's "blue-eyed hag," we need to remember that the whole rickety twentieth-century superstructure of historical investigation of "blue eyes" was reared on a base of nineteenth-century assumptions about what was acceptably English as opposed to unacceptably alien and threatening. To unedit the phrase "blue-eyed hag" is to cast off a set of strict cultural delimitations by which the witch has been kept under control in modern editions of *The Tempest*. It is to declare a preference for variability over fixity of meaning. It is to open the play once more to an unsettling, polysemous menace that Prospero and modern editors have worked very hard to contain.

The Challenge of Postcolonial Criticism

As we noted in our last section, though the New Critical reading of *The Tempest* by Reuben Brower differs from the traditional historical reading by Frank Kermode, both critics agree that the play is a fully unified work of art. Indeed, going back to Aristotle and the Greeks, it has usually been assumed that formal and thematic *unity* is a fundamental criterion of artistic excellence, and a central aim of critics has been to demonstrate how this unity is achieved in a given work of art. The critics in this section, however, who are influenced by postmodern psychoanalytic and social theory, argue that *The Tempest* — and, indeed, all texts and human beings themselves — are fundamentally disunified and contradictory.

The essays by Paul Brown and by Francis Barker and Peter Hulme both argue that Shakespeare tries to tell a unified story in *The Tempest* but ultimately fails to do so. Shakespeare tries to resolve the conflict between the different "stories" of the action — and of European colonialism — that come from different characters in the play. On the one hand, we have Prospero's story, given largely in his account to Miranda in act 1, scene 2, of the usurpation by Antonio of his dukedom and his consequent banishment to the island. On the other hand, we have the very different and conflicting story told by Caliban in the same scene, in which Prospero is the usurper in his dispossession and enslavement of Caliban.

Brown and Barker and Hulme maintain that Prospero's version of the story echoes the official defense of colonial rule assumed by cultivated European society, whereas Caliban's opposing version of the story radically challenges the legitimacy of European rule over natives like himself. According to these postcolonial readings, then, *The Tempest* (in Brown's words) seeks "to harmonize" these clashing stories and thereby to "transcend irreconcilable contradictions" largely by giving Prospero's story the last word at the end of the play and condemning Caliban to shame and humiliation. Yet the play, in Brown's words again, "ultimately fails to deliver that containment and instead may be seen to foreground precisely those problems which it works to efface or overcome" (p. 269 in this volume).

Since Barker and Hulme's essay can be difficult for readers new to the world of literary criticism, we would like to highlight and further emphasize some of its distinctive elements. Barker and Hulme resemble earlier historical critics like Kermode and E. M. W. Tillyard (see pp. 215 and 168) who argue that *The Tempest* — and by extension any literary work or cultural product — cannot be understood unless we temporarily set aside our modern assumptions and reconstruct the contemporary assumptions relevant to that cultural product. For both Kermode and Tillyard, the assumptions relevant to *The Tempest* constitute a vision of a clear cosmic order in which every being should stay in its naturally assigned place. Barker and Hulme depart from this earlier historical approach in two significant ways. First, Barker and Hulme — like both Ronald Takaki (see p. 180) and Leah Marcus (see p. 244) — see the culture and outlook of the Elizabethan period not as unified and completely coherent, but as deeply riven by clashes of belief and power. Second, whereas Tillyard and Kermode take the Elizabethan outlook at face value and therefore do not challenge its values, Barker and Hulme view that outlook from a critical distance informed by their own contemporary populist and prodemocratic (and thus pro-Caliban) perspective.

More specifically, Barker and Hulme's key move in their analysis of the play is to separate Prospero's own view of his legitimacy and right to rule from the play's view of them. That is, they establish a distance between Prospero and his role as orchestrator of events in the play, especially events involving Caliban, and the play's attitudes toward the events and characters. As they put it, "Prospero's play and *The Tempest* are not necessarily the same thing" (p. 301). Thus, when Barker and Hulme analyze Prospero's interruption of his masque in act 4, they note that his reaction to Caliban's rebellion seems over-the-top, far in excess of the actual threat that Caliban, with his buffoonishly ineffectual allies Stephano and Trinculo, presents to Prospero's power. Barker and Hulme read Prospero's strange overreaction as the play's way of marking his — and by extension the dominant order's — profound discomfort over having usurped Caliban's position on the island.

Barker and Hulme build on their distinction between Prospero's disapproval of Caliban's rebellion and the play's more conflicted attitude toward it by moving from their description of the values of Shakespeare's culture represented by the play to their judgment of those values from their own modern perspective. Barker and Hulme's prodemocratic perspective emerges as they argue that the play, though sometimes critical of Prospero, is ultimately in the final scene complicit with his power and his view of Caliban. Though the play sometimes gives Caliban's rebellion an eloquent voice, it does not invite us to take that rebellion seriously but instead relegates it to a comic subplot. They suggest that this uneasy formal resolution of the conflict that reaffirms Prospero's right to rule Caliban is "symptomatic of the text's own anxiety about the threat posed to its decorum by its New World materials" (p. 305).

Postcolonial readings of *The Tempest* such as Brown's and Barker and Hulme's have led many readers — and stage directors — to see Caliban in a new and more sympathetic light as a victim of oppression and an exemplar of revolutionary consciousness. This view of Caliban has begun to influence the way the part is acted and performed, and in some cases has even inspired the rewriting of the play itself. Our final selection here is an excerpt from one such rewriting, by the Martinique playwright Aimé Césaire, an exponent during the 1960s of the theory of "Negritude" or black cultural nationalism. Whether Césaire's *A Tempest* represents a reversal of the play's original intention or simply draws out implications that are latent but not fully developed in the original would be a ripe topic for debate.

PAUL BROWN

"This Thing of Darkness I Acknowledge Mine": *The Tempest* and the Discourse of Colonialism

Paul Brown wrote his doctoral thesis at the University of Sussex. The selection reprinted in this volume is a chapter from that thesis, which appeared in the controversial anthology *Political Shakespeare: New Essays in Cultural Materialism* (1985) edited by Jonathan Dollimore and Alan Sinfield. Paul Brown has since left the academy and resumed an earlier career in banking and finance.

It has long been recognized that *The Tempest* bears traces of the contemporary British investment in colonial expansion. Attention has been drawn to Shakespeare's patronal relations with prominent members of the Virginia Company and to the circumstances of the play's initial production at the expansionist Jacobean court in 1611 and 1612–13. Borrowings from a traditional and classical stock of exotic stereotypes, ranging from the wild man, the savage, and the masterless man to the tropology of the pastoral *locus amoenus* and the wilderness, have been noted. Semi-quotations from contemporary propagandist pamphlets and Montaigne's essay on cannibals have been painstakingly logged.[1] However, a sustained historical and theoretical analysis of the play's involvement in the colonialist project has yet to be undertaken.[2] This chapter seeks to demonstrate that *The Tempest* is not simply a reflection of colonialist practices but an intervention in an ambivalent and even contradictory discourse.[3] This intervention takes the form of a

[1] Such scholarship is summarized in Frank Kermode's Introduction to his edition of William Shakespeare, *The Tempest* (London: Methuen, 6th ed., corrected, 1964), *passim*.

[2] Some of the major incursions into this field are to be found in the notes below. At a late stage in the production of this paper I learnt of Peter Hulme's and Francis Barker's collaboration on an analysis of *The Tempest* in the forthcoming *Alternative Shakespeares,* ed. John Drakakis (London: Methuen, 1985) [reprinted in this volume, p. 292]. I was very pleased to see a draft of this important intervention which, unfortunately, I have not space to comment fully upon here. However, I hope I have begun to answer their call for a historical "con-textual" analysis of the play.

[3] By "discourse" I refer to a domain or field of linguistic strategies operating within particular areas of social practice to effect knowledge and pleasure, being produced by and reproducing or reworking power relations between classes, genders, and cultures.

powerful and pleasurable narrative which seeks at once to harmonize disjunction, to transcend irreconcilable contradictions, and to mystify the political conditions which demand colonialist discourse. Yet the narrative ultimately fails to deliver that containment and instead may be seen to foreground precisely those problems which it works to efface or overcome. The result is a radically ambivalent text which exemplifies not some *timeless* contradiction internal to the discourse by which it inexorably undermines or deconstructs its "official" pronouncements, but a moment of *historical* crisis. This crisis is the struggle to produce a coherent discourse adequate to the complex requirements of British colonialism in its initial phase. Since accounts of the miraculous survival of members of the company of the *Sea Adventure,* wrecked off Bermuda in 1609, are said to have provided Shakespeare with an immediate source for his production, let an incident in the later life of one of those survivors serve as a ground for this analysis.

In 1614 John Rolfe, a Virginia planter, wrote a letter seeking the Governor's blessing for his proposed marriage with Pocahontas, abducted daughter of Powhatan, chief-of-chiefs. This remarkable document announces a victory for the colonialist project, confirming Rolfe in the position of colonizer and Pocahontas in the position of a savage other. The letter is an exposure of Rolfe's inner motives to public scrutiny, a production of his civilized "self" as a text to be read by his superiors, that is, his Governor and his God. What lurks in Rolfe's "secret bosome" is a desire for a savage female. He has had "to strive with all my power of body and minde, in the undertaking of so mightie a matter, no way led (so farre forth as mans weaknesse may permit) with the unbridled desire of carnall affection: but for the good of this plantation, for the honour of our countrie, for the glory of God, for my own salvation, and for the converting to the true knowledge of God and Jesus Christ, an unbeleeving creature, namely Pokahuntas."[4] As the syntax of the sentence indicates, the whole struggle, fought on the grounds of psychic order, social cohesion, national destiny, theological mission, redemption of the sinner, and the conversion of the pagan, is conducted in relation to the female body. "Carnall affection" would appear, despite Rolfe's disavowal, to have been a force which might disrupt commitments to conscience, Governor, and God.

[4]The text is reproduced in Warren M. Billings, ed., *The Old Dominion in the Seventeenth Century: A Documentary History of Virginia* (Chapel Hill: University of North Carolina Press, 1975), pp. 216–19.

Pocahontas had posed a problem that was "so intricate a laborinth, that I was even awearied to unwinde my selfe thereout." Yet whether good or evil, Pocahontas cannot fail to operate as a sign of Rolfe's election, since if reformable, she is the space to be filled with the saintly seed of civility, if obdurately irreformable, she assures the godliness of him who is called to trial (the whole ethos of the godly community in the wilderness depended upon such proximity and exposure to evil). Rolfe's supposedly problematic letter may therefore be said to *produce* Pocahontas as an other in such a way that she will always affirm Rolfe's sense of godly duty and thus confirm him as a truly civil subject.

Inexorably, the text moves from the possible beleaguerments of carnality — variously constituted as the threat of the tempting wilderness, the charge that Rolfe's own interests in this matter are purely sexual, and the possible detraction of "depravers and turbulent spirits" within the colony — towards a more positive presentation. Now the carnal affection which might fracture Rolfe's sense of duty becomes re-encoded as a vital part of God's commandments: "why was I created? If not for transitory pleasures and worldly vanities, but to labour in the Lord's vineyard, there to sow and plant, to nourish and increase the fruites thereof, daily adding with the good husbandman in the Gospell, somewhat to the tallent, that in the end the fruites may be reaped, to the comfort of the laborer in this life, and his salvation in the world to come?" Given this imperative, mutual sexual desire, including the female's "own inticements," can be admitted. Now it would be unmasterly not to desire her, as husbandman. The other incites the godly project: the godly project is embodied in the other. With the word thus made flesh and with Rolfe's self-acquittal in the court of conscience, all that remains to be achieved is the reorientation of those potential detractors into public witnesses of Rolfe's heroism, that "all the world may truly say: this is the work of God, and it is marvelous in our eies."

The threats of disruption to Rolfe's servitude to conscience, Governor and God have thus become the site of the affirmation of psychic, social, and cosmic order. The encounter with the savage other serves to confirm the civil subject in that self-knowledge which ensures self-mastery. Of his thoughts and desires he can say: "I know them all, and have not rashly overslipped any." The letter, then, rehearses the power of the civil subject to maintain self-control and to bring the other into his service, even as it refers to a desire which might undermine that mastery.

After his initial calls for Rolfe to be denounced as a traitor, James I allowed the "princess," newly christened "Lady Rebecca," into court as visible evidence of the power of civility to transform the other.

Pocahontas was to die in England a nine day wonder; Rolfe returned to his tobacco plantation, to be killed in the great uprising of the Indians in 1622. The Pocahontas myth was only beginning, however.[5]

Even this partial analysis of one aspect of such myth-making serves to demonstrate the characteristic operations of the discourse of colonialism. This complex discourse can be seen to have operated in two main areas: they may be called "masterlessness" and "savagism." Masterlessness analyzes wandering or unfixed and unsupervised elements located in the internal margins of civil society (in the above example, Rolfe's subjective desire and potential detractors within the colony). Savagism probes and categorizes alien cultures on the external margins of expanding civil power (in the same example, the Amerindian cultures of Virginia). At the same time as they serve to define the other, such discursive practices refer back to those conditions which constitute civility itself. Masterlessness reveals the mastered (submissive, observed, supervised, deferential) and masterful (powerful, observing, supervising, teleological) nature of civil society. Savagism (a-sociality and untrammelled libidinality) reveals the necessity of psychic and institutional order and direction in the civil regime. In practice these two concepts are intertwined and mutually reinforcing. Together they constitute a powerful discourse in which the non-civil is represented to the civil subject to produce for Rolfe a "laborinth" out of which, like Theseus escaping from the Minotaur's lair, he is to "unwinde" his "selfe."

That such an encounter of the civil and non-civil should be couched in terms of the promulgation/resistance of fulfilling/destructive sexual desire, as it is in Rolfe's case, deserves careful attention, as this strategy is common in colonialist discourse. Such tropes as that of the colonizer as husbandman making the land fruitful, or of the wilderness offering a dangerous libidinal attraction to the struggling saint, are ubiquitous. The discourse of sexuality in fact offers the crucial nexus for the various domains of colonialist discourse which I have schematized above. Rolfe's letter reorients potentially truant sexual desire within the confines of a duly ordered and supervised civil relationship. *The Tempest* represents a politicization of what for Rolfe is experienced as primarily a crisis of his individual subjectivity. For example, the proof of Prospero's power to order and supervise his little colony is manifested in his capacity to control not *his,* but his *subjects'* sexuality, particularly that of his slave and his daughter. Rolfe's personal triumph of reason over passion

---

[5]See Grace Steele Woodward, *Pocahontas* (Norman: University of Oklahoma Press, 1969), especially pp. 153–89.

or soul over body is repeated publicly as Prospero's triumphant ordering of potentially truant or subversive desires in his body politic. Similarly, Prospero's reintegration into the political world of Milan and
Naples is represented, in Prospero's narrative, as an elaborate courtship,
a series of strategic maneuvers with political as well as "loving" intentions and effects. This will be examined further in due course. For the
moment I am simply seeking to show connection between a class discourse (masterlessness), a race discourse (savagism), and a courtly and
politicized discourse on sexuality. This characteristically produces an
encounter with the other involving the colonizer's attempts to dominate, restrict, and exploit the other even as that other offers allurements
which might erode the order obtaining within the civil subject or the
body politic. This encounter is truly a labyrinthine situation, offering
the affirmation or *ravelling up* of the civil subject even as it raises the
possibility of its undoing, its erosion, its *unravelling*.[6] A brief survey of
British colonial operations will help us to establish a network of relations or discursive matrix *within and against which* an analysis of *The
Tempest* becomes possible.

Geographically, the discourse operated upon the various domains of
British world influence, which may be discerned roughly, in the terms
of Immanuel Wallerstein, as the "core," "semiperiphery" and "periphery."[7] Colonialism therefore comprises the expansion of royal hegemony in the English-Welsh mainland (the internal colonialism of the
core), the extension of British influence in the semiperiphery of Ireland,
and the diffuse range of British interests in the extreme periphery of the
New World. Each expansive thrust extended British power beyond
existing spheres of influence into new margins. In the core, these areas
included the North, Wales, and other "dark corners" such as woods,
wastes, and suburbs. In the semiperiphery, the Pale around Dublin was
extended and other areas subdued and settled. In America, official and
unofficial excursions were made into "virgin" territory. I have given
one example of the production of an American other; the production of
core and Irish others will exemplify the enormous scope of contemporary colonialist discourse.

In his "archaeology" of the wild man type, Hayden White discusses
the threat to civil society posed by the very proximity of anti-social
man: "he is just out of sight, over the horizon, in the nearby forest,

---

[6]Actually "ravelling" is a radically ambivalent term, meaning both to entangle and
disentangle. It has peculiar descriptive relevance for my analysis of *The Tempest*.

[7]See Immanuel Wallerstein, *The Modern World System: vol. I* (New York: Academic
Press, 1974), ch. 2, *passim*.

desert, mountains, or hills. He sleeps in crevices, under great trees, or in the caves of wild animals."[8] Many of these characteristics are shared by the more socially specific production of the "masterless man," the ungoverned and unsupervised man without the restraining resources of social organization, an embodiment of directionless and indiscriminate desire.[9] Masterless types were discerned in royal proclamations to exist in the very suburbs of the capital.[10] These and other texts produce a counter-culture within the margins of civility, living in disorder, requiring surveillance, classification, expulsion, and punishment. A typical example is Richard Johnson's *Look Upon Me London* (1613) in which warnings against the city's many "alectives to unthriftinesse" are given. To counter such traps for the ingenuous sons of the gentry, Johnson produces a taxonomy of bad houses, hierarchically arranged according to the social standing of their clientele, of which the worst are "out of the common walkes of the magistrates."[11] These are "privy houses," privy in that they are hidden and secret and also in that they attract the dirt or excremental elements of the body politic. Such dirt is continually viewed as a dire threat to civil order in this literature. Johnson specifically warns that "if the shifters in, and within the level of London, were truly mustered, I dare boldly say they would amaze a good army" (20). The masterless are, here, produced as an other, that "many-headed multitude" common in such writing.[12]

This other is a threat around which the governing classes might mobilize, that is, around which they might recognize their common class position, as governors, over and against the otherwise ungoverned and dangerous multitudes. In *The Tempest* Stephano the "drunken butler" and the "jester" Trinculo obviously represent such masterless men,

---

[8]Hayden White, "The Forms of Wildness: Archaeology of an Idea," in Edward Dudley and Maximillian Novak, eds., *The Wild Man Within: An Image in Western Thought from the Renaissance to Romanticism* (Pittsburgh University Press, 1972), pp. 20–21.

[9]On the masterless classes see particularly Christopher Hill, *The World Turned Upside Down* (1972; rpt. Harmondsworth: Penguin, 1975), ch. 3, *passim*.

[10]See Paul L. Hughes and James F. Larkin, ed., *Tudor Royal Proclamations* (New Haven: Yale University Press, 1969), vol. II, no. 622, and vol. III, nos. 762 and 809, for examples.

[11]Richard Johnson, "Look Upon Me London . . ." in J. Payne Collier, ed., *Illustrations of Early English Popular Literature* (1863; rpt. New York: Benjamin Blom, 1966), part 7, p. 19. Jonathan Dollimore, above p. 76, quotes a remarkably similar phrase in George Whetstone's *Mirror for Magistrates,* which is undoubtedly the most important immediate source for Johnson's plagiarism and serves to underline the chronic ubiquity of such a trope.

[12]See Christopher Hill, "The Many-Headed Monster in Late Tudor and Early Stuart Political Thinking," in Charles H. Carter, ed., *From the Renaissance to the Counter-Reformation* (New York: Random House, 1965), pp. 296–324.

whose alliance with the savage Caliban provides an antitype of order, issuing in a revolt requiring chastisement and ridicule. The assembled aristocrats in the play, and perhaps in the original courtly audiences, come to recognize in these figures their own common identity — and the necessity for a solidarity among the ruling class in face of such a threat. This solidarity must take priority over any internecine struggles; the masterless therefore function to bind the rulers together in hegemony. They were produced as a counter-order, sometimes classified according to rigid hierarchies of villainy in some demonic parody of good order,[13] sometimes viewed as a reserve army of potential recruits for rebellion, sometimes offered as a mere negative principle, the simple absence of the requirements of civility, attracting the sons of the gentry through its very spaciousness, irresponsibility, and dirtiness.

Johnson's text produces a complex pleasure beyond the simple production of an instrumental knowledge of the masterless other. This knowledge is certainly offered for the services of magistracy and no doubt produces the antitype by which good order might be defined. Yet this moral and serviceable discourse displays in its descriptive richness precisely the intense and voyeuristic fascination for the other which it warns the gentry against. The text ostensibly avoids the taint of voyeurism by declaring that since this probing and exposing of dirt is required for the sober gaze of magistracy, a certain specular pleasure may be allowed. Again, at least officially, a potentially disruptive desire provoked by the "alective" other of masterlessness is channelled into positive civil service. This encoding of pleasure within the production of useful knowledge for the advantage of civil power is specifically described by Francis Bacon in his essay "Of Truth" as an erotic and courtly activity: the pursuit of knowledge is a "love-making or wooing."[14] Bacon implicitly offers an ideal of Renaissance sovereignty which can unite what Foucault terms "power-knowledge-pleasure."[15] Here pleasure is not simply disruptive, something produced by the other to deform or disturb the civil subject; it is a vital adjunct to power, a utilization of the potentially disruptive to further the workings of power. In courtly fictions we can see this movement in operation: the other is incorporated into the service of sovereignty by reorienting *its* desires.

[13]See for example the collection of A. V. Judges, ed., *The Elizabethan Underworld* (1930; rpt. London: Routledge, 1965).

[14]In Francis Bacon, *Essays (1625),* ed. Michael Hawkins (London: Dent, 1973), p. 4.

[15]See the theorization of power–knowledge–pleasure in Michel Foucault, *The History of Sexuality: vol. I: An Introduction,* trans. Robert Hurley (Harmondsworth: Penguin, 1981), *passim.*

Such fictions include celebrations which center upon the figure of the good sovereign. In these, the mere presence of the royal personage and the power of the royal gaze are able to transmute hitherto recalcitrant elements of the body politic, engendering in the place of disorderly passion a desire for service that is akin to an erotic courtship. In progresses, processions, and masques such powers were continually complimented. In 1575, for example, at Kenilworth, Elizabeth I was confronted by an "Hombre Salvagio." In dangerous marginal space, beyond the confines of the great house, at the edge of the wild woods, at a most dangerous hour (nine o'clock in the evening), the Virgin Queen encountered the very emblem of marginality. But at this moment of maximum threat the wild man is metamorphosed into her eloquent and loving subject. He says:

> O queen, I must confesse it is not without cause
> These civile people so rejoice, that you should give them lawes.
> Since I, which live at large, a wilde and savage man,
> And have ronne out a wilfull race, since first my life began,
> Do here submit my selfe, beseeching yow to serve.[16]

The Hombre's entry into a loving relationship with Elizabeth is also his entry into interpersonal language (he has hitherto only spoken to his echo) and into subjection to a lawful sovereign: his very capacity to represent himself as "I" is in the gift of the sovereign. She confers on him the status of a linguistic and a legal subject, he now operates in a courtly idiom and in the "sentence" of the sovereign law.[17] Such taming of the wild man by a courtly virgin is a ubiquitous trope in medieval and Renaissance literature, as Richard Bernheimer has shown.[18] It serves as an emblem of courtly power, of the capacity to reorient masterlessness and savagism into service without recourse to the naked exercise of

[16]In John Nichols, ed., *The Progresses and Public Processions of Queen Elizabeth* (1823; rpt. New York: Burt Franklin, 1966), vol. I, pp. 436–38.

[17]On the assimilation of the language of the other for the service of colonialism see Stephen J. Greenblatt, "Learning to Curse: Aspects of Linguistic Colonialism in the Sixteenth Century," in Fredi Chiapelli, ed., *First Images of America: The Impact of the New World on the Old* (Berkeley and Los Angeles: University of California Press, 1970), pp. 561–80. This article and that of Peter Hulme, "Hurricanes in the Caribbees: The Constitution of the Discourse of English Colonialism," in Francis Barker *et al.*, eds., *Literature and Power in the Seventeenth Century: Proceedings of the Essex Conference on the Sociology of Literature, July 1980* (Colchester: University of Essex, 1981), pp. 55–83, offer important commentary on Caliban and civil language.

[18]Richard Bernheimer, *Wild Men in the Middle Ages: A Study in Art, Sentiment and Demonology* (1952; rpt. New York: Octagon Press, 1970), pp. 136–55.

coercive power. This tropology is of great importance in the delineation of the Miranda–Caliban relationship, as I shall show later.

The discourse of masterlessness was embodied also in proclamations and statutes requiring that the bodies of vagrant classes, for example, should be modified.[19] Those condemned as persistent vagrants could literally be marked (whipped, bored, branded) with public signs announcing their adulteration, the hallmark of vice. Alternatively they could suffer the discipline of the work-house or the Bridewell. Yet no apparatus seemed sufficient to keep their numbers down. The constant vilification and punishment of those designated masterless by the ruling classes was not simply a strategy designed to legitimate civil rule: it also evidences a genuine anxiety. This took several forms: a real fear of the power of the governed classes should they mobilize against their betters; a complex displacement of the fear of aristocratic revolt on to the already vilified; a realization that the increasing numbers of mobile classes evidenced a fundamental social change and a great threat to traditional modes of deference; and, finally, perhaps, a recognition of the restrictive nature of that deference society registered precisely in the continuous fascination for the disorderly other.

The thrust into Ireland from the 1530s sought to consolidate and expand British political control and economic exploitation of a strategic marginal area previously only partially under British authority.[20] D. B. Quinn has shown that the major policies of this expansion included plantation of British settlements in key areas, the establishment of a docile landed elite, the fossilization of the social order in areas under British control, the conversion of Gaelic customs into their "civil" counterparts, and the introduction of English as the sole official language.[21] These policies were exercised partly through a vast discursive production of Ireland and the Irish. The virtuous and vicious potentialities that were attributed to Pocahontas predominate in such discourse. Ireland was therefore a savage land that might yet be made to flow with milk and honey like a new Canaan. Similarly the Irish were seen as both savage Gaels and lapsed civil subjects. This arose out of

---

[19]For a listing of the acts relating to vagrancy see Ken Powell and Chris Cook, *English Historical Facts: 1485–1603* (London: Macmillan, 1977), pp. 56–58.

[20]For a short account of this bloody history see Grenfell Morton, *Elizabethan Ireland* (London: Longmans, 1971), *passim*.

[21]See David Beers Quinn, *The Elizabethans and the Irish* (Ithaca: Cornell University Press, 1966), especially ch. 10; and Michael Hechter, *Internal Colonialism: The Celtic Fringe in British Colonial Development 1536–1966* (London: Routledge and Kegan Paul, 1975), especially part 2.

historic claims that the land was *both* a feudal fief under British lordship (then, under the Tudors, under direct British sovereignty), whose truant subjects needed reordering and pacification *and* also a colony, where the savage other needed to be civilized, conquered, dispossessed.[22] The discourse afforded a flexible ensemble to be mobilized in the service of the varying fortune of the British in their semiperiphery.

In this highly complex discourse an "elementary ethnology" was formulated in which the various cultures of Ireland might be examined, and evidence gathered to show their inferiority to civility even as their potential for exploitation was assessed (Quinn 20). As with the Negro or Amerindian, the Irish might be constituted as bestial or only marginally human and, as such, totally irreformable. For example, in 1594 Dawtrey drew upon a whole stock of commonplaces to give his opinion of the possibility of change in the Irish: "an ape will be an ape though he were clad in cloth of gold" (quoted in Quinn 36–37). It should be noted that Stephano's and Trinculo's masterless aping of the aristocrats in 4.1, where they steal rich clothes off a line, bears the weight of this stereotypicality — and their subsequent punishment, being hunted with dogs, draws full attention to their bestiality.

Even if granted human status, Gaelic modes of social behavior were viewed as the antithesis of civil codes. In Spenser's account of booleying (the seasonal migration of livestock and owners to summer pasture), this wandering and unsupervised operation enables its practioners to "grow thereby the more barbarous and live more licentiously than they could in towns, . . . for there they think themselves half exempted from law and obedience, and having once tasted freedom do, like a steer that hath long been out of his yoke, grudge and repine ever after to come under rule again."[23] Barbarity is opposed to the life of the town or *polis,* and the booleyers evade the law, conferring upon themselves the status of truants or outlaws — masterless men. Each social relegation marks the Irish off again as beast-like, requiring the management of the British husbandman.

Within this general delineation of masterless barbarity, particular classes of footloose Irish were specifically targeted, especially jesters

---

[22]Hence the discourses regarding the Irish and the Amerindians were mutually reinforcing. See on this issue Nicholas P. Canny, "The Ideology of English Colonization," *William and Mary Quarterly,* 30 (1973), pp. 575–98. Throughout this section I am indebted to the work of Bernard W. Sheehan, *Savagism and Civility: Indians and Englishmen in Colonial Virginia* (Cambridge University Press, 1980), *passim.*

[23]Edmund Spenser, *A View of the Present State of Ireland* (1596), ed. W. L. Renwick (Oxford: Clarendon Press, 1970), p. 50.

(again notice how Trinculo is related to such exemplary antitypes), "carrows" (or gamblers), wolvine "kernes" (or foot soldiers), and bards. Such figures literally embodied the masterless/savage threat and their suppression became a symbolic statement of British intent for the whole of uncivil Ireland.

More positive versions of Ireland were also produced, particularly in those texts which advocated plantation of the English beyond the Pale. Such versions produce Irish culture, generally, along the lines of a "negative formula," in which the alien is afforded no positive terms but merely displays the absence of those qualities that connote civility, for example, no law, no government, no marriage, no social hierarchy, no visible mode of production, no permanent settlement.[24] Again *The Tempest* is implicated in such a strategy. Gonzalo's description of his imagined island kingdom in 2.1, culled from Montaigne, rehearses the standard formula by which the colonized is denigrated even as it appears to be simply the idle thoughts of a stranded courtier.

At its most optimistic the negative formula represents the other as a natural simplicity against which a jaded civility might be criticized, yet even here the other is produced for the use of civility, to gauge *its* present crisis. Nevertheless, the other's critical function must not be overlooked, as I hope to demonstrate with *The Tempest*. The more typical orientation of the other around the negative formula, however, is the production of a *tabula rasa*. Eden's translation of Peter Martyr's *Decades* (1555) provides a central statement of such a strategy. The Amerindians are "Gentiles" who "may well be likened to a smooth, bare table unpainted, or a white paper unwritten, upon the which you may at the first paint or write what you list, as you cannot upon tables already painted, unless you raze or blot out the first forms."[25] Here the other is an empty space to be inscribed at will by the desire of the colonizer. In some accounts of Ireland the land and the bulk of its peasantry were this unpainted table. Yet contradictorily, for instance in the version of Sir John Davies, before it could be painted at will certain obdurate forms, tyrannical lords, and customs had to be razed.[26]

[24]See Sheehan, ch. 1, *passim*, and Margaret T. Hogden, *Early Anthropology in the Sixteenth and Seventeenth Centuries* (Philadelphia: University of Pennsylvania Press, 1964), *passim*.

[25]Quoted in H. C. Porter, *The Inconstant Savage: Englishmen and the North American Indian* (Duckworth, 1979), p. 28.

[26]Sir John Davies, "A Discovery of the True Causes Why Ireland Was Never Subdued . . . Until the Beginning of His Majesty's Happy Reign," in Henry Morley, ed., *Ireland under Elizabeth and James* (London: George Routledge, 1890), p. 341.

So vacuous or vicious, docile or destructive, such stereotypical production announced the triumph of civility or declared the other's usefulness for its purposes. But a dark countertruth needed to be acknowledged. The inferior culture of the Gaels had absorbed the Old English invaders, as Davies noted with horror: "The English, who hoped to make a perfect conquest of the Irish, were by them perfectly and absolutely conquered" (290). The possibility of "going native" was constantly evidenced in this example, which Davies likened to the vicious transformation of Nebudchadnezzar or the Circean swine (297). The supposed *binary* division of civil and other into virtue/vice, positive/negative, etc., was shown to be erodable as the forces of the subordinate term of the opposition seeped back into the privileged term. The blank spaces of Ireland provided not only an opportunity for the expansion of civility; they were also sites for the possible undoing of civil man, offering a "freedom" (Spenser's term for the avoidance of civility in the quotation above) in which he might lapse into masterlessness and savagism. The same discourse which allows for the transformation of the savage into the civil also raises the possibility of a reverse transformation. As Davies could announce a hope for the homogenization of the Irish into civility "so that we may conceive a hope that the next generation will in tongue and heart and every way else become English" (Davies 335), so Spenser could remark of civil man: "Lord, how quickly doth that country alter men's natures" (51).

Given the importance of the colonization of Ireland for British expansionism, together with its complex discursive formation which I have outlined briefly, it is surprising that such scant attention has been paid to such material in relation to *The Tempest*. I am not suggesting that Irish colonial discourse should be ransacked to find possible sources for some of the play's phraseology. Rather (as Hulme and Barker suggest) we should note a general analogy between text and context; specifically, between Ireland and Prospero's island. They are both marginally situated in semiperipheral areas (Ireland is geographically semiperipheral, its subjects both truant civilians and savages, as Prospero's island is ambiguously placed between American and European discourse). Both places are described as "uninhabited" (that is, connoting the absence of civility) and yet are peopled with a strange admixture of the savage and masterless other, powerfully controlling and malcontentedly lapsed civil subjects. Both locations are subject to powerful organizing narratives which recount the beleaguerments, loss, and recovery — the ravelling and unravelling — of colonizing subjects.

Such discourse provides the richest and the most fraught discussion of colonialism at the moment of the play's inception.

Much of my analysis above has been theoretically informed by Edward Said's account of orientalist discourse.[27] Orientalism is not simply a discourse which produces a certain knowledge of the East, rather it is a "western style for dominating, restructuring and having authority over the Orient" (3). Although it cannot be simply correlated with the process of *material* exploitation of the East, the discourse produces a form of knowledge which is of great utility in aiding this process — serving to define the West as its origin, serving to relegate alien cultures, serving even the voyeuristic and libidinal desire of the western man who is denied such expression elsewhere.

Homi K. Bhabha's recent account of the colonialist stereotype effects a critique of Said, suggesting that even in the stereotype there is something which prevents it from being *totally* useful for the colonizer.[28] Bhabha says the stereotype "connotes rigidity and an unchanging order as well as disorder, degeneracy and demonic repetition" (18). This is to say that at the heart of the stereotype, a discursive strategy designed to locate or "fix" a colonial other in a position of inferiority to the colonizer, the potentiality of a disruptive threat must be admitted. For example, if a stereotype declares the black to be rapacious, then even as it marks him as inferior to the self-controlled white, it announces his power to violate, and thus requires the imposition of restraint if such power is to be curtailed: so the stereotype cannot rest, it is always impelled to *further* action.

To summarize, I have begun to suggest that colonialist discourse voices a demand both for order and disorder, producing a disruptive other in order to assert the superiority of the colonizer. Yet that production is itself evidence of a struggle to restrict the other's disruptiveness to that role. Colonialist discourse does not simply announce a triumph for civility, it must continually *produce* it, and this work involves struggle and risk. It is this complex relation between the intention to produce colonialist stereotypicality, its beleaguerments, and even its possible erosion in the face of the other that I now wish to trace through *The Tempest*.

The play begins in an apparent disruption of that social deference and elemental harmony which characterize the representation of

[27]Edward W. Said, *Orientalism* (London: Routledge, 1978), p. 2.
[28]Homi K. Bhabha, "The Other Question," *Screen* 24, no. 6 (1983), pp. 18–36.

courtly authority in Renaissance dramaturgy. Yet this initial "tempest" becomes retroactively a kind of antimasque or disorderly prelude to the assertion of that courtly authority which was supposedly in jeopardy. From Prospero's initial appearance it becomes clear that disruption was produced to create a series of problems precisely in order to effect their resolution. The dramatic conflict of the opening of the play is to be reordered to declare the mastery of Prospero in being able to initiate and control such dislocation and dispersal. This narrative intention is a correlate of the courtly masque proper, in which, conflict having been eradicated, elaborate and declarative compliment might be made to the supervising sovereign (as in the Hombre Salvagio episode, above). Prospero's problems concerning the maintenance of his power on the island are therefore also problems of representation, of his capacity to "forge" the island in his own image. The production of narrative, in this play, is always related to questions of power.

In his powerful narrative, Prospero interpellates the various listeners — calls to them, as it were, and invites them to recognize themselves as subjects of his discourse, as beneficiaries of his civil largesse. Thus for Miranda he is a strong father who educates and protects her; for Ariel he is a rescuer and taskmaster; for Caliban he is a colonizer whose refused offer of civilization forces him to strict discipline; for the shipwrecked he is a surrogate providence who corrects errant aristocrats and punishes plebeian revolt. Each of these subject positions confirms Prospero as master.

The second scene of the play is an extended demonstration of Prospero's powerful narration as it interpellates Miranda, Ariel, and Caliban. It is recounted as something importantly rescued out of the "dark backward and abysm of time" (1.2.50), a remembrance of things past soon revealed as a mnemonic of power. This is to say, Prospero's narrative demands of its subjects that they should accede to *his* version of the past. For Miranda, Prospero's account of her origins is a tale of the neglect of office, leading to a fraternal usurpation and a banishment, followed by a miraculous landfall on the island. Prospero first tells of his loss of civil power and then of its renewal, in magic, upon the marginal space of the island. This reinvestiture in civil power through the medium of the non-civil is an essentially colonialist discourse. However, the narrative is fraught because it reveals internal contradictions which strain its ostensible project and because it produces the possibility of sites of resistance in the other precisely at the moment when it seeks to impose its captivating power.

In the recitation to Miranda, for example, Prospero is forced to remember his own past *forgetfulness*, since it was his devotion to private study that allowed his unsupervised brother, masterlessly, to seize power. He is forced to recall a division between liberal and stately arts which are ideally united in the princely magus of masquing fiction. However as the recitation continues, this essentially political disjunction becomes simply the pretext or initial disruption that is replaced by a mysterious account of the recovery of civil power, the reunification of the liberal artist and the politic sovereign. It is re-presented as a *felix culpa*, a fortunate fall, in which court intrigue becomes reinscribed in the terms of romance, via a shift from the language of courtiership to that of courtship, to a rhetoric of love and charity.

This is marked by a series of tropes deriving from courtly love conventions, as Kermode notes (18). The deposed duke becomes a helpless exile who cries into the sea, which charitably responds, as does the wind, with pity (148–50). The deposition becomes a "loving wrong" (151) — again the very form of oxymoron is typical of Petrarchan love sonnetry. These romance tropes effect a transition from a discourse of power to one of powerlessness. This mystifies the origin of what is after all a colonialist regime on the island by producing it as the result of charitable acts (by the sea, the wind and the honest courtier, Gonzalo, alike) made out of pity for powerless exiles. Recent important work on pastoral and amatory sonnet sequences has shown how such a rhetoric of love, charity, and romance is always already involved in the mediation of power relations.[29] Prospero's mystifying narrative here has precisely these effects. Further, his scheme for the resumption of his dukedom and his reintegration with the larger political world is also inscribed in such terms, as a courtship of "bountiful Fortune," his "dear lady," or of an auspicious star which "If now I court her not, but omit, my fortunes / Will ever after droop" (178–84). And, of course, a major strategy of this scheme is to engineer another courtship, between Miranda and the son of his old enemy — his daughter having been duly educated for such a role in the enclosed and enchanted space of the island. The

[29]On the relation of courtship and courtiership see Peter Stallybrass and Ann Rosalind Jones, "The Politics of *Astrophil and Stella*," *Studies in English Literature*, 24 (1984), pp. 53–68. On the mediation and effacement of power relations in courtly discourse see Louis A. Montrose, " 'Eliza, Queene of Shepheardes,' and the Pastoral of Power," *English Literary Renaissance*, 10 (1980), pp. 153–82. For a short account of courtly theater see Stephen Orgel, *The Illusion of Power: Political Theatre in the English Renaissance* (Berkeley and Los Angeles: University of California Press, 1975), *passim*.

entire production of the island here, ostensibly an escape or exile from the world of statism, is thoroughly instrumental, even if predicated upon an initial loss of power.

In the same scene Prospero reminds Ariel of his indebtedness to the master, an act of memory which it is necessary to repeat monthly (262–64). This constant reminding operates as a mode of "symbolic violence":[30] What is really at issue is the underlining of a power relation. Ariel is, paradoxically, *bound* in service by this constant reminder of Prospero's gift of *freedom* to him, in releasing him from imprisonment in a tree. That bondage is reinforced by both a promise to repeat the act of release when a period of servitude has expired and a promise to repeat the act of incarceration should service not be forthcoming. In order to do this, Prospero utilizes the previous regime of Sycorax as an evil other. Her black, female magic ostensibly contrasts with that of Prospero in that it is remembered as viciously coercive, yet beneath the apparent voluntarism of the white, male regime lies the threat of precisely this coercion. This tends to produce an identification between the regimes, which is underscored by biographical similarities such as that both rulers are magicians, both have been exiled because of their practices, both have nurtured children on the isle. The most apparent distinction between black and white regimes[31] would seem to be that the latter is simply more powerful and more flexible. Part of its flexibility is its capacity to produce and utilize an other in order to obtain the consent of Ariel to his continued subjugation.

Caliban, on the other hand, is nakedly enslaved to the master. The narrative of 1.2 legitimizes this exercise of power by representing Caliban's resistance to colonization as the obdurate and irresponsible refusal of a simple educative project. This other, the offspring of a witch and a devil, the wild man and savage, the emblem of morphological ambivalence (see Hulme, "Hurricanes in the Caribees," 67ff), was even without language before the arrival of the exiles. It was Miranda, the civil virgin, who, out of pity, taught Caliban to "know thine own meaning" (359). Yet, as with the Hombre Salvagio above, the "gift" of language also inscribes a power relation as the other is hailed and recognizes himself as a linguistic subject of the master language. Caliban's refusal marks him as obdurate yet he must voice this in a curse in the

---

[30]On this concept see Pierre Bourdieu, *Outline of a Theory of Practice*, trans. Richard Nice (Cambridge University Press, 1977), pp. 190–97.

[31]As noted in Leslie A. Fiedler, *The Stranger in Shakespeare* (St. Albans: Paladin, 1974), p. 64.

language of civility, representing himself as a subject of what he so accurately describes as "*your* language" (368, emphasis added). Whatever
Caliban does with this gift announces his capture by it.

Yet within the parameters of this capture Caliban is able to create a
resistance. Ostensibly *produced* as an other to provide the pretext for
the exercise of naked power, he is also a *producer*, provoking reaction in
the master. He does not come when called, which makes Prospero
angry (316–23). Then he greets the colonizers with a curse, provoking
the master to curse in reply, reducing the eloquent master of civil language to the raucous registers of the other (324–33). Third, he ignores
the civil curse and proceeds with his own narrative, in which Prospero
himself is designated as usurping other to Caliban's initial monarchy
and hospitality (333–47). Such discursive strategies show that Caliban
has indeed mastered enough of the lessons of civility to ensure that its
interpellation of him as simply savage, "a born devil, on whose nature /
Nurture can never stick" (4.1.188–89), is inadequate. Paradoxically, it
is the eloquent power of civility which allows him to know his *own*
meaning, offering him a site of resistance even as civility's coercive
capacities finally reduce him to silence (374–77).

The island itself is an "uninhabited" spot, a *tabula rasa* peopled for-
tuitously by the shipwrecked. Two children, Miranda and Caliban, have
been nurtured upon it. Prospero's narrative operates to produce in
them the binary division of the other, into the malleable and the
irreformable, that I have shown to be a major strategy of colonialist discourse. There is Miranda, miraculous courtly lady, virgin prospect (cf.
Virginia itself) and there is Caliban, scrambled "cannibal," savage
incarnate. Presiding over them is the cabalist Prospero, whose function
it is to divide and demarcate these potentialities, arrogating to the male
all that is debased and rapacious, to the female all that is cultured and
needs protection.

Such a division of the "children" is validated in Prospero's narrative
by the memory of Caliban's attempted rape of Miranda (1.2.347–54),
which immediately follows Caliban's own account of his boundless hospitality to the exiles on their arrival (333–47). The issue here is not
whether Caliban is actually a rapist or not, since Caliban accepts the
charge. I am rather concerned with the political effects of this charge at
this moment in the play. The first effect is to circumvent Caliban's version of events by reencoding his boundlessness as rapacity: his inability
to discern a concept of private, bounded property concerning his own
dominions is reinterpreted as a desire to violate the chaste virgin, who
epitomizes courtly property. Second, the capacity to divide and order is

shown to be the prerogative of the courtly ruler alone. Third, the memory legitimizes Prospero's takeover of power.

Such a sexual division of the other into rapist and virgin is common in colonialist discourse. In *The Faerie Queene,* for example, Ireland is presented as both Irene, a courtly virgin, and Grantorto, a rapacious woodkerne from whom the virgin requires protection, thus validating the intervention of the British knight, Artegall, and his killing machine, Talus.[32] Similarly, in Purchas's *Virginia's Verger* of 1625 the uprising of 1622 is shown to be an act of incestuous rape by native sons upon a virgin land, and this declares the rightfulness of the betrothal of that land to duly respectful civil husbandmen, engaged in "presenting her as a chaste virgin to Christ" (see Porter, *The Inconstant Savage,* 480). Miranda is represented as just such a virgin, to be protected from the rapist native and presented to a civil lover, Ferdinand. The "fatherly" power of the colonizer, and his capacity to regulate and utilize the sexuality of his subject "children," is therefore a potent trope as activated in *The Tempest* and again demonstrates the crucial nexus of civil power and sexuality in colonial discourse. The other is here presented to legitimate the seizure of power by civility and to define by antithesis (rape) the proper course of civil courtship — a channelling of desire into a series of formal tasks and maneuvers and, finally, into courtly marriage. Such a virtuous consummation is predicated upon the disruptive potential of carnality, embodied in the rapist other and in the potentially truant desires of the courtly lovers themselves, which Prospero constantly warns them against (as at 4.1.15–23 and 51–54). With little evidence of such truancy, Prospero's repeated warnings reassert his power to regulate sexuality just at the point when such regulatory power is being transferred from father to husband. Yet his continued insistence on the power of desire to disrupt courtly form surely also evidences an unease, an anxiety, about the power of civility to deliver control over a force which it locates both in the other and in the civil subject.

A capacity to divide and demarcate groups of subjects along class lines is also demonstrated. The shipwrecked courtiers are dispersed on the island into two groups, aristocrats and plebians. The usurping "men of sin" in the courtly group are first maddened, then recuperated; the drunken servants, unmastered, are simply punished and held up to ridicule. This division of masterless behavior serves a complex hegemonic function: the unselfmastered aristocrats are reabsorbed, after

---

[32]Edmund Spenser, *The Faerie Queene,* ed. T. P. Roche and C. P. O'Donnell (Harmondsworth: Penguin, 1978), book V, cantos xi–xii, *passim.*

correction, into the governing class, their new solidarity underscored by their collective laughter at the chastened revolting plebians. The class joke acts as a recuperative and defusive strategy which celebrates the renewal of courtly hegemony and displaces its breakdown on to the ludicrous revolt of the masterless.

Such binarism is also apparent in productions such as Ben Jonson's *Irish Masque at Court* (first put on in December, 1613).[33] Here indecorous stage-Irish plebeians are banished from the royal presence, to be replaced with the courtly exemplars of newly-converted Anglo-Irish civility. In this James I's coercive power is celebrated as music. Now Ireland has stooped to "the music of his peace, / She need not with the spheres change harmony." This harmonics of power causes the Irish aristocrats to slough off their former dress and customs to emerge as English court butterflies; the ant-like rabble are precluded from such a metamorphosis.

This last example demonstrates another strategy by which sovereign power might at once be praised and effaced *as power* in colonialist discourse. In this masque, power is represented as an *aesthetic* ordering. This correlates with Prospero's investment in the power of narrative to maintain social control and with *The Tempest's* production of the origins of colonialism through the rhetoric of romance, its representation of colonial power as a gift of freedom or of education, its demonstration of colonialist organization as a "family romance" involving the management and reordering of disruptive desire. The play's observation of the classical unities (of space, time, and action), its use of harmonious music to lead, enchant, relax, restore, its constant reference to the leisured space of pastoral[34] and the dream, all underline this aesthetic and disinterested, harmonious, and non-exploitative representation of power. In a sermon of Richard Crashaw (1610), the latent mechanisms of power which actually promote the metamorphosis of jaded civil subjects is acknowledged: the transplanted, if "subject to some pinching miseries and to a strict form of government and severe discipline, do often become new men, even as it were cast in a new mould" (quoted in Porter 369–70). *The Tempest* is, therefore, fully implicated in the process of "euphemization," the effacement of power — yet, as I have begun to demonstrate, the play also reveals precisely "the strict form of

[33]Ben Jonson, *The Complete Masques,* ed. Stephen Orgel (New Haven: Yale University Press, 1968), pp. 206–12.

[34]For the use of pastoral in colonialist discourse see Howard Mumford Jones, *O Strange New World: American Culture: The Formative Years* (New York: Viking Press, 1964), pp. 185–93.

government" which actually underpins the miraculous narrative of "sea change." The play oscillates uneasily between mystification and revelation and this is crucially demonstrated in the presentation of the plebeian revolt.

The process of euphemization depends upon the rebellious misalliance of Caliban and Stephano and Trinculo being recognized as a kind of antimasque, yet there are features of this representation which disrupt such a recognition. Ostensibly the "low" scenes of the play ape courtly actions and demonstrate the latter's superiority. The initial encounter of the masterless and the savage, for example, is analogous to the encounter between the civil and the savage narrated by Prospero, and to the encounter of the New World virgin and the gallant courtier enacted before the audience. Caliban's hospitality to Prospero is repeated as an act of voluntary subjection to the actually powerless exile, Stephano. This act is a bathetic version of the idealized meeting of civil and savage epitomized in the Hombre Salvagio episode — Caliban misrecognizes *true* sovereignty and gives his fealty rather to a drunken servant. Unlike the immediate recognition of a common courtly bond which Miranda and Ferdinand experience, the savage and the masterless reveal a spontaneous *non-civil* affinity. More locally, as the courtly exiles brought Caliban the gift of language, so the masterless donate "that which will give language to you, cat"— a bottle, the former imposes linguistic capture and restraint, the latter offers release.

Yet the issue is more complex, for what this misalliance mediates, in "low" terms, is precisely a colonizing situation. Only here can the colonizing process be viewed as nakedly avaricious, profiteering, perhaps even pointless (the expense of effort to no end rather than a proper teleological civil investment). Stephano, for example, contemplates taming and exhibiting Caliban for gain (2.2.72–74). Also, the masterless do not lead but are led around by the savage, who must constantly remind them of their rebellious plans (4.1.229–31). This low version of colonialism serves to displace possibly damaging charges which might be levied against properly constituted civil authority on to the already excremental products of civility, the masterless. This allows those charges to be announced and defused, transforming a possible anxiety into pleasure at the ludicrous antics of the low who will, after all, be punished in due course.

This analysis still produces the other as being in the (complex) service of civility, even if the last paragraph suggests that a possible anxiety is being displaced. Yet there is a manifest contradiction in the representation of the misalliance which I have not considered so far: in denigrating the masterless, such scenes foreground more positive qualities in the savage. The banter of the drunkards serves to counterpoint moments of great eloquence in the obdurate slave. Amid all the comic business, Caliban describes the effects of the island music:

> the isle is full of noises,
> Sounds and sweet airs, that give delight, and hurt not.
> Sometimes a thousand twangling instruments
> Will hum about mine ears; and sometimes voices,
> That, if I then had wak'd after long sleep,
> Will make me sleep again: and then, in dreaming,
> The clouds methought would open, and show riches
> Ready to drop upon me: that, when I wak'd,
> I cried to dream again
>
>   (3.2.130–38)

Here the island is seen to operate not for the colonizer but for the colonized. Prospero utilizes music to charm, punish, and restore his various subjects, employing it like James I in a harmonics of power. For Caliban, music provokes a dream wish for the riches which in reality are denied him by colonizing power. There seems to be a quality in the island beyond the requirements of the colonizer's powerful harmonics, a quality existing for itself, which the other may use to resist, if only in dream, the repressive reality which hails him as villain — both a feudalized bonded workhorse and evil incarnate.

This production of a site beyond colonial appropriation can only be represented through colonialist discourse, however, since Caliban's eloquence is after all "your language," the language of the colonizer. Obviously the play itself, heavily invested in colonialist discourse, can only represent this moment of excess through that very discourse: and so the discourse itself may be said to produce this site of resistance. Yet what precisely is at stake here?

The answer I believe is scandalously simple. Caliban's dream is not the *antithesis* but the *apotheosis* of colonialist discourse. If this discourse seeks to efface its own power, then here at last is an eloquent spokesman who is powerless; here such eloquence represents not a desire to control and rule but a fervent wish for release, a desire to escape reality and return to dream. Caliban's production of the island as a pastoral space, separated from the world of power, takes *literally* what the discourse in the hands of a Prospero can only mean *metaphorically*. This is to say, the colonialist project's investment in the processes of euphemization of what are really powerful relations here has produced a utopian moment where powerlessness represents *a desire for powerlessness*. This is the danger that any metaphorical system faces, that vehicle may be taken for tenor and used against the ostensible meanings intended. The play registers, if only momentarily, a radical ambivalence at the heart of colonialist discourse, revealing that it is a site of *struggle* over meaning.

Prospero's narrative can be seen, then, to operate as a reality principle, ordering and correcting the inhabitants of the island, subordinating their discourse to his own. A more potent metaphor, however, might be the concept of dreamwork[35] — that labor undertaken to represent seamlessly and palatably what in reality is a contest between a censorship and a latent drive. The masterful operations of censorship are apparent everywhere in *The Tempest*. In the terminology of the analysis of dreamwork developed by Freud, these political operations may be discerned as displacement (for example, the displacement of the fear of noble insurrection on to the easily defeated misalliance), condensation (the condensation of the whole colonial project into the terms of a patriarchal demarcation of sexuality), symbolization (the emblems of the vanishing banquet, the marriage masque, the discovery of the lovers at chess), and secondary revision (the ravelling up of the narrative dispersal of the storm scene, the imposition of Prospero's memory over that of his subjects, etc.). As I have attempted to show above with specific examples, such operations encode struggle and contradiction even as they, or *because* they, strive to insist on the legitimacy of colonialist narrative.

Further, as this narrative progresses, its master appears more and more to divest himself of the very power he has so relentlessly sought. As Fiedler brilliantly notes, in the courtship game in which Miranda is a pawn, even as Prospero's gameplan succeeds he himself is played out, left without a move as power over his daughter slips away (Fiedler,

[35]On dreamwork see Sigmund Freud, *Introductory Lectures in Psychoanalysis: The Pelican Freud Library Vol. I*, trans. James Strachey, ed. James Strachey and Angela Richards (Harmondsworth: Penguin, 1973), especially chs. 9–11. Stephen Greenblatt notes in his *Renaissance Self-Fashioning: From More to Shakespeare* (University of Chicago Press, 1980), p. 173, that it was Freud who first drew the analogy between the political operations of colonialism and the modes of psychic repression. My use of Freudian terms does not mean that I endorse its ahistorical, Eurocentric, and sexist models of psychical development. However, a materialist criticism deprived of such concepts as displacement and condensation would be seriously impoverished in its analysis of the complex operations of colonialist discourse and its addressing of subjects of its power. This paper attempts to utilize psychoanalytic concepts for a strictly historical analysis of a particular text, foregrounding the representation of the embattled subjectivity of the (white, governing, patriarchal) colonizer.

The Stranger in Shakespeare, 206). So the magus abjures his magic, his major source of coercive power (5.1.33–57). This is ostensibly replaced by civil power as Prospero resorts to his "hat and rapier," twin markers of the governor (the undoffed hat signifying a high status in a deference society, as the rapier signifies the aristocratic right to carry such weaponry). Yet this resumption of power entails the relinquishing of revenge upon the usurpers, an end to the exploitation and punishment of the masterless and the savage, even an exile from the island. Further, he goes home not to resume public duty but to retire and think of death (5.1.310–11). The completion of the colonialist project signals the banishment of its supreme exponent even as his triumph is declared.

Is this final distancing of the master from his narrative an unravelling of his project? Or is this displacement merely the final example of that courtly euphemization of power outlined above? One last example must serve to demonstrate that the "ending" of the play is in fact a struggle between the apotheosis and the aporia of colonialist discourse. The marriage masque of 4.1 demonstrates Prospero's capacity to order native spirits to perform a courtly narrative of his own design. In addition, this production is consented to by the audience of the two courtly lovers, whose pleasure itself shows that they are bound by the narrative. As such, the masque is a model of ideological interpellation, securing chastity, a state which the master continually *demands* of the lovers, through active consent rather than coercive power. Further, Prospero's instructions to his audience before the masque begins implicitly rehearse his ideal subject-audience. "No tongue! All eyes! be silent." Yet the masque is disrupted, as Prospero is drawn back from this moment of the declaration of his triumph into the realm of struggle, for Caliban's plot must be dealt with. Although the plot is allowed for in his timetable (4.1.141–42) and is demonstrably ineffectual, this irruption of the antimasque into the masque proper has a totally disproportionate effect to its actual capacity to seize power. The masque is dispelled and Prospero utters a monologue upon the illusory nature of all representation, even of the world itself (4.1.148–58). Hitherto he has insisted that his narrative be taken as real and powerful — now it is collapsed, along with everything else, into the "stuff" of dreams. The forging of colonialist narrative is, momentarily, revealed as a forgery. Yet, Prospero goes on to meet the threat and triumph over it, thus completing his narrative. What is profoundly ambivalent here is the relation between narrative declaration and dramatic struggle. Prospero requires a struggle with the forces of the other in order to show his power: struggle is therefore the precondition for the announcement of his victory. Yet here the moment of declaration is disrupted as a further contest arises: Prospero must repeat the process of struggle. It is *he* who largely produces the ineffectual challenge as a dire threat. This is to say, the colonialist narrative requires and produces the other — an other which continually destabilizes and disperses the narrative's moment of conviction. The threat must be present to validate colonialist discourse; yet if present it cannot but impel the narrative to further action. The process is interminable. Yet the play has to end.

Given this central ambivalence in the narrative, and given Prospero's problematic relationship to the restitution of civil power, it falls upon the honest old courtier, Gonzalo, actually to announce the closure of the narrative. He confirms that all is restored, including "all of us ourselves / When no man was his own" (5.1.206–13). True civil subjectivity is declared: the encounter with the forces of otherness on the island produces a signal victory. Yet the architect of that victory is to retire and die, his narrative a mere entertainment to while away the last night on the isle, his actor reduced in the epilogue to beg for the release of applause. When apportioning the plebeians to the masters, he assigns Caliban to himself, saying "this thing of darkness I / Acknowledge mine" (5.1.275–76). Even as this powerfully designates the monster as his property, an object for his own utility, a darkness from which he may rescue self-knowledge, there is surely an ironic identification *with* the other here as both become interstitial. Only a displacement of the narrating function from the master to a simpler, declarative civilian courtier can hope to terminate the endless struggle to relate self and other so as to serve the colonialist project. At the "close" of the play, Prospero is in danger of becoming the other to the narrative declaration of his own project, which is precisely the ambivalent position Caliban occupies.

The Tempest, then, declares no all-embracing triumph for colonialism. Rather it serves as a limit text in which the characteristic operations of colonialist discourse may be discerned — as an instrument of exploitation, a register of beleaguerment and a site of radical ambivalence. These operations produce strategies and stereotypes which seek to impose and efface colonialist power; in this text they are also driven into contradiction and disruption. The play's "ending" in renunciation and restoration is only the final ambivalence, being at once the apotheosis, mystification, and potential erosion of the colonialist discourse. If this powerful discourse, thus mediated, is finally reduced to the stuff of dreams, then it is still dreamwork, the site of a struggle for meaning.

My project has been to attempt a repunctuation of the play so that it
may reveal its involvement in colonial practices, speak something of the
ideological contradictions of its *political* unconscious.[36]

[36]The term is that of Fredric Jameson in his *The Political Unconscious: Narrative as a
Socially Symbolic Act* (London: Methuen, 1983), *passim*. This represents the most profound attempt to assimilate psychoanalytic concepts into a materialist account of narrative
production.

I would like to record my deepest thanks to the editors and to Peter Stallybrass, Ann
Jones, Andrew Crozier, Alan Fair, Eric Woods, and especially Barry Taylor for their enormous help in the preparation of this paper. My main debt, as ever, is to Lesly Brown.

FRANCIS BARKER
PETER HULME

Nymphs and Reapers Heavily Vanish:
The Discursive Con-texts of *The Tempest*

Francis Barker (1952–1999) taught at the University of Essex,
England, from 1978 until his sudden death in 1999. His research
included work on early modern culture and on modernism and
postmodernism. He is the author of *Solzhenitsyn: Politics and
Form* (1976), *The Tremulous Private Body: Essays on Subjection*
(1984), and *The Culture of Violence: Essays on Tragedy and History* (1993). He edited *Uses of History: Marxism, Postmodernism
and the Renaissance* (1991), and he coedited with Peter Hulme
and Margaret Iversen *Postmodernism and the Re-Reading of
Modernity* (1991), *Colonial Discourse, Postcolonial Theory* (1994),
and *Cannibalism and the Colonial World* (1998).

Peter Hulme (b. 1948) is professor in the Department of
Literature, Film, and Theatre Studies at the University of Essex,
where he has taught since 1975. He is the author of *Colonial
Encounters: Europe and the Native Caribbean, 1492–1797*
(1986; paperback 1992). In addition to the books he coedited
with Francis Barker and Margaret Iversen mentioned above, he
also coedited *The Tempest and Its Travels* (2000) and *The Cambridge Companion to Travel Writing* (2002). The following
essay appeared in *Alternative Shakespeares* (1985), edited by
John Drakakis.

I

No one who has witnessed the phenomenon of midsummer tourism at Stratford-upon-Avon can fail to be aware of the way in which "Shakespeare" functions today in the construction of an English past: a past which is picturesque, familiar, and untroubled. Modern scholarly editions of Shakespeare, amongst which the Arden is probably the most influential, have seemed to take their distance from such mythologizing by carefully locating the plays against their historical background. Unfortunately such a move always serves, paradoxically, only to highlight in the foregrounded text preoccupations and values which turn out to be not historical at all, but eternal. History is thus recognized and abolished at one and the same time. One of the aims of this essay is to give a closer account of this mystificatory negotiation of "history," along with an examination of the ways in which the relationship between text and historical context can be more adequately formulated. Particular reference will be made to the way in which, in recent years, traditional notions of the historical sources of the text have been challenged by newer analyses which employ such terms as "intertextuality" and "discourse." To illustrate these, a brief exemplary reading will be offered of *The Tempest*. But to begin with, the new analyses themselves need setting in context.

II

The dominant approach within literary study has conceived of the text as autotelic, "an entity which always remains the same from one moment to the next" (Hirsch 46); in other words a text that is fixed in history and, at the same time, curiously free of historical limitation. The text is acknowledged as having been produced at a certain moment in history; but that history itself is reduced to being no more than a background from which the single and irreducible meaning of the text is isolated. The text is designated as the legitimate object of literary criticism, *over against* its contexts, whether they be arrived at through the literary-historical account of the development of particular traditions and genres or, as more frequently happens with Shakespeare's plays, the study of "sources." In either case the text has been separated from a surrounding ambit of other texts over which it is given a special pre-eminence.

In recent years, however, an alternative criticism, often referred to as "structuralist" and "post-structuralist," has sought to displace radically the primacy of the autotelic text by arguing that a text indeed "cannot be limited by or to . . . the originating moment of its production, anchored in the intentionality of its author."[1] For these kinds of criticism exclusive study of the moment of production is defined as narrowly "historicist" and replaced by attention to successive *inscriptions* of a text during the course of its history.[2] And the contextual background — which previously had served merely to highlight the profile of the individual text — gives way to the notion of *intertextuality,* according to which, in keeping with the Saussurean model of language, no text is intelligible except in its differential relations with other texts.[3]

The break with the moment of textual production can easily be presented as liberatory; certainly much work of importance has stemmed from the study of inscription. It has shown for example that texts can never simply be *encountered* but are, on the contrary, repeatedly constructed under definite conditions: *The Tempest* read by Sir Walter Raleigh in 1914 as the work of England's national poet is very different from *The Tempest* constructed with full textual apparatus by an editor/critic such as Frank Kermode, and from the "same" text inscribed institutionally in that major formation of "English Literature" which is the school or university syllabus and its supporting practices of teaching and examination.[4]

If the study of the inscription and reinscription of texts has led to important work of historical description, it has also led to the formulation of a political strategy in respect of literary texts, expressed here by Tony Bennett when he calls for texts to be "articulated with new texts, socially and politically mobilized in different ways within different class practices" (Bennett 224). This strategy also depends, therefore, on a form of intertextuality which identifies in all texts a potential for new linkages to be made and thus for new political meanings to be constructed. Rather than attempting to derive the text's significance from the moment of its production, this politicized intertextuality emphasizes the present *use* to which texts can now be put. This approach undercuts itself, however, when, in the passage from historical description

---

[1]Bennett 1982, p. 227; drawing on the argument of Derrida 1977.

[2]For the theory behind the concept of inscription see Balibar 1974 and 1983; Macherey and Balibar 1978; and Davies 1978. For an accessible collection of essays which put this theory to work on the corpus of English literature, see Widdowson 1982.

[3]Intertextuality is a term coined by Julia Kristeva 1970, from her reading of the seminal work of Mikhail Bakhtin 1968, 1973, 1981.

[4]For Raleigh's *Tempest* see Terence Hawkes, 1985, pp. 26–46; Kermode is editor of the Arden edition of *The Tempest* (Shakespeare 1964); on the formation of "English" see Davies 1978.

to contemporary rearticulation, it claims for itself a radicalism which it cannot then deliver. Despite speaking of texts as always being "installed in a field of struggle" (Bennett 229), it denies to itself the very possibility of combating the dominant orthodoxies. For if, as the logic of Bennett's argument implies, "the text" were wholly dissolved into an indeterminate miscellany of inscriptions, then how could any confrontation between different but contemporaneous inscriptions take place: what would be the ground of such a contestation?[5] While a genuine difficulty in theorizing "the text" does exist, this should not lead inescapably to the point where the only option becomes the voluntaristic ascription to the text of meanings and articulations derived simply from one's own ideological preferences. This is a procedure only too vulnerable to pluralistic incorporation, a recipe for peaceful co-existence with the dominant readings, not for a contestation of those readings themselves. Struggle can only occur if two positions attempt to occupy the same space, to appropriate the "same" text; "alternative" readings condemn themselves to mere irrelevance.

Our criticism of this politicized intertextuality does not however seek to reinstate the autotelic text with its single fixed meaning. Texts are certainly not available for innocent, unhistorical readings. Any reading must be made *from* a particular position, but is not *reducible* to that position (not least because texts are not infinitely malleable or interpretable, but offer certain constraints and resistances to readings made of them). Rather, different readings struggle with each other on the site of the text, and all that can count, however provisionally, as knowledge of a text, is achieved through this discursive conflict. In other words, the onus on new readings, especially radical readings aware of their own theoretical and political positioning, should be to proceed by means of a *critique* of the dominant readings of a text.

We say critique rather than simply criticism, in reference to a powerful radical tradition which aims not merely to disagree with its rivals but to *read their readings:* that is, to identify their inadequacies and to explain why such readings come about and what ideological role they play.[6] Critique operates in a number of ways, adopting various strategies

---

[5]Stanley Fish (1980, p. 165), whose general argument is similar to Bennett's, admits that in the last analysis he is unable to answer the question: what are his interpretative acts interpretations *of*?

[6]Marx's work was developed out of his critique of the concepts of classical political economy that had dominated economic thought in the middle of the nineteenth century. We choose here to offer a critique of Kermode's introduction to the Arden *Tempest* (Shakespeare 1964) because of the *strengths* of his highly regarded and influential work.

and lines of attack as it engages with the current ideological formations, but one aspect of its campaign is likely to have to remain constant. Capitalist societies have always presupposed the naturalness and universality of their own structures and modes of perception, so, at least for the foreseeable future, critiques will need to include an *historical* moment, countering capitalism's self-universalization by reasserting the rootedness of texts in the contingency of history. It is this particular ground that what we have been referring to as alternative criticism runs the risk of surrendering unnecessarily. As we emphasized earlier, the study of successive textual inscriptions continues to be genuinely important, but it must be recognized that attention to such inscriptions is not logically dependent on the frequent presupposition that *all* accounts of the moment of production are either crudely historicist or have recourse to claims concerning authorial intentionality. A *properly* political intertextuality would attend to successive inscriptions without abandoning that no longer privileged but still crucially important *first* inscription of the text. After all, only by maintaining our right to make statements that we can call "historical" can we avoid handing over the very notion of history to those people who are only too willing to tell us "what really happened."

III

In order to speak of the Shakespearean text as an historical utterance, it is necessary to read it with and within a series of *con-texts*.[7] These con-texts are the precondition of the plays' historical and political signification, although literary criticism has operated systematically to close down that signification by a continual process of occlusion. This may seem a strange thing to say about the most notoriously bloated of all critical enterprises, but in fact "Shakespeare" has been force-fed behind a high wall called Literature, built out of the dismantled pieces of other seventeenth-century discourses. Two particular examples of the occlusive process might be noted here. First, the process of occlusion is accomplished in the production of critical meaning, as is well illustrated by the case of Caliban. The occlusion of his political claims — one of the subjects of the present essay — is achieved by installing him at the very center of the play, but only as the ground of a

---

[7]Con-texts with a hyphen, to signify a break from the inequality of the usual text/context relationship. Con-texts are themselves *texts* and must be *read with:* they do not simply make up a background.

nature/art confrontation, itself of undoubted importance for the Renaissance, but here, in Kermode's account, totally without the historical contextualization that would locate it among the early universalizing forms of incipient bourgeois hegemony (Shakespeare xxxiv–lxiii). Secondly, source criticism, which might *seem* to militate against autotelic unity by relating the text in question to other texts, in fact only obscures such relationships. Kermode's paragraphs on "The New World" embody the hesitancy with which Shakespearean scholarship has approached the problem. Resemblances between the *language* of the Bermuda pamphlets and that of *The Tempest* are brought forward as evidence that Shakespeare "has these documents in mind" but, since this must remain "inference" rather than "fact," it can only have subsidiary importance, "of the greatest interest and usefulness," while clearly not "fundamental to [the play's] structure of ideas." Such "sources" are then reprinted in an appendix so "the reader may judge of the verbal parallels for himself," and the matter closed (Shakespeare xxvii–xxviii).

And yet such closure proves premature since, strangely, source criticism comes to play an interestingly crucial role in Kermode's production of a site for *The Tempest*'s meaning. In general, the fullness of the play's unity needs protecting from con-textual contamination, so "sources" are kept at bay except for the odd verbal parallel. But occasionally, and on a strictly *singular* basis, that unity can only be protected by recourse to a notion of source as explanatory of a feature otherwise aberrant to that posited unity. One example of this would be Prospero's well-known irascibility, peculiarly at odds with Kermode's picture of a self-disciplined, reconciliatory white magician, and therefore to be "in the last analysis, explained by the fact that [he] descend[s] from a bad-tempered giant-magician" (Shakespeare lxiii). Another would be Prospero's strange perturbation which brings the celebratory masque of Act 4 to such an abrupt conclusion, in one reading (as we will demonstrate shortly) the most important scene in the play, but here explained as "a point at which an oddly pedantic concern for classical structure causes it to force its way through the surface of the play" (Shakespeare lxxv). In other words the play's unity is constructed only by shearing off some of its "surface" complexities and explaining them away as irrelevant survivals or unfortunate academicisms.

Intertextuality, or con-textualization, differs most importantly from source criticism when it establishes the necessity of reading *The Tempest* alongside congruent texts, irrespective of Shakespeare's putative knowledge of them, and when it holds that such congruency will become apparent from the constitution of discursive networks to be traced independently of authorial "intentionality."

IV

Essential to the historico-political critique which we are proposing here are the analytic strategies made possible by the concept of *discourse*. Intertextuality has usefully directed attention to the relationship *between* texts: discourse moves us towards a clarification of just what kinds of relationship are involved.[8]

Traditionally *The Tempest* has been related to other texts by reference to a variety of notions: *source,* as we have seen, holds that Shakespeare was influenced by his reading of the Bermuda pamphlets. But the play is also described as belonging to the *genre* of pastoral romance and is seen as occupying a particular place in the *canon* of Shakespeare's works. Intertextuality has sought to displace work done within this earlier paradigm, but has itself been unable to break out of the practice of connecting text with text, of assuming that single texts are the ultimate objects of study and the principal units of meaning.[9] Discourse, on the other hand, refers to the *field* in and through which texts are produced. As a concept wider than "text" but narrower than language itself (Saussure's *langue*), it operates at the level of the enablement of texts. It is thus not an easy concept to grasp because discourses are never simply observable but only approachable through their effects just as, in a similar way, grammar can be said to be *at work* in particular sentences (even those that are ungrammatical), governing their construction but never fully present "in" them. The operation of discourse is implicit in the regulation of what statements can and cannot be made and the forms that they can legitimately take. Attention to discourse therefore moves the focus from the interpretative problem of meaning to questions of

---

[8]MacCabe 1979 offers a helpful guide through some of discourse's many usages. The concept of discourse at work in the present essay draws on Michel Foucault's investigation of the discursive realm. A useful introduction to his theorization of discourse is provided by Foucault's essays, 1978 and 1981. His most extended theoretical text is *The Archaeology of Knowledge,* 1972. However, a less formal and in many ways more suggestive treatment of discourse is practiced and, to a certain extent theorized, in his early work on "madness" and in more recent studies of the prison and of sexuality, where discourse is linked with both the institutional locations in which it circulates and the power functions it performs: see Foucault 1967, 1977, 1979a. For a cognate approach to discourse see the theory of "utterance" developed by Valentin Vološinov 1973.

[9]On the weakness of Kristeva's own work in this respect see Culler 1981, pp. 105–07.

instrumentality and function. Instead of *having* meaning, statements should be seen as *performative of* meaning; not as possessing some portable and "universal" content but, rather, as instrumental in the organization and legitimation of power-relations — which of course involves, as one of its components, control over the constitution of meaning. As the author of one of the first modern grammars said, appropriately enough in 1492, "language is the perfect instrument of empire."[10] Yet, unlike grammar, discourse functions effectively precisely because the question of codifying its rules and protocols can never arise: the utterances it silently governs speak what appears to be the "natural language of the age." Therefore, from within a given discursive formation no general rules for its operation will be drawn up except against the ideological grain; so the constitution of the discursive fields of the past will, to some degree, need comprehending through the excavatory work of historical study.

To initiate such excavation is of course to confront massive problems. According to what we have said above, each individual text, rather than a meaningful unit in itself, lies at the intersection of different discourses which are related to each other in a complex but ultimately hierarchical way. Strictly speaking, then, it would be meaningless to talk about the unity of any given text — supposedly the intrinsic quality of all "works of art." And yet, because literary texts *are* presented to us as characterized precisely by their unity, the text must still be taken as a point of purchase on the discursive field — but in order to demonstrate that, athwart its alleged unity, the text is in fact marked and fissured by the interplay of the discourses that constitute it.

V

The ensemble of fictional and lived practices, which for convenience we will simply refer to here as "English colonialism," provides *The Tempest*'s dominant discursive con-texts.[11] We have chosen here to

[10]Antonio de Nebrija, quoted in Hanke 1959, p. 8.

[11]In other words we would shift the emphasis from the futile search for the texts Shakespeare "had in mind" to the establishment of significant patterns within the larger discursive networks of the period. The notion of "English colonialism" can itself be focused in different ways. The widest focus would include present con-texts, the narrowest would concentrate on the con-texts associated with the initial period of English colonization of Virginia, say 1585 to 1622. In the first instance many of the relevant texts would be found in the contemporary collections of Hakluyt (1903–05) and Purchas (1905–07). For congruent approaches see J. Smith 1974; Frey 1979; Greenblatt 1980, chapter 4; and Hulme 1981.

concentrate specifically on the figure of usurpation as the nodal point of the play's imbrication into this discourse of colonialism. We shall look at the variety of forms under which usurpation appears in the text, and indicate briefly how it is active in organizing the text's actual diversity.[12]

Of course conventional criticism has no difficulty in recognizing the importance of the themes of legitimacy and usurpation for *The Tempest*. Indeed, during the storm-scene with which the play opens, the issue of legitimate authority is brought immediately to the fore. The boatswain's peremptory dismissal of the nobles to their cabins, while not, according to the custom of the sea, strictly a mutinous act, none the less represents a disturbance in the normal hierarchy of power relations. The play then proceeds to recount or display a series of actual or attempted usurpations of authority: from Antonio's successful palace revolution against his brother, Prospero, and Caliban's attempted violation of the honor of Prospero's daughter — accounts of which we hear retrospectively; to the conspiracy of Antonio and Sebastian against the life of Alonso and, finally, Caliban's insurrection, with Stephano and Trinculo, against Prospero's domination of the island. In fact it could be argued that this series *is* the play, in so far as *The Tempest* is a dramatic action at all. However, these rebellions, treacheries, mutinies and conspiracies, referred to here collectively as usurpation, are not *simply* present in the text as extractable "Themes of the Play."[13] Rather, they are differentially embedded there, figural traces of the text's anxiety concerning the very matters of domination and resistance.

Take for example the play's famous *protasis*, Prospero's long exposition to Miranda of the significant events that predate the play. For Prospero, the real beginning of the story is his usurpation twelve years previously by Antonio, the opening scene of a drama which Prospero intends to play out during *The Tempest* as a comedy of restoration. Prospero's exposition seems unproblematically to take its place as the indispensable prologue to an understanding of the present moment of Act 1, no more than a device for conveying essential information. But to see it simply as a neutral account of the play's prehistory would be to occlude the contestation that follows insistently throughout the rest of the first act, of Prospero's version of true beginnings. In this narration the crucial early days of the relationship between the Europeans and the

---

[12]See Macherey 1978. Macherey characterizes the literary text not as unified but as plural and diverse. Usurpation should then be regarded not as the center of a unity but as the principle of a diversity.

[13]Kermode's second heading (Shakespeare 1964, p. xxiv).

island's inhabitants are covered by Prospero's laconic "Here in this island we arrived" (1.2.171). And this is all we would have were it not for Ariel and Caliban. First Prospero is goaded by Ariel's demands for freedom into recounting at some length how his servitude began, when, at their first contact, Prospero freed him from the cloven pine in which he had earlier been confined by Sycorax. Caliban then offers his compelling and defiant counter to Prospero's single sentence when, in a powerful speech, he recalls the initial mutual trust which was broken by Prospero's assumption of the political control made possible by the power of his magic. Caliban, "Which first was mine own king," now protests that "here you sty me / In this hard rock, whiles you do keep from me / The rest o' th' island" (1.2.345–47).

It is remarkable that these contestations of "true beginnings" have been so commonly occluded by an uncritical willingness to identify Prospero's voice as direct and reliable authorial statement, and therefore to ignore the lengths to which the play goes to dramatize its problems with the proper beginning of its own story. Such identification hears, as it were, only Prospero's play, follows only his stage directions, not noticing that Prospero's play and *The Tempest* are not necessarily the same thing.[14]

But although different beginnings are offered by different voices in the play, Prospero has the effective power to impose his construction of events on the others. While Ariel gets a threatening but nevertheless expansive answer, Caliban provokes an entirely different reaction. Prospero's words refuse engagement with Caliban's claim to original sovereignty ("This island's mine, by Sycorax my mother, / Which thou tak'st from me," 1.2.334–35). Yet Prospero is clearly disconcerted. His sole — somewhat hysterical — response consists of an indirect denial ("Thou most lying slave," 1.2.347) and a counter accusation of attempted rape ("thou didst seek to violate / The honor of my child," 1.2.350–51), which together foreclose the exchange and serve in practice as Prospero's only justification for the arbitrary rule he exercises over the island and its inhabitants. At a stroke he erases from what we have called Prospero's play all trace of the moment of his reduction of Caliban to slavery and appropriation of his island. For, indeed, it could be argued that the series of usurpations listed earlier as constituting the dramatic action all belong to that play alone, which is systematically

---

[14]This is a weak form of the critical fallacy that, more chronically, reads Prospero as an autobiographical surrogate for Shakespeare himself. On some of the theoretical issues involved here see Foucault 1979b.

silent about Prospero's own act of usurpation: a silence which is curious, given his otherwise voluble preoccupation with the theme of legitimacy. But, despite his evasiveness, this moment ought to be of decisive *narrative* importance since it marks Prospero's self-installation as ruler, and his acquisition, through Caliban's enslavement, of the means of supplying the food and labor on which he and Miranda are completely dependent: "We cannot miss him. He does make our fire, / Fetch in our wood, and serves in offices / That profit us" (1.2.314–16). Through its very occlusion of Caliban's version of proper beginnings, Prospero's disavowal is itself performative of the discourse of colonialism, since this particular reticulation of denial of dispossession with retrospective justification for it, is the characteristic trope by which European colonial regimes articulated their authority over land to which they could have no conceivable legitimate claim.[15]

The success of this trope is, as so often in these cases, proved by its subsequent invisibility. Caliban's "I'll show thee every fertile inch o' th' island" (2.2.141) is for example glossed by Kermode with "The colonists were frequently received with this kindness, though treachery might follow," as if this were simply a "fact" whose relevance to *The Tempest* we might want to consider, without seeing that to speak of "treachery" is already to interpret, from the position of colonizing power, through a purported "description." A discursive analysis would indeed be alive to the use of the word "treachery" in a colonial context in the early seventeenth century, but would be aware of how it functioned for the English to explain to themselves the *change* in native behavior (from friendliness to hostility) that was in fact a *reaction* to their increasingly disruptive presence. That this was an explanatory trope rather than a description of behavior is nicely caught in Gabriel Archer's slightly bemused comment: "They are naturally given to trechery, howbeit we could not finde it in our travell up the river, but rather a most kind and loving people" (Archer 1979). Kermode's use of the word is of course by no means obviously contentious: its power to shape readings of the play stems from its continuity with the grain of unspoken colonialist assumptions.

So it is not just a matter of the occlusion of the play's initial colonial moment. Colonialist legitimation has always had then to go on to tell its own story, inevitably one of native violence: Prospero's play performs this task within *The Tempest*. The burden of Prospero's play is

[15]This trope is studied in more detail in Hulme [1986], chapters 3 and 4. See also Jennings 1976.

already deeply concerned with producing legitimacy. The purpose of Prospero's main plot is to secure recognition of his claim to the usurped duchy of Milan, a recognition sealed in the blessing given by Alonso to the prospective marriage of his own son to Prospero's daughter. As part of this, Prospero reduces Caliban to a role in the supporting sub-plot, as instigator of a mutiny that is programmed to fail, thereby forging an equivalence between Antonio's initial *putsch* and Caliban's revolt. This allows Prospero to annul the memory of his failure to prevent his expulsion from the dukedom, by repeating it as a mutiny that he will, this time, forestall. But, in addition, the playing out of the colonialist narrative is thereby completed: Caliban's attempt — tarred with the brush of Antonio's supposedly self-evident viciousness — is produced as final and irrevocable confirmation of the natural treachery of savages.

Prospero can plausibly be seen as a playwright only because of the control over the other characters given him by his magic. He can freeze Ferdinand in mid-thrust, immobilize the court party at will, and conjure a pack of hounds to chase the conspirators. Through this physical control he seeks with considerable success to manipulate the mind of Alonso. Curiously though, while the main part of Prospero's play runs according to plan, the sub-plot provides the only real moment of drama when Prospero calls a sudden halt to the celebratory masque, explaining, aside:

> I had forgot that foul conspiracy
> Of the beast Caliban and his confederates
> Against my life. The minute of their plot
> Is almost come.
>
> (4.1.139–42)

So while, on the face of it, Prospero has no difficulty in dealing with the various threats to his domination, Caliban's revolt proves uniquely disturbing to the smooth unfolding of Prospero's plot. The text is strangely emphatic about this moment of disturbance, insisting not only on Prospero's sudden vexation, but also on the "strange hollow, and confused noise" with which the Nymphs and Reapers — two lines earlier gracefully dancing — now "heavily vanish"; and the apprehension voiced by Ferdinand and Miranda:

> FERDINAND: This is strange: your father's in some passion
>   That works him strongly.
> MIRANDA: Never till this day
>   Saw I him touched with anger, so distempered.
>
> (4.1.143–45)

For the first and last time Ferdinand and Miranda speak at a distance from Prospero and from his play. Although this disturbance is immediately glossed over, the hesitation, occasioned by the sudden remembering of Caliban's conspiracy, remains available as a site of potential fracture.

The interrupted masque has certainly troubled scholarship, introducing a jarring note into the harmony of this supposedly most highly structured of Shakespeare's late plays. Kermode speaks of the "apparently inadequate motivation" for Prospero's perturbation (Shakespeare 1964, p. lxxv), since there is no obvious reason why he should so excite himself over an easily controllable insurrection.

What then is the meaning of this textual excess, this disproportion between apparent cause and effect? There are several possible answers, located at different levels of analysis. The excess obviously marks the recurrent difficulty that Caliban causes Prospero — a difficulty we have been concerned to trace in some detail. So, at the level of character, a psychoanalytic reading would want to suggest that Prospero's excessive reaction represents his disquiet at the irruption into consciousness of an unconscious anxiety concerning the grounding of his legitimacy, both as producer of his play and, *a fortiori*, as governor of the island. The by now urgent need for action forces upon Prospero the hitherto repressed contradiction between his dual roles as usurped and usurper. Of course the emergency is soon contained and the colonialist narrative quickly completed. But, nonetheless, if only for a moment, the effort invested in holding Prospero's play together as a unity is laid bare.

So, at the formal level, Prospero's difficulties in staging his play are themselves "staged" by the play that we are watching, this moment presenting for the first time the possibility of distinguishing between Prospero's play and *The Tempest* itself.

Perhaps it could be said that what is staged here in *The Tempest* is Prospero's anxious determination to keep the sub-plot of his play in its place. One way of distinguishing Prospero's play from *The Tempest* might be to claim that Prospero's carefully established relationship between main and sub-plot is reversed in *The Tempest*, whose *main* plot concerns Prospero's anxiety over his *sub*-plot. A formal analysis would seem to bear this out. The climax of Prospero's play is his revelation to Alonso of Miranda and Ferdinand playing chess. This is certainly a true *anagnorisis* for Alonso, but for us a merely theatrical rather than truly dramatic moment. *The Tempest*'s dramatic climax, in a way its only dramatic moment at all, is, after all, this sudden and strange disturbance of Prospero.

But to speak of Prospero's anxiety being staged by *The Tempest* would be, on its own, a recuperative move, preserving the text's unity by the familiar strategy of introducing an ironic distance between author and protagonist. After all, although Prospero's anxiety over his sub-plot may point up the *crucial* nature of that "sub" plot, a generic analysis would have no difficulty in showing that *The Tempest* is ultimately complicit with Prospero's play in treating Caliban's conspiracy in the fully comic mode. Even before it begins, Caliban's attempt to put his political claims into practice is arrested by its implication in the convention of clownish vulgarity represented by the "low-life" characters of Stephano and Trinculo, his conspiracy framed in a grotesquerie that ends with the dubiously amusing sight of the conspirators being hunted by dogs, a fate, incidentally, not unknown to natives of the New World. The shakiness of Prospero's position is indeed staged, but in the end his version of history remains *authoritative*, the larger play acceding as it were to the containment of the conspirators in the safely comic mode, Caliban allowed only his poignant and ultimately vain protests against the venality of his co-conspirators.

That this comic closure is necessary to enable the European "reconciliation" which follows hard on its heels — the patching up of a minor dynastic dispute within the Italian nobility — is, however, itself symptomatic of the text's own anxiety about the threat posed to its decorum by its New World materials. The lengths to which the play has to go to achieve a legitimate ending may then be read as the quelling of a fundamental disquiet concerning its own functions within the projects of colonialist discourse.

No adequate reading of the play could afford not to comprehend *both* the anxiety and the drive to closure it necessitates. Yet these aspects of the play's "rich complexity" have been signally ignored by European and North American critics, who have tended to listen exclusively to Prospero's voice: after all, he speaks their language. It has been left to those who have suffered colonial usurpation to discover and map the traces of that complexity by reading in full measure Caliban's refractory place in both Prospero's play and *The Tempest*.[16]

[16]See for example Lamming 1960 and Fernández Retamar 1973. Aimé Césaire's rewriting of the play, *Une Tempête,* 1969, has Caliban as explicit hero. For an account of how Caliban remains refractory for contemporary productions of *The Tempest* see Griffiths 1983. [Reprinted in part in this volume, p. 309.]

VI

We have tried to show, within the limits of a brief textual analysis, how an approach via a theory of discourse can recognize *The Tempest* as, in a significant sense, a play imbricated within the discourse of colonialism; and can, at the same time, offer an explanation of features of the play either ignored or occluded by critical practices that have often been complicit, whether consciously or not, with a colonialist ideology.

Three points remain to be clarified. To identify dominant discursive networks and their mode of operation within particular texts should by no means be seen as the end of the story. A more exhaustive analysis would go on to establish the precise articulation of discourses within texts: we have argued for the discourse of colonialism as the articulatory *principle* of *The Tempest*'s diversity but have touched only briefly on what other discourses are articulated and where such linkages can be seen at work in the play.

Then again, each text is more than simply an *instance* of the operation of a discursive network. We have tried to show how much of *The Tempest*'s complexity comes from its *staging* of the distinctive moves and figures of colonialist discourse. Discourse is always performative, active rather than ever merely contemplative; and, of course, the mode of the theater will also inflect it in particular ways, tending, for example, through the inevitable (because structural) absence of any direct authorial comment, to create an effect of distantiation, which exists in a complex relationship with the countervailing (and equally structural) tendency for audiences to identify with characters presented — through the language and conventions of theater — as heroes and heroines. Much work remains to be done on the articulation between discursive performance and mode of presentation.

Finally, we have been concerned to show how *The Tempest* has been severed from its discursive con-texts through being produced by criticism as an autotelic unity, and we have tried therefore to exemplify an approach that would engage with the fully dialectical relationship between the detail of the text and the larger discursive formations. But nor can theory and criticism be exempt from such relationships. Our essay too must engage in the discursive struggle that determines the history within which the Shakespearean texts will be located and read: it matters what kind of history that is.

WORKS CITED

Archer, Louis (1979) "The description of the now discovered river and county of Virginia . . ." [1607], in Quinn, D., *et al.* (eds.), *New American World*, vol. 5, London: Macmillan.

Bakhtin, Mikhail (1968) *Rabelais and His World.* Cambridge, Mass.: MIT Press.

———. (1973) *Problems of Dostoevsky's Poetics.* Ann Arbor, Mich.: Ardis.

———. (1981) *The Dialogic Imagination.* Austin: University of Texas Press.

Balibar, Renée (1974) *Les Français fictifs: Le rapport des styles littéraires au français national.* Paris: Hachette.

———. (1983) "National language, education, literature," in Barker, F., *et al.* (eds.), *The Politics of Theory.* Colchester: University of Essex, 79–99.

Bennett, T. (1982) "Text and history," in Widdowson, P. (ed.), *Re-Reading English.* London: Methuen, 223–36.

Césaire, Aimé (1969) *Une Tempête.* Paris: Seuil.

Culler, J. (1981) *The Pursuit of Signs.* London: Routledge & Kegan Paul.

Davies, Tony (1978) "Education, ideology and literature," *Red Letters*, 7, 4–15.

Derrida, Jacques (1977) "Signature event context," *Glyph*, 1, 172–98.

Fernández Retamar, Roberto (1973) *Caliban: Apuntes sobre la Cultura de Nuestra América.* Buenos Aires: Editorial la Pleyade.

Fish, Stanley (1980) *Is There a Text in This Class?: The Authority of Interpretive Communities.* Cambridge, Mass.: Harvard University Press.

Foucault, Michel (1967) *Madness and Civilization: A History of Insanity in the Age of Reason.* London: Tavistock Publications.

———. (1970) *The Order of Things.* London: Tavistock Publications.

———. (1972) *The Archaeology of Knowledge.* London: Tavistock Publications.

———. (1977) *Discipline and Punish: The Birth of a Prison.* London: Allen Lane.

———. (1978) "Politics and the study of discourse," *Ideology and Consciousness*, 3, 7–26.

———. (1979a) *The History of Sexuality*, vol. 1. London: Allen Lane.

———. (1979b) "What is an author?," in Harari, J. V. (ed.), *Textual Strategies: Perspectives in Post-structuralist Criticism.* London: Methuen, 141–60.

————. (1981) "The order of discourse," in Young, Robert (ed.) *Untying the Text: A Post-structuralist Reader.* London: Routledge & Kegan Paul, 48–78.

Frey, Charles (1979) "*The Tempest* and the New World," *Shakespeare Quarterly,* 30, 29–41.

Greenblatt, Stephen (1980) *Renaissance Self-Fashioning from More to Shakespeare.* Chicago: University of Chicago Press.

Griffiths, Trevor (1983) "'This island's mine': Caliban and colonialism," *The Yearbook of English Studies,* 13, 159–80.

Hakluyt, Richard (1903–05) *The Principal Navigations, Voyages Traffiques and Discoveries of the English Nation* [1589], 12 vols. Glasgow: James MacLehose and Sons.

Hanke, Lewis (1959) *Aristotle and the American Indians.* Bloomington: Indiana University Press.

Hawkes, Terence (1985) "Swisser-Swatter: Making a man of English letters." in Drakakis, J. (ed.), *Alternative Shakespeares,* London: Methuen, 26–46.

Hirsch, E. D. (1967) *Validity in Interpretation.* New Haven: Yale University Press.

Hulme, Peter (1981) "Hurricanes in the Caribbees: The constitution of the discourse of English colonialism," in Barker, F., *et al.* (eds.), *1642: Literature and Power in the Seventeenth Century.* Colchester: University of Essex, 55–83.

————. (1986) *Colonial Encounters: Europe and the Native Caribbean, 1492–1797.* London: Methuen.

Jennings, Francis (1976) *The Invasion of America: Indians, Colonialism and the Cant of Conquest.* New York: Norton.

Kristeva, Julia (1970) *Le Texte du roman.* The Hague: Mouton.

Lamming, George (1960) *The Pleasures of Exile.* London: Michael Joseph.

MacCabe, Colin (1979) "On discourse," *Economy and Society,* 8, 4, 279–307.

Macherey, P. (1978) *A Theory of Literary Production,* trans. Geoffrey Wall. Reprinted London: Routledge & Kegan Paul, 1980.

Macherey, P., and Balibar, E. (1978) "On literature as an ideological form: Some Marxist propositions," *Oxford Literary Review,* 3, 4–12.

Purchas, Samuel (1905–07) *Purchas His Pilgrimes* [1625], 20 vols. Glasgow: James MacLehose.

Shakespeare, William (1964) *The Tempest,* ed. Frank Kermode. London: Methuen.

Smith, James (1974) *"The Tempest,"* in *Shakespearian and Other Essays.* Cambridge: Cambridge University Press, 159–261.

Vološinov, Valentin (1973) *Marxism and the Philosophy of Language.* New York: Seminar Press.

Widdowson, Peter (ed.) (1982) *Re-Reading English.* London: Methuen.

AIMÉ CÉSAIRE

From A Tempest

Aimé Césaire (1913–2008) was born in Martinique in the West Indies and was educated at the Ecole Normale Supérieure in Paris, where he was active in efforts to restore the cultural identity of black Africans. He began his career in literature as a revolutionary poet, protesting French oppression, writing such works as *Cahier d'un retour au pays natal* (1939; *Return to My Native Land*). He later turned to drama, and his plays include *Le tragédie du Roi Christophe* (1963; *The Tragedy of King Christophe*), *Une saison au Congo* (1966; *A Season in the Congo*), and *Une tempête* (1969; *A Tempest*, which had its American premier in 1991). He served as mayor of Fort-de-France, Martinique, and as Martinique's representative in the French National Assembly. The scenes we have selected from *A Tempest* were translated by Richard Miller (New York: Ubu Repertory Theater, 1992).

ACT I, SCENE 2

MIRANDA: Oh God! Oh God! A sinking ship! Father, help!

PROSPERO: (*enters hurriedly carrying a megaphone.*) Come daughter, calm yourself! It's only a play. There's really nothing wrong. Anyway, everything that happens is for our own good. Trust me, I won't say any more.

MIRANDA: But such a fine ship, and so many fine, brave lives sunk, drowned, laid waste to wrack and ruin . . . A person would have to have a heart of stone not to be moved . . .

PROSPERO: Drowned . . . hmmm. That remains to be seen. But draw near, dear Princess. The time has come.

MIRANDA: You're making fun of me, father. Wild as I am, you know I am happy — like a queen of the wildflowers, of the streams and paths, running barefoot through thorns and flowers, spared by one, caressed by the other.

PROSPERO: But you are a Princess . . . for how else does one address the daughter of a Prince? I cannot leave you in ignorance any longer. Milan is the city of your birth, and the city where for many years I was the Duke.

MIRANDA: Then how did we come here? And tell me, too, by what ill fortune did a prince turn into the reclusive hermit you are now, here, on this desert isle? Was it because you found the world distasteful, or through the perfidy of some enemy? Is our island a prison or a hermitage? You've hinted at some mystery so many times and aroused my curiosity, and today you shall tell me all.

PROSPERO: In a way, it is because of all the things you mention. First, it is because of political disagreements, because of the intrigues of my ambitious younger brother. Antonio is his name, your uncle, and Alonso the name of the envious King of Naples. How their ambitions were joined, how my brother became the accomplice of my rival, how the latter promised the former his protection and my throne . . . the devil alone knows how all that came about. In any event, when they learned that through my studies and experiments I had managed to discover the exact location of these lands for which many had sought for centuries and that I was making preparations to set forth to take possession of them, they hatched a scheme to steal my as-yet-unborn empire from me. They bribed my people, they stole my charts and documents and, to get rid of me, they denounced me to the Inquisition as a magician and sorcerer. To be brief, one day I saw arriving at the palace men to whom I had never granted audience: the priests of the Holy Office.

Flashback: Standing before Prospero, who is wearing his ducal robes, we see a friar reading from a parchment scroll.

THE FRIAR: The Holy Inquisition for the preservation and integrity of the Faith and the pursuit of heretical perversion, acting through the special powers entrusted to it by the Holy Apostolic See, informed of the errors you profess, insinuate and publish against God and his Creation with regard to the shape of the Earth and the possibility of discovering other lands, notwithstanding the fact that the Prophet

Isaiah stated and taught that the Lord God is seated upon the circle of the Earth and in its center is Jerusalem and that around the world lies inaccessible Paradise, convinced that it is through wickedness that to support your heresy you quote Strabus, Ptolemy and the tragic author Seneca, thereby lending credence to the notion that profane writings can aspire to an authority equal to that of the most profound of the Holy Scriptures, given your notorious use by both night and day of Arabic calculations and scribblings in Hebrew, Syrian and other demonic tongues and, lastly, given that you have hitherto escaped punishment owing to your temporal authority and have, if not usurped, then transformed that authority and made it into a tyranny, doth hereby strip you of your titles, positions and honors in order that it may then proceed against you according to due process through a full and thorough examination, under which authority we require that you accompany us.

PROSPERO: (*back in the present*) And yet, the trial they said they were going to hold never took place. Such creatures of darkness are too much afraid of the light. To be brief: instead of killing me they chose — even worse — to maroon me here with you on this desert island.

MIRANDA: How terrible, and how wicked the world is! How you must have suffered!

PROSPERO: In all this tale of treason and felony there is but one honorable name: Gonzalo, counsellor to the King of Naples and fit to serve a better master. By furnishing me with food and clothing, by supplying me with my books and instruments, he has done all in his power to make my exile in this disgusting place bearable. And now, through a singular turn, Fortune has brought to these shores the very men involved in the plot against me. My prophetic science had of course already informed me that they would not be content merely with seizing my lands in Europe and that their greed would win out over their cowardice, that they would confront the sea and set out for those lands my genius had discovered. I couldn't let them get away with that, and since I was able to stop them, I did so, with the help of Ariel. We brewed up the storm you have just witnessed, thereby saving my possessions overseas and bringing the scoundrels into my power at the same time.

Enter Ariel.

PROSPERO: Well, Ariel?
ARIEL: Mission accomplished.

PROSPERO: Bravo; good work! But what seems to be the matter? I give you a compliment and you don't seem pleased? Are you tired?

ARIEL: Not tired; disgusted. I obeyed you but — well, why not come out with it? — I did so most unwillingly. It was a real pity to see that great ship go down, so full of life.

PROSPERO: Oh, so you're upset, are you! It's always like that with you intellectuals! Who cares! What interests me is not your moods, but your deeds. Let's split: I'll take the zeal and you can keep your doubts. Agreed?

ARIEL: Master, I must beg you to spare me this kind of labor.

PROSPERO: (*shouting*) Listen, and listen good! There's a task to be performed, and I don't care how it gets done!

ARIEL: You've promised me my freedom a thousand times, and I'm still waiting.

PROSPERO: Ingrate! And who freed you from Sycorax, may I ask? Who rent the pine in which you had been imprisoned and brought you forth?

ARIEL: Sometimes I almost regret it . . . After all, I might have turned into a real tree in the end . . . Tree: that's a word that really gives me a thrill! It often springs to mind: palm tree — springing into the sky like a fountain ending in nonchalant, squid-like elegance. The baobab — twisted like the soft entrails of some monster. Ask the calao bird that lives a cloistered season in its branches. Or the Ceiba tree — spread out beneath the proud sun. O bird, o green mansions set in the living earth!

PROSPERO: Stuff it! I don't like talking trees. As for your freedom, you'll have it when I'm good and ready. In the meanwhile, see to the ship. I'm going to have a few words with Master Caliban. I've been keeping my eye on him, and he's getting a little too emancipated. (*Calling*) Caliban! Caliban! (*He sighs.*)

Enter Caliban.

CALIBAN: Uhuru!

PROSPERO: What did you say?

CALIBAN: I said, Uhuru!

PROSPERO: Mumbling your native language again! I've already told you, I don't like it. You could be polite, at least; a simple "hello" wouldn't kill you.

CALIBAN: Oh, I forgot . . . But make that as froggy, waspish, pustular and dung-filled a "hello" as possible. May today hasten by a decade the day when all the birds of the sky and beasts of the earth will feast upon your corpse!

PROSPERO: Gracious as always, you ugly ape! How can anyone be so ugly?

CALIBAN: You think I'm ugly . . . well, I don't think you're so handsome yourself. With that big hooked nose, you look just like some old vulture. (*Laughing*) An old vulture with a scrawny neck!

PROSPERO: Since you're so fond of invective, you could at least thank me for having taught you to speak at all. You, a savage . . . a dumb animal, a beast I educated, trained, dragged up from the bestiality that still clings to you.

CALIBAN: In the first place, that's not true. You didn't teach me a thing! Except to jabber in your own language so that I could understand your orders: chop the wood, wash the dishes, fish for food, plant vegetables, all because you're too lazy to do it yourself. And as for your learning, did you ever impart any of *that* to me? No, you took care not to. All your science you keep for yourself alone, shut up in those big books.

PROSPERO: What would you be without me?

CALIBAN: Without you? I'd be the king, that's what I'd be, the King of the Island. The king of the island given me by my mother, Sycorax.

PROSPERO: There are some family trees it's better not to climb! She's a ghoul! A witch from whom — and may God be praised — death has delivered us.

CALIBAN: Dead or alive, she was my mother, and I won't deny her! Anyhow, you only think she's dead because you think the earth itself is dead . . . It's so much simpler that way! Dead, you can walk on it, pollute it, you can tread upon it with the steps of a conqueror. I respect the earth, because I know that it is alive, and I know that Sycorax is alive.

Sycorax. Mother.
Serpent, rain, lightning.
And I see thee everywhere!
In the eye of the stagnant pool which stares back at me,
through the rushes,
in the gesture made by twisted root and its awaiting thrust.
In the night, the all-seeing blinded night,
the nostril-less all-smelling night!
. . . Often, in my dreams, she speaks to me and warns me . . . Yesterday, even, when I was lying by the stream on my belly lapping at

the muddy water, when the Beast was about to spring upon me with that huge stone in his hand . . .

PROSPERO: If you keep on like that even your magic won't save you from punishment!

CALIBAN: That's right, that's right! In the beginning, the gentleman was all sweet talk: dear Caliban here, my little Caliban there! And what do you think you'd have done without me in this strange land? Ingrate! I taught you the trees, fruits, birds, the seasons, and now you don't give a damn . . . Caliban the animal, Caliban the slave! I know that story! Once you've squeezed the juice from the orange, you toss the rind away!

PROSPERO: Oh!

CALIBAN: Do I lie? Isn't it true that you threw me out of your house and made me live in a filthy cave. The ghetto!

PROSPERO: It's easy to say "ghetto"! It wouldn't be such a ghetto if you took the trouble to keep it clean! And there's something you forgot, which is that what forced me to get rid of you was your lust. Good God, you tried to rape my daughter!

CALIBAN: Rape! Rape! Listen, you old goat, you're the one that put those dirty thoughts in my head. Let me tell you something: I couldn't care less about your daughter, or about your cave, for that matter. If I gripe, it's on principle, because I didn't like living with you at all, as a matter of fact. Your feet stink!

PROSPERO: I did not summon you here to argue. Out! Back to work! Wood, water, and lots of both! I'm expecting company today.

CALIBAN: I've had just about enough. There's already a pile of wood that high . . .

PROSPERO: Enough! Careful, Caliban! If you keep grumbling you'll be whipped. And if you don't step lively, if you keep dragging your feet or try to strike or sabotage things, I'll beat you. Beating is the only language you really understand. So much the worse for you: I'll speak it, loud and clear. Get a move on!

CALIBAN: All right, I'm going . . . but this is the last time. It's the last time, do you hear me? Oh . . . I forgot: I've got something important to tell you.

PROSPERO: Important? Well, out with it.

CALIBAN: It's this: I've decided I don't want to be called Caliban any longer.

PROSPERO: What kind of rot is that? I don't understand.

CALIBAN: Put it this way: I'm *telling* you that from now on I won't answer to the name Caliban.

PROSPERO: Where did you get that idea?

CALIBAN: Well, because Caliban *isn't* my name. It's as simple as that.

PROSPERO: Oh, I suppose it's mine!

CALIBAN: It's the name given me by your hatred, and everytime it's spoken it's an insult.

PROSPERO: My, aren't we getting sensitive! All right, suggest something else . . . I've got to call you something. What will it be? Cannibal would suit you, but I'm sure you wouldn't like that, would you? Let's see . . . what about Hannibal? That fits. And why not . . . they all seem to like historical names.

CALIBAN: Call me X. That would be best. Like a man without a name. Or, to be more precise, a man whose name has been stolen. You talk about history . . . well, that's history, and everyone knows it! Every time you summon me it reminds me of a basic fact, the fact that you've stolen everything from me, even my identity! Uhuru! (*He exits.*)

Enter Ariel as a sea-nymph.

PROSPERO: My dear Ariel, did you see how he looked at me, that glint in his eye? That's something new. Well, let me tell you, Caliban is the enemy. As for those people on the boat, I've changed my mind about them. Give them a scare, but for God's sake don't touch a hair of their heads! You'll answer to me if you do.

ARIEL: I've suffered too much myself for having made them suffer not to be pleased at your mercy. You can count on me, Master.

PROSPERO: Yes, however great their crimes, if they repent you can assure them of my forgiveness. They are men of my race, and of high rank. As for me, at my age one must rise above disputes and quarrels and think about the future. I have a daughter. Alonso has a son. If they were to fall in love, I would give my consent. Let Ferdinand marry Miranda, and may their marriage bring us harmony and peace. That is my plan. I want it executed. As for Caliban, does it matter what that villain plots against me? All the nobility of Italy, Naples and Milan henceforth combined, will protect me bodily. Go!

ARIEL: Yes, Master. Your orders will be fully carried out.

Ariel sings:

> Sandy seashore, deep blue sky,
> Surf is rising, sea birds fly
> Here the lover finds delight,
> Sun at noontime, moon at night.

> Join hands lovers, join the dance,
> Find contentment, find romance.
> Sandy seashore, deep blue sky,
> Cares will vanish . . . so can I . . .

FERDINAND: What is this music? It has led me here and now it stops . . .
No, there it is again . . .

ARIEL: (*singing*)
> Waters move, the ocean flows,
> Nothing comes and nothing goes . . .
> Strange days are upon us . . .
>
> Oysters stare through pearly eyes
> Heart-shaped corals gently beat
> In the crystal undersea
>
> Waters move and ocean flows,
> Nothing comes and nothing goes . . .
> Strange days are upon us . . .

FERDINAND: What is this that I see before me? A goddess? A mortal?

MIRANDA: I know what *I'm* seeing: a flatterer. Young man, your ability to pay compliments in the situation in which you find yourself at least proves your courage. Who are you?

FERDINAND: As you see, a poor shipwrecked soul.

MIRANDA: But one of high degree!

FERDINAND: In other surroundings I might be called "Prince," "son of the King". . . But, no, I was forgetting . . . not "Prince" but "King," alas . . . "King" because my father has just perished in the shipwreck.

MIRANDA: Poor young man! Here, you'll be received with hospitality and we'll support you in your misfortune.

FERDINAND: Alas, my father . . . Can it be that I am an unnatural son? Your pity would make the greatest of sorrows seem sweet.

MIRANDA: I hope you'll like it here with us. The island is pretty. I'll show you the beaches and the forests, I'll tell you the names of fruits and flowers, I'll introduce you to a whole world of insects, of lizards of every hue, of birds . . . Oh, you cannot imagine! The birds! . . .

PROSPERO: That's enough, daughter! I find your chatter irritating . . . and let me assure you, it's not at all fitting. You are doing too much honor to an impostor. Young man, you are a traitor, a spy, and a woman-chaser to boot! No sooner has he escaped the perils of the sea than he's sweet-talking the first girl he meets! You won't get round me that way. Your arrival is convenient, because I need more manpower: you shall be my house servant.

FERDINAND: Seeing the young lady, more beautiful than any wood-nymph, I might have been Ulysses on Nausicaa's isle. But hearing you, Sir, I now understand my fate a little better . . . I see I have come ashore on the Barbary Coast and am in the hands of a cruel pirate. (*Drawing his sword*) However, a gentleman prefers death to dishonor! I shall defend my life with my freedom!

PROSPERO: Poor fool: your arm is growing weak, your knees are trembling! Traitor! I could kill you now . . . but I need the manpower. Follow me.

ARIEL: It's no use trying to resist, young man. My master is a sorcerer: neither your passion nor your youth can prevail against him. Your best course would be to follow and obey him.

FERDINAND: Oh God! What sorcery is this? Vanquished, a captive — yet far from rebelling against my fate, I am finding my servitude sweet. Oh, I would be imprisoned for life if only heaven will grant me a glimpse of my sun each day, the face of my own sun. Farewell, Nausicaa.

They exit.

ACT II, SCENE 1

Caliban's cave. Caliban is singing as he works when Ariel enters. He listens to him for a moment.

CALIBAN: (*singing*)
> May he who eats his corn heedless of Shango
> Be accursed! May Shango creep beneath
> His nails and eat into his flesh!
> Shango, Shango ho!
>
> Forget to give him room if you dare!
> He will make himself at home on your nose!
>
> Refuse to have him under your roof at your own risk!
> He'll tear off your roof and wear it as a hat!
> Whoever tries to mislead Shango
> Will suffer for it!
> Shango, Shango ho!

ARIEL: Greetings, Caliban. I know you don't think much of me, but after all we *are* brothers, brothers in suffering and slavery, but brothers in hope as well. We both want our freedom. We just have different methods.

CALIBAN: Greetings to you. But you didn't come to see me just to make that profession of faith. Come on, Alastor! The old man sent you, didn't he? A great job: carrying out the Master's fine ideas, his great plans.

ARIEL: No, I've come on my own. I came to warn you. Prospero is planning horrible acts of revenge against you. I thought it my duty to alert you.

CALIBAN: I'm ready for him.

ARIEL: Poor Caliban, you're doomed. You know that you aren't the stronger, you'll never be the stronger. What good will it do you to struggle?

CALIBAN: And what about you? What good has your obedience done you, your Uncle Tom patience and your sucking up to him. The man's just getting more demanding and despotic day by day.

ARIEL: Well, I've at least achieved one thing: he's promised me my freedom. In the distant future, of course, but it's the first time he's actually committed himself.

CALIBAN: Talk's cheap! He'll promise you a thousand times and take it back a thousand times. Anyway, tomorrow doesn't interest me. What I want is (*shouting*) "Freedom now!"

ARIEL: Okay. But you know you're not going to get it out of him "now," and that he's stronger than you are. I'm in a good position to know just what he's got in his arsenal.

CALIBAN: The stronger? How do you know that? Weakness always has a thousand means and cowardice is all that keeps us from listing them.

ARIEL: I don't believe in violence.

CALIBAN: What *do* you believe in, then? In cowardice? In giving up? In kneeling and groveling? That's it, someone strikes you on the right cheek and you offer the left. Someone kicks you on the left buttock and you turn the right . . . that way there's no jealousy. Well, that's not Caliban's way . . .

ARIEL: You know very well that that's not what I mean. No violence, no submission either. Listen to me: Prospero is the one we've got to change. Destroy his serenity so that he's finally forced to acknowledge his own injustice and put an end to it.

CALIBAN: Oh sure . . . that's a good one! Prospero's conscience! Prospero is an old scoundrel who has no conscience.

ARIEL: Exactly — that's why it's up to us to give him one. I'm not fighting just for *my* freedom, for *our* freedom, but for Prospero too, so that Prospero can acquire a conscience. Help me, Caliban.

CALIBAN: Listen, kid, sometimes I wonder if you aren't a little bit nuts. So that Prospero can acquire a conscience? You might as well ask a stone to grow flowers.

ARIEL: I don't know what to do with you. I've often had this inspiring, uplifting dream that one day Prospero, you, me, we would all three set out, like brothers, to build a wonderful world, each one contributing his own special thing: patience, vitality, love, will-power too, and rigor, not to mention the dreams without which mankind would perish.

CALIBAN: You don't understand a thing about Prospero. He's not the collaborating type. He's a guy who only feels something when he's wiped someone out. A crusher, a pulveriser, that's what he is! And you talk about brotherhood!

ARIEL: So then what's left? War? And you know that when it comes to that, Prospero is invincible.

CALIBAN: Better death than humiliation and injustice. Anyhow, I'm going to have the last word. Unless nothingness has it. The day when I begin to feel that everything's lost, just let me get hold of a few barrels of your infernal powder and as you fly around up there in your blue skies you'll see this island, my inheritance, my work, all blown to smithereens . . . and, I trust, Prospero and me with it. I hope you'll like the fireworks display — it'll be signed Caliban.

ARIEL: Each of us marches to his own drum. You follow yours. I follow the beat of mine. I wish you courage, brother.

CALIBAN: Farewell, Ariel, my brother, and good luck.

Responding to the Challenge

As we have seen, postcolonial critics have disputed and sought to overthrow a set of received ideas about *The Tempest*, ideas that celebrate the power of art and order and downplay or ignore the implicit politics of that power. In this chapter, we present three essays that attempt to change the conversation about the play once more. Deborah Willis, David Scott Kastan, and Meredith Anne Skura do not, however, argue for a return to an emphasis on universal themes; instead, they contend that the postcolonial critics have some of the same critical shortcomings as the formalists and the traditional historicist critics, especially a tendency to ignore or distort details of the play that do not fit their preferred readings.

From this shared starting point, the three critics go in different directions as they each focus on a different set of significant details that need to be accounted for. Deborah Willis engages directly with the arguments of Paul Brown's essay " 'This Thing of Darkness I Acknowledge Mine': *The Tempest* and the Discourse of Colonialism." Willis endorses Brown's attention to the politics of the play, but argues that his reading conflates Prospero with Shakespeare, and thus fails to see both Shakespeare's attention to Prospero's defects and the "qualified endorsement" the play gives to the colonialist project. In Willis's view, Brown also mistakenly identifies Caliban as Prospero's Other, when the play clearly puts Antonio in that role. Furthermore, for Willis, if the play ends by leaving some political threat "contained but not dissolved," as Brown maintains, it is the threat of Antonio, not of Caliban. Finally, for Willis, Brown fails to account for Caliban's complexity, and especially for the fact that he is not a threat in the eyes of the audience. The result of Willis's essay is a very different view of the politics of the play.

David Scott Kastan also wants to retain the focus on *The Tempest*'s politics, but in his view, postcolonial critics have gone astray by supposing that Shakespeare is primarily interested in England's activities in the New World. Through a careful tracing of parallels between important moments in the play and England's relation to the broader context of European politics at the time of the play's composition, Kastan argues that Shakespeare "effectively stages and manages . . . anxieties about European politics and England's role within them" (p. 350 in this volume). Kastan's argument thus tends to support Willis, who maintains that the anxiety expressed in the play is directed not at rebellious Indian natives but at "factious and rebellious artistocrats" (p. 333) like Antonio.

Where Willis and Kastan argue that postcolonial critics get the politics of the play wrong, Meredith Anne Skura contends that attention to politics needs to be supplemented by "traditional insights about the text, its immediate sources, its individual author — and his individual psychology" (p. 358). She proceeds, first, to complicate the postcolonial readings by calling attention to details those readings have overlooked; she argues, for example, that a close look at Caliban's traits shows that his "name seems more like a mockery of stereotypes than a mark of monstrosity" (p. 364). In the second half of the essay, Skura joins these revised political understandings to her more traditional concerns. The results are especially striking in her discussion of the multiple motives — both political and psychological — behind Prospero's anger with Caliban.

DEBORAH WILLIS

Shakespeare's *Tempest* and the Discourse of Colonialism

Deborah Willis (b. 1952) is associate professor of English at the University of California, Riverside. She is the author of *Malevolent Nurture: Witch-hunting and Maternal Power in Early Modern England* (1995) and many essays on Renaissance drama. The essay that follows first appeared in *Studies in English Literature 1500–1900* 29.2 (1989).

Recent historicist critics of Shakespeare have been energetically producing a body of work on state power and cultural forms. Such critics often seek to distance themselves from an older, "monological" historicism that assumed literature passively reflected its social or political context. Yet despite their commitment to a more complex theory of cultural production, some of these critics reproduce the very reductiveness they want to avoid. Literature, instead of passively reflecting society or power relations, now too often passively repeats a single, all-consuming discourse.

I would like to focus my complaint by examining a recent essay on *The Tempest* by Paul Brown.[1] According to Brown, this play may be seen as Shakespeare's "intervention in an ambivalent and even contradictory [colonialist] discourse" (p. 268). This discourse operates in part by "producing" a threatening "other" that can be used to confirm colonial power. In *The Tempest*, otherness is embodied by the "masterless" men, Stephano and Trinculo, by the sexuality of Miranda and Ferdinand, and especially by Caliban. The threatening "other" is used by colonial power to display its own godliness, to insure aristocratic class solidarity, to justify the colonial project morally, and to "further its workings" through the reorientation of desire. But by representing the "other" in terms that suggest its disruptive potential, colonial discourse also indicates the inherent instability of the colonial project. Masterlessness, savagism, and illicit sexuality retain qualities alluring to "civil" man, and in the process of representing otherness as a threat, colonial discourse inevitably reveals "internal contradictions which strain its ostensible project" (p. 281). Colonial discourse, according to Brown, cannot rest; it is always being impelled to further action in order to contain the threatening "other" upon which it depends.

Brown's discussion of connections between *The Tempest* and colonial discourse is often powerful as a gloss on Prospero's view of the characters he seeks to bring under his control. Yet in other ways his essay is more troubling. In the course of his argument, Shakespeare's

---

[1]Paul Brown, "'This thing of darkness I acknowledge mine': *The Tempest* and the discourse of colonialism," in *Political Shakespeare: New Essays in Cultural Materialism*, ed. Jonathan Dollimore and Alan Sinfield (Ithaca: Cornell Univ. Press, 1985), pp. 48–71. [Reprinted in this volume, p. 268; hereafter, all quotations from Brown correspond to page numbers in this volume.]

play becomes almost wholly engulfed by colonial discourse, retaining little separate identity of its own.[2] Though Brown speaks at first of the play as an "intervention," thereby suggesting an act of aggressive, masterful penetration, he soon follows this with suggestions of the play's dissolution; as his argument unfolds, the play vanishes almost completely into the "domain" of colonial discourse. Both *The Tempest* and other products of colonial discourse share "the intention to produce colonialist stereotypicality" but both end inevitably in "beleaguerement." Both use a threatening "other" to assert the superiority of the colonizer, but in so doing reveal the "other" as a site of potential disruption. Shakespeare has done little more than repeat ambivalences already present in the materials he is working with, ambivalences which, in Brown's view, arise inevitably from the nature of the colonial project itself.

Furthermore, Brown's account implies an author whose most powerful effects are those which have eluded his control. Shakespeare's intervention in colonial discourse, Brown writes,

> takes the form of a powerful and pleasurable narrative which seeks at once to harmonize disjunction, to transcend irreconcilable contradictions, and to mystify the political conditions which demand colonialist discourse. Yet the narrative ultimately fails to deliver that containment and instead may be seen to foreground precisely those problems which it works to efface or overcome. The result is a radically ambivalent text.[3]

Here, Shakespeare's play "seeks" to harmonize disjunction, transcend, and mystify, but it "ultimately fails" to do so, offering instead "radical ambivalence." Later, Brown states that the play is "fully implicated" in the "euphemization of power" characteristic of forms such as the Jacobean masque, yet at the same time is irresistibly drawn to expose the coercive methods upon which that power depends. Brown would have us think of *The Tempest* as a kind of masque manqué; apparently, Shakespeare wants to endorse unequivocally the colonial enterprise,

---

[2]In this regard, *Tempest* criticism has gone from one extreme to another — that is, from considering colonialism to be a non-issue to considering it to be the only issue. Geoffrey Bullough sums up the attitude of an earlier generation when, in his essay on the sources of this play, he states that "*The Tempest* is not a play about colonization." See *Narrative and Dramatic Sources of Shakespeare*, 8 vols. (London: Routledge & Kegan Paul, 1975), 8:241. Bullough, it should be noted, goes on to express some reservations about this claim.

[3]Brown, p. 268–69.

but, like a helpless giant, he is unable to do so, forced by the very nature of his project into revealing its inadequacy.

By representing the play's "ambivalences" as unintended by-products of an attempt to endorse colonialism unequivocally, Brown makes it difficult to see the more qualified endorsement the play is really making; he also makes it difficult to distinguish the play from other texts that *do* deliver such endorsements. His argument, it seems to me, reproduces an error that has haunted criticism of *The Tempest* — that is, the conflation of Prospero with Shakespeare. Though Prospero dominates this play in a way few Shakespearean characters do in others, the play cannot be said to endorse fully Prospero's most blatant expressions of colonial ideology. It invites us to look at Prospero from other angles, Caliban's especially, and draws our attention to questionable aspects of Prospero's conduct and beliefs in ways that seem to be a function of the play's design. While Prospero clearly views Caliban as a threatening "other," the audience does not; the play invites us to sympathize with and to laugh at Caliban, but not to perceive him as a real threat. No necessity compels Shakespeare to give Caliban a speech giving him a persuasive claim to legitimate ownership of the island, or to undermine Prospero's claim that Caliban is ineducable by having Caliban state his intention to "seek for grace" in the play's final scene (5.1.295). He might have easily displayed Prospero's mastery by means of a much cruder, less engaging character. Shakespeare clearly wants us to feel Caliban's claim on us and to sense Prospero's limitations.

But if the play does not uncritically submit to colonial discourse, what is the play's relation to it?[4] Brown's understanding of colonialism

---

[4]Other recent treatments of this question include Francis Barker and Peter Hulme, "Nymphs and reapers heavily vanish: The discursive con-texts of *The Tempest*," in *Alternative Shakespeares,* ed. John Drakakis (London: Methuen, 1985), pp. 191–205 [reprinted in this volume, p. 292; hereafter, all quotations from Barker and Hulme correspond to page numbers in this volume]; Walter Cohen, *Drama of a Nation: Public Theater in Renaissance England and Spain* (Ithaca: Cornell Univ. Press, 1985), pp. 398–404; and Stephen Orgel, "Shakespeare and the Cannibals," in *Cannibals, Witches, and Divorce: Estranging the Renaissance,* ed. Marjorie Garber, Selected Papers from the English Institute, 1985, n.s., no. 11 (Baltimore: Johns Hopkins Univ. Press, 1987), pp. 40–66. Though these critics take different approaches, all three assume, as I do, that Shakespeare in *The Tempest* is more self-consciously critical of the colonial enterprise than Brown represents him to be. Stephen Orgel also explores the interesting possibility that Europeans could view the New World natives not only as "other" but also as reflections of themselves and their ancestors. For earlier treatments of *The Tempest* and colonialist writings, see Charles Frey, "*The Tempest* and the New World," *SQ* 30 (1979): 29–41; Stephen J. Greenblatt, "Learning to Curse: Aspects of Linguistic Colonialism in the Sixteenth Century," in *First Images of America: The Impact of the New World on the Old,* 2 vols., ed. Fredi Chiappelli, et al. (Berkeley: Univ. of California Press, 1976), 2:561–80; and Peter

is shaped in part by categories he borrows from Immanuel Wallerstein.[5] To Wallerstein, the colonial enterprise may be seen to operate in three domains, the "core," "semiperiphery," and "periphery." The colonialism of the core involves the reinforcement and expansion of royal hegemony within England itself; that of the semiperiphery involves its expansion into areas (such as Ireland) only partially under English control; that of the periphery, into the New World. The "production of the other" takes place in all three domains, and Brown finds all three relevant to *The Tempest*. Brown uses Wallerstein's categories to explore a "general analogy between text and context" and to draw suggestive parallels between the play's subplots. Yet he does so in ways that obscure important distinctions. Prospero's colonial project is, for Brown, embodied not only in his "regime" on the island (periphery and semiperiphery) but also in his dukedom in Milan (core); when Brown comes to make general statements about the play's treatment of colonial relations, he is presumably referring to all three domains. Because Prospero's "colonial project" can include not only his "regime" on the island but also his dukedom in Milan, Brown's general statements about the play's treatment of colonial relations can be confusing: does he mean one, two, or all three domains? We may wish to think of colonialism in Wallerstein's terms, yet, in applying them to *The Tempest*, we should not let them prevent us from seeing that Shakespeare's treatment of the "colonialism of the core" is not identical to his treatment of the "colonialism of the periphery."[6] Shakespeare, in fact, to a large extent plays core *against* periphery: *The Tempest* registers tensions between Prospero's role as colonist-magician and his role as duke; it self-consciously explores problematic aspects of Prospero's rule on the

---

Hulme, "Hurricanes in the Caribbees: The Constitution of the Discourse of English Colonialism," in *1642: Literature and Power in the Seventeenth Century: Proceedings of the Essex Conference on the Sociology of Literature, July 1980*, ed. Francis Barker, et al. (Cochester: Univ. of Essex, 1981), pp. 55–83. Since this essay was written, several other studies that deal with *The Tempest*'s relation to colonialism have appeared, including Stephen Orgel's introduction to the Oxford edition of *The Tempest* (Oxford: Oxford Univ. Press, 1987); Thomas Cartelli, "Prospero in Africa: *The Tempest* as colonialist text and pretext" in *Shakespeare Reproduced: The Text in History and Ideology*, ed. Jean E. Howard, et al. (New York: Methuen, 1987), pp. 99–115; and Stephen Greenblatt, "Martial Law in the Land of Cockaigne" in *Shakespearean Negotiations: The Circulation of Social Energy in Renaissance England* (Berkeley: Univ. of California Press, 1988), pp. 129–63.

[5]Brown, p. 271.

[6]To avoid confusion I will use the terminology of colonialism only when I am referring to the "colonialism of the periphery."

island; and it raises questions about his view of Caliban. At the same time, the play declares Prospero's restoration of Milanese political order to be unequivocally legitimate. Prospero works to restore order by gaining back his dukedom, bringing Antonio under his control, engineering Alonso's repentance, and marrying Miranda to the son of his old enemy. The play strongly suggests these goals have the blessing of heaven; and at no time does it bring into question the legitimacy of Prospero's rule as duke, his right to reclaim and expand his dukedom, or his right to arrange a marriage for Miranda.

Thus, *The Tempest* celebrates what Wallerstein calls the "colonialism of the core" while rendering the "colonialism of the periphery" in more problematic terms. Rather than a failed attempt to endorse a vaguely defined colonialism unequivocally, the play should be understood as an extremely successful endorsement of the core's political order. At the same time, the play registers anxiety about the legitimacy of peripheral colonial ventures and their ability to further core interests. Brown, then, is right when he suggests that the play shares with many masques the intention to celebrate an ideal ruler. He is also right to suggest that the play's celebration of an ideal ruler depends, in part at least, upon the disclosure of a threatening "other." Yet, as I will argue below, the play's true threatening "other" is not Caliban, but Antonio. Furthermore, though the play may be said to help create a context in which a colonial venture might be condoned, it is more significantly engaged in arousing the desire for, and displaying the power of, a ruler at the core who can contain a tendency toward oligarchy and division. The colonial venture is subordinate to this larger aim and is given up when it has served its purpose.

ANTONIO AS "OTHER"

Oddly, Brown scarcely refers to Antonio or to Prospero's attitude toward him. Yet it is Antonio whom Prospero first invests with the qualities of a threatening "other." Prospero's narration to Miranda of their history reveals that he discerns in Antonio's betrayal an "evil nature" at work:

> I, thus neglecting worldly ends, all dedicated
> To closeness and the bettering of my mind
> With that which, but by being so retir'd,
> O'er-priz'd all popular rate, in my false brother
> Awak'd an evil nature; and my trust,

Like a good parent, did beget of him
A falsehood in its contrary, as great
As my trust was; which had indeed no limit,
A confidence sans bound.

(1.2.89–97)

Here, Prospero turns himself and his brother into stark opposites; Antonio's falseness is "in its contrary, as great" as Prospero's large-hearted "trust." Prospero is a blameless "good parent," whereas, in subsequent lines, Antonio demonstrates his evil nature by his deceit and violent seizure of Prospero's dukedom; his overreaching aggression is simultaneously an act of rebellion against the state and a betrayal of family bonds.

The rest of the play faithfully endorses Prospero's production of his brother as a threatening "other." (Its success in doing so is partially indicated by the fact that, while Caliban has had numerous defenders in the critical tradition, no one, to my knowledge, has taken up Antonio's cause.) Antonio's incitement of Sebastian to usurpation and murder of Alonso suggests that he has a kind of pathological addiction to treason and fratricide; Antonio seems to be a permanent enemy of state and family order. But it is, perhaps, his seeming incapacity for bonding that makes him an especially sinister figure. In addition to attributing an "evil nature" to Antonio, Prospero also calls him "unnatural" (5.1.75–79), suggesting that Antonio's evil is not only indicated by the active presence of an evil desire, but also by the absence of a bond that would lead him to contain it: Antonio feels none of the "natural" affection supposed to arise from their fraternal tie. His incapacity for bonding is further underscored by his arrogance, his contempt for conscience, and his cold, cynical humor. It is perhaps these aspects of his character, even more than his silence in the final scene, that lead the audience to suspect Antonio has not repented, and probably cannot repent of his crimes. Prospero can induce repentance in Alonso by making use of Alonso's feeling for his son Ferdinand; we cannot imagine Antonio capable of feeling any tie intensely enough to make him responsive to such a maneuver.

The play does not fully endorse Prospero's construction of himself as Antonio's absolute opposite, however. As Brown notes in passing, Prospero's language in his narration of the past also makes visible his own abdication of authority. If Antonio possesses an "evil nature," is trust the appropriate strategy of the "good parent"? Such trust, we are told, "Awak'd" Antonio's evil and "did beget" his falsehood. By representing their relation in terms that suggest cause and effect, Prospero's own metaphors hint at a greater responsibility than he ever acknowledges openly. His actions later in the play do indicate he has assumed some responsibility, however. Antonio's temptation of Sebastian reenacts the past in a way that makes it possible for Prospero to replace his earlier "trust" with a hidden surveillance that will bring Antonio under his control. Furthermore, Prospero "abjures" the magic that led him to neglect his office. And though at the end of the play Prospero does not seem much inclined to return to the active duties of a duke, he has made sure his dukedom will fall into the hands of people more trustworthy than Antonio.

Because Antonio functions so powerfully as a threatening "other," Shakespeare can display Prospero's imperfections without seriously jeopardizing Prospero's claim to be a "good master." That Prospero's representation of himself has an element of denial, that his neglect of office may have contributed to Antonio's fall — these offenses as well as others pale in comparison to those of Antonio. Antonio clearly would be a much worse "master" than Prospero, and the audience is encouraged to feel that a controlling authority is needed to contain his overreaching.

A good deal of what Brown has to say about "savagism" and "masterlessness," then, can easily be used to illuminate the play's characterization of Antonio. Antonio's apparently constitutional evil helps to confirm the moral legitimacy of Prospero's rule, much as the savage is used to confirm the "civilized" and "godly" character of colonial authority. And like the rebellion of the "masterless" man or lapsed civil subject, Antonio's occurs when the state's structures of supervision break down (i.e., when Prospero neglects "worldly ends"). Moreover, Antonio remains a potential "site of disruption" even after Prospero has brought him back under his control. In the final scene, Antonio is the only character who refuses to participate in the general atmosphere of reconciliation. Many critics have noted Antonio's ominous silence here, as well as the grudging, incomplete quality of Prospero's "forgiveness." Perhaps Shakespeare is dramatizing the difficulty of exacting justice upon a once-beloved relative; in confronting the brother who betrayed him, Prospero seems understandably torn between retaliatory impulses and more merciful ones. Yet Prospero would also be in danger of self-contradiction by punishing Antonio more severely: if one mark of a "good nature" is to feel strong family bonds, Prospero would risk appearing "unnatural" were he to send Antonio to the executioner's block. Because Antonio's evil is conceived as an innate quality, or something close to it, he cannot be redeemed via repentance in the final scene; because Antonio is Prospero's once-beloved brother, his evil cannot be banished decisively by a retributive justice. The threat posed by Antonio is contained but not dissolved; as in Brown's analysis, the very terms Prospero uses to produce Antonio as "other" help to insure that he will remain a "site of disruption" in need of continued surveillance and control.

CALIBAN

Prospero invests Caliban with much the same qualities as Antonio. Caliban, we hear early on, will not take the "print of goodness"; his "vile race / . . . had that in't which good natures / Could not abide to be with" (1.2.355, 361–63; most editors give Miranda these lines, but she is clearly speaking the views of her father). Or, as Prospero puts it later, Caliban is "a born devil, on whose nature / Nurture can never stick" (4.1.188–89). Yet, while the play clearly endorses Prospero's construction of Antonio as threatening "other," it is by no means clear that it endorses Caliban as such. The play's early scenes, particularly in performance, work especially to Caliban's advantage. While we are at first led to see Prospero as a wonder-working and benevolent "god of power," his displays of bad temper, to Miranda and Ariel as well as to Caliban, raise doubts in subsequent scenes (1.2.78, 87–88, 106; 1.2.246–97) and his censure of Caliban must be viewed in this light. In addition, Caliban has a child-like exuberance that is likely to soften our judgment of him, and his response to Prospero's reminder of his rape attempt is disarming: "O ho, O ho! wouldn't had been done! / Thou didst prevent me; I had peopled else / This isle with Calibans" (1.2.352–54). Caliban manages to make even Prospero's defense of Miranda's chastity sound sanctimonious.

More importantly, Prospero's enslavement of Caliban is undermined by his precarious claim to legitimate rule of the island. Caliban's speeches encourage the audience to sympathize with his suffering, and also make it apparent that the history of Prospero and Caliban reverses that of Prospero and Antonio in at least one important respect. To Caliban, Prospero is the usurper: "This island's mine, by Sycorax my mother, / Which thou tak'st from me . . . / I am all the subjects that you have, / Which first was mine own King" (1.2.334–35, 344–45). Prospero makes no direct response to Caliban's accusation. His implicit claim to the island rests on Caliban's degenerate nature. In a sense, Prospero plays Bolingbroke to Caliban's Richard II: Caliban can claim the title of King of the island by inheritance; Prospero's claim rests solely on superior virtue and fitness for rule. Here, Prospero undercuts the basis of his own title, inconsistently assuming the position of Antonio, who argued that Prospero's withdrawal from office showed him to be "incapable" of rule and justified his takeover. Caliban's claim to legitimacy is at least as powerful as Prospero's own.[7]

The scene, then, draws us to criticize Prospero's actions: we also are led to criticize Prospero's assessment of Caliban's character. As many critics have pointed out, descriptions of Caliban in the text are varied and suggest that indeterminacy is an essential feature of his character. He crosses several boundaries: half-human, half-devil, or perhaps half-human, half-fish; abnormal mentally and physically; savage, "strange beast," and "moon-calf." As "wild man," he is also a composite, possessing qualities of the "noble savage" as well as the monster. He is capable of learning language, of forming warm attachments; he is sensitive to beauty and music; he speaks — like the aristocratic characters — in the rhythms of verse, in contrast to the prose of Stephano and Trinculo; he can follow a plan and reason; yet he is also physically deformed, "vile," credulous, and capable of rape and brutality.[8]

The audience's response to Caliban is likely to have a similarly composite character. Caliban's credulousness in the scenes with Stephano and Trinculo, for example, evokes both sympathy and derision. We are invited to laugh at Caliban for his conversion to Stephano and his drunkenness, and yet as the mean-spiritedness of Stephano and Trinculo becomes more evident, Caliban's superiority becomes so as

[7]Stephen Orgel also discusses this point in "Shakespeare and the Cannibals," arguing that "Caliban does constitute a significant counterclaim to Prospero's authority" (p. 54). See also his comments in "Prospero's Wife," in *Representations* 8 (Fall 1984): 1–13 (esp. 7–9).

[8]On Caliban's composite character, see Stephen J. Greenblatt, "Learning to Curse." Greenblatt shows how Caliban's character is shaped by seemingly opposed attitudes toward native speech in New World writings. On Caliban and the "wild man," see Hayden White, "The Forms of Wildness: Archaeology of an Idea," in *The Wild Man Within; an Image in Western Thought from the Renaissance to Romanticism*, ed. Edward Dudley and Maximillian Novak (Pittsburgh: Pittsburgh Univ. Press, 1972), pp. 3–38; on Caliban's antecedents, see Richard Bernheimer, *Wild Men in the Middle Ages: A Study in Art, Sentiment and Demonology* (1952; rpt. New York: Octagon Press, 1970); on Caliban and pastoral, see Frank Kermode's introduction to the Arden edition of *The Tempest*. For a review of different ways Caliban has been imagined in performance, see Virginia M. Vaughan, "'Something Rich and Strange': Caliban's Theatrical Metamorphoses" in *SQ* 36 (Spring 1985): 390–405.

well. Moreover, in first encountering the spirits of the island, Gonzalo has raised the possibility that those who appear monstrous may in fact possess civilized traits: though the "islanders" are "of monstrous shape" he urges the King's party to note that "Their manners are more gentle, kind, than of / Our human generation" (3.3.29, 31–33). Prospero, overlooking the scene, comments "Honest lord, / Thou hast said well; for some of you there present / Are worse than devils" (lines 34–36). Prospero himself, then, implicitly ranks the evil of Antonio below that of Caliban, and in the final scene, he softens his earlier characterization of Caliban: Caliban is a "demi-devil" rather than a "devil" (5.1.272).

The audience must also reckon with Caliban's final conversion. At the end of the play, Caliban's reaction to the sight of Prospero in his duke's robes and to the other Milanese provokes a response that echoes Miranda's vision of a "brave new world": "O Setebos, these be brave spirits indeed! / How fine my master is!" (5.1.261–62). When Prospero directs Caliban to his cell, saying "as you look / To have my pardon, trim it handsomely" (5.1.292–93), Caliban responds dutifully:

> Ay, that I will; and I'll be wise hereafter,
> And seek for grace. What a thrice-double ass
> Was I, to take this drunkard for a god,
> And worship this dull fool!
>
> (5.1.294–97)

While perhaps not a full conversion — Caliban seems more motivated by his dislike of appearing ridiculous than by remorse — his change of heart largely undermines Prospero's statement that "nurture can never stick" upon the "born devil." At the very least, it suggests that Prospero has applied the wrong strategies in his dealings with Caliban. Neither "humane education" nor punishment and enslavement have produced virtue in him; rather, his transformation is the product of events largely outside Prospero's control.

Brown passes over Caliban's conversion, which does not fit with his claim that the "other" must remain a continual "site of disruption." He uses this moment to argue that Caliban's function in the final act is to insure aristocratic class solidarity, and focuses instead on the laughter that accompanies Caliban's entrance:

> SEBASTIAN: Ha, ha!
> What things are these, my lord Antonio?
> Will money buy 'em?

ANTONIO: Very like; one of them
     Is a plain fish, and no doubt, marketable.
                          (5.1.263–66)

The moment, however, is more complex. We are probably drawn to
laugh at Caliban — but uneasily. These remarks recall the cynical, sneer-
ing humor Sebastian and Antonio have displayed in earlier scenes, reaf-
firming their sinister character and setting them apart from the "good"
aristocrats. The remarks also link Sebastian and Antonio with the language and exploitive attitudes of Trinculo and Stephano. Indeed, the
general tendency of the final scene is to use this division within the aristocracy to produce a solidarity that cuts across class lines. Caliban, along
with Stephano, Trinculo, and the blasphemous Boatswain, all take their
place in a restored political order to which only Antonio refuses to be
reconciled, an order confirmed primarily by disclosing the threat, not of
masterlessness or savagism, but of aristocratic overreaching.

What then can we conclude about the play's relation to colonial
discourse? As Brown says, a "sustained historical and theoretical analysis of the play's involvement in the colonialist project has yet to be
undertaken."[9] Such an analysis will need to take into account the fact
that Caliban is not, to the audience, an embodiment of threat. Indeed,
Caliban is by turns sympathetic and ridiculous; the play's racism in-
heres most clearly in its linking of Caliban's "vile race" to a "nature"
that is conceived of as comically grotesque rather than demonic.[10]

---

[9]Brown, p. 268.

[10]Caliban, we should note, is still produced as "other"— but not in accordance with
Brown's pattern, the pattern that he insists is the characteristic mechanism of colonial discourse. By the play's end, Caliban is neither a threat nor a continuing "site of disruption."
But why should colonial discourse always speak the same way, according to the same set
of rules? Brown adapts his pattern from Edward Said and others, who are analyzing the
colonial discourse of a later period, a discourse which also focuses on a different culture.
Why should this analysis necessarily apply to *The Tempest*, a text written at a time when
the colonizing of the New World was still in its early stages, before its structures were
fully in place? Brown's representation of otherness in colonialist discourse seems one-
dimensional and, at times, ahistorical.

To be sure, Brown does, at the beginning of his essay, acknowledge the presence in
colonialist writings of the "reformable" native as well as the irreducibly savage. But this
discussion gives way quickly to his preoccupation with a "colonialist stereotype" that typically produces "a disruptive other in order to assert the superiority of the colonizer,"
who by definition is always provoking the colonizer to further efforts at control (p. 280).
Brown does not explain the relation of the "reformable" native to this stereotype. Both
the reformable native and the irreformable "born devil" confirm the civilized and godly
character of the colonialist, as Brown points out (p. 271); but the former, once con-
verted, no longer is likely to function as a "site of disruption."

Ultimately, the play trivializes Caliban's plight. Caliban's conversion insures that the moral and logical problems attendant upon Prospero's seizure of the island are simply forgotten as the play shifts focus and celebrates the regeneration of the Milanese political order. Yet we may find ourselves wondering about Caliban's fate. What good can come to him if Prospero leaves him to his island, now that he has become a "servant-monster," a creature of civilization? What good can come to him if they take him to Milan? The play in its final moments focuses briefly on Ariel's coming freedom, which we know Ariel will enjoy; it is eloquent in its silence about Caliban.

An analysis of the play's involvement in the colonial project will also need to consider the role of the far more sinister figure of Antonio. Shakespeare fashions Antonio out of his culture's anxieties about factious and rebellious aristocrats, about the exclusion of younger brothers from power by primogeniture, and about aggression unmodulated by a sense of familial or communal bonds. He locates the origin of Prospero's colonial project in a crisis that besets the political order of the "core," that is, in the failure of that order to contain the threats embodied by Antonio. As Prospero moves toward greater mastery of self and "others" (and toward the successful containment of these threats), he is forced by the emergency nature of his situation to use the "peripheral" space provided by the island — despite its risks, its moral dangers, its subversive magic. When the emergency is over, he must give the island up.

DAVID SCOTT KASTAN

"The Duke of Milan / And His Brave Son": Old Histories and New in *The Tempest*

David Scott Kastan (b. 1946) is the Old Dominion Foundation Professor in the Humanities and chair of the Department of English at Columbia University. He is the author of *Shakespeare and the Shapes of Time* (1982), *Shakespeare after Theory* (1999), and *Shakespeare and the Book* (2001). He has coedited *Staging the Renaissance: Essays on Elizabethan and Jacobean Drama* (1991) and *The New History of Early English Drama* (1997). In addition, he is the editor of *Critical Essays on Shakespeare's "Hamlet"* (1995) and *A Companion to Shakespeare* (1999) as well as two Norton Critical editions, Christopher Marlowe's

Doctor Faustus (2005) and John Milton's *Paradise Lost* (2006). He serves as a general editor of the Arden Shakespeare and his edition of *1 Henry IV* for that series was published in 2002. The following piece is a chapter from *Shakespeare after Theory*.

Every image of the past that is not recognized by the present as one of its own concerns threatens to disappear irretrievably.

—WALTER BENJAMIN

It is, of course, *The Comedy of Errors* that alone among Shakespeare's plays mentions "America" (which the Syracusan Dromio exhuberantly locates "upon [Nell's] nose, all o'er embellished with rubies, carbuncles, sapphires, declining their rich aspect to the hot breath of Spain"[1]), but it is Shakespeare's other comedy observing the unities of time and place, *The Tempest,* that has almost inescapably become his play of Europe's engagement with the New World. Since Malone in 1808 first called attention to the play's relation to the Virginia Company pamphlets, offering the closest thing we have to something that might be thought of as a source for *The Tempest,* the experience of Thomas Gates and his men in Bermuda has been taken to give a local habitation and a name to the stereotypical narrative of shipwreck and deliverance articulating the play's romance form.[2]

Following Malone, critics have long claimed that the accounts of the miraculous escape of Gates's ship from "the most dreadful tempest," as Strachey's report terms it, that drove it from the Virginia coast provided the material that stimulated Shakespeare's dramatic imagination. The texts of the various reports from Virginia have come to seem the determining source and subtext of the play itself. In 1901, Morton Luce, editor of the first Arden edition, argued that the wreck of the *Sea-Venture* "must have suggested the leading incidents of *The Tempest*"; "indeed," he continues, "we may fairly say that fully nine-tenths of the subjects touched upon by Shakespeare in *The Tempest* are suggested by the new enterprise of colonisation."[3] And critics have

---

[1] *The Comedy of Errors,* 3.2.133–35. It is worth noting that "America," perhaps inevitably for a play written in the early 1590s, is here associated with a Spanish colonial interest rather than an English one.

[2] Edmond Malone, *An account of the incidents from which the title and part of the story of Shakespeare's "Tempest" were derived and its true date determined* (London: C. and R. Baldwin, 1808).

[3] *The Tempest,* ed. Morton Luce (London: Methuen, 1901), pp. xii, xlii.

continued to insist, as John Gillies has recently put it, that the play is "vitally rather than casually implicated in the discourses of America and the Virginia Company," whose directors included the Earl of Southampton, to whom Shakespeare dedicated *Venus and Adonis* and *The Rape of Lucrece*, and the Earl of Pembroke, one of the dedicatees of the First Folio, making such a connection to Shakespeare plausible if not absolutely compelling.[4]

Recently, of course, criticism of *The Tempest*, while reasserting the New World context, has effectively wrested the play from the idealizations of romance (as Gillies's word "implicated" no doubt signals). The experience of the Virginia colonists is no longer merely a timely reminder of the timeless structures of a romance mode in which the world of "mortal accident" is discovered to "suffer a sea-change / Into something rich and strange" (1.2.404–05), in which the hand of "great creating nature" can be felt organizing the turbulence of earthly existence, reestablishing love and human continuance. No longer is *The Tempest* a play of social reconciliation and moral renewal, of benevolent artistry and providential design; it now appears as a telling document of the first phase of English imperialism, implicated in the will-to-power of the Jacobean court, even as an "instrument of empire" itself.[5]

Prospero is no longer an inspiring magus but an arrogant and ill-tempered magistrate (not even the "good, authoritarian Governor" that Geoffrey Bullough saw[6]); and the romance form is no longer a utopian spectacle of wonder but itself a participant in the ideological activity of imperialism — performing the necessary act of colonialist legitimation by naturalizing domination as the activity of a "Providence divine" (1.2.159). Coleridge found *The Tempest* to be one of those

[4]John Gillies, *Shakespeare and the Geography of Difference* (Cambridge: Cambridge University Press, 1994), p. 149. On Shakespeare's relations with the Virginia Company, see Charles Mills Gayley, *Shakespeare and the Founders of Liberty in America* (New York: Macmillan, 1917).

[5]The phrase, now a staple of *Tempest* criticism, derives from Antonio de Nebrija's justification to Queen Isabella for his Spanish grammar: "language is the perfect instrument of empire" (quoted from Louis Hanke, *Aristotle and the American Indians* [Bloomington: Indiana Univ. Press, 1959], p. 8). Nebrija (or, more properly, Lebrija) was, however, a bit less explicit about the instrumental relation of language and empire; "siempre la lengua fue compañera del imperio" (sig. a2ʳ) is what he wrote in his *Grammatica Castellana* (1492). For the play's "implication" in the English colonial project, see, for example, Paul Brown, " 'This thing of darkness I acknowledge mine': *The Tempest* and the Discourse of Colonialism," *Political Shakespeare: New Essays in Cultural Materialism,* ed. Jonathan Dollimore and Alan Sinfield (Ithaca: Cornell Univ. Press, 1985), esp. pp. 56 and 64. [Reprinted in this volume, p. 268; see pp. 278 and 286.]

[6]*Narrative and Dramatic Sources of Shakespeare* (London: Routledge and Kegan Paul, 1975), vol. 8, p. 245.

plays "where the ideal is predominant,"[7] but for us the "ideal" usually now seems only the name that the powerful give to their desire. In our anxious postcolonial moment, the power of Prospero's art, once confidently viewed as benevolently civilizing, has become the colonizer's technology of domination and control. Prospero's magic in the play now appears, in Stephen Greenblatt's phrase, as "the romance equivalent of martial law," or, in Peter Hulme's version, marking out "the space really inhabited in colonial history by gunpowder."[8] And Caliban and, if somewhat less truculently, Ariel are the natives of the new world who have been unwillingly subjected to the coercive power of European knowledge.

This is the current orthodoxy of *Tempest* criticism, but not, it should be said, of *Tempest* performance, which most often has chosen, for obvious reasons, to emphasize the theme and spectacle of artistry, even as it has come to recognize the contradictions and stresses of the text. Nonetheless, there have been memorable "colonial" interpretations, as Jonathan Miller's production of the play at the Mermaid in 1970, casting black actors as Caliban and Ariel and explicitly depending, as Miller wrote, on "the whole colonial theme as knowledge which the audience brought to bear on Shakespeare's play."[9] But though undoubtedly "colonial," this was not a "new world" *Tempest*. Miller was thinking explicitly of the then current political situation in Nigeria, and he based his characterizations upon Octave Mannoni's analysis in *La psychologie de la colonisation* (1950) of the 1947 revolt in Madagascar. And, more recently, George Wolfe's 1995 *Tempest* in Central Park (and then on Broadway), starring Patrick Stewart, did stage the play as a third-world fantasy and made its colonial theme explicit, if uncertainly located both temporally and geographically. But these productions are, in any case, more the exception than the rule.

If on stage *The Tempest*'s relation to the new world is still optional, the critical assertion of the play's relation to the colonial enterprise in the Americas is now seemingly inescapable, even historically extendable, as in Leslie Fiedler's claim that in the play "the whole history of

---

[7] *Coleridge on Shakespeare: The Text of the Lectures of 1811–1812*, ed. R. A. Foakes (Charlottesville: Univ. Press of Virginia, 1971), p. 106.

[8] Greenblatt, *Shakespearean Negotiations: The Circulation of Social Energy in Renaissance England* (Berkeley and Los Angeles: Univ. of California Press, 1988), p. 156; and Hulme, "Hurricanes in the Caribbees: The Constitution of the Discourse of English Colonialism," in *1642: Literature and Power in the Seventeenth Century*, ed. Francis Barker, et al. (Colchester: Univ. of Essex, 1981), p. 74.

[9] Ralph Berry, *On Directing Shakespeare: Interviews with Contemporary Directors* (London: Croom Helm, 1977), p. 34.

imperialist America has been prophetically revealed to us."[10] Fiedler at least has the good grace not to see the play as solely a document of *English* imperialism; but clearly for Fiedler, as for most of us who have read it in his wake, the play unsettlingly defines the encounter of the old world with the new, of the powerful with the powerless, its bad faith evident in Prospero's bitter denunciation of Antonio's usurpation of his dukedom but his complete blindness to his own usurpation of the sovereignty of the island. "This island's mine," protests Caliban, "by Sycorax my mother, / Which thou tak'st from me . . . I am all the subjects that you have, / Which first was mine own King: and here you sty me / In this hard rock, whiles you do keep from me / the rest o' th' island" (1.2.334–47). Prospero responds angrily: "thou most lying slave," not, however, angry about Caliban's claim of alienated sovereignty but at his assertion of undeserved hard-treatment: "I have us'd thee, / Filth thou art, with human care; and lodg'd thee / In mine own cell, till thou didst seek to violate / The honor of my child" (1.2.347–51). What Prospero calls a lie is only the claim that he is an oppressor; Caliban's claim that he is a usurper is not contested, indeed, not even heard, so fully does Prospero feel his own right to rule to be beyond any question.

No doubt Prospero's bad faith (a bad faith not canceled out by the fact that Caliban's sovereign claim is itself based upon his Algerian mother's parallel domination of a native "spirit" population) is relevant to any understanding of the encounter with the new world, whose native inhabitants could have said to their putative "discoverers," no less tellingly than Prospero to Miranda, "'Tis new to thee" (5.1.184). But it is worth reminding ourselves how thin is the thread on which the play's relation to the new world hangs.

The play is obviously set in the old world; the tempest is called up as the Italian nobles are returning from Africa to Italy, and those who have escaped the storm are said to return "sadly" to Naples "upon the Mediterranean flote" (1.2.234). Ariel does refer to Bermuda, but pointedly as the place they are not: the Italian's ship, he tells Prospero, is safe in the harbor "where once / Thou call'dst me up at midnight to fetch dew / From the still-vex'd Bermoothes" (1.2.227–29). The only other explicit textual connections are the two references to "Setebos," who Caliban identifies as "my dam's god" (1.2.376) and editors have identified in accounts of Magellan's voyages as a "great devil" of the

---

[10]Leslie A. Fiedler, *The Stranger in Shakespeare* (New York: Stein and Day, 1972), p. 238.

Patagonian religion. Trinculo observes that the English who "will not give a doit to relieve a lame beggar . . . will lay out ten to see a dead Indian" (2.2.31–32), but Trinculo never takes the creature hiding beneath the cloak for an Indian; it is some kind of "monster" that "smells like a fish." That's it. Some would add Gonzalo's use of the word "plantation," its only appearance in Shakespeare, though "plantation" is a word apparently coined for *old* world domination, to describe the English colonial project in Ireland, and even when applied to the new world is used to describe an exclusively English enclave: "a plantation of the people of your owne English nation," as John Hooker writes to Raleigh.[11] And, of course, Gonzalo's utopian fantasy is based on a passage in Montaigne's essay on the cannibals of Brazil. But its primitivist vision has little relevance to the dreams and desires of the Italian courtiers, as is revealed by its self-contradiction, where Gonzalo's imaginings of a world with "no sovereignty" (2.1.153) originate in its opposite, in a fantasy of power: "Had I plantation of this isle, my lord . . . And were the king on't . . ." (2.1.140, 142).

In all there is very little to go on, especially to validate the now commonplace insistence that new world colonialism provides the play's "dominant discursive con-texts."[12] Though Prospero does locate Caliban in anthropological, social, moral, even theological discourses — "beast," "slave," "demi-devil"— that sanction and support his own hierarchical superiority, we might note that Caliban is described as "freckled" and of a "blue-ey'd" dam (1.2.284, 270; and though editors regularly remind us that "blue-eyed" may well refer to the dark blue of the eyelid understood as a mark of pregnancy or even be an error for "blear-eyed," to an English audience for whom blue eyes were not at all unusual the term must inevitably have been heard, if not necessarily intended, conventionally, as an indication of the color of the iris). Caliban is not, therefore, easily imagined either as an indigenous American or African slave. Indeed, as long ago as 1927, E. E. Stoll would emphatically deny that the play had any relation to the new world at all. "There is not a word in *The Tempest*," he writes, "about America or

---

[11]Epistle Dedicatory to *The Second Volume of Chronicles* in *The First and Second Volumes of Chronicles*, ed. Raphael Holinshed, et al. (London, 1586), sig. A3ᵛ.

[12]Francis Barker and Peter Hulme, "Nymphs and reapers heavily vanish: The Discursive Con-texts of *The Tempest*," in *Alternative Shakespeares,* ed. John Drakakis (London: Routledge, 1985), p. 198. [Reprinted in this volume, p. 292; see p. 299.] Richard Halpern similarly says that "colonialism has established itself as a dominant, if not the dominant code for interpreting *The Tempest*," in his "'The Picture of Nobody': White Cannibalism in *The Tempest*," in *The Production of English Renaissance Culture,* ed. David Lee Miller, Sharon O'Dair, and Harold Weber (Ithaca: Cornell Univ. Press, 1994), p. 265.

Virginia, colonies or colonizing, Indians or tomahawks, maize, mocking-birds, or tobacco. Nothing but the Bermudas, once barely mentioned as faraway places, like Tokio or Mandalay."[13] And more recently Geoffrey Bullough stated bluntly: "*The Tempest* is not a play about colonization."[14]

Stoll and Bullough are, of course, too absolute, but if the play has a relation to the new world colonial activity it is not writ deep into its texture; the relation is allusive and elusive, existing primarily in the negations, like Ariel's or Trinculo's, that deny that the experience on the island is the experience of the Americas. The negations, of course, make the new world present, in a sense, but we may wonder why, if colonialism is, as Francis Barker and Peter Hulme put it, "the articulatory *principle* of *The Tempest*" the principle is almost completely effaced and when present is established negatively rather than by a direct engagement with the material of Virginia.[15]

Possibly this is evidence of the play's uneasy conscience about the colonial project, or possibly our hypersensitivity to it is evidence merely of our own uneasy conscience in the postcolonial world we inhabit. In any case, part of the desire to locate the play within the discourses of early colonialism, to return the play to a historical moment, is evidence of the degree to which the imagination of the past now enthralls us as once we were enthralled by the imagination of the future, and seems worthily motivated by the felt need to rescue the play from the banality of the moral claims made for it in the name of its putative timelessness and transcendence. Yet one might ask about the specific historicizing gesture: why this moment, why these discourses that are arguably no less eccentric in the play than they were in the culture of Jacobean England? Certainly, it is possible to suggest other and more obvious contexts, and then perhaps to wonder about why they do not appear to us the play's "articulatory principle," if only to suggest that the Americanization of *The Tempest* may be itself an act of cultural imperialism.

The play is much more obviously a play about European dynastic concerns than European colonial activities, but this has largely slipped

[13]"Certain Fallacies and Irrelevancies in the Literary Scholarship of the Day," *Studies in Philology* 24 (1927): 484.

[14]*Narrative and Dramatic Sources of Shakespeare*, vol. 8, p. 241.

[15]Barker and Hulme, "Nymphs," p. 306. Greenblatt, while basing his account of *The Tempest* upon its relation to the Virginia Company narratives, does see the play's "swerve away from these materials," though he sees this swerve as evidence "of the process by which the Bermuda material is made negotiable"; that is, even as the play transforms the source material, for Greenblatt, it remains centrally grounded in the new world and "colonial discourse" (*Shakespearean Negotiations*, pp. 154–55).

from view — or at least from critical comment. The Italian courtiers have no interest in colonizing the island on which they find themselves, no desire to "plant a nation / Where none before had stood," as Rich's *Newes From Virginia* (1610, sig. B2ʳ) defines the goals of the first English settlers. The Italians' journey was not to explore or settle a new world but was intended as a return home, a return from a royal wedding of Alonso's daughter Claribel to the King of Tunis. And only Trinculo and Stephano worry about sovereignty on the island: "the King and all our company else being drowned," says Stephano, "we will inherit *here*" (2.2.167–68); Antonio and Sebastian, on the contrary, think only about crowns in Europe: "As thou got'st Milan, / I'll come by Naples" (2.1.286–87), Sebastian eagerly declares, urging Antonio to draw his sword and murder the Neapolitan king. Even Ferdinand immediately understands and articulates his situation in the explicitly dynastic terms of the world he has come from. When he hears Miranda speak, he responds with amazement: "My language! heavens! / I am the best of them that speak this speech" (1.2.432–33), instantly locating his sorrow in a set of political relations: "myself am Naples, / Who with mine eyes, never since at ebb, beheld / The King my father wrack'd" (1.2.438–40), just as he, with the same alacrity, finds political measure for his love for Miranda: "I'll make you / The Queen of Naples" (1.2.452–53). And Alonso at the end, hearing that Prospero has "lost" *his* daughter, thinks of her and his own lost son as a royal couple to provide the terms of loss for the tragic cutting off of their children's too brief lives: "O heavens, that they were living both in Naples, / The King and Queen there" (5.1.149–50).

Indeed, the critical emphasis upon the new world not only obscures the play's more prominent discourses of dynastic politics but also blinds us to disturbances in the text that should alert us to this aspect of the play's engagement with its own historical moment. When Alonso mourns the apparent death of his son, he, perhaps predictably, identifies him not by name but by his dynastic position: "O thou mine heir / Of Naples and Milan" (2.1.108–09). No edition of the play feels the line worthy of comment, but it seemingly poses a problem. As son of the Neapolitan King, Ferdinand is obviously heir to the crown of Naples, but why is he heir of "Milan"? Antonio has replaced Prospero as duke — and Antonio has a son who presumably would be his successor: reporting on his experience of the tempest, Ferdinand reports his dismay at seeing Antonio "and his brave son being twain" (1.2.442), a line that editors usually gloss by predicating some earlier and then abandoned conception of the play in which this dynastic relation would have been developed. Thus Dover Wilson writes in his note in the New Cambridge edition (now, of course, the "old" New Cambridge) that "he must be one of the Alonso group in an earlier version" of the play, as if a prior, and differing, version of *The Tempest* is certain to have existed. Stephen Orgel in his Oxford edition more cautiously writes that "possibly a parallel to Ferdinand was originally contemplated by Shakespeare, and then abandoned as the drama took shape." And Frank Kermode, in his Arden edition, somewhat despairingly concludes that "Shakespeare began writing with a somewhat hazy understanding of the dynastic relationships he was to deal with."

But the "dynastic relations" are adequately, indeed tellingly, developed here. Antonio's arrangement with Naples, in which, in return, as Prospero says, for "homage and I know not how much tribute" (1.2.124), Alonso has conferred "fair Milan, / With all the honors, on my brother" (1.2.126–27), clearly reserves Milanese sovereignty for Naples, alienating Antonio's son from the succession. Indeed, when Alonso at the end begs Prospero to "pardon" his wrongs, it is he, not Antonio, who offers: "Thy dukedom I resign" (5.1.118), another line that has generally escaped critical comment. The romance action is to rescue Milan from vassalage to Naples and yet still allow the merging of national interests that James's fantasy of European peace and coherence would demand. As the truth of the strange events of the play emerges fully, leading those who will to "rejoice / Beyond a common joy" (5.1.206–07), even the utopian Gonzalo recognizes that the true source of wonder is the political miracle that has been performed: "Was Milan thrust from Milan, that his issue / Should become Kings of Naples?" (5.1.205–06). It is this happy dynastic resolution that he would see set down "With gold on lasting pillars" (5.1.208), invoking the imperial iconography of Charles V, which was soon adopted by other European monarchies.[16] Ariel's terms for the success of Prospero's tempest are thus homonymically apt; in the play's magical rewriting of history there is "not so much perdition as an hair" (1.2.30). Indeed the only thing that apparently is lost in the tempest is the usurper Antonio's disinherited son, the one "hair"— or heir — that can be cut from the restorative action of the play.

[16]Dennis Kay identifies the allusion here to the pillars of Hercules, adopted as an imperial emblem first by Charles V and then by other European rulers, including Elizabeth. See his "Gonzalo's 'Lasting Pillars': *The Tempest,* V.i.208," *Shakespeare Quarterly* 35 (1984): 322–24.

Certainly, for the audience of *The Tempest* at Court in 1613, when the play was performed as one of fourteen plays selected for the festivities leading up to the marriage of the King's daughter, Elizabeth, to Frederick, the Elector Palatine (this was, it should be noted, the second recorded performance of the play, the first on Hallowmas night of 1611 at Whitehall before "ye kinges Maiestie"[17]), the play's events were more likely to resonate with political issues in Europe rather than in the Americas. Alonso's sadness at having apparently lost his son and married his daughter to a foreign prince might well have seemed a virtual mirror of the situation of their King, whose son, Henry, had died the previous year, and who now was marrying his daughter, Elizabeth, to a foreign prince (and who would, exactly as Alonso feared for himself, never see his daughter again).

The marriage of the Princess Elizabeth was, like all royal weddings, politics by other means, designed primarily to serve the political interests of the nation or at least its king, rather than the emotional needs of the marrying couple. The match had long been rumored, and negotiations for it had begun as early as 1608, though there were always other prominent candidates for Elizabeth's hand, most notably the Prince of Piedmont, heir of the Duke of Savoy, and the recently widowed King of Spain, Philip III. A contemporary discussion of "suitable alliances" for Elizabeth interestingly comments: "the Prince of Piedmont an unequal match for the Princess, unless the King of Spain will give him the Duchy of Milan on his marriage, which is not likely, as that King is said to want her for himself. She could not marry him without changing her religion, and such a marriage would be dangerous to the two that are between her and the Crown. A match with Sweden or the Prince Palatine suggested for her . . ." (*CSPD* [*Calendar of State Papers*] 1611–18, p. 97).

It was the match with the Prince Palatine to which James finally agreed. In many ways the "most suitable" (*CSPD* 1611–18, p. 97), the choice, of course, was designed not least to satisfy the interests of the Protestant nation and more immediately to tie James to the Union of Protestant Princes in the struggle against the Austrian Habsburgs and the states of the Catholic League. Though James's original hope had been to avoid sectarian alliance — or rather, while Henry lived, to pair sectarian alliances — Henry to the Spanish Infanta; Elizabeth to the

[17]See E. K. Chambers, *William Shakespeare: A Study of Facts and Problems* (Oxford: Clarendon Press, 1930), vol. 2, p. 342.

Palatine prince — in order to play his planned role as mediator of Europe's religious conflicts, with Henry's death in 1612, that particular balancing act was impossible. While the Treaty of Antwerp in 1609, reconciling Spain to the United Provinces, seemed initially to promise peace in Europe, within a few weeks a dispute over succession in the Rhine principality of Cleves — Jülich divided the Protestant and Catholic States and again pushed Europe toward full-scale religious war, "a generall altercacion in Christendome," as Salisbury feared.[18] James had little choice then but to side with the Protestant princes — and, indeed, the marriage of Elizabeth to the Palatine Prince was finally agreed to as a result of the negotiations with the Evangelical Union for English support in their struggle against the Catholic League.[19]

England seemed now fully committed to the international Protestant cause. Dudley Carleton reported that "all well-affected people take great pleasure and contentment in this Match, as being a firm foundation and stablishing of religion . . . and the Roman Catholics malign it as much, as being the ruin of their hopes."[20] Though, in fact, as James's almost immediate search for a Spanish match for Prince Charles reveals, the King never abandoned his fantasy of being Rex Pacificus, to play the role of mediator between the rival religious blocs to secure a lasting peace. His willingness to side with the Evangelical Union was motivated less by his commitment to international Protestantism than by the desire to counterbalance the destabilizing aggressions of the Habsburg monarchy.

This all may seem to be taking us far from the island world of *The Tempest,* even farther than the new world narratives claimed as the play's source; but it may well bring us closer to the historical center of the play — and possibly to the heart of the interpretive problem it poses — than do the tracts of the Virginia Company. While southern Europe, including the Kingdom of Naples and the Dukedom of Milan, was largely at peace under the administration of the Spanish monarchy, the Holy Roman Empire was marked by a crisis of authority. In 1606,

---

[18] *Parliamentary Debates in 1610,* ed. S. R. Gardiner (London: Camden Society, 1861), p. 53.

[19] See Roger Lockyer, *The Early Stuarts: A Political History of England* (London and New York: Longman, 1989), esp. p. 15. It is perhaps of interest here that Pembroke and Southampton, to both of whom Shakespeare had connections, were proponents of an aggressive pro-Protestant foreign policy. See Thomas Cogswell, *The Blessed Revolution: English Politics and the Coming of War, 1621–1624* (Cambridge: Cambridge Univ. Press, 1989), esp. pp. 12–50.

[20] John Nichols, *Progresses of King James the First* (1828; rpt. New York: AMS Press, n.d.), vol. 2, 601–02.

the Habsburg archdukes stripped administrative control from the Emperor, Rudolf II, conferring it upon his brother Matthias. In 1608, Rudolf was forced to surrender to his brother the crowns of Austria, Hungary, and Moravia, keeping only the imperial crown and the crown of Bohemia. In April 1611, Rudolf was deposed from the throne of Bohemia as his brother was proclaimed Emperor.[21]

Rudolf turned to the Evangelical Union for support, and to James. Envoys were sent to England from the Diet of Protestant Princes in November asking James to back the reinstatement of the deposed Habsburg and to agree to the marriage of Elizabeth with the Elector Palatine to secure his commitment. While James's respect for the authority of princes could perhaps alone be reasonably expected to produce support for the reinstatement — and James had dedicated his own 1609 *Apology for the Oath of Allegiance* to "the Most Sacred and invincible Prince, Rudolf the II"— the English King certainly knew that the Emperor had brought about his own troubles by being irascible, indecisive, and increasingly unavailable. As early as 1591, Sir Henry Wotton had observed that Rudolf seems "now rather to bear the title of Emperor for fashion sake, than authority to command by virtue of it."[22] Gradually the Emperor withdrew from the affairs of state, shutting himself up in his palace, dedicating himself to scientific and occult study. Indeed, in 1606 the archdukes justified the reassignment of authority to Matthias by commenting that "[h]is majesty is interested only in wizards, alkymists, Kabbalists, and the like, sparing no expense to find all kinds of treasure, learn secrets, and use scandalous ways of harming his enemies" and noted his "whole library of magic books."[23] The responsibilities of government of little interest and increasingly beyond his control, Rudolf took refuge in his books behind the walls of his palace, uncannily like another ruler "transported / And rapt in secret studies" (1.2.76–77) who would be deposed by his brother for "neglecting worldly ends" (1.2.89).

---

[21]Henry Wotton wrote in May 1611 of how Rudolf was forced "to make Matthias King of the Romans." Commenting on the treatment of Rudolf by the supporters of Matthias, Wotton notes, "having first spoiled him of obedience and reverence, next of his estates and titles, they have now reduced him to so low a case, that he is no longer patron of his voice." See *Life and Letters of Sir Henry Wotton*, ed. Logan Pearsall Smith (Oxford: Clarendon Press, 1907), vol. 1, p. 507.

[22]*Life and Letters of Sir Henry Wotton*, vol. 1, p. 268.

[23]Quoted in R. J. W. Evans, *Rudolph II and His World* (Oxford: Clarendon Press, 1973), p. 196. See also Hugh Trevor-Roper, *Princes and Artists: Patronage and Ideology at Four Habsburg Courts 1517–1633* (London: Thames and Hudson, 1976), esp. pp. 122–23.

Part Two of John Barclay's popular *roman à clef, Euphormionis Lusinini Satyricon,* published in Paris in 1609 (but circulating widely in England, so much so that it is named as what any "Young Gentleman of the Universitie" would be reading in the character in John Earle's *MicroCosmographie*), has a readily identifiable portrait of Rudolf in the Theban ruler Aquilius who "abandons all thoughts of public matters, foreign and domestic" (sig. K2^r; translation mine) for "voluntary solitude" (sig. Ia^r) in his "beloved laboratory" (sig. K5^r) where he "searches into nature's secret places" (sig. K2^r). Similarly, Jonson's *Alchemist,* performed in 1610, reveals the English knowledge of Rudolf's habits in its reference to the alchemist and medium Edward Kelly, who, along with John Dee, was, like Jonson's "divine instructor" Subtle, "courted" by "the Emp'ror" (4.1.90–92) in Prague with the extraordinary commitment to alchemy and magic.

Though Rudolf's interests and political fate would inevitably have been known to many, I certainly am not claiming that Rudolf II is the sole inspiration for Shakespeare's Duke.[24] Here I am primarily concerned with showing the relevance of an available and unquestionably urgent European courtly context for the concerns of the play, and one that accounts for more of its textual density than the colonial theme that has come to dominate our readings. This is perhaps merely the move of the old historicism, eurocentric and courtly; though James, of course, would never have approved of either Rudolf's or Prospero's interest in magic or neglect of the concerns of state. Though George Marcelline hailed James as "The king of wonders, or the wonder of Kings" (1610, sig. H3^v), what "wonders" James achieved and his own appeal as an object of admiration were far more predictably worldly than the arcane interests and attractions of Rudolf's court in Prague or, more modestly, in Prospero's island cell.

In his *Daemonologie,* James explicitly condemns "diuerse Christian Princes" who allow magicians to live in their realms, and "euen sometimes delight to see them prooue some of their practicques"; these princes, he says "sinne heavilie against their office in that poynt."[25] And

---

[24]Michael Srigley's *Images of Regeneration: A Study of Shakespeare's "The Tempest" and Its Cultural Background* (Uppsala: Academiae Upsaliensis, 1985) does make an argument for such topical allegory, though, of course, we should remember that as early as *Loves Labor's Lost* Shakespeare had begun thinking about rulers who preferred the study to the affairs of state.

[25]*Daemonologie (1597) and Newes from Scotland,* ed. G. B. Harrison (London: Bodley Head, 1924), pp. 24–25.

in *Basilikon Doron* he instructs his son that "it is necessarie yee delight in reading and seeking the knowledge of all lawful things, but with these two restrictions. First, that yee choose idle houres for it, not interfering therewith the discharge of your office: and next, that yee studie not for knowledge nakedly, but that your principall ende be, to make you able thereby to vse your office."[26] The renunciation of magic to return to the reponsibilities of rule allows Prospero to redeem Rudolf's kingship — or rather allows him to escape the damning parallel with Rudolf and achieve a saving one with James himself. Prospero drowns his magic book, not, of course, the only reading matter with which Gonzalo had provided him, and returns to the teachings of the *speculum principiis,* like James's own *Basilikon Doron,* which always knows the priority of the arts of rule over the rules of magical art.

All interpretation is in a sense allegorical, offering a meaning other than the literal. But I am not suggesting here that we should substitute another allegory, not the biographical one of Prospero as Shakespeare, or the humanistic one of his magic as art, or in its recent, suspicious form as colonial domination, in order to see Prospero now as the Holy Roman Emperor; though certainly I am arguing that the world of European politics has receded too far from our view. In *The Winter's Tale,* Shakespeare may well have, in following Greene's *Pandosto,* mistakenly given Bohemia a sea-coast, but the complex politics of Bohemia and the other Habsburg states were arguably more deeply connected to the hopes and anxieties of the Jacobean court than were the struggling settlements in the new world.

This shift in focus from the new world to the old is not to evade or erase the history of colonialism as it has left its traces in the play but to individualize and clarify that history — perhaps indeed to motivate it. The colonial activity of seventeenth-century Europe must itself be understood in relation to the politics of the great European powers, to recognize at once England's deep involvements in Europe (a historical dimension that has worryingly dropped out of our recent attentions to the politics of early modern England) and the differing forms of colonial activity produced by its differing impulses and circumstances in England, Spain, and the Netherlands. If our attention to early modern colonialism is to be more than reflexive it must see its practices for what they were, as various and admittedly overdetermined activities within

---

[26] *The Political Works of James I,* ed. Charles Howard McIlwain (Cambridge, Mass.: Harvard Univ. Press, 1918), p. 38.

the conflicts of seventeenth-century European absolutism rather than as examples of a unified and transhistorical imperial desire and administration.[27]

Certainly, European expansionism is evident in the play, but more, it must be insisted, in the marriage of Claribel to the King of Tunis or Alonso's support of Antonio in exchange for Milan's vassalage than in Prospero's domination of the island. Or rather, the old world examples reveal the old technologies of expansion; the action on the island is symbolic of the new. And the two were always understood to support one another. Even as Europe looked west, it was mainly as it sought to thrive at home. Thinking about the incredible riches available in the new world, Hakluyt, that quintessential voice of English imperialism, observes enthusiastically (and in terms that uncannily explain something of the geo-politics of *The Tempest*): "with this great treasure, did not the emperor Charles get from the French king the kingdom of Naples, the dukedom of Milan, and all other his dominions in Italy, Lombardy, Piedmont, and Savoy."[28]

But though I would say (and have said) that the play clearly engages the social and political concerns of seventeenth-century Europe, concerns that the insistent focus on the new world in recent criticism has largely obscured, I am not now claiming that European court politics must replace new world colonialism as the "dominant discursive context" that reveals the meaning of *The Tempest*. Indeed, I am as much interested in the process by which a historical reading of a text is generated and grounded as I am in any particular reading, especially given the familiar charge of the arbitrariness of New Historicism's strategies of contextualization (in its most expansive form, evident in Dominick LaCapra's laundry-list of disparaging epithets: "facile associationism, juxtaposition or pastiche . . . weak montage, or, if you prefer, cut-and-paste bricolage"[29]).

Facile or not, New Historicism has often brilliantly connected apparently disparate cultural moments and practices to reveal their

---

[27]Even Marc Ferro's ambitious synthesis, *Colonization: A Global History* (London and New York: Routledge, 1997), admits that "it is true that one colonization was different from another" (p. viii).

[28]*The Original Writings and Correspondence of the Two Richard Hakluyts*, ed. Eva G. R. Taylor (London: Hakluyt Society, 1935), p. 243. See Jeffrey Knapp's fine *An Empire Nowhere: England, America, and Literature from "Utopia" to the "The Tempest"* (Berkeley: Univ. of California Press, 1992), esp. pp. 231–34.

[29]*Soundings in Critical Theory* (Ithaca: Cornell Univ. Press, 1989), p. 193.

common participation in a cultural system. In part, this has worked to erase the familiar opposition of text and context. Where the context once served as the flat backdrop against which the text's verbal display showed brilliantly in all of its artistic and intellectual complexity, now context and text are not so easily distinguished. Literary texts are no longer understood as repositories of meaning, but are seen as places where meanings are being made — places no more necessarily efficacious or valuable in this construction of social meaning than any other discursive form. It is this refusal to privilege automatically the literary over other discursive activities that has produced much of the hostility to New Historicism (and other poststructural critical modes). The literary text, however, is seen to be imbricated with a range of material and symbolic practices that make its distinction, in both senses of the word, from what formerly was understood as its context no longer sustainable.

The notion of context has thus been usefully problematized, understood now not as the static ground external to the text and reflected by it, but as the set of discourses that the literary text intersects and is intersected by. Texts and contexts are thus related dynamically rather than hierarchically: the text inevitably serves as a context for other texts, while the context is itself revealed as a text demanding interpretation before it yields its meanings. Many critics have therefore grown uncomfortable with the very term "context," fearing that its use reinstates the autonomy and presumptive value of the literary text that has been pointedly called into question.

Yet clearly the notion of context cannot be dispensed with. Indeed, once the meaning of the literary work is no longer sought in its aesthetic autonomy and formal perfection, all that is left is context. The text as it is both written and read is necessarily context-rich and context-dependent, and this is the source of its meaning. The written text takes meaning from the discourses that circulate through it; the text as read becomes meaningful through the contexts that structure the reader's engagement. That is, the text "means" only through the processes by which its particularities are seen to exist in relation to something outside it. Meaning may be of "different kinds," as Richard Palmer recognizes, "but it is always a kind of cohesion, relationship, or binding force; it is always in a context."[30]

---

[30]Richard E. Palmer, *Hermeneutics* (Evanston: Northwestern Univ. Press, 1969), p. 120.

But if meaning is necessarily context-bound, the number of meaningful contexts is apparently boundless.[31] By definition they can be neither singular nor inevitable. Certainly the frames in which one chooses to see a text, the horizons of interpretation, to use Gadamer's term, through which an interpreter engages it,[32] logically are virtually infinite (a single point can be intersected by an infinite number of lines), and they are valuable as they — and only as they — serve the interests and needs of the interpreter.

Once this is granted, however, it must be worth asking more about the contexts that appear to us to be relevant. *The Tempest* can profitably be viewed in relation to various historical and non-historical (e.g., ethical, psychological, theological, even, may I say it, aesthetic) contexts, and no one is inevitable and determining. If, however, one's interpretive desire is to reinsert the play into its own historical moment, into the space of its diegetic setting[33] as well as the performative space of its earliest productions (and this is a thoroughly reasonable and productive desire, though hardly the only useful interpretive desire we might have), it seems to me that we should look more closely at the old world than the new, at the wedding of Elizabeth and Frederick rather than of Pocahontas and John Rolfe, at James's own writings rather than the writings from Jamestown. This seems to me so both because old world history marks the play (context as discourse) more insistently than does the history of the new world that has dominated recent criticism — a history which, in fact, the play conspicuously avoids — and because the European history allows a reader to make sense of more in the text (context as frame) that would otherwise seem arbitrary or inexplicable. If, however, one's interpretive desire is to locate the play in *our* historical moment — also a reasonable and productive desire — then the colonial reading has more purchase; plays absorb history as much as they are marked by it at their inception.[34]

---

[31]The terms here are familiar. Jonathan Culler writes, "meaning is context-bound, but context is boundless" in his *On Deconstruction: Theory and Criticism after Structuralism* (Ithaca: Cornell Univ. Press, 1982), p. 123. But, for example, Susan Horton invokes the same wordplay ("although meaning itself may be 'context bound'. . . context itself is boundless") in her *Interpreting Interpreting: Interpreting Dicken's "Dombey"* (Baltimore: The Johns Hopkins Univ. Press, 1979), p. x.

[32]Hans-Georg Gadamer, *Truth and Method,* trans. Garrett Barden and John Cumming (London: Sheed and Ward, 1975), p. 269.

[33]**diegetic setting:** time and place of the play's main action.

[34]It is in the work of George Lamming, Roberto Fernández Retamar, Aimé Césaire, and others writing from within the anticolonial struggles of the mid-twentieth century that *The Tempest* suffers its sea-change and becomes the paradigmatic drama of colonialism.

In either case, the critical attention to the new world is not, of course merely willful; the play does find its source in the narrative accounts of a shipwreck of would-be colonists bound for Jamestown. But Shakespeare's relocation of the narrative from the new world to the old is not the unconscious displacement of this imperial theme as much as it is its deliberate erasure. In *The Tempest,* Shakespeare actively chooses *not* to tell the new world story that was before him. And if a later history has insisted that we restore the tale of colonial adventurism to the play, it is at least as much because we know we can use Shakespeare's cultural authority to claim a hearing for our political interests as because Shakespeare's political interests demand it from us. Certainly, such readings tell us something important, but arguably more about our world than about Shakespeare's. But if the shift in focus from Bermuda to Bohemia, from Harriot to Habsburg, removes the play from the colonial encounter of Europe with the Americas, it is not to evade or dull its political edges. Indeed, arguably it is to sharpen them, but it is to find them less in the conquest of the new world than in the killing religious conflicts and territorial ambitions of the old, where tragically they can be still found.[35]

The Tempest effectively stages and manages these anxieties about European politics and England's role within them, harmonizing and securing absolutist desire through the marriage of Miranda and Ferdinand. The play drives purposefully to fulfill Gonzalo's prayer: "look down, you gods, / And on this couple drop a blessed crown" (5.1.201–02). But this utopian solution to the problem of political conflict — a solution that by temperament, ideology, and financial limitation appealed to James and led him to conduct his foreign policy through marriage negotiation — is vulnerable, if only to irony. If the

---

[35]Howard Felperin has recently argued similarly that "the colonialism of the New World" has been overemphasized. Its traces in the play, he argues, have been "overread," mistaking "the part for the whole." Felperin, however, wants finally to see the "whole" not as a larger historical picture but "as a projection of nothing less than a historical totality" itself, or, as he says, "a vision of history as a cycle of repetition." This, however, seems to me to return the play to the very idealism that historical criticism has tried to counter. See his "Political Criticism at the Crossroads: The Utopian Historicism of *The Tempest,*" in *The Tempest,* ed. Nigel Wood (Buckingham and Philadelphia: Open University Press, 1995), esp. pp. 47–55. For a different relocation of *The Tempest* in relation to new world colonial activity, see Meredith Anne Skura's "Discourse and the Individual: The Case of Colonialism in *The Tempest,*" *Shakespeare Quarterly* 40 (1989): pp. 42–69 and reprinted in *Critical Essays on Shakespeare's "The Tempest,"* ed. Alden and Virginia Vaughan (New York: G. K. Hall, 1998). [Reprinted in this volume, p. 351.]

crown is "blessed," we should remember that the impending marriage
will accomplish precisely what the "inveterate" (1.2.122) hatred of
Alonso for Prospero attempted: the dissolution of Milanese sovereignty
into Neapolitan dynastic rule. However, in the reparative fantasy of the
The Tempest, nothing — nothing, that is, except the brave son of
Antonio, who has no place in its ambitious political relations — is
finally lost.

MEREDITH ANNE SKURA

Discourse and the Individual:
The Case of Colonialism in *The Tempest*

Meredith Anne Skura (b. 1944) is Libbic Shearn Moody Professor of English at Rice University. A scholar of Renaissance
drama, she is particularly interested in autobiography, performance, and psychoanalysis. She is the author of *The Literary
Uses of the Psychoanalytic Process* (1981), *Shakespeare the Actor
and the Purposes of Playing* (1993), and numerous essays on
Shakespeare, the Renaissance, and psychoanalysis. Her most
recent project is on English autobiographical writing in the
Renaissance. The essay that follows was originally published in
the *Shakespeare Quarterly* 40 (Spring 1989).

For many years idealist readings of *The Tempest* presented Prospero
as an exemplar of timeless human values. They emphasized the way in
which his hard-earned "magical" powers enable him to re-educate the
shipwrecked Italians to heal their civil war — and, even more important, to triumph over his own vengefulness by forgiving his enemies;
they emphasized the way he achieves, if not a wholly "brave," at least a
harmoniously reconciled new world. Within the last few years, however, numbers of critics have offered remarkably similar critiques of
this reading. There is an essay on *The Tempest* in each of three recent
anthologies of alternative, political, and reproduced Shakespeare
criticism, and another in the volume on estranging Renaissance criticism; *The Tempest* was a focus for the 1988 SAA session on "Shakespeare and Colonialism" and was one of the masthead plays in the

Folger Institute's 1988 seminar on new directions in Shakespeare studies.[1] Together, the revisionists call for a move to counteract some "deeply ahistorical readings" of *The Tempest*,[2] a play that is now seen to be not simply an allegory about "timeless"[3] or universal experience but rather a cultural phenomenon that has its origin in and effect on "historical" events, specifically in English colonialism. "New historicist" criticism in general, of which much recent work on *The Tempest* is a part, has itself begun to come under scrutiny, but the numerous historical reinterpretations of *The Tempest* deserve closer attention in their own right,[4] and they will be the subject of the rest of this essay.

[1]Two of the earliest of these critiques were actually written, although not published, by 1960: George Lamming, "A monster, a child, a slave" (1960) in *The Pleasures of Exile* (London: Allison and Busby, 1984); James Smith, "The Tempest" (1954) in *Shakespearian and Other Essays*, ed. E. M. Wilson (Cambridge: Cambridge Univ. Press, 1974), pp. 159–261. Two more articles, less politicized, followed in the sixties: Philip Brockbank, "*The Tempest*: Conventions of Art and Empire" in *Later Shakespeare*, eds. J. R. Brown and B. Harris (London: Edward Arnold, 1966), pp. 183–201; and D. G. James, "The New World" in *The Dream of Prospero* (Oxford: Clarendon Press, 1967), pp. 72–123.

The recent group, returning to the political perspective of the first two, includes: Stephen Greenblatt, "Learning to Curse: Aspects of Linguistic Colonialism in the Sixteenth Century" in *First Images of America*, ed. Fredi Chiappelli, 2 vols. (Los Angeles: Univ. of California Press, 1976), Vol. 2, 561–80; Bruce Erlich, "Shakespeare's Colonial Metaphor: On the Social Function of Theatre in *The Tempest*," *Science and Society*, 41 (1977), 43–65; Lorie Leininger, "Cracking the Code of *The Tempest*," *Bucknell Review*, 25 (1980), 121–31; Peter Hulme, "Hurricanes in the Caribbees: The Constitution of the Discourse of English Colonialism in *1642: Literature and Power in the Seventeenth Century*, Proceedings of the Essex conference on the Sociology of Literature, eds. Francis Barker et al. (Colchester: Univ. of Essex, 1981), pp. 55–83; Paul N. Siegel, "Historical Ironies in *The Tempest*," *Shakespeare Jahrbuch*, 119 (Weimar: 1983), 104–11; Francis Barker and Peter Hulme, "Nymphs and reapers heavily vanish: the discursive con-texts of *The Tempest*" in *Alternative Shakespeares*, ed. John Drakakis (London and New York: Methuen, 1985), pp. 191–205 [reprinted in this volume, p. 292]; Terence Hawkes, "Swisser-Swatter: Making a man of English letters" in *Alternative Shakespeares*, pp. 26–46; Paul Brown, "'This thing of darkness I acknowledge mine': *The Tempest* and the discourse of colonialism" in *Political Shakespeare: New essays in cultural materialism* (Ithaca, N.Y., and London: Cornell Univ. Press, 1985), pp. 48–71 [reprinted in this volume, p. 268]; Peter Hulme, *Colonial Encounters: Europe and the native Caribbean, 1492–1797* (London and New York: Methuen, 1986), pp. 89–134; Thomas Cartelli, "Prospero in Africa: *The Tempest* as colonialist text and pretext" in *Shakespeare Reproduced: The text in history and ideology*, eds. Jean Howard and Marion O'Conner (New York: Methuen, 1987), pp. 99–115; I would include two essays by Stephen Orgel somewhat different in their focus but nonetheless related: "Prospero's Wife" in *Rewriting the Renaissance*, eds. Margaret Ferguson et al. (Chicago: Univ. of Chicago Press, 1986), pp. 50–64, and "Shakespeare and the Cannibals" in *Cannibals, Witches, and Divorce: Estranging the Renaissance*, ed. Marjorie Garber (Baltimore and London: Johns Hopkins Univ. Press, 1987), pp. 40–66.

[2]Hulme, *Colonial Encounters*, p. 94.

[3]See, for example, Paul Brown, "This thing of darkness," p. 269.

[4]In fact Edward Pechter, in one of the earliest of such scrutinies, cited several of the

In assessing the "new" historicist version of the play, it is important to realize that here, even more than in other new historical criticism, an historical emphasis in itself is not new. Since the early nineteenth century *The Tempest* has been seen in the historical context of the New World, and Frank Kermode, citing the early scholars, argued in the fifties that reports of a particular episode in British efforts to colonize North America had precipitated the play's major themes.[5] In 1609 nine ships had left England to settle the colony in Jamestown, Virginia, and the *Sea Venture,* carrying all of the colonial officers, had disappeared. But its passengers reappeared in Virginia one year later, miraculously saved; they had wrecked off the Bermudas, until then believed demonically dangerous but now found to be providentially mild and fruitful. These events, much in the news in the year just preceding *The Tempest,* have long been seen as a relevant context for the play by all but a very few critics.[6] These earlier historical interpretations generally placed the play and its immediate source in the context of voyaging discourse in general, which stressed the romance and exoticism of discoveries in the Old as well as the New World. Even the "factual" reports in this discourse, as Charles Frey notes, were themselves colored by the romance of the situation, for better and for worse; and the traditional view was that *The Tempest*'s stylized allegory abstracts the romance core of all voyagers' experience.[7]

Nor had traditional criticism entirely ignored either Prospero's flaws[8] or their relation to the dark side of Europe's confrontation with the Other. Kermode had identified Caliban as the "core" or "ground"

---

recent *Tempest* articles as especially problematic. See "The New Historicism and Its Discontents: Politicizing Renaissance Drama," *PMLA,* 102 (1987), 292–303. See also Howard Felperin, "Making it 'neo': The new historicism and Renaissance literature," *Textual Practice,* 1 (1987), 262–77; Jean Howard, "The New Historicism in Renaissance Studies," *English Literary Renaissance,* 16 (1986), 13–43; and Anthony B. Dawson, "*Measure for Measure,* New Historicism, and Theatrical Power," *Shakespeare Quarterly,* 39 (1988), 328–41.

[5] *The Tempest,* The Arden Shakespeare, ed. Frank Kermode (London: Methuen, 1954), p. xxv. For an account of the work of earlier scholars exploring the connection between the play and these documents, see Kermode, pp. xxv–xxxiv, and Charles Frey, "*The Tempest* and the New World," *SQ* 30 (1979), 29–41.

[6] E. E. Stoll and Northrop Frye are the only exceptions I have seen cited.

[7] Recently there has been a renewed emphasis on the romance elements. See Gary Schmidgall, "*The Tempest* and *Primaleon:* A New Source," *SQ* 37 (1986), 423–39, esp. p. 436; and Robert Wiltenberg, "The '*Aeneid*' in *The Tempest,*'" *Shakespeare Survey,* 39 (1987), 159–68.

[8] See, for example, Harry Berger's important essay, "Miraculous Harp: A Reading of Shakespeare's *Tempest,*" *Shakespeare Studies,* 5 (1969), 253–83.

of the play, insofar as confrontation with this strange representative of "uncivilized" man prompts the play's reexamination of "civilized" human nature. Harry Levin, Leslie Fiedler, Leo Marx, and others had suggested that in trying to understand the New World representatives of "uncivilized" human nature, Prospero, like other Europeans, had imposed Old (and New) World stereotypes of innocence and monstrosity on the Native Americans, distorting perception with hope and fear.[9] Fiedler's landmark book had indeed placed *The Tempest* suggestively in the context of a series of plays about the Other (or, as he called it in 1972, the "Stranger") in Shakespeare, showing Caliban's resemblance to the demonized women, Moors, and Jews in the canon. O. Mannoni had added that, in this process, Prospero displayed the psychology of colonials who projected their disowned traits onto New World natives.[10]

Why, then, so many recent articles? In part they are simply shifting the emphasis. Revisionists claim that the New World material is not just present but is right at the center of the play, and that it demands far more attention than critics have been willing to grant it. They argue that the civil war in Milan that had ousted Prospero should be recognized as merely an episode in a minor dispute between Italian dynasties, of little import compared to the transatlantic action;[11] they show how the love story can be seen as a political maneuver by Prospero to ensure his return to power in Milan,[12] and how even Caliban's attempted rape of Miranda can be seen as an expression not merely of sexual but also of territorial lust, understandable in its context.[13]

These recent critics are not simply repeating the older ones, however; they are making important distinctions. First and most explicitly, they are not calling attention to history in general but rather to one aspect of history: to power relations and to the ideology in which power relations are encoded.[14] The revisionists look not at the New World

[9]Harry Levin, *The Myth of the Golden Age in the Renaissance* (Bloomington: Indiana Univ. Press, 1969); Leslie A. Fiedler, *The Stranger in Shakespeare* (New York: Stein and Day 1972); Leo Marx, "Shakespeare's American Fable," *The Machine in the Garden* (London and New York: Oxford Univ. Press, 1964), pp. 34–72.

[10]O. Mannoni, *Prospero and Caliban: The Psychology of Colonization*, trans. Pamela Powesland (1950; rpt. New York: Praeger, 1964).

[11]Hulme, *Colonial Encounters*, p. 133.

[12]Hulme, *Colonial Encounters*, p. 115; Barker and Hulme, p. 303; Orgel, "Prospero's Wife," pp. 62–63.

[13]Orgel, "Shakespeare and the Cannibals," p. 55.

[14]As Paul Werstine wrote in the brochure announcing the NEH Humanities Institute on "New Directions in Shakespeare Criticism" (The Folger Shakespeare Library, 1988), "To appreciate *The Tempest* . . . today . . . we must understand discourses of colonialism, power, legitimation."

material in the play but to the play's effect on power relations in the New World. What matters is not just the particular Bermuda pamphlets actually echoed in the play but rather the whole "ensemble of fictional and lived practices" known as "English colonialism," which, it is now being claimed, provides the "dominant discursive con-texts"[15] for the play. (Though the term "colonialism" may allude to the entire spectrum of New World activity, in these articles it most often refers specifically to the use of power, to the Europeans' exploitative and self-justifying treatment of the New World and its inhabitants — and I shall use it in that sense.) If Caliban is the center of the play, it is not because of his role in the play's self-contained structure, and not even because of what he reveals about man's timeless tendency to demonize "strangers," but because Europeans were at that time exploiting the real Calibans of the world, and *The Tempest* was part of the process. It is no longer enough to suggest that Europeans were trying to make sense of the Indian; rather, the emphasis is now on the way Europeans subdued the Indian to "make sense/order/money — not of him, so much as out of him."[16] Revisionists argue that when the English talked about these New World inhabitants, they did not just innocently apply stereotypes or project their own fears: they did so to a particular effect, whether wittingly or unwittingly. The various distortions were discursive strategies that served the political purpose of making the New World fit into a schema justifying colonialism.[17] Revisionists therefore emphasize the discursive strategies that the play shares with all colonial discourse, and the ways in which *The Tempest* itself not only displays prejudice but fosters and even "enacts" colonialism by mystifying or justifying Prospero's power over Caliban.[18] The new point is that *The Tempest* is a political act.

Second, this shift in our attitude toward the object of interpretation entails a less explicit but extremely important move away from the psychological interpretation that had previously seemed appropriate for the play (even to its detractors) largely because of its central figure who,

---

[15]Barker and Hulme, p. 299.

[16]Hawkes, "Swisser-Swatter," p. 28.

[17]Thus stereotypes, for example, served as part of a "discursive strategy . . . to locate or 'fix' a colonial other in a position of inferiority . . ." (Paul Brown, modifying Edward Said on orientalism, p. 280).

[18]Actually, this point too is a matter of emphasis. R. R. Cawley ("Shakespeare's Use of the Voyagers in *The Tempest*," *PMLA*, 41 [1926], 688–726) and Kermode, among others, had noted in passing some similarities between the play's view of Caliban and the distortions of colonialist self-serving rhetorical purposes; but revisionists take this to be the important point, not to be passed over.

so like Shakespeare, runs the show. Where earlier criticism of Prospero talked about his "prejudice," the more recent revisionists talk about "power" and "euphemization." Thus, a critic writing in 1980 argued that *The Tempest*'s "allegorical and Neoplatonic overlay masks some of the most damaging prejudices of Western civilization";[19] but by 1987 the formulation had changed: "*The Tempest* is . . . fully implicated in the process of 'euphemization,' the effacement of power," in "operations [that] encode struggle and contradiction even as they, or *because* they, strive to insist on the legitimacy of colonialist narrative."[20]

Psychological criticism of the play is seen as distracting at best; one recent critic, for example, opens his argument by claiming that we need to conceive *The Tempest* in an historical context that is not "hamstrung by specious speculations concerning 'Shakespeare's mind.'"[21] Even in less polemical examples the "political unconscious" often replaces, rather than supplements, any other unconscious; attention to culture and politics is associated with an implicit questioning of individuality and of subjective experience. Such a stance extends beyond an objection to wholesale projections of twentieth-century assumptions onto sixteenth-century subjects, or to psychological interpretations that totally ignore the cultural context in which psyches exist. As Fredric Jameson argued in a work that lies behind many of these specific studies, it derives from the desire to transcend personal psychology altogether, because Freud's psychology remains "locked into the category of the individual subject."[22] The emphasis now is on psychology as a product of culture, itself a political structure; the very concept of a

[19]Leininger, "Cracking the Code of *The Tempest*," p. 122.

[20]Paul Brown, pp. 286, 289. Brown also contends that *The Tempest* "exemplifies . . . a moment of *historical* crisis. This crisis is the struggle to produce a coherent discourse adequate to the complex requirements of British colonialism in its initial phase" (p. 269).

[21]Hulme, *Colonial Encounters,* p. 93. Later he does grant a little ground to the psychological critics in allowing that their "totally spurious" identification of Prospero with Shakespeare yet "half grasps the crucial point that Prospero . . . is a dramatist and creator of theatrical effects" (p. 115).

[22]"From the point of view of a political hermeneutic, measured against the requirements of a 'political unconscious,' we must conclude that the conception of wish-fulfillment remains locked in a problematic of the individual subject . . . which is only indirectly useful to us." The objection to wish-fulfillment is that it is "always outside of time, outside of narrative" and history; "what is more damaging, from the present perspective, is that desire . . . remains locked into the category of the individual subject, even if the form taken by the individual in it is no longer the ego or the self, but the individual body. . . . *the need to transcend individualistic categories and modes of interpretation is in many ways the fundamental issue for any doctrine of the political unconscious*" (*The Political Unconscious: Narrative as a Socially Symbolic Act* [Ithaca, N.Y.: Cornell Univ. Press, 1981], pp. 66, 68, italics added).

psyche is seen to be a product of the cultural nexus evolved during the Renaissance, and indeed, psychoanalysis itself, rather than being a way of understanding the Renaissance psyche, is a marginal and belated creation of this same nexus.[23] Thus the revisionists, with Jameson, may look for a "political unconscious" and make use of Freud's insights into the "logic of dreams"[24] — the concepts of displacement, condensation, the management of desire[25] — but they do not accept Freud's assumptions about the mind — or the subject — creating that logic.[26] The agent who displaces or manages is not the individual but the "collective or associative" mind; at times it seems to be the text itself, seen as a "libidinal apparatus" or "desiring machine"[27] independent of any individual creator.

The revisionist impulse has been one of the most salutary in recent years in correcting New Critical "blindness" to history and ideology. In particular it has revealed the ways in which the play has been "reproduced" and drafted into the service of colonialist politics from the nineteenth century through G. Wilson Knight's twentieth-century celebration of Prospero as representative of England's "colonizing, especially her will to raise savage peoples from superstition and blood-sacrifice, taboos and witchcraft and the attendant fears and slaveries, to a more enlightened existence."[28] But here, as critics have been suggesting about new historicism in general, it is now in danger of fostering blindness of its own. Granted that something was wrong with a commentary that focused on *The Tempest* as a self-contained project of a self-contained individual and that ignored the political situation in 1611. But something seems wrong now also, something more than the rhetorical excesses characteristic of any innovative critical movement. The recent criticism not only flattens the text into the mold of colonialist discourse and eliminates what is characteristically "Shakespearean" in order to foreground what is "colonialist," but it is also — paradoxically — in

---

[23]Stephen Greenblatt, "Psychoanalysis and Renaissance Culture," *Literary Theory/Renaissance Texts,* eds. Patricia Parker and David Quint (Baltimore: Johns Hopkins Univ. Press, 1986), 210–24.

[24]Jameson, p. 12. So, too, Freud's "hermeneutic manual" can be of use to the political critic (p. 65).

[25]"Norman Holland's suggestive term," Jameson, p. 49.

[26]Jameson, p. 67. Cf. Paul Brown, "My use of Freudian terms does not mean that I endorse its ahistorical, Eurocentric, and sexist models of psychical development. However, a materialist criticism deprived of such concepts as displacement and condensation would be seriously impoverished . . ." (p. 289, n. 35).

[27]Jameson discussing Althusser (p. 30) and Greimas (p. 48).

[28]*The Crown of Life* (1947; rpt. New York: Barnes & Noble, 1966), p. 255.

danger of taking the play further from the particular historical situation in England in 1611 even as it brings it closer to what we mean by "colonialism" today.

It is difficult to extrapolate back from G. Wilson Knight's colonialist discourse to seventeenth-century colonialist discourse without knowing more about the particulars of that earlier discourse. What is missing from the recent articles is the connection between the new insights about cultural phenomena like "power" and "fields of discourse" and the traditional insights about the text, its immediate sources, its individual author — and his individual psychology. There is little sense of how discourse is related to the individual who was creating, even as he was participating in, that discourse. The following discussion will suggest how such a relation might be conceived. Sections I and II briefly elaborate on *The Tempest*'s versions of problems raised by new historicist treatment of the text and its relation to the historical context; sections III and IV go on to suggest that the recognition of the individuality of the play, and of Shakespeare, does not counter but rather enriches the understanding of that context. Perhaps by testing individual cases, we can avoid the circularity of a definition that assumes that "colonialism" was present in a given group of texts, and so "discovers" it there.

I

How do we know that *The Tempest* "enacts" colonialism rather than merely alluding to the New World? How do we know that Caliban is part of the "discourse of colonialism"? To ask such a question may seem perversely naive, but the play is notoriously slippery. There have been, for example, any number of interpretations of Caliban,[29] including not only contemporary postcolonial versions in which Caliban is a Virginian Indian but also others in which Caliban is played as a black slave or as "missing link" (in a costume "half monkey, half coco-nut"[30]), with the interpretation drawing on the issues that were being debated at the time — on the discursive contexts that were culturally operative — and articulated according to "changing Anglo-American attitudes toward primitive man."[31] Most recently one teacher has suggested that *The*

[29]See Trevor R. Griffiths, " 'This Island's mine': Caliban and Colonialism," *Yearbook of English Studies*, 13 (1983), 159–80.

[30]Griffiths, p. 166.

[31]Virginia Mason Vaughan, " 'Something Rich and Strange': Caliban's Theatrical Metamorphoses," *SQ* 36 (1985), 390–405, esp. p. 390.

Tempest is a good play to teach in junior colleges because students can identify with Caliban.

Interpretation is made even more problematic here because, despite the claims about the play's intervention in English colonialism,[32] we have no *external* evidence that seventeenth-century audiences thought the play referred to the New World. In an age when real voyages were read allegorically, the status of allegorical voyages like Prospero's can be doubly ambiguous, especially in a play like *The Tempest,* which provides an encyclopedic context for Prospero's experience, presenting it in terms of an extraordinary range of classical, biblical, and romantic exiles, discoveries, and confrontations.[33] Evidence for the play's original reception is of course extraordinarily difficult to find, but in the two nearly contemporary responses to Caliban that we do know about, the evidence for a colonialist response is at best ambiguous. In *Bartholomew Fair* (1614) Jonson refers scornfully to a "servant-monster," and the Folio identifies Caliban as a "salvage and deformed slave"[34] in the cast list. Both "monster" and "salvage" are firmly rooted in the discourse of Old World wild men, though the latter was of course also applied to the New World natives. In other words, these two seventeenth-century responses tend to invoke the universal and not the particular implications of Caliban's condition. A recent study of the play's history suggests that "if Shakespeare, however obliquely, meant Caliban to personify America's natives his intention apparently miscarried almost completely."[35]

Despite this lack of contemporary testimony, the obvious reason for our feeling that the play "is" colonialist — more so than *The Winter's Tale* or *Henry VIII,* for example, which were written at roughly the same time — is, of course, the literal resemblance between its plot and certain events and attitudes in English colonial history: Europeans arrive in the New World and assume they can appropriate what properly belongs to the New World Other, who is then "erased." The similarities

---

[32]Erlich, "Shakespeare's Colonial Metaphor," p. 49; Paul Brown, pp. 268–69.

[33]Even St. Paul in his travels (echoed in the play) met natives who — like Caliban — thought him a god.

[34]Hulme produces as evidence against Shakespeare these four words from the cast list, which Shakespeare may or may not have written ("Hurricanes in the Caribbees," p. 72).

[35]Alden T. Vaughan, "Shakespeare's Indian: The Americanization of Caliban," *SQ* 39 (1988), 137–53. He argues that the intention miscarried not only at the time but also for the three centuries following. He adds, "Rather, from the Restoration until the late 1890s, Caliban appeared on stage and in critical literature as almost everything but an Indian" (p. 138).

are clear and compelling — more so than in many cases of new historical readings; the problem, however, is that while there are also many
literal differences between *The Tempest* and colonialist fictions and practice, the similarities are taken to be so compelling that the differences
are ignored. Thus Caliban is taken to "be" a Native American despite
the fact that a multitude of details differentiate Caliban from the Indian
as he appeared in the travelers' reports from the New World.[36] Yet it
does seem significant that, despite his closeness to nature, his naiveté,
his devil worship, his susceptibility to European liquor, and, above all,
his "treachery"— characteristics associated in writings of the time with
the Indians — he nonetheless lacks almost all of the defining external
traits in the many reports from the New World — no superhuman
physique, no nakedness or animal skin (indeed, an English "gaberdine"
instead), no decorative feathers,[37] no arrows, no pipe, no tobacco, no
body paint, and — as Shakespeare takes pains to emphasize — no love
of trinkets and trash. No one could mistake him for the stereotyped
"Indian with a great tool," mentioned in passing in *Henry VIII*. Caliban in fact is more like the devils Strachey expected to find on the
Bermuda island (but didn't) than like the Indians whom adventurers
did find in Virginia, though he is not wholly a monster from the explorers' wild tales either.[38]

[36]Hulme, while noting Caliban's "anomalous nature," sees the anomaly as yet
another colonialist strategy: "In ideological terms [Caliban is] a compromise formation
and one achieved, like all such formations, only at the expense of distortion elsewhere"
("Hurricanes in the Caribbees," pp. 71, 72). This begs the question: Caliban can only be
a "distortion" if he is intended to represent someone. But that is precisely the question —
is he meant to represent a Native American? Sidney Lee noted that Caliban's method of
building dams for fish reproduces the Indians'; though he is often cited by later writers as
an authority on the resemblance, the rest of his evidence is not convincing ("The Call of
the West: America and Elizabethan England," *Elizabethan and Other Essays*, ed. Frederick
S. Boas [Oxford: Clarendon Press, 1929], pp. 263–301). G. Wilson Knight has an
impressionistic essay about the relationship between Caliban and Indians ("Caliban as
Red Man" [1977] in *Shakespeare's Styles*, eds. Philip Edwards, Inga-Stina Ewbank, and
G. K. Hunter [London: Cambridge Univ. Press, 1980]). Hulme lists Caliban's resemblances to Caribs ("Hurricanes in the Caribbees"), and Kermode cites details taken from
natives visited during both the Old and the New World voyages.

[37]The Indians who would appear in Chapman's 1613 masque would be fully
equipped with feathers. See R. R. Cawley, *The Voyagers and Elizabethan Drama* (Boston:
D. C. Heath; London: Oxford Univ. Press, 1938), p. 359, and Orgel, "Shakespeare and
the Cannibals," pp. 44, 47.

[38]Shakespeare had apparently read up on his monsters (R. R. Cawley, "Shakespeare's
Use of the Voyagers," p. 723, and Frey, passim), but he picked up the stereotypes only to
play with them ostentatiously (in Stephano's and Trinculo's many discredited guesses
about Caliban's identity) or to leave them hanging (in Prospero's identification of
Caliban as "devil").

In other ways, too, it is assumed that the similarities matter but the differences do not: thus Prospero's magic occupies "the space *really inhabited in colonial history* by gunpowder"[39] (emphasis mine); or, when Prospero has Caliban pinched by the spirits, he shows a "similar sadism" to that of the Haitian masters who "roasted slaves or buried them alive";[40] or, when Prospero and Ariel hunt Caliban with spirit dogs, they are equated to the Spaniards who hunted Native Americans with dogs.[41] So long as there is a core of resemblance, the differences are irrelevant. The differences, in fact, are themselves taken to be evidence of the colonialist ideology at work, rationalizing and euphemizing power — or else inadvertent slips. Thus the case for colonialism becomes stronger insofar as Prospero *is* good and insofar as Caliban *is* in some ways bad — he did try to rape Miranda — or is *himself* now caught trying to falsify the past by occluding the rape and presenting himself as an innocent victim of Prospero's tyranny. Prospero's goodness and Caliban's badness are called rationalizations, justifications for Prospero's tyranny. Nor does it matter that the play seems *anti*colonialist to the degree that it qualifies Prospero's scorn by showing Caliban's virtues, or that Prospero seems to achieve some kind of transcendence over his own colonialism when at the end of the play he says, "This thing of darkness I acknowledge mine."[42] Prospero's acknowledgement of Caliban is considered a mistake, a moment of inadvertent sympathy or truth, too brief to counter Prospero's underlying colonialism: in spite of the deceptively resonant poetry of his acknowledgement, Prospero actually does nothing to live up to the meaning which that poetry suggests;[43] it has even been argued that Prospero, in calling Caliban "mine," is simply claiming possession of him: "It is as though, after a public disturbance, a slaveowner said, 'Those two men are yours; this darkie's mine.'"[44]

---

[39]Hulme, "Hurricanes in the Caribbees," p. 74.

[40]Lamming (n. 1, above), pp. 98–99.

[41]Lamming, p. 97; Erlich, p. 49.

[42]The play also seems anti-colonialist because it includes the comic sections with Stephano and Trinculo, which show colonialism to be "nakedly avaricious, profiteering, perhaps even pointless"; but this too can be seen as a rationalization: "This low version of colonialism serves to displace possibly damaging charges . . . against properly constituted civil authority on to the already excremental products of civility, the masterless" (Paul Brown, p. 287).

[43]Greenblatt, "Learning to Curse," pp. 570–71; Leininger (n. 1, above), pp. 126–27.

[44]Leininger, p. 127.

Nonetheless, in addition to these differences that have been seen as rationalizations, there are many other differences as well that collectively raise questions about what counts as "colonialist discourse" and about what, if anything, might count as a relevant "difference." Thus, for example, any attempt to cast Prospero and Caliban as actors in the typical colonial narrative (in which a European exploits a previously free — indeed a reigning — native of an unspoiled world) is complicated by two other characters, Sycorax and Ariel. Sycorax, Caliban's mother, through whom he claims possession of the island, was not only a witch and a criminal, but she came from the Old World herself, or at least from eastern-hemisphere Argier.[45] She is a reminder that Caliban is only half-native, that his claim to the island is less like the claim of the Native American than the claim of the second generation Spaniard in the New World.[46] Moreover, Caliban was not alone when Prospero arrived. Ariel either came to the island with Sycorax or was already living on the island — its true reigning lord[47] — when Sycorax arrived and promptly enslaved him, thus herself becoming the first colonialist, the one who established the habits of dominance and erasure before Prospero ever set foot on the island. Nearly all revisionists note some of these differences before disregarding them, though they are not agreed on their significance — on whether they are "symptoms" of ideological conflict in the discourse, for example, or whether Shakespeare's "insights exceeded his sympathies."[48] But however they are explained, the differences *are* discarded. For the critic interested only in counteracting earlier blindness to potentially racist and ideological elements in the play, such ignoring of differences is understandable; for his or her purposes, it *is* enough to point out that *The Tempest* has a "political unconscious" and is connected in *some* way to colonialist discourse without specifying further.

---

[45]As Fiedler's book implies (n. 9, above), she is less like anything American than like the Frenchwoman Joan of Arc, who also tried to save herself from the law by claiming she was pregnant with a bastard; Joan simply wasn't as successful (see pp. 43–81, esp. p. 77).

[46]See Brockbank, p. 193. Even these details can be discounted as rationalizations, of course. Paul Brown, for example, explains Sycorax's presence as a rationalization: by degrading her black magic, he argues, Shakespeare makes Prospero seem better than he is (p. 283). Hulme notes that Sycorax may be Prospero's invention, pointing out that we never see any direct evidence that she was present (*Colonial Encounters,* p. 115). Orgel links Caliban's claims of legitimacy by birth to James I's claims ("Prospero's Wife," pp. 58–59).

[47]See Fiedler, p. 205.

[48]Erlich, "Shakespeare's Colonial Metaphor," p. 63.

But if the object is, rather, to understand colonialism, instead of simply identifying it or condemning it, it is important to specify, to notice how the colonial elements are rationalized or integrated into the play's vision of the world. Otherwise, extracting the play's political unconscious leads to the same problems Freud faced at the beginning of his career when he treated the personal unconscious as an independent entity that should be almost surgically extracted from conscious discourse by hypnotizing away the "defenses." But, as is well known, Freud found that the conscious "defenses" were as essential — and problematic — as the supposedly prior unconscious "wish," and that they served purposes other than containment.[49] Indeed, in most psychoanalytic practice since Freud, the unconscious — or, rather, unconscious mentation — is assumed to exist in texts rather than existing as a reified "id," and interpretation must always return to the text.

As in the case of the personal unconscious, the political unconscious exists only in texts, whose "defenses" or rationalizations must be taken into account. Otherwise interpretation not only destroys the text — here *The Tempest* — as a unique work of art and flattens it into one more example of the master plot — or master ploy — in colonialist discourse; it also destroys the evidence of the play as a unique cultural artifact, a unique voice in that discourse. Colonialist discourse was varied enough to escape any simple formulation, even in a group of texts with apparent thematic links. It ranged from the lived Spanish colonialist practice of hunting New World natives with dogs to Bartholomew Las Casas's "factual" account lamenting and exposing the viciousness of that hunt,[50] to Shakespeare's possible allusion to it in *The Tempest,* when Prospero and Ariel set spirit dogs on Caliban, to a still earlier Shakespearean allusion — or possible allusion — in the otherwise

---

[49]The trend, moreover, is to move away from anthropomorphic terms like "repression" or "censorship," themselves inherited from the political terminology on which Freud drew for his own. Like the vocabulary of "scientific" hydraulics on which Freud also drew for his notions of libido flowing and damming up, the older terms are being replaced by contemporary terminologies more appropriate to describing a conflict among meanings or interpretations, rather than between anthropomorphized forces engaged in a simple struggle "for" and "against."

[50]Spaniards, he writes, "taught their Hounds, fierce Dogs, to teare [the Indians] in peeces" (*A briefe Narration of the destruction of the Indies by the Spaniards* [1542 (?)], Samuel Purchas, *Purchas His Pilgrimes,* 20 vols. [Glasgow: Maclehose and Sons, 1905–1907], Vol. XVIII, 91). This was apparently a common topos, found also in Eden's translation of Peter Martyr's *Decades of the New Worlde* (1555), included in Eden's *Historie of Trauaile* (1577), which Shakespeare read for *The Tempest*. It was also used by Greene and Deloney (Cawley, *Voyagers and Elizabethan Drama,* pp. 383–84).

non-colonialist *A Midsummer Night's Dream*, when Puck (who has come from India himself) chases Greek rude mechanicals with illusory animals in a scene evoking an entirely English conflict. The same "colonialist" hunt informs radically different fictions and practices, some of which enact colonialism, some of which subvert it, and some of which require other categories entirely to characterize its effect.

It is not easy to categorize the several links between *The Tempest* and colonialist discourse. Take the deceptively simple example of Caliban's name. Revisionists rightly emphasize the implications of the cannibal stereotype as automatic mark of Other in Western ethnocentric colonialist discourse,[51] and, since Shakespeare's name for "Caliban" is widely accepted as an anagram of "cannibal," many read the play as if he *were* a cannibal, with all that the term implies. But an anagram is not a cannibal, and Shakespeare's use of the stereotype is hardly automatic.[52] Caliban is no cannibal — he barely touches meat, confining himself more delicately to roots, berries, and an occasional fish; indeed, his symbiotic harmony with the island's natural food resources is one of his most attractive traits. His name seems more like a mockery of stereotypes than a mark of monstrosity, and in our haste to confirm the link between "cannibal" and "Indian" outside the text, we lose track of the way in which Caliban severs the link *within* the text.[53] While no one would deny *some* relation between Caliban and the New World natives to whom such terms as "cannibal" were applied, what that relation is remains unclear.

To enumerate differences between *The Tempest* and "colonialist discourse" is not to reduce discussion of the play to a counting contest, pitting similarities against differences. Rather, it is to suggest that inherent in any analysis of the play as colonialist discourse is a particular assumption about the relation between text and discourse — between one man's fiction and a collective fiction — or, perhaps, between one man's fiction and what we take for "reality." This relation matters not only to New Critics trying to isolate texts from contexts but to new

[51]Hulme. "Hurricanes in the Caribbees," pp. 63–66; see also Orgel on this "New World topos" in "Shakespeare and the Cannibals," pp. 41–44.

[52]Neither was Montaigne's in the essay that has been taken as a source for the play. Scholars are still debating about Montaigne's attitude toward cannibals, though all agree that his critical attitude toward *Europeans* was clear in the essay.

[53]This blend of Old and New World characteristics, earlier seen as characteristic of New World discourse, is acknowledged in many of the revisionist studies but is seen as one of the rhetorical strategies used to control Indians.

historicists (or just plain historicists) trying to put them back together. The relation is also vital to lived practices like censorship and inquisitions — and there are differences of opinion about what counts in these cases. Such differences need to be acknowledged and examined, and the method for reading them needs to be made more explicit before the implications of *The Tempest* as colonialist discourse can be fully understood.

II

Similar problems beset the definition of the "discourse" itself, the means of identifying the fictional — and the "lived"— practices constituting "English colonialism" in 1611. Given the impact of English colonialism over the last 350 years, it may again seem perversely naive to ask what colonialist discourse was like in 1611, as opposed to colonialism in 1911 or even in 1625, the year when Samuel Purchas asked, alluding to the "treachery" of the Virginian Indians, "Can a Leopard change his spots? Can a Savage remayning a Savage be civill?" Purchas added this comment when he published the 1610 document that Shakespeare had used as his source for *The Tempest,* and Purchas has been cited as an example of "colonialist discourse."[54] Purchas does indeed display the particular combination of exploitative motives and self-justifying rhetoric — the "effacement of power"[55] — that revisionists identify as colonialist and which they find in *The Tempest.* But, one might reasonably ask, was the discursive context in 1611, when Shakespeare was writing, the same as it would be fourteen years later, when Purchas added his marginal comment?[56]

There seems, rather, to have been in 1611 a variety of what we might call "New World discourses" with multiple points of view, motives, and effects, among which such comments as Purchas's are not

---

[54]William Strach[e]y, "A true reportorie . . . ," *Purchas,* Vol. XIX, p. 62. For the citation of Purchas as colonialist, see Hulme, "Hurricanes in the Caribbees," p. 78, n. 21.

[55]Paul Brown, p. 286.

[56]This is an entirely separate question from another that one might ask: How comparable were Purchas's remarks, taken from the collection of travelers' tales which he edited, censored, and used to support his colonialist ideal, on the one hand, and a play, on the other? In *Purchas,* Richard Marienstras argues, "the multiplicity of interpretations modulates and reinforces a single ideological system. The same can certainly not be said of . . . *The Tempest*" (*New Perspectives on the Shakespearean World,* trans. Janet Lloyd [Cambridge: Cambridge Univ. Press 1985], p. 169). This entire book, which devotes a chapter to *The Tempest,* is an excellent study of "certain aspects of Elizabethan ideology and . . . the way these are used in Shakespeare" (p. 1).

as common as the revisionist emphasis implies. These are "colonialist" only in the most general sense in which all ethnocentric cultures are always "colonialist": narcissistically pursuing their own ends, oblivious to the desires, needs, and even the existence of the Other. That is, if this New World discourse is colonialist, it is so primarily in that it *ignores* Indians, betraying its Eurocentric assumptions about the irrelevance of any people other than white, male, upper-class Europeans, preferably from England. It thus expresses not an historically specific but a *time-less* and universal attitude toward the "stranger," which Fiedler described in so many of Shakespeare's plays. We might see this discourse as a precondition[57] for colonialism proper, which was to follow with the literal rather than the figurative colonizing of New World natives. But to assume that colonialism was already encoded in the anomalous situation in 1611 is to undermine the revisionist effort to understand the historical specificity of the moment when Shakespeare wrote *The Tempest.*

It is not easy to characterize the situation in 1611. On the one hand, Spain had long been engaged in the sort of "colonialist discourse" that revisionists find in *The Tempest*; and even in England at the time there were examples of colonialist discourse (in the rhetoric, if not yet often in the lived practices) produced by those directly involved in the colonialist project and expecting to profit from it. The official advertisements in the first rush of enthusiasm about Virginia, as well as the stream of defenses when the Virginia project began to fail, often have a euphemistic ring and often do suggest a fundamental greed and implicit racism beneath claims to be securing the earthly and spiritual well-being of the Virginia natives.[58] ("[We] doe buy of them the pearles

---

[57]See Pechter (n. 4, above). This kind of "condition," he argues, is really a precondition in the sense that it is assumed to be logically (if not chronologically) prior. It is assumed to have the kind of explanatory power that "the Elizabethan world view" was once accorded (p. 297).

[58]See, for example, the following contemporary tracts reprinted in *Tracts and Other Papers Relating Principally to the Origin, Settlement, and Progress of . . . North America,* ed. Peter Force, 4 vols. (1836–47; rpt. New York: Peter Smith, 1947): R. I., " *Nova Brittania:* OFFERING MOST Excellent fruites by Planting IN VIRGINIA. Exciting all such as be well affected to further the same" (1609), Vol. 1, No. 6; "Virginia richly valued" (1609), Vol. 4, No. 1; "A TRVE DECLARATION of the estate of the Colonie in Virginia, With a confutation of such scandalous reports as haue tended to the disgrace of so worthy an enterprise" (1610), Vol. 3, No. 1; Sil. Jourdan, "A PLAINE DESCRIPTION OF THE BARMVDAS, NOW CALLED SOMMER ILANDS" (1613), Vol. 3, No. 3.

In *The Genesis of the United States,* ed. Alexander Brown, 2 vols. (New York: Russell & Russell, 1964), see also: Robert Gray, "A GOOD SPEED to Virginia" (1609), Vol. 1, 293–302; "A True and Sincere declaration of the purpose and ends of the *Plantation* begun in

of earth, and sell to them the pearles of heauen."[59]) These documents efface not only power but most practical problems as well, and they were supplemented by sermons romanticizing hardships as divine tribulation.[60] Scattered throughout this discourse are righteous defenses of taking land from the Indians, much in the spirit — and tone — of Rabbi Zeal-of-the-Land Busy defending his need to eat pig. (This was also the tone familiar from the anti-theatrical critics — and, indeed, occasional colonialist sermons included snipes at the "Plaiers," along with the Devil and the papists, as particular enemies of the Virginia venture.[61])

On the other hand, even in these documents not only is the emphasis elsewhere but often there are important contradictory movements. For example, "A True Declaration," the official record of the Bermuda wreck, refers once to the Indians as "humane beasts" and devotes one paragraph of its twenty-four pages to the "greedy Vulture" Powhattan and his ambush. It notes elsewhere, however, that some of the English settlers themselves had "created the *Indians* our implacable enemies by some violence they had offered," and it actually spends far more time attacking the lazy "scum of men" among the settlers, who had undermined the colony from within, than demonizing the less relevant Indians.[62]

Virginia of the degrees which it hath received; and meanes by *which it hath beene advanced:* and *the . . . conclusion of His Majesties Councel* of that Colony . . . untill by the mercies of GOD it shall *retribute a fruitful harvest to the Kingdome of heaven, and this Common-Wealth*" (1609), Vol. 1, 337–53; "A Publication of the Counsell of Virginea," touching the Plantation there" (1609), Vol. 1, 354–56; R. Rich, "NEWES FROM VIRGINIA. THE LOST FLOCKE TRIUMPHANT . . ." (1610), Vol. 1, 420–26.

[59]"A Trve Declaration," p. 6.

[60]Alexander Brown, in *The Genesis of the United States,* reprints extracts from the following pertinent documents: William Symonds, "VIRGINIA: A SERMON PREACHED AT WHITE CHAPPEL . . ." (1609), Vol. 1, 282–91; Daniel Price, "SAVLES PROHIBITION STAIDE . . . And to the Inditement of all that persecute Christ with a reproofe of those that traduce the Honourable Plantation of Virginia" (1609), Vol. 1, 312–16; and, most important, William Crashaw's sermon titled "A New-yeeres Gift to Virginea," and preached, as the title page announced, before "Lord La Warre Lord Governour and Captaine Generall of Virginia, and others of [the] Counsell . . . At the said Lord Generall his . . . departure for Virginea . . . Wherein both the lawfulnesses of that action is maintained and the necessity thereof is also demonstrated, not so much out of the grounds of Policie, as of Humanity, Equity and Christianity" (1610), Vol. 1, 360–75.

[61]In Alexander Brown, see William Crashaw for two of these references (in "A New-yeeres Gift to Virginea [1610], and "Epistle Dedicatory" to Alexander Whitaker's *"Good Newes from Virginia"* [1613], Vol. 2, 611–20); and see Ralphe Hamor in *A True Discourse of the Present Estate of Virginea* (1615), Virginia State Library Publications, No. 3 (Richmond: Virginia State Library, 1957).

[62]Pp. 16, 17.

And on the whole, the exploitative and self-justifying rhetoric is only one element in a complex New World discourse. For much of the time, in fact, the main conflict in the New World was not between whites and Native Americans but between Spain and England. Voyages like Drake's (1577–80) were motivated by this international conflict, as well as by the romance of discovery and the lure of treasure — but not by colonizing.[63] Even when Raleigh received the first patent to settle and trade with the New World (1584), necessitating more extended contact with Native Americans, the temporary settlements he started in the 1580s were largely tokens in his play for fame and wealth rather than attempts to take over sizable portions of land from the natives.[64]

Only when the war with Spain was over (1604) and ships were free again did colonization really begin; and then "America and Virginia were on everyone's lips."[65] But this New World discourse still reflects little interest in its inhabitants. Other issues are much more widely discussed. For example, what would the New World government be like? Would James try to extend his authoritarianism to America? *Could* he? This was the issue, for example, most energizing Henry Wriothesley, Shakespeare's Southampton, who led the "Patriot" faction on the London Virginia Council, pushing for more American independence.[66]

[63]For the general history of the period, see David Beers Quinn, *England and the Discovery of America, 1481–1620* (New York: Alfred A. Knopf, 1974); Alexander Brown's *Genesis* identifies similar shifting motives in the history of colonization. Such voyages were made famous by often-reprinted accounts, especially in collections by Richard Eden and Richard Hakluyt, both of whose anthologies Shakespeare would consult for *The Tempest*. In the introductory material in these collections, as in the voyages themselves, the self-interest is obvious but so mixed with excitement and utopian hopes, and so focused on competition with Spain, that the issue of relation to Indians was dwarfed by comparison.

[64]If he didn't succeed in establishing a settlement, he would lose his patent. His interest in the patent rather than the colony was shown by his apparent negligence in searching for his lost colony (Quinn, n. 63, above, p. 300). He could hold onto his patent only so long as there was hope that the colonists were still alive; clearly the hope was worth more to Raleigh than the colony.

[65]Matthew P. Andrews, *The Soul of a Nation: The Founding of Virginia and the Projection of New England* (New York: Scribner's, 1943), p. 125. An entire popular literature developed, so much so that the Archbishop of York complained that "of Virginia there be so many tractates, divine, human, historical, political, or call them as you please, as no further intelligence I dare desire" (quoted in Andrews, p. 125).

[66]It is this issue rather than colonialism that stimulated an earlier period of political commentary on the New World material in *The Tempest:* Charles M. Gayley, *Shakespeare and the Founders of Liberty in America* (New York: Macmillan, 1917); A. A. Ward, "Shakespeare and the makers of Virginia," *Proceedings of the British Academy,* 9 (1919); see also E. P. Kuhl, "Shakespeare and the Founders of America: *The Tempest,*" *Philological Quarterly,* 41 (1962), 123–46.

(As for James's own "colonial discourse," it seems to have been devoted to worries about how it would all affect his relations with Spain,[67] and to requests for flying squirrels and other New World "toyes."[68]) Of more immediate interest, perhaps, to the mass of real or armchair adventurers were the reports of New World wealth that at first made Virginia known as a haven for bankrupts and spendthrifts, as well as for wild dreamers — followed by the accounts of starvation, rebellion, and hardship brought back by those who had escaped from the reality of colonial existence. Now the issue became "Is it worth it?" The official propaganda, optimistic about future profits, was soon countered by a backlash from less optimistic scoffers challenging the value of the entire project, one which sent money, men, and ships to frequent destruction and brought back almost no profit.[69]

Even the settlers actually living with the natives in the New World itself were — for entirely non-altruistic reasons — not yet fully engaged in "colonialist" discourse as defined by revisionists. In 1611 they had not managed to establish enough power to euphemize; they had little to be defensive about. They were too busy fighting mutiny, disease, and the stupidities of the London Council to have much energy left over for Indians. It is true that no writer ever treated Native Americans as equals — any more than he treated Moors, Jews, Catholics, peasants, women, Irishmen, or even Frenchmen as equals; travellers complacently recorded kidnapping natives to exhibit in England, as if the natives had no rights at all.[70] And it is true that some of their descriptions are distorted by Old World stereotypes of wild men or cannibals — though these descriptions are often confined to earlier *pre*-colonial explorers' reports.[71] Or, far more insidiously, the descriptions

---

[67]Contributing to the welter of contradictory discourses was the Spanish ambassador's flow of letters to Spain insisting, not irrationally, that the whole purpose of maintaining a profitless colony like Jamestown was to establish a base for pirate raids against Spanish colonies.

[68]Letter from Southampton to the Earl of Salisbury, 15 December 1609, in Alexander Brown, Vol. 1, 356–57.

[69]The quantity and quality of the objections, which have not on the whole survived, has been judged by the nature of the many defenses thought necessary to answer them. See notes 58, 60, 61.

[70]A practice that Shakespeare did not admire if Stephano and Trinculo are any indication.

[71]As are the two monsters cited as possible prototypes for Caliban by Geoffrey Bullough (*Narrative and Dramatic Sources of Shakespeare*, 8 vols. [New York: Columbia Univ. Press, 1958], Vol. 8, 240). There were exceptions, of course, as in George Percy's *Observations . . . of the Plantation of . . . Virginia* (1606), in *Purchas*, Vol. XVIII, 403–19.

were distorted by stereotypes of unfallen innocent noble savages — stereotypes that inevitably led to disillusionment when the settlers had to realize that the Indians, like the land itself, were not going to fulfill their dreams of a golden world made expressly to nurture Englishmen. The "noble savage" stereotype thus fueled the recurring accusation of Indian treachery, a response to betrayal of settlers' fantasies as well as to any real Indian betrayal,[72] and one to which I will return in discussing *The Tempest*.

But, given the universality of racial prejudice towards New World natives along with all "Others," in this early period the movement was to loosen, not to consolidate, the prejudices brought from the Old World. The descriptions of these extended face-to-face encounters with Native Americans were perhaps even more varied than contemporary responses to Moors and Jews, who were usually encountered on the white man's own territory, where exposure could be limited and controlled. The very terms imported from the Old World to name the natives — "savages" or "naturals"— began to lose their original connotations as the differing descriptions multiplied and even contradicted themselves. The reports range from Harriot's widely republished attempt at scientific, objective reporting (1588), which viewed natives with great respect, to Smith's less reliable adventure stories (1608–31), disputed even in his own time by Purchas. And although these do not by any means live up to our standards for non-colonialist discourse, their typical attitude is a wary, often patronizing, but live-and-let-live curiosity, rather than the exploitative erasure which would later become the mark of colonialist discourse. So long as the conflicts remained minimal, Native Americans were seen as beings like the writers;[73] further, tribes were distinguished from one another, and recognition was granted to their different forms of government, class structure,

---

[72]See Karen Ordahl Kupperman, *Settling with the Indians: The Meeting of English and Indian Cultures in America, 1580–1640* (Totowa, N.J.: Rowman and Littlefield, 1980), pp. 127–29. The origins of this nearly universal belief in Indian treachery are of course multiple, ranging from the readiness of the English to project their fears onto any available victim, whether Indians or mariners (who were also regularly accused of treachery in these narratives), to the prevailing stereotypes of the Other, to specific English acts of provocation, to the general tensions inherent in the situation. Without arguing for any one of these, I merely wish to suggest that the notion of "colonialist discourse" simplifies a complex situation.

[73]Even as proto-white men, their skin as tanned rather than naturally black, etc. See Kupperman, and Orgel, "Shakespeare and the Cannibals."

dress codes, religion, and language.[74] And when conflict did trigger the recurring accusation of "treachery," the writers never presented the Indians as laughable Calibans, but rather as capable, indeed formidable, enemies whose skill and intelligence challenged that of the settlers.

Horrors had already been perpetrated by the Spanish in the name of colonialism; not learning from these — or perhaps learning all too well — the English would soon begin perpetrating their own. But that lay in the future. When *The Tempest* was written, what the New World seems to have meant for the majority of Englishmen was a sense of possibility and a set of conflicting fantasies about the wonders to be found there; these were perhaps the preconditions for colonialism — as for much else — but not yet the thing itself.

To place colonialist discourse as precisely as possible within a given moment (like stressing the differences between *The Tempest* and colonialist discourse) is not to reduce the discussion to a numbers game. What is at stake here is not a quibble about chronology but an assumption about what we mean by the "relevant discursive context," about how we agree to determine it, and about how we decide to limit it. Here too there are differences of opinion about what counts, and these differences need to be acknowledged, examined, and accounted for.

III

My point in specifying Shakespeare's precise literal and temporal relation to colonialist discourse — in specifying the unique mind through which the discourse is mediated — is not to deny that the play has *any* relation to its context but to suggest that the relation is problematic. In

---

[74]Greenblatt, in his study of the ways in which white men verbally "colonized" Indians, emphasizes the degree to which whites assumed that the Indians had *no* language. Although he notes that there were exceptions, he makes it sound as if these exceptions were rare and were largely confined to the "rough, illiterate sea dog, bartering for gold trinkets on a faraway beach," rather than to the "captains or lieutenants whose accounts we read" ("Learning to Curse," pp. 564–65). On the contrary, even the earliest travelers had often included glossaries of Indian terms in their reports (e.g., the Glossary in the introductory material of Eden's translation of Martyr's *Decades* [1555], as well as in various later English reports reprinted in *Purchas His Pilgrimes* [1625]); and in reading through Purchas's helter-skelter collection, one is struck by the number of writers who grant automatic respect to the Indians' language. A possibly figurative rather than literal force for comments on the Indians' "want of language" is suggested by Gabriel Archer's account of a 1602 voyage. Here it is the English, not the Indians, who are deficient in this respect: they "spake divers Christian words, and seemed to understand much *more than we, for Want of Language, could comprehend*" ("Relation of Captain Gosnold's voyage," *Purchas*, Vol. XVIII, 304, italics mine).

the effort to identify Caliban as one more colonialist representation of the Other, we fail to notice how remarkable it is that such a Caliban should exist. In 1611 there were in England no literary portrayals of New World inhabitants and certainly no fictional examples of colonialist discourse.[75] Insofar as *The Tempest* does in some way allude to an encounter with a New World native (and I will for the remainder of this essay accept this premise), it is the very first work of literature to do so. There may be Indians, more or less demonized, in the nonliterary discourse. Outside of Shakespeare, however, there would be none in literature until two years after *The Tempest,* when they began to appear — feathers and all — in masques.[76] And Shakespeare went out of his way to invent Caliban: Strachey's account of the wreck on the uninhabited Bermuda islands — Shakespeare's main New World source — contains, of course, no island natives.[77] For these Shakespeare had to turn elsewhere in Strachey and in others who described the mainland colony in Virginia. Shakespeare was the first to show one of *us* mistreating a native, the first to represent a native from the inside, the first to allow a native to complain onstage, and the first to make that New World encounter problematic enough to generate the current attention to the play.

[75]See R. R. Cawley, *Voyagers and Elizabethan Drama,* passim, and *Unpathed Waters: Studies in the Influence of the Voyagers on Elizabethan Literature* (Princeton, N.J.: Princeton Univ. Press, 1940), pp. 234–41. Neither of R. R. Cawley's two books about the voyagers' influence on contemporary English literature cites any pre-1611 passage of more than a few lines. It is true that in the 1580s Marlowe's plays took off from the general sense of vastness and possibility opened up by voyages to the New as well as to the Old World. In addition Drayton wrote an "Ode to the Virginia Voyage," perhaps expressly for the settlers leaving for Jamestown in 1606; and one line in Samuel Daniel's "Musophilis" has a colonialist ring: he speaks of "vent[ing] the treasure of our tongue . . . T' inrich unknowing Nations with our stores." True, too, that in a quite different spirit Jonson, Marston, and Chapman collaborated in *Eastward Ho* (1605) to make fun of gallants flocking to Virginia with expectations as great as those bringing foolish victims to Face and Subtle's alchemical chimeras. But while Marlowe participates in the spirit of romantic adventure associated with voyaging and treasure-hunting, and *Eastward Ho* satirizes it, neither deals at all with the New World or with the New World natives.

[76]The three brief exceptions are references to Spanish cruelty to Indians, all published before the truce with Spain. The Stationers' Register lists "The crueltie of ye Spaniardes toward th[e] Indians, a ballad" (1586) and "Spanishe cruelties" (1601), now lost. Robert Greene notes in passing that the Spaniards hunted Indians with dogs, while by contrast the English treated the natives with "such courtesie, as they thought the English Gods, and the Spaniardes both by rule and conscience halfe Devils" (*The Spanish Masquerado* [1589], *Life and . . . Works,* ed. Alexander B. Grosart, 15 vols. [London and Aylesbury: privately printed, 1881–86], Vol. V, 282–83). See Cawley, *Voyagers and Elizabethan Drama,* pp. 385–86.

[77]When Strachey finishes with his account of the Bermuda episode and turns to a description of Virginia, he does devote one sentence to the Indians' treachery.

To argue for Shakespeare's uniqueness is not to argue that as fiction *The Tempest* is above politics, or that as a writer of fiction Shakespeare transcended ideology. It does imply, however, that if the play is "colonialist," it must be seen as "prophetic" rather than descriptive.[78] As such, the play's status immediately raises important questions. Why was Shakespeare — a man who had no direct stake in colonization — the first writer of fiction to portray New World inhabitants? Why then? Shakespeare had shown no signs of interest in the New World until *The Tempest,* despite the fact that there had been some colonial activity and some colonialist rhetoric for several years among those who did have a stake in it. How did the colonialist phenomenon spread?

To hasten over Shakespeare's relation to colonialism as if it were not a question but a conclusion is to lose one of the most important bits of data we may ever have about how such things as colonialism — and discourse — work. Problematic as it may be to speculate about an individual mind, it is even more problematic to speculate about the discourse of an entire nation or an entire period. One way to give substance to such large generalizations is to trace, in as much detail as may be available, the particulars on which they are based. Here the particulars include the individuals who produced, as well as reproduced, the larger cultural discourse — especially individuals like Shakespeare, who, more than almost any other, both absorbed and shaped the various conflicting discourses of the period.

To do this, as I have been arguing, it is necessary to consider the entire play, without deciding prematurely what is "only a distortion" or "only an irrelevance." In addition, however, we must also look to a context for *The Tempest* that is as relevant as colonialist discourse and perhaps even more essential to the presence of colonialism in *The Tempest* in the first place — that is, to the context of Shakespeare's own earlier "discourse." Only then can we see how the two fields of discourse intersect. In making use of the New World vocabulary and imagery, Shakespeare was in part describing something much closer to home — as was Jonson when he called the London brothel district "the Bermudas,"[79] or as would Donne when he found his America, his "newfounde land," in the arms of his mistress. Or as was Dudley Carleton in a gossipy letter from

---

[78]See Frey, p. 31.

[79]In his edition of *The Tempest,* Kermode notes this parallel with *Bartholomew Fair* (2.6.76–77), "Looke into any Angle o' the towne, (the Streights, or the Bermuda's) . . ." (p. 24, n. 223).

London about Lord Salisbury enduring a "tempest" of reproof from a lady; or Sir Ralph Winwood in trying to "begin a new world by setting himself and his wife here at home."[80]

Long before writing *The Tempest,* Shakespeare had written another play about a ruler who preferred his books to government. Navarre's academy in *Love's Labor's Lost* was no island, but, like an island, it was supposed to be isolated from territorial negotiations. And Navarre, oblivious to colonial issues, though certainly not exempt from timeless aristocratic prejudice, brought his own version of Ariel and Caliban by inviting Armado and Costard to join him. Like Prospero, he asked his "Ariel" to make a pageant for him, and he imprisoned his "Caliban" for trying to "do" a wench. His relation to the two is not a matter of colonization but rather of condescension and ironic recognition, as Navarre is forced to see something of himself in the conflict between fiery Armado's over-active imagination and earthy Costard's lust.[81] Only much later did this pattern come to be "colonial."

The Tempest is linked in many other ways not only to *Love's Labor's Lost* but also to the rest of the canon, as continued efforts of critics have shown,[82] and it is revealing to see how, in each case, the non-colonial structures become associated with colonialist discourse. Indeed, the

---

[80]Letter from Carleton to Chamberlain, August 1607, in Alexander Brown, Vol. 1, 111–13.

[81]Many other similarities link *The Tempest* to the earlier play, including some which might have been taken to suggest *The Tempest*'s focus on the New World. Thus, for example, Stephano cries out when he first sees Caliban, "Do you put tricks upon's with salvages and men of Inde, ha?" (2.2.55–56). But Berowne, though rooted in the Old World, resorts to similarly exotic analogies to describe the passion which Rosaline should inspire in his colleagues. Who sees her, he says,

> That, (like a rude and savage man of Inde),
> At the first op'ning of the gorgeous east,
> Bows not his vassal head. . . ?
>   (*Love's Labor's Lost,* 4.3.218–20)

See Kermode's note on the line in *The Tempest.*

[82]Specific resemblances between subplots here and the plots of other plays have been noted (between the plot to murder Alonso and *Macbeth,* between Ferdinand's courtship of Miranda and *Romeo and Juliet,* etc.). See Alvin B. Kernan, "The great fair of the world and the ocean island: *Bartholomew Fair* and *The Tempest,*" in *The Revels History of Drama in English,* 8 vols., eds. J. Leeds Barroll, Alexander Leggatt, Richard Hosley, Alvin Kernan (London: Methuen, 1975), Vol. III, 456–74. G. Wilson Knight has described the place of *The Tempest* in Shakespeare's overarching myth of the tempest. Even more suggestive, Leslie Fiedler has traced the less obvious personal mythology that provides a context for the play. Drawing on marginal details, he shows the play's concern with themes that pervade the entire canon, such as the interracial marriage that here, not accidentally, initiates the action of the play. His work is the starting point for mine.

very details of *The Tempest* that revisionists see as marking the "nodal point of the play's imbrication into this discourse of colonialism"[83] are reworkings of similar moments in earlier and seemingly precolonial plays. The moment I will focus on for the rest of this paper is the one that many revisionists take as the strongest evidence in the play for the falseness of Prospero's position — the moment when the hidden colonialist project emerges openly,[84] when the "*political* unconscious" is exposed.[85] It occurs when Caliban's plot interrupts the pageant Prospero is staging for Ferdinand and Miranda, and Prospero is so enraged that Miranda says she has never seen him so angry. The explanation, it has been suggested, is that if psychology matters at all, Prospero's anger here, like his anger earlier when Caliban tried to rape Miranda, derives from the politics of colonialism. It reveals Prospero's political "disquiet at the irruption into consciousness of an unconscious anxiety concerning the grounding of his legitimacy" on the island.[86]

But the dramatic context counters the assumption that politics is primary in this episode. Like Caliban, Prospero differs in significant ways from the stereotyped "real life" characters in colonial political drama. Unlike the single-minded colonial invader, Prospero is both an exile and a father; and the action of the play is initiated when both these roles are newly activated by the arrival of Prospero's old enemies, those who had exiled him as well as his daughter's husband-to-be. At the moment of Prospero's eruption into anger, he has just bestowed Miranda on his enemy's son Ferdinand[87] and is in the midst of presenting his pageant as a wedding gift, wrapped in a three-fold warning about chastity.[88] If Prospero is to pass on his heritage to the next generation, he must at this moment repress his desire for power and for revenge at home, as well as any sexual desire he feels toward Miranda.[89] Both desires are easily projected onto the fishily phallic Caliban, a

---

[83]Barker and Hulme, p. 300.

[84]Hulme, *Colonial Encounters*, p. 133.

[85]Paul Brown, p. 292.

[86]Barker and Hulme, p. 304.

[87]The last time Prospero got so angry that Miranda had to apologize was when Ferdinand began to court Miranda.

[88]See A. D. Nuttall's discussion of the blend of colonialist and sexual tensions in *The Tempest*, "Two Unassimilable Men," in *Shakespearian Comedy*, Stratford-upon-Avon Studies 14 (London: Edward Arnold, 1972), pp. 210–40, esp. p. 216.

[89]The incestuous impulse implicit in the situation is even clearer in Shakespeare's own earlier romances; both Fiedler and Nuttall, among others, have explored these in the context of the vast literature of romance that lies behind the play. See also Mark Taylor, *Shakespeare's Darker Purpose: A Question of Incest* (New York: AMS Press, 1982).

walking version of Prospero's own "thing" of darkness. Not only has Caliban already tried to rape Miranda; he is now out to kill Prospero so that he can turn Miranda over to Stephano ("she will give thee brave brood"); and Caliban does not even feel guilty. Caliban's function as a walking screen for projection may help explain why Caliban's sin does not consist in cannibalism, to which, one assumes, Prospero was never tempted, but rather in Prospero's own repressed fantasies of omnipotence and lust.[90] Of course Prospero is also angry that Caliban is now threatening both his authority on the island and his justification of that authority; but the extraordinary intensity of Prospero's rage suggests a conjunction of psychological as well as political passion.

This conjunction of the psychological and the political not only appears here in *The Tempest* but also characterizes a surprising number of Prospero-like characters in Shakespeare's earlier plays who provide a suggestive context for *The Tempest*. All through the canon one finds characters who escape from active lives to some kind of pastoral retreat, who step aside from power and aggression — and usually from sexuality as well — and from all the forbidden fantasies in which these are enacted. But while each adopts a disinterested stance, as if having retired behind the scenes, each sees life as a play and manipulates others still on stage in a way that suggests a fascination with what he has rejected and assigned to the "Others." And each of these has his "Caliban" and his moment of sudden, irrational anger when his "Caliban" threatens to overstep the limits defining him as "other" and separating him from "Prospero." At this moment of confrontation, boundaries threaten to disappear and hierarchies are menaced. And in each of the earlier plays, this moment is indicative of inner conflict, as the earlier "Prospero" figure confronts someone who often has neither property nor power to colonize, and whose threat is largely symbolic. In all these plays Shakespeare is dealing not just with power relations but also with the psychology of domination, with the complicated ways in which personal psychology interacts with political power.

As early as the mid-1590s, two figures show some resemblance to Prospero. Antonio, the merchant of Venice, sees the world as "A stage where every man must play a part, / And mine a sad one" (1.1.78–79). Almost eagerly accepting his passive lot, he claims to renounce both profit and love. But, as Marianne Novy suggests, a repressed self-assertion is hinted at in the passive/aggressive claims he makes on Bassanio and comes out clearly when he lashes out at the greedy and self-assertive

---

[90]Fiedler, p. 234.

Shylock with a viciousness like Prospero's towards Caliban, a viciousness he shows nowhere else.[91] He admits calling the Jew a dog and says,

> I am as like to call thee so again
> To spet on thee again. . . .
>   (1.3.130–31)[92]

A related and similarly problematic exchange occurs in the *Henry IV* plays, written a year or so later, where role-playing Prince Hal, during his temporary retreat from power, had found a version of pastoral in Falstaff's tavern. After reclaiming his throne, when he finds that Falstaff has also come from the tavern to claim a role in the new kingdom, Hal suddenly repudiates Falstaff with a cruelty as cold as Prospero's anger at Caliban — and equally excessive: "I know thee not, old man." In both these cases, though the resemblance to Prospero is clear, the relation to an historically specific colonialism is hard to establish.

Then in *As You Like It* (1599) and *Measure for Measure* (1604) come the two exiled or self-exiled Dukes who leave home — one to "usurp" the deer in the forest (2.1.21–28), the other to "usurp" the beggary in the Vienna streets (3.2.93) — and who most resemble Prospero. Duke Senior in *As You Like It* is banished to the pastoral forest of Arden, where he professes himself utterly content to live a life notable for the absence of both power and women (a "woeful pageant," he calls it cheerfully [2.7.138]). He is saved from having to fight for power when his evil brother (unlike the one in Shakespeare's source) conveniently repents and hands back the dukedom; but an ambivalence about sexuality is at least suggested when this mildest of men lashes out at Jaques, precisely when Jaques returns from melancholy withdrawal and claims the fool's license to satirize society's ills — to "cleanse the foul body of the infected world."[93] "Fie on thee!" says the Duke,

> . . . thou thyself hast been a libertine,
> As sensual as the brutish sting itself,

[91]Marianne Novy, *Love's Argument: Gender Relations in Shakespeare* (Chapel Hill and London: Univ. of North Carolina Press, 1984), pp. 63–82.

[92]All Shakespeare quotations [except those from *The Tempest*, which correspond to this volume] are from *The Riverside Shakespeare*, ed. G. Blakemore Evans (Boston: Houghton Mifflin, 1974). The earlier group of critics who had pointed out the racist assumptions in Antonio's behavior made many of the same points recently made on Caliban's behalf. The two cases are indeed similar, and although both can be seen as examples of "colonialism"— with the word "colonialism" used very loosely as it is today for any exploitative appropriation — the more historically specific "colonialist discourse" does not seem to be the appropriate context for Shylock.

[93]Nuttall (n. 88, above) notes the strangeness of the Duke's explosion and the fact that Jaques's request for a fool's license "has shaken Duke Senior" (p. 231).

And all th' embossed sores, and headed evils,
That thou with license of free foot hast caught,
Wouldst thou disgorge into the general world.
                                        (2.7.65–69)

Jaques seems to have touched a nerve. Elsewhere Jaques makes a claim
on behalf of the deer in the forest rather like the claim Caliban makes
for himself on the island, complaining that Duke Senior has "usurped"
these "velvet friends"; he even makes it "most invectively," having, like
Caliban, learned how to curse. Just as in the case of Caliban, we cannot
laugh away the claim the way the Duke does. But Jaques's complaint
seems intended more as an insight into the Duke than a comment on
the deer — whom Jaques later kills anyway.

The touchiest of these precursors, Vincentio in *Measure for Measure*
(1604), is the one who most closely resembles Prospero. He too prefers
study to government, and he turns over his power to Angelo, claiming
"[I] do not like to stage me to their eyes" (1.1.68) — but then he steps
behind the scenes to manipulate the action. Like Prospero, Vincentio
sees his manipulation as an altruistic means of educating his wayward
subjects into chastity, repentance, and merciful mildness; but it seems
to serve more private needs of self-definition as well. For it first allows
him, as "ghostly father," to deny any aggressive or sexual motives of his
own, and then allows him to return at the end to claim both power and
sexual rewards as he resumes his dukedom and claims Isabel.[94] Vincentio's "Caliban" is the libidinous and loose-tongued Lucio, who not
only indulges his own appetites but openly accuses the Duke of
indulging his, so that it is unusually clear in this case that the "Caliban"
figure is a representation of the Duke's own disowned passions. Lucio's
slanders include the claim that the Duke has "usurp[ed] the beggary he
was never born to," but, like Jaques speaking for the deer, he is more
concerned with revealing the Duke's contradictory desires here than
with defending beggars' rights. Goaded by Lucio's insubordination,
the Duke lashes out at him as he does at no one else and threatens a
punishment much worse than the one he assigned to the would-be
rapist and murderer Angelo or to the actual murderer Barnardine.

In the case of all of these "Prosperos," it is hard to see the attack on
"Caliban" as part of a specifically colonialist strategy, as a way of
exploiting the Other or of rationalizing illegitimate power over him

---

[94]See Richard P. Wheeler's analysis in *Shakespeare's Development and the Problem
Comedies: Turn and Counter-turn* (Berkeley and Los Angeles: Univ. of California Press,
1981).

rather than over what he represents in "Prospero" himself. To a logical observer, the Prospero-attack seems at best gratuitous — and the more frightening for being so. It has no political rationale. The "political" attack always takes place outside the play's old world, after the characters' withdrawal to a second world that is not so much a new world as one that projects, exaggerates, turns upside down, or polarizes the conflicts that made the old world uninhabitable. In the case of each earlier "Prospero," the conflicts seem internal as well as external, so that when he moves out to meet his "Caliban," he is always meeting himself. Political exile is also presented as self-estrangement, a crisis of selfhood expressed in social and geographical divisions. And in each case, Shakespeare exposes the fragility of such arrangements, whether they take the form of the pastoralization of the forest of Arden, or of the scapegoating of Shylock in Venice, or of Falstaff's carnival misrule in the tavern, or of the theatricalizing of the prison in Vincentio's Vienna, or of Prospero's "colonizing" of a utopian island.

Whatever varying political role each earlier "Caliban" plays as inhabitant of his second — or second-class — world, each seems to embody a similar psychological quality. In each case he displays the overt self-assertion that the retired or retiring "Prospero" cannot — or wishes not to — muster for himself, and that for Shakespeare seems to be the mark of the Other. Each is an epitome of what Shakespeare (perhaps in his own punning ambivalence about acknowledging it as his own) elsewhere calls "will."[95] This "will" includes a range of forbidden desires and appetites often attributed to the Other and always associated with the "foul body," as Jaques calls it; or with the fat appetitive body, as in Hal's picture of Falstaff; or with the body as mere pounds of flesh and blood; perhaps with what we might call, after Bakhtin, the "grotesque" body. And it is defined in opposition to the ethereal, or ariel, virtues such as "mercy," "honor," and "chastity" characterizing the various "Prosperos."

The "will" of these "Calibans" can carry suggestions of primitive oral greed, as in Shylock's desire to "feed fat" his revenge with a pound of human flesh, in Falstaff's voracious appetite, or in Caliban's name. Or it emerges in a rampant sexual greed, as in Falstaff, in Jaques's past, in Lucio, perhaps even in Shylock's reproductive miracles with sheep, and of course in Caliban himself. But the most alien aspect of self-assertion or "will" in these plays emerges in a primitive vengefulness.

---

[95]Primarily of course in the sonnets, but in the plays as well. See Novy's discussion of self-assertiveness in Shylock.

This vengefulness is associated with an infantile need to control and dominate and with the scatological imagery of filth — with a disgust at the whole messy, physical world that always threatens to get out of control. Thus Shylock's drive for revenge is linked to his Jonsonian "anal" virtues ("fast bind, fast find"), to his fecal gold, and to his tightly locked orifices ("stop my house's ears, I mean my casements" {2.5.34}). Thus, too, Duke Senior's description of Jaques "disgorging" his "embossed sores" suggests that he is projecting onto Jaques his disgust at the idea of "the foul body of the infected world"— and his fear that Jaques will "disgorge" and overflow his boundaries rather than cleanse; Jaques's very name associates him with this scatological vision. Caliban, very much concerned with revenge, also takes on a taint of anality through the words of Trinculo and Stephano. The latter sees Caliban hiding under his gabardine with Trinculo and takes Caliban for a monster whose first act is to "vent" a Trinculo — a Gargantuan act of defecation; Trinculo elsewhere complains that Caliban led them to a "foul lake" that o'erstunk their feet till they smelled "all horse-piss."[96]

Thus, although Caliban is like the New World natives in his "otherness," he is linked at least as closely to Shakespeare's earlier "Calibans." What is interesting in any attempt to understand *The Tempest*'s uniqueness in other aspects is that in Caliban for the first time Shakespeare shows "will," or narcissistic self-assertion, in its purest and simplest form as the original "grandiosity" or "megalomania" of a child;[97] for the first time he makes the representative of bodily existence a seeming child whose ego is a "body ego," as Freud said, a "subject" whose "self" is defined by the body. There is a childishly amoral — and almost asexual — glee in Caliban's sexuality ("O ho, O ho, would't had been done!" he says of the attempted rape [1.2.352]) and a childish exaggeration in his dreams of revenge ("brain him / . . . or with a log / Batter his skull, or paunch him with a stake, / Or cut his wezand with thy knife" [3.2.83–86]).[98] Like a child he thinks often about his mother,[99] and now that she is gone, he dreams of riches dropping from heaven and cries to dream again; like a child he was taught language and shown the man in the moon.[100] And like an imperious child he is enraged

---

[96]Caliban later joins the two courtly servants in appropriately scatological double entendres.

[97]Norman Holland, "Caliban's Dream," *The Design Within: Psychoanalytic Approaches to Shakespeare*, ed. M. D. Faber (New York: Science House, 1970), pp. 521–33.

[98]Compare Antonio's cold calculations as he plans to kill Alonso.

[99]Albeit in a "My mommy is going to get you" fashion.

[100]Nuttall, p. 225.

when his pie in the sky does not appear. If he rebukes Prospero for first stroking and then disciplining him, if he objects to being made a subject when he was "mine own king" (1.2.345), this is the rebuke made by every child, who begins life as "His Majesty the Baby," tended by his mother, and who is then subjected to the demands of the community,[101] represented by the father. Childhood is the period in which anyone — even the most powerful Elizabethan aristocrat — can experience the slave's side of the master/slave relation, its indignities, and the dreams of reversal and revenge it can imbue. Appropriate and acceptable in a baby, all these traits (like Caliban himself) "with age [grow] uglier" (4.1.191) — and far more dangerous.

Caliban's childishness has been dismissed as a defense, another rationalization of Prospero's illegitimate power.[102] But if it is a defense, it is one which itself is revealing. Caliban's childishness is a dimension of the Other in which Shakespeare seems extremely interested.[103] It is a major (not peripheral) source both of Caliban's defining characteristics and of what makes his relation to Prospero so highly charged. Caliban's childish innocence seems to have been what first attracted Prospero, and now it is Caliban's childish lawlessness that enrages him. To a man like Prospero, whose life has been spent learning a self-discipline in which he is not yet totally adept, Caliban can seem like a child who must be controlled, and who, like a child, is murderously enraged at being controlled. Prospero treats Caliban as he would treat the willful child in himself.

The importance of childishness in defining Caliban is suggested by the final *Tempest* precedent to be cited here, one that lies behind

[101] So, too, any child might complain that he was taught to speak and now his "profit on 't" is to be trapped in the prison house of language.

[102] See Leininger, p. 125, for the most effective presentation of this view; also Paul Brown, pp. 284–85.

[103] Here, too, Shakespeare seems unusual. Not until our child-centered, post-Freudian age do we find writers so directly representing the aliens on our galactic frontier as children — whether as innocents like Steven Spielberg's E. T. or as proto-savages like his Gremlins. Others had associated the primitive with metaphorical childhood: De Bry's 1590 edition of Harriot's *Briefe and true report* and, later, Purchas's version of Strachey associated the primitive Indians with the childhood of the English nation, and writers spoke of the Indians as "younger brethren" (Kupperman, n. 72, above, p. 170). What is unusual in Shakespeare is the emphasis and the detailed portrayal of emotional as well as cognitive childishness. Leah Marcus argues, in another context, that the English in the chaotic and disorienting intellectual context of the seventeenth century were especially susceptible to dreams of the golden age — and to sympathetic portrayals of childhood wholeness (*Childhood and Cultural Despair* [Pittsburgh, Pa.: Univ. of Pittsburgh Press, 1978]). Most of the instances of such portrayals did not appear until later in the century, however.

Prospero's acknowledgement of Caliban as his own thing of darkness — and in which the Caliban figure is literally a child. This figure is found in *Titus Andronicus,* where a bastard child, called "devil" and "slave," is cast out by his mother but rescued by his father, who promises — in language foreshadowing Caliban's imagery in *The Tempest* — to raise him in a cave and feed him on berries and roots.[104] Here the father is black Aaron the Moor, and the childish thing of darkness, whom Aaron is at some pains to acknowledge his, is his own literally black son. What is remarkable about this portrait of a barbarian father and son is that Aaron's is the only uncomplicated parental love in a play-world where civilized white men like Titus kill their own children on principle. It is a world, by the way, which contains the only literal (if unwitting) cannibal in Shakespeare's plays, the child's white mother. Unlike Titus, Aaron can love his child because he can identify with him; as an "uncivilized" black man, he can accept the greedy, sensual, lawless child in himself: "This is my self, the vigor and the picture of my youth," he says (4.2.108). This love, which comes easily to Aaron in acknowledging his own flesh and blood, is transformed in *The Tempest* to Prospero's strained and difficult recognition of a tribal Other whose blackness nonetheless figures his own.

The echoes of Aaron not only suggest the family resemblance between Prospero and Caliban. They also suggest that here Shakespeare is changing his earlier vision of authority. In the earlier play it is white Titus who — like Prospero — gives away his power and is betrayed; but it is black Aaron who is stigmatized as the vengeful villain. And Titus maintains this black-and-white distinction even while savagely carrying out his own revenge. But distinctions in *The Tempest* have become less rigid. By merging his fantasy about a "white" (but exiled and neurotically puritanical) duke with his fantasy about a villainous (but loving) "black" father, Shakespeare for the first time shows, in Prospero, a paternal leader who comes back to power by admitting rather than denying the "blackness" in himself. Prospero may not, as several revisionists point out, physically *do* much for Caliban at the end; however, what he *says* matters a great deal indeed, for his original transgression, when he first defined Caliban as the Other, was intellectual as well as physical. When Prospero finally acknowledges Caliban, although he is a long way from recognizing the equality of racial "others," he comes closer than any of Shakespeare's other "Prosperos" to acknowledging

[104]Edward A. Armstrong, *Shakespeare's Imagination* (Lincoln: Univ. of Nebraska Press, 1963), p. 52.

the otherness within, which helps generate all racism — and he comes closer than anyone else in colonialist discourse. Prospero acknowledges the child-like Caliban as his own, and although he does not thus undo hierarchy, he moves for the first time towards accepting the child in himself rather than trying to dominate and erase that child (along with random vulnerable human beings outside himself) in order to establish his adult authority.

Thus, although Shakespeare may, as the revisionists claim, to some degree reproduce Prospero's colonialist vision of the island, the play's emphasis lies not so much in justifying as in analyzing that vision, just as Shakespeare had analyzed the origins of dominance in the earlier plays. The play insists that we see Prospero's current relation to Caliban in terms of Prospero's own past; it contains the "colonial" encounter firmly within the framing story of his own family history. And though that history does not extend backward to Prospero's own childhood, it does begin with family ties and Miranda's memory of "the dark backward and abysm of time" (1.2.50), before either she or Prospero had known the Other. Prospero was then, he thought, in total harmony with his world and himself, happy in his regressive retreat to his library-Eden; he was buffered from reality, he thought, by a "lov'd" brother so linked to himself and his own desires that Prospero had in him a trust with no "limit, / A confidence sans bound" (1.2.96–97), like the trust that Miranda must have had in the women who "tended" her then. Only when Antonio's betrayal shattered that trust and Prospero was ousted from Eden — newly aware of both the brother as Other and of himself as a willful self in opposition — did he "discover" the island and Caliban. In a sense, then, Caliban emerged from the rift between Prospero and Antonio,[105] just as Ariel emerged from Sycorax's riven pine. Once the brother has shown that he is not identical to the self, reflecting back its own narcissistic desire, then he becomes the Other — and simultaneously rouses the vengeful Other in the self. In *The Tempest* the distance that a "colonialist" Prospero imposes between self and Other originated in a recoil from the closest relation of all; it was a recoil that in fact *defined* both the "distant" and the "close," the public and the private — the political and the personal — as separate realms. When Prospero acknowledges Caliban, he thus partly defuses an entire dynamic that began long before he had ever seen the island.

---

[105]Might the brothers' definition by opposition perhaps have influenced Shakespeare's choice of names: *Pro*spero and *An*tonio?

IV

When Shakespeare created a childish "Caliban," he was himself rounding out a dynamic process that had begun as long ago as the writing of *Titus Andronicus*. We will never "know" why Shakespeare gave to this final version of his exile story a local habitation incorporating aspects of colonialist discourse. But the answer lies not only in that discourse but also in him and in what was on his mind. Some of the most "specious" speculations about Shakespeare's mind have been stimulated by his presumed resemblance to Prospero at the end of the play: past his zenith, on the way to retirement, every third thought turned to his grave. Without trying speciously to read minds, however, it seems safe to say that to some degree Shakespeare had been for several years concerned with the aging, loss, mortality, and death that recur in so much of what we know he was writing and reading at the time. To this degree, both the play and its context deal with the end of the individual self, the subject and the body in which it is located. It is the end of everything associated with the discovery of self in childhood, the end of everything Caliban represents — and thus the greatest threat to infantile narcissism since His Majesty the Baby was first de-throned. John Bender has noted that the occasion of the play's presumed court debut in 1611 was Hallowmas, the feast of winter and the time of seasonal celebrations figuring the more final endings and death associated with winter.[106] As part of the celebrations, Bender suggests, the play might have served to structure a communal response to the recurring "seasonal mentality" brought on by the reminder of mortality. Whether or not this is true, that which "recurs" in seasons and communities comes only once to individuals; and as the final stage in Shakespeare's own "seasonal" movement from *A Midsummer Night's Dream* to *The Winter's Tale,* the play can be seen as staging a final "crisis of selfhood" and of betrayal like those in the earlier exile plays — but this time a far more extreme one.[107] For those who rage against the dying of the light, it is a crisis that awakens the old infantile narcissistic demand for endless

---

[106]John B. Bender, "The Day of *The Tempest,*" *English Literary History,* 47 (1980), 235–58.

[107]It also marks Shakespeare's return to the pattern of withdrawal from active life used in *Love's Labor's Lost* — but this time with a difference. The earlier play had shown young men hoping to conquer death by forswearing the body and all it represents. *The Tempest* shows an old man coming to terms with death by acknowledging the body and what it represents.

fulfillment and the narcissistic rage and vengefulness against a world that denies such satisfactions.[108]

To one on the threshold of retirement from the Old World, the New World is an appropriate stage on which to enact this last resurgence of the infantile self. We take for granted the historical conditions generating utopian visions in the voyagers' reports outside the play. What the example of Caliban's childish presence in the play suggests is that for Shakespeare the desire for such utopias — the golden worlds and fountains of youth — has roots in personal history as well as in "history." The desire has been shaped by the most local as well as by the largest, collective, material constraints: by being born small and weak in a world run by large, strong people with problems of their own; by being born in "a sexed and mortal body"[109] that must somehow become part of a social and linguistic community. Caliban's utopia of sweet voices and clouds dropping riches (3.2.130–38) draws most directly on the infantile substratum that colored Columbus's report when he returned from his third voyage convinced "that the newly discovered hemisphere was shaped like a woman's breast, and that the Earthly Paradise was located at a high point corresponding to the nipple."[110] But the play's other "utopias" draw on it too. Gonzalo's utopia is more socialized ("nature should bring forth, / . . . all abundance, / To feed my innocent people" [2.1.159–61]); Prospero's pageant utopia is more mythic (a world without winter, blessed by nurturing Ceres); but, like Caliban's, their utopias recreate a union with a bounteous Mother Nature. And, like every child's utopia, each is a fragile creation, easily destroyed by the rage and violence that constitute its defining alternative — a dystopia of murderous vengeance; the interruption of Prospero's pageant is only the last in a series of such interruptions.[111] Each is the creation of a childish mind that operates in binary divisions: good mother/bad mother, love/rage, brother/Other.

That Shakespeare was drawn to the utopian aspects of the New World is suggested by the particular fragment of New World discourse that most directly precipitated (Kermode's suggestive term) the play — the

---

[108]Elliot Jacques offers a related account, in Kleinian terms, of the role of infantile demands and emotions in the effort to come to terms with death in "Death and the Midlife Crisis," *International Journal of Psychoanalysis,* 46 (1965), 502–14.

[109]John Forrester, "Psychoanalysis or Literature?" *French Studies,* 35 (1981), 170–79, esp. p. 172.

[110]Cited in Levin (n. 9, above), p. 183.

[111]See Bender (n. 106, above) on the way dreams are always followed by violence in the play; the violence is not a cause of the problem on the island but rather an effect.

Bermuda pamphlets, which record what was "perhaps the most romantic incident associated with America's beginnings."[112] What attracted Shakespeare, that is, was the story in which a "merciful God," a loving and fatherly protector, rescued a whole shipload of people from certain death; it was a story that countered thoughts of winter with reports of magical bounty in the aptly named "Summer Islands."

The concerns that made Shakespeare's approach to colonialist discourse possible may have been operative later in other cases as well. In analyzing the colonialist discourse growing out of political motives, it is important not to lose touch with the utopian discourse growing out of a different set of motives. Without reducing colonialism to "the merely subjective and to the status of psychological projection,"[113] one can still take account of fantasies and motives that, though now regarded as secondary, or as irrelevant to politics, may interact with political motives in ways we have not yet begun to understand — and cannot understand so long as we are diverted by trying to reduce psychology to politics or politics to psychology. The binary dynamics of infantile utopian fantasies can, for example, help explain why frustrated settlers succumbed *so easily* to the twin stereotypes of the Native Americans as innocent primitives who would welcome and nurture the settlers, and as hopelessly treacherous Others. They can serve as a reminder that the desire for friendship and brotherhood can be as destructive as a desire to exploit. Reference to irrational, outdated infantile needs can help explain why the settlers, once they actually did begin colonizing, set out with such gratuitous thoroughness to "reduce" the savage to civility. As James Axtell describes the process, "In European eyes, no native characteristic was too small to reform, no habit too harmless to reduce."[114] Such behavior seems to go beyond any immediate political or material motive and seems rather to serve more general psychological needs stirred up by conflict with the natives. The recent emphasis on the colonists' obvious material greed and rational self-interest — or classinterest — has unnecessarily obscured the role of these less obvious irrational motives and fantasies that are potentially even more insidious.

---

[112]Andrews (n. 65, above), p. 126.

[113]Jameson cites as being "very much in the spirit of [his] present work" the concern of Deleuze and Guattari "to reassert the specificity of the political content of everyday life and of individual fantasy-experience and to reclaim it from . . . reduction to the merely subjective and to the status of psychological projection" (*The Political Unconscious*, n. 22, above, p. 22).

[114]*The Invasion Within: The Contest of Cultures in North America* (Oxford: Oxford Univ. Press, 1985), p. 54.

Shakespeare's assimilation of elements from historical colonialist discourse was neither entirely isolated from other uses or innocent of their effects. Nonetheless, the "colonialism" in his play is linked not only to Shakespeare's indirect participation in an ideology of political exploitation and erasure but also to his direct participation in the psychological aftereffects of having experienced the exploitation and erasure inevitable in being a child in an adult's world. He was not merely reproducing a preexistent discourse; he was also crossing it with other discourses, changing, enlarging, skewing, and questioning it. Our sense of *The Tempest*'s participation in "colonialist discourse" should be flexible enough to take account of such crossings; indeed our notion of that in which such discourse consisted should be flexible enough to include the whole of the text that constitutes the first English example of fictional colonialist discourse.[115]

[115]The original version of this essay was presented at a session on "Psychoanalysis and Renaissance History," chaired by Richard Wheeler at the 1987 MLA annual meeting. The current version has greatly benefited from careful readings by Janet Adelman, Anne and Rob Goble, Carol Neely, Marianne Novy, Martin Wiener, and several anonymous readers.

The Challenge of
Feminist Criticism

In this chapter, we present two essays that bring a feminist perspective into the debate, one that challenges traditional interpretations of *The Tempest* but also calls attention to the "gender-blindness," in Ania Loomba's phrase, of postcolonial interpretations. At the same time, both essays grapple with the problem posed by *The Tempest* for feminist critics. As Ann Thompson succinctly puts the problem, "I want to ask what feminist criticism can do in the face of a male-authored canonical text which seems to exclude women" (p. 404 in this volume).

As Loomba shows in our excerpt from her book *Gender, race, Renaissance Drama* (1989), this problem remains acute even when the play is appropriated for purposes of anticolonial and antiracist rebellion. Loomba focuses on "the gender politics" that have been ignored by such appropriations. She notes that critics who celebrate Caliban as a spokesperson for the oppressed have a problem with his attempted rape of Miranda. Loomba points out that this element of the play reflects "the racist assumption that Caliban's subordinate status will naturally lead him to desire (and hence rape) Miranda"; it also however reflects a sexist image of the woman as a figure of "passive purity" (pp. 391; 392).

This set of concerns enables Loomba to see striking new importance in the otherwise seemingly marginal character Sycorax. For Loomba, Sycorax is a figure of latent rebellion, whose "licentious black femininity" (p. 392) and whose black magic stand in contrast both "to

388

the white, virginal and obedient Miranda" (p. 393) and to the white magic of Prospero. Finally, Loomba, in Ann Thompson's words, illuminates "the contradictory position of Miranda as typical of that of all white women in the colonial adventure: the nature of her participation confirms her subordination to white men" (p. 412).

Thompson addresses similar concerns in her own essay here as she explores "the ideology of femininity" in the play and its critical interpretations. Noting the importance and apparent approval accorded to "male control" over female chastity and fertility in the play — seen for instance in Prospero's obsessive concern to keep Miranda a virgin before marriage — Thompson asks "what kind of pleasure can a woman and a feminist take in this text beyond the rather grim one of mapping its various patterns of exploitation?" (p. 412). Thompson does not attempt to answer this question, but her raising it suggests that she would agree with the critics in our previous section ("Responding to the Challenge") that there is something unsatisfactory about political readings of the play that dismiss it on purely political grounds.

ANIA LOOMBA

From Gender, race, Renaissance Drama

Ania Loomba (b. 1955), who has taught at Jawaharal Nehru University in New Delhi, the University of Tulsa, and the University of Illinois, is currently the Catherine Bryson Professor of English at the University of Pennsylvania. She is the author of *Gender, race, Renaissance Drama* (1989), *Colonialism-Postcolonialism* (1998), and *Shakespeare, Race, and Colonialism* (2007). In addition, she has coedited *Postcolonial Shakespeares* (1998), *Postcolonial Studies and Beyond* (2005), and *Race in Early Modern England: A Documentary Companion* (2007). The following selection is from *Gender, race, Renaissance Drama*.

THE BLACK RAPIST[1]

One of the reasons for the play's declining pertinence to contemporary third world politics has been identified as

[1]I am indebted to work on *The Tempest* by Barker and Hulme, Paul Brown, and Rob Nixon, all of which has made this chapter possible.

the difficulty of wresting from it any role for female defiance or leadership in a period when protest is coming increasingly from that quarter. Given that Caliban is without a female counterpart in his oppression and rebellion, and given the largely autobiographical cast of African and Caribbean appropriations of the play, it follows that all the writers who quarried from *The Tempest* an expression of their lot should have been men. (Nixon 577)

It is true that the play poses a problem for a feminist, and especially a nonwestern feminist appropriation, if by "appropriation" we mean an amplification of the anti-colonial voices within the text. But such a difficulty does not arise simply from the lack of a strong female presence, black or white, in the play, but also from the play's representation of black male sexuality.

Caliban contests Prospero's account of his arrival on the island but not the accusation of attempted rape of Miranda. Identifying the political effects of Prospero's accusation, Paul Brown comments that "the issue here is not whether Caliban is actually a rapist or not, since Caliban accepts the charge" (p. 284 in this volume). On the contrary, I suggest that this acceptance is important for assessing both colonial and anti-colonial readings of the play. An article written in 1892, which later became what Griffiths calls "a standard defence of Caliban" speaks of the rape as "an offence, an unpardonable offence, but *one that he was fated to commit*" (166; emphasis added) and goes on to see Caliban as unfortunate, oppressed, but "like all these lower peoples, easily misled." This implies that sexual violence is part of the black man's inferior nature, a view that amalgamates racist common-sense notions about black sexuality and animalism, and sexist assumptions about rape as an inevitable expression of frustrated male desire.

These notions were complexly employed in the influential *Psychologie de la colonisation* (1948) by Octave Mannoni, who seriously reassessed the play in order to propound a controversial view of the psychology of the colonised subject. Mannoni advocated the notion of the "Caliban complex" which he analyzed as the desire for dependency on the part of the native. Caliban (and the Madagascans, whose uprising of 1947–48 provided the impetus for the work) revolts not against slavery but because he is abandoned by Prospero. Analyzing Caliban's speech in Act 2, Mannoni came to the conclusion that "Caliban does not complain of being exploited: he complains of being betrayed." As other Caribbean and African intellectuals pointed out, Mannoni posited Caliban as an eager partner in his own colonization (Nixon 562–65).

Crucially, Mannoni traces the roots of racism to sexual guilt. The antagonism between Caliban and Prospero hinged on Miranda's presence as the sole woman on the island. Accordingly, a definition of the colonizer's psyche, or what Mannoni called the "Prospero complex" was based on the notion of racism as a pseudo-rational construct used to rationalize feelings of sexual guilt.

Both dependency and racism by this account are connected to politics of sexual desire, but in a way that preserves the patriarchal exclusion of sexuality from economics as well as the racist assumption that Caliban's subordinate status will naturally lead him to desire (and hence rape) Miranda. The supposed desire of the native for European care has been advanced by nearly every imperialist regime. That Mannoni's theories could be used to legitimize colonization was demonstrated by the publication of Philip Mason's *Prospero's Magic: Some Thoughts on Class and Race* in 1962 (Nixon 564–65). Mannoni was severely criticized for his psychological reductionism by, among others, Frantz Fanon, who pointed out that economic motivations for plunder were omitted in the former's account.

Fanon's own explanation of the sexual encounter between the black man and white woman in *Black Skins, White Masks*, . . . attributes both sexual insecurity and racist hatred to the white father who is antagonized by the black lover of his daughter. Fanon also describes the ways in which a black man who has internalized the value system of white society may view his liaison with a white woman as a pathway to acceptance and I have used this explanation to describe Othello's love for Desdemona [see *Gender, race, Renaissance Drama,* chapter 2]. A Fanonian explanation of black men's desire for white women is useful only in specific situations and with some qualifications. Firstly, to extend it to the consciousness of all black men would be to assume "too readily that black men have necessarily internalized the white man's view of things" (see Lawrence, "Just plain common-sense," 71). Secondly, in Fanon's account, the white woman is only an *object* of the black man's desire; her own subjectivity is markedly absent. This is a serious limitation of Fanon's work, for racist common-sense (although from a totally different perspective) also posits that black men lust after white women, and also erases the desire of white women. By doing so, racism moves from the black man's desire to his bestiality and concludes that black men will seek to *enforce* a liaison upon white women. Hence the myth of the black rapist. In *Othello*, such a myth hovers on the margins of Brabantio's accusations, but is undercut by Desdemona's own powerfully articulated desire for Othello.

In *The Tempest*, Prospero's accusation of rape and its corroboration by Caliban upholds such a myth, which derives from the idea that, aware of the damage they can do by making sexual advances towards white women, black men have all conceived "a peculiar lust for white womanhood" (Lawrence 71). Of course, rape has been articulated as a weapon by black militants: Eldridge Cleaver called it an "insurrectionary act" against white society. Imamu Baraka wrote: "Come up, black dada nihilismus. Rape the white girls. Rape their fathers. Cut the mother's throats" (cited Angela Davis 197). If varieties of feminism are guilty of racist practices, it needs hardly to be detailed here that sexist versions of anti-racism abound as well. The result of these has strengthened the fiction, often presented as "facts," of black animalism. Susan Brownmiller's influential study of rape, *Against Our Will,* has argued that black men's historical oppression has placed many of the "legitimate" expressions of male supremacy beyond their reach, resulting in their open sexual violence. Quoting Jean McKellar's *Rape: The Bait and the Trap,* which claims that ninety percent of all reported rapes in the United States are by black men, Angela Davis points out that even official FBI figures place it at forty percent (179). The point here is not that black men do not rape, but that their dominant fictional representation has legitimized both patriarchal and racist myths of female and black sexuality.

Gerda Lerner rightly says that "the myth of the black rapist of white women is the turn of the myth of the bad black woman — both designed to apologize for and facilitate the continued exploitation of black men and women" (quoted Angela Davis 174). And of white women, one may add — the construction of the black rapist also includes that of the passive white woman, whose potential desire for black men is thus effaced. In *The Tempest,* therefore, we must read Caliban's rapacity as set against Sycorax's licentious black femininity and the passive purity of Miranda, whose own desire, like Portia's, corroborates the will of the father; although Miranda can be seen to "slip away" from Prospero (see Paul Brown, p. 281 in this volume; Fiedler 206), this slippage does not erode fatherly authority in the same way as Desdemona's passion for Othello. Moreover, this juxtaposition of Miranda, Sycorax, and Caliban focuses both on the economic aspects that were erased by Mannoni, and on the gender politics that have been ignored in some other appropriations.

SYCORAX

Mannoni, significantly, edited out these opening lines of Caliban's version of Prospero's arrival on the island:

This island's mine, by Sycorax my mother,
Which thou tak'st from me.
                        (1.2.334–35)

These lines had elicited the first recorded anti-imperialist response to the play in 1904, which found that in them "the whole case of the aboriginal against aggressive civilisation [was] dramatised before us" (Nixon 561–62). They were also focused by subsequent Caribbean and African appropriations, but although some of these indicated the matrilinear nature of many pre-colonial societies, gender was hardly ever seized upon by anti-colonial intellectuals as a significant dimension of racial oppression.

Sycorax is more than the justification for Caliban's territorial rights to the island — she operates as a powerful contrast to Miranda. Both Prospero and Caliban testify to her power; the former draws upon the language of misogyny as well as racism to construct her as a "foul witch" (1.2.258), the latter invokes her strength to express his hatred of his master (1.2.324–26, 342–43). Prospero's descriptions of Sycorax emphasize both her non-European origins — she's "from Argier"— and her fertility —"This blue-ey'd hag was hither brought with child" (1.2.266, 270). She is also "so strong / That could control the moon, make flows and ebbs, / And deal in her command without her power" (5.1.269–71). Hence she stands in complete contrast to the white, virginal, and obedient Miranda. Between them they split the patriarchal stereotype of woman as the white devil — virgin and whore, goddess (Miranda is mistaken for one by Ferdinand) and witch.

But Sycorax is also Prospero's "other"; his repeated comparisons between their different magics and their respective reigns of the island are used by him to claim a superior morality, a greater strength and a greater humanity, and hence legitimize his takeover of the island and its inhabitants; but they also betray an anxiety that Sycorax's power has not been fully exorcised, for Caliban still invokes it for his own rebellion: "All the charms / Of Sycorax, toads, beetles, bats, light on you!" (1.2.342–43). As George Lamming pointed out in *The Pleasures of Exile*, while Miranda is like many an African slave child in never having known her mother, "the actual Caliban of *The Tempest* has the advantage . . . of having known the meaning and power of his mother Sycorax" (111).

Prospero's takeover is both *racial* plunder and a transfer to *patriarchy*. The connections between witches and transgressive women, between witch-trials with the process of capital accumulation, and between the economic, ideological and sexual subordination of native women by colonial rule, have already been discussed [in *Gender, race, Renaissance Drama*, chapters 1 and 3]. The restructuring of the colonized economy not only involved the export of raw material to factories in England, but also a redefinition of men and women's work, which economically dislocated women, and calcified patriarchal tendencies in the native culture (see Lawrence, "Sociology and black 'pathology,'" 113–14). In Burma, for example, British colonialists acknowledged that Burmese women had property and sexual rights unheard of in England. Accordingly, Fielding Hall, Political Officer in the British Colonial Administration in Burma, suggested that in order to "civilise" the Burmese people:

1. The men must be taught to kill and to fight for the British colonialists.
2. Women must surrender their liberty in the interests of men.
(Mies, quoted by Rughani, 19)

Colonized women were also subjected to untold sexual harassment, rape, enforced marriage, and degradation, both under direct slavery and otherwise. Sycorax's illegitimate pregnancy contrasts with Miranda's chastity and virginity, reminding us that the construction of the promiscuity of non-European women served to legitimize their sexual abuse and to demarcate them from white women.

Therefore Prospero as colonialist consolidates power which is specifically white and male, and constructs Sycorax as a black, wayward, and wicked witch in order to legitimize it. If Caliban's version of past events prompts us to question Prospero's story, then this interrogation should include the re-telling of Sycorax's story. The distinctions drawn by generations of critics between his "white magic" and Sycorax's "black magic" only corroborate Prospero's narrative. African appropriations emphasized the brutality of Prospero's "reason" and its historical suppression of black culture, but they did not bring out the gender-value of these terms; they read the story of colonized and colonizing men but not of colonized and colonizing women, which is also told by Miranda's lonely presence on the island.

MIRANDA'S SCHOOLING

It is ironical but not entirely inappropriate that one of the oldest of Delhi's colleges for women should have been called "Miranda House," after the daughter of the university's colonial founder, Sir Maurice Gwyer. Miranda's schooling in *The Tempest* demonstrates the contradictory position occupied by white women in the colonial adventure. Paul Brown has discussed how "the discourse of sexuality . . . offers the crucial nexus for the various domains of colonialist discourse" (p. 271) and the ways in which control of his subjects' sexuality is crucial for Prospero's exercise of power. Patriarchalism alternately asserts its *knowledge* (the father's wisdom: Prospero's magic, his schooling of Miranda, his civilizing of Caliban); its *humanity* (parental concern and love: Prospero's reiteration of his "care" of Miranda, his liberation of "my Ariel," and of his "humanely taken" pains over Caliban); its *power* (the father's authority: Miranda cannot choose but obey Prospero, he can torture both Caliban and Ariel); and often all three together (Prospero's aside to the rebels that he will "tell no tales" is simultaneously a disclosure of his knowledge of their plans, a favor, and a warning). In the colonial situation, patriarchalism makes specific, and often apparently contradictory demands of its "own" women.

Miranda is the most solitary of Renaissance woman protagonists, and moves on an exclusively male stage — "I do not know / One of my sex; no woman's face remember" (3.1.48–49) — where references are made to only three other women. She indicates the apparent exclusion of women from the colonial arena, but at the same time, their actual and sinister inclusion, together with other images of femininity in the play, propels the narrative even when posited as an absence. Miranda provides the ideological legitimation of each of Prospero's actions; at the beginning of the play he tells her that his "Art" is prompted by his concern for her: "I have done nothing but in care of thee" (1.2.16). Next, in the same scene, he claims that his enslavement of Caliban was prompted by the latter's attempted rape of Miranda (1.2.347–51). Later she is described by him as "a third of mine own life, / Or that for which I live" (4.1.3–4); therefore after she is married he will "retire me to my Milan, where / Every third thought shall be my grave" (5.1.310–11).

Prospero's complaint against Antonio is that he "new created / The creatures that were mine, I say or chang'd 'em, / Or else new form'd 'em" (1.2.81–83). His own enterprise is precisely the same, and Miranda is the most successful of his creations. For twelve years "have I, thy schoolmaster, made thee more profit / Than other princess' can, that have more time / For vainer hours, and tutors not so careful" (1.2.172–74). This education has had two main and diverse purposes. On the one hand it has schooled her to obedience; Prospero proudly affirms that Miranda is "ignorant of what thou art; nought knowing / Of whence I am." She obeys in silence and has been taught not to question why, despite the fact that Prospero has left his story tantalizingly incomplete: "More to know / Did never meddle with my thoughts" (1.2.18–22). She has therefore been well prepared to accept his version of the past (unlike Caliban, who questions it). Gratitude to her father mingles with a self-depreciation and she repeatedly perceives herself as a nuisance to him (1.2.63–64; 1.2.151–52). Prospero never takes this control for granted, however, and is anxious to secure her attention and obedience. His story-telling is punctuated by repeated orders to "sit down," "Obey, and be attentive," "Dost thou attend me?", "I pray thee, mark me," "Thou attend'st not?" "Dost thou hear?" (1.2). Miranda is ordered to sleep, awake, come on, see, speak, be quiet, obey, be silent, hush, and be mute. She is his property, to be exchanged between father and husband: "Then, as my gift, and thine own acquisition / Worthily purchas'd, take my daughter" (4.1.13–14).

On the other hand, Miranda's schooling calls upon her to *participate* actively in the colonial venture. Although she does not "love to look upon" Caliban, she must be educated about the economics of the situation:

> We cannot miss him: he does make our fire.
> Fetch in our wood, and serves in offices
> That profit us.
>
> (1.2.314–16)

Editors of *The Tempest* have often sought to transfer Miranda's verbal assault on Caliban beginning "Abhorred slave" (1.2.354–65) to Prospero on the grounds that Miranda is too delicate and not philosophical enough to speak so harshly (*The Tempest* 32; Barton 137). On the contrary, these lines underline Miranda's implication in the colonialist project. She has been taught to be revolted by Caliban ("abhorred slave"); to believe in his natural inferiority ("thy vile race") and inherent incapacity to be bettered ("which any print of goodness will not take"); to feel sorry for the inferior native ("I pitied thee") and to try and uplift him ("took pains to make thee speak"); and to concur totally in his "deserv'd" confinement. Miranda thus conforms to the dual requirements of femininity within the master-culture: by taking on aspects of the white man's burden the white woman only confirmed her own subordination.

"Miranda House" was a school for Indian women and its naming was not a careful colonial conspiracy. I do not want to ignore the contradictions of such institutions, and the space for alternative stances within them; yet the name betrays some of the assumptions underlying female education in the colonies and indicates the effort to create a native *female* intelligentsia which would be schooled to ignore its gendered and racial alienation from the prevailing status quo.[2] Two other women are mentioned in *The Tempest,* and the references to them reinforce racial and sexual power relations. The first of these is Miranda's mother, who is dismissed as "a piece of virtue" (1.2.56) and remembered solely for her capacity to ensure the pure descent of the Duke of Milan. Later we hear of Claribel, daughter of Alonzo, King of Naples, who has been married to the King of Tunis. The tempest wrecked the ship while it was returning from the wedding celebrations. While he laments the death of his son, Alonzo is told:

> Sir, you may thank yourself for this great loss,
> That would not bless our Europe with your daughter,
> But rather loose her to an African.
>
> (2.1.120–22)

Thus women and black men, and particularly a combination of the two, are posited as the cause of misfortune. We are also told that Claribel herself, "the fair soul," oscillated between "loathness" at this union and "obedience" to her father (2.1.126–27). Her marriage is abnormal and the source of ill-luck but she, a true European daughter, is subservient to patriarchal will. The references to the marriage also serve to distinguish between different non-Europeans, between the King of Tunis and Caliban, underlining the way that class positions, power, and regional differences can alter the meaning of racial difference. In this respect, one may recall also that whereas Cleopatra's status can allow her frankly to acknowledge her dark color —"Think on me, / That am with Phoebus'

---

[2]The English department of Miranda House has been instrumental in initiating (in Delhi) the critical examination of English studies in India; it has also provided a forum for regular discussion of critical theory and its applicability in the Indian classroom and published feminist criticism by university lecturers in Delhi. This perhaps bears out my contention that, given the increasing feminization of English studies, and women's alienation from the dominant concerns of the discipline, a Third World feminist criticism will play a central role in overhauling English studies in India.

amorous pinches black" (1.5.27–28) — Zanche as a lowly servant girl must attempt, with a dowry of "a hundred thousand crowns," to "wash the Ethiop white" (Webster 259; see also Newman 142).[3]

A DOOMED DIALECTIC?

The "rape" amplifies the doomed dialectic which might be detected in Caliban's ability to curse *in the colonizer's tongue,* which exerted the greatest fascination for anti-colonial appropriations and became a symbol both for the internalization of European values by the African and Caribbean intellectual and for his subversion (hers was not considered) of them. George Lamming's *The Pleasures of Exile* points out that the "gift" of language is "not English, in particular, but speech and concept as a way . . . [it] is the very prison in which Caliban's achievements will be realised and restricted" (109–10). Caliban presents the rape as his attempt to "people . . . This isle with Calibans" (1.2.353–54). But even by positing himself as worthy of duplication, Caliban's revolt boomerangs to confirm the shaping power of dominant culture. Lamming wonders why Caliban is so sure that his children by Miranda would be like him, and not like her or Prospero. But he does not consider the phallocentricism of Caliban's confidence, nor how it is ironically undercut by his subordinate racial position. Moreover, he constantly simplifies both Caliban and Miranda. "Caliban is in his way a kind of Universal. Like the earth he is always there, generous in his gifts, inevitable, yet superfluous and dumb . . . Caliban can never reach perfection, not even the perfection implicit in Miranda's privileged ignorance" (108–10). The political effect of Prospero's accusation and Caliban's acceptance is to make the potential revolutionary a rapist, and I have tried to suggest that it is crucially interrelated with the other ways in which Caliban's spaces are limited by the boundaries of colonial discourse. Although the connection between Caliban's linguistic and sexual rebellion is hinted at by Lamming, it is not fully developed; this omission is typical of the gender-blindness of many anti-colonial appropriations and criticism.

---

[3]Femininity and race are picked up in the references to other women, as in the apparently trivial banter about Dido "which has never properly been explained" (*The Tempest* 46). This exchange both differentiates between African Tunis and Carthage, center of the Old World, and introduces the idea of identification between the two worlds: "Tunis, sir was Carthage" (2.1.81).

Can Caliban ever exist outside the territories allowed him by *The Tempest*? Feminists have found the "masculine will" of disorderly women in Renaissance drama unsatisfactory, and I have tried to show that no other pure feminist consciousness is possible from within the masculine arena available to them. Homi Bhabha writes: "it is always in relation to the place of the Other that colonial desire is articulated: that is, in part, the fantasmatic space of 'possession' that no one subject can singly occupy which permits the dream of the inversion of role" (Bhabha xv). This implicates both the colonizer and the colonized: while it would be idealist to imagine spaces outside such a dialectic in the colonial situation, the interlocking is increasingly dissatisfying in the post-colonial reality. Even within the colonial struggle, the evocation of native culture has been important — Aimé Césaire, for example, tried to locate his Caliban in indigenous space — he is rooted in African religion and culture and draws on traditions uncontaminated by colonialism.

Here *The Tempest* brings us to the center of a crucial controversy surrounding current theories of colonial discourse. Benita Parry has suggested that recent work in this area has concentrated on the complexity, ambiguity, and "hybridity" of colonial discourse at the expense of obscuring what Fanon called the "murderous and decisive struggle between two protagonists" (Parry 43). This problem has been identified in relation to *The Tempest* by Thomas Cartelli, who counterposes those "who quarrel with the notion of a *Tempest* that speaks the predatory language of colonialism" and "another nonwestern interpretative community for whom *The Tempest* has long served as the embodiment of colonial presumption." As he sees it, the first group "problematize[s] the traditionally stereotyped critical estimate of the relationship of Prospero and Caliban," while the second resists this "by recuperating the starkness of the master/slave configuration" (101).

It is true that the limits of the "radical ambivalence" of *The Tempest* are marked by the confinement of Caliban to the space structured by the colonizer; the play does not allow him to visualize what Parry calls "another condition beyond imperialism." But we can question a simple opposition between the two groups identified by Cartelli by arguing that the play functions as "the embodiment of colonial presumption" only when the tensions and ambivalence which Brown points to are erased. What do we mean by "the starkness of the master/slave configuration"? Surely not that either of the two opponents, their stances and psyches, are simple or monolithic? The harshness of the colonial conflict cannot be stressed by ignoring the complexity of the adversaries.

This project has tried to emphasize this point in relation to our own encounter with the European text, including the agenda for its alternative teaching. The colonial conflict intersects with others — those of class, gender, caste, and ethnicity — and "the colonial subject" is not a simple being. Moreover, three centuries of colonial history have shaped complex institutions, such as the Indian education system, which cannot be dismantled unless we take into account the interpenetration of colonial, indigenous, and patriarchal power structures. But this is precisely the point at which Parry's criticism becomes crucial: she attributes the concentration on "hybridity" to a "programme marked by the exorbitation of discourse and a related incuriosity about the enabling socio-economic and political institutions and other forms of social praxis" (43). Whereas in *The Tempest* Caliban is simply left on his island, we know that in reality Prospero rarely simply sails away. To curse in "your language" (1.2.368) is not to appropriate the European text on its own terms or to limit ourselves to the spaces allowed by it. Not only will it center around a disclosure of the similarity and dissimilarity, usefulness and irrelevance of the Western text, but it must extend to the economic, sociopolitical, and institutional realities in which our academic practice exists.

WORKS CITED

Barker, Francis, and Hulme, Peter, "Nymphs and reapers heavily vanish: The discursive contexts of *The Tempest*" in Drakakis, 1985, pp. 191–205. [Reprinted in this volume, p. 292.]

Barton, Anne, "Leontes and the spider: Language and speaker in Shakespeare's last plays," in P. Edwards, I. S. Ewbank, and G. K. Hunter, eds., *Shakespeare's Styles: essays in honour of Kenneth Muir* (Cambridge, Cambridge University Press, 1980), pp. 131–50.

Bhabha, Homi, "Introduction" to Fanon, 1986.

Brown, Paul, "This thing of darkness I acknowledge mine: *The Tempest* and the discourse of colonialism," in Dollimore and Sinfield, eds., 1985, pp. 48–71. [Reprinted in this volume, p. 268.]

Brownmiller, Susan, *Against Our Will: Men, Women, and Rape* (London, Secker and Warburg, 1975).

Cartelli, Thomas, "Prospero in Africa: *The Tempest* as colonial text and pretext," in Howard and O'Connor, eds., 1987, pp. 99–115.

CCCS (Centre for Contemporary Cultural Studies), *The Empire Strikes Back: Race and racism in 70s Britain* (London, etc., Hutchinson, 1982).

Davis, Angela, *Women, Race and Class* (London, Women's Press, 1982).

Dollimore, Jonathan, and Sinfield, Alan, eds., *Political Shakespeare: New essays in cultural materialism* (Manchester University Press, 1985).

Drakakis, John, ed., *Alternative Shakespeares* (London, Metheun, 1985).

Fanon, Frantz, *Black Skins, White Masks,* trans. Charles Lam Markmann (London and Sydney, Pluto Press, 1986).

Fiedler, Leslie A., *The Stranger in Shakespeare* (Hertfordshire, Paladin, 1974).

Griffiths, Trevor R., "This island's mine: Caliban and Colonialism," *Yearbook of English Studies* 13 (1983), pp. 159–80.

Howard, Jean E., and O'Connor, Marian F., eds., *Shakespeare Reproduced: The text in history and ideology* (New York and London, Metheun, 1987).

Lamming, George, *The Pleasures of Exile* (London and New York, Allison and Busby, 1984).

Lawrence, Errol, "Just plain common-sense: The 'roots' of racism," in CCCS, 1982, pp. 47–94.

———. "In abundance of water the fool is thirsty; sociology and black 'pathology,'" in CCCS, 1982, pp. 95–142.

Mannoni, O., *Prospero and Caliban: The Psychology of Colonization,* trans. Pamela Powesland (New York, Praeger, 1964).

Mies, Maria, *Patriarchy and Accumulation on a World Scale: Women in the International Division of Labor* (London, Zed Books, 1986).

Newman, Karen, "'And wash the Ethiop white'— Femininity and the monstrous in *Othello,*" in Howard and O'Connor, eds., 1987, pp. 143–62.

Nixon, Rob, "Caribbean and African appropriations of *The Tempest,*" *Critical Inquiry* 13 (Spring 1987), pp. 557–77.

Parry, Benita, "Problems in current theories of colonial discourse," *Oxford Literary Review* 9 (1987), pp. 27–58.

Rughani, Pratap, "Kipling, India and Imperialism" (unpublished paper).

Shakespeare, William. *The Complete Works of William Shakespeare,* ed. Peter Alexander (London and Glasgow, Collins, 1951).

The Tempest, ed. Frank Kermode (London, Metheun, 1954).

Webster, John, *The White Devil,* ed. Elizabeth M. Brennan, in *Elizabeth and Jacobean Tragedies* (Kent, Ernest Benn, 1984).

ANN THOMPSON

"Miranda, Where's Your Sister?":
Reading Shakespeare's *The Tempest*

Ann Thompson (b. 1947) is currently head of the School of Humanities at King's College, London. An experienced textual editor, she is a general editor of the Arden Shakespeare and in that series has coedited *Hamlet* (2006) and *Hamlet: The Texts of 1603 and 1623* (2006). In addition she has coedited *In Arden: Editing Shakespeare* (2003) and *Reading Shakespeare's Dramatic Language* (2001) and edited *Women Reading Shakespeare, 1600–1900* (1997). The following selection appeared in *Feminist Criticism: Theory and Practice,* edited by Susan Sellers (1991).

These are Prospero's first words in *The Tempest, or The Enchanted Island,* the adaptation of Shakespeare's play created for the most part by William Davenant, with some input from John Dryden, in 1667. They act as a clear signal to a knowing audience or reader that this is not the original. Davenant's Miranda does indeed have a younger sister, Dorinda, and the two are described in the *Dramatis Personae* as "Daughters to Prospero, that never saw Man." Dorinda is balanced, and ultimately partnered, by another new character, Hippolito, heir to the dukedom of Mantua, "one that never saw Woman." In the insistent pattern of parallels and repetitions which characterizes Davenant's version, Ariel has a female consort, Milcha, and even Caliban has a twin sister named after their mother, Sycorax, whom he proposes as a bride for Trinculo.[1] This proliferation of female roles can presumably be attributed in part to the need to provide employment for actresses on the Restoration stage.

In contrast, women are notably absent from Shakespeare's *Tempest.* Miranda at one point stresses her isolation and lack of female companionship by saying "I do not know / One of my sex, no woman's face remember, / Save from my glass, mine own" (3.1.48–50), though at the beginning of the play she had claimed at least a vague recollection:

---

[1]Maximilian E. Novak and George Robert Guffey, eds., *The Works of John Dryden* (vol. X, Berkeley, CA and London: University of California Press, 1970). I would like to thank Andrew Gurr for drawing my attention to the line which forms my title.

"Had I not / Four or five women once that tended me?" (1.2.46–47).
Apart from Miranda herself, the only females mentioned in the First
Folio's list of the "Names of the Actors" are Iris, Ceres, Juno and the
Nymphs, all of whom are "spirits" explicitly impersonated by Ariel and
his "fellows." While Ariel is clearly a male spirit, he is also required to
impersonate a "nymph of the sea" (1.2.303) and a half-female harpy
(stage direction at 3.3.52), indicating a degree of ambiguity about his
gender. The part has often been performed by women or by androgy-
nous youths. Conversely, the part of Miranda would in actuality have
been performed by a boy actor on Shakespeare's stage.

Miranda, in Shakespeare's play, has no sister and apparently no
mother. It is odd that she does not even inquire about the fate of the
latter, though she might have been prompted to do so by Prospero's
reply to her question "Sir, are not you my father?" In his only reference
to his wife Prospero says "Thy mother was a piece of virtue, and / She
said thou wast my daughter" (1.2.56–57). This is apparently all that
needs to be said about her. Some fifty lines later, Miranda demonstrates
that she has fully internalized the patriarchal assumption that a
woman's main function is to provide a legitimate succession when
asked to comment on the wickedness of Prospero's brother: "I should
sin / To think but nobly of my grandmother: / Good wombs have
borne bad sons" (1.2.118–20).

The worldly cynicism of such standard jokes was formerly thought
inappropriate to the innocent Miranda, and they were often omitted
from performances from the late eighteenth century to the early twentieth century; Davenant's Miranda more explicitly denies that she had a
mother when she remarks with a coy naiveté to Dorinda that she thinks
Prospero "found us when we both were little, and grew within the
ground" (1.2.332–33). In Shakespeare's version, Miranda's destined
spouse, Ferdinand, is also motherless, and *his* sister's absence is curiously stressed: although the distance from Naples to North Africa is not
enormous, Alonso insists that Claribel is "so far from Italy removed / I
ne'er again shall see her" (2.1.107–8), and Antonio expresses her
remoteness even more extravagantly:

> She that is Queen of Tunis; she that dwells
> Ten leagues beyond man's life; she that from Naples
> Can have no note unless the sun were post —
> The Man i' th' Moon's too slow — till newborn chins
> Be rough and razorable;
>
> (2.1.240–44)

Claribel had to wait until 1949 for the female poet H.D. to make her
visible and give her a voice.[2] Shakespeare's Caliban has no sister and his
mother, Sycorax, is long dead by the time the play's events take place.
Sycorax also has a North African connection, having been banished by
the Algerians, who apparently spared her life because she was pregnant.
Her power is at least recognized by Prospero, Ariel, and Caliban,
though she is vilified by the two former characters as a "hag" and a
"foul witch." Oddly, Shakespeare draws on the lines Ovid gave another
notorious female enchantress, Medea, for Prospero's big "conjuring"
speech, "Ye elves of hills, brooks, standing lakes, and groves" (5.1.33
ff.), but Medea herself is not mentioned.

The fact that I have chosen nevertheless to discuss *The Tempest* in
the context of this book [*Feminist Criticism: Theory and Practice*, ed.
Susan Sellers] may seem perverse, but my choice is a deliberate one and
relates precisely to the *absence* of female characters. I want to ask what
feminist criticism can do in the face of a male-authored canonical text
which seems to exclude women to this extent. Much early feminist
criticism consisted merely in privileging female characters and identifying with their viewpoints, especially if they could be claimed to be in
any way subversive or protofeminist. This is clearly impossible in *The
Tempest*: even nineteenth-century female critics, who on the whole participated enthusiastically in the trend of aggrandizing and romanticizing Shakespeare's heroines, could not find a great deal to say for
Miranda. Anna Jameson wrote in *Shakespeare's Heroines* (first published
in 1833) that in Ophelia and Miranda Shakespeare had created two
beings in whom "the feminine character appears resolved into its very
elementary principles — as modesty, grace, tenderness," but added
that by the same token Miranda resembles nothing on earth";[3] and
Mrs. M. L. Elliott remarked in *Shakespeare's Garden of Girls* (1885)
that Miranda was too ethereal and thus tended to be more popular with
male than with female readers.[4] Anyone who has taught the play
recently will know that these seem very moderate views compared to
the opinions of twentieth-century female students, who find Miranda

---

[2] See *By Avon River* (New York: Macmillan, 1949). For a discussion of H.D.'s transformation of *The Tempest* in this experimental work, see Susan Stanford Friedman,
"Remembering Shakespeare Differently: H.D.'s *By Avon River*," in Marianne Novy, ed.,
Women's Revisions of Shakespeare (Urbana and Chicago: University of Illinois Press,
1990), pp. 143–64.

[3] *Shakespeare's Heroines*, 1897 reprint (London: George Bell & Sons), pp. 134, 149.

[4] *Shakespeare's Garden of Girls*, published anonymously (London: Remington & Co.,
1885), p. 265.

an extremely feeble heroine and scorn to identify with her. Perhaps, then, *The Tempest* can be used as something of a test case for discovering what else a feminist approach may offer beyond this character-based level.

Faced with a comparable problem in relation to *King Lear,* where modern readers hesitate to identify with either the stereotype of the bad woman represented by Goneril and Regan or with the stereotype of the good woman represented by Cordelia, Kathleen McLuskie writes:

> Feminist criticism need not restrict itself to privileging the woman's part or to special pleading on behalf of female characters. It can be equally well served by making a text reveal the conditions in which a particular ideology of femininity functions and by both revealing and subverting the hold which such an ideology has for readers both female and male.[5]

I shall attempt in the remainder of this essay to explore the "ideology of femininity" at work in *The Tempest,* both through a reading of the play and through a survey of some of the most influential ways in which it is currently being reproduced in literary criticism.

Despite her small and comparatively passive role, the text claims that Miranda is nevertheless crucial to the play. Explaining the storm, Prospero tells her: "I have done nothing but in care of thee" (1.2.16). A feminist critic might ask in what sense this is true, and whether Miranda's gender is significant: would the play have worked in the same way if Prospero had had a son? How does sexuality, and especially female sexuality, function in this narrative? Reading the play with an explicit focus on issues of gender, one is immediately struck by its obsession with themes of chastity and fertility, which occur in its figurative language as well as in its literal events. These themes are often specifically associated with female sexuality. In the first, rather startling metaphor of this kind, Gonzalo imagines the very ship which seems to founder in the opening scene as being "as leaky as an unstanched wench" (1.1.43–44), a phrase interpreted as alluding either to a sexually aroused (insatiable) woman or to one menstruating "without the use of absorbent padding," as the Oxford editor puts it. In his long narrative speech to Miranda in the second scene, Prospero uses a metaphor of birth to describe Antonio's treachery —"my trust, / Like

---

[5]"The Patriarchal Bard: Feminist Criticism and Shakespeare: *King Lear* and *Measure for Measure,*" in Jonathan Dollimore and Alan Sinfield, eds., *Political Shakespeare* (Manchester: Manchester University Press, 1985), pp. 88–108.

a good parent, did beget of him / A falsehood" (1.2.93–95), and seems almost to claim that he gave a kind of second birth to Miranda in his sufferings on the voyage to the island:

> When I have decked the sea with drops full salt,
> Under my burden groaned, which raised in me
> An undergoing stomach to bear up
> Against what should ensue.
>
> (1.2.155–58)

This scene also introduces the literal contrast between the chaste Miranda and the "earthy and abhorred" Sycorax who arrived on the island pregnant (by the devil himself, according to Prospero at 1.2.322) and there "littered" or "whelped" her subhuman son. It is notable that the acknowledged, if evil, power of Sycorax is effectively undermined by the bestial stupidity of her son, rather as the power of Tamora is defused in *Titus Andronicus* and that of the Queen in *Cymbeline*. As in the earlier plays, the son of the witch like woman is a rapist (or would-be rapist); Caliban is accused of attempting to rape Miranda, and he does not deny the charge:

> O ho, O ho! Would't had been done!
> Thou didst prevent me — I had peopled else
> This isle with Calibans.
>
> (1.2.352–54)

He later promises Stephano that Miranda, seen as one of the spoils of victory, will "bring thee forth brave brood" (3.2.100). It is perhaps not surprising, therefore, that Ferdinand's "prime request" to Miranda on first seeing her is "If you be maid or no" (1.2.431), a topic to which he returns twenty lines later, ignoring Prospero's intervention in the dialogue.

Miranda's chastity apparently has a quasi-mystical power. She herself swears "by my modesty, / The jewel in my dower" (3.1.53–54), and tells Ferdinand: "I am your wife if you will marry me; / If not, I'll die your maid" (3.1.83–84). Prospero warns Ferdinand in what seem to be unnecessarily harsh terms against breaking her "virgin-knot before / All sanctimonious ceremonies" (4.1.15–16), threatening dire consequences:

> No sweet aspersion shall the heavens let fall
> To make this contract grow; but barren hate,
> Sour-eyed disdain, and discords shall bestrew
> The union of your bed with weeds so loathly

That you shall hate it both. Therefore take heed,
As Hymen's lamps shall light you.

(4.1.18–23)

Ferdinand's reply is comparably graphic:

> As I hope
> For quiet days, fair issue, and long life,
> With such love as 'tis now, the murkiest den,
> The most opportune place, the strong'st suggestion
> Our worser genius can, shall never melt
> Mine honor into lust, to take away
> The edge of that day's celebration
> When I shall think or Phoebus' steeds are foundered,
> Or Night kept chained below.

(4.1.23–31)

Ostensibly reassuring, such language seems to suggest that the minds of both men are dwelling in morbid detail on the possibilities of completing Caliban's attempted violation: the image of Miranda as a rape victim interferes disturbingly with the image of Miranda as a chaste and fertile wife. The masque which Prospero organizes for the entertainment of the young couple in this scene explicitly banishes lust in the form of Venus and Cupid, and emphasizes the blessed fertility of honorable marriage. And yet, reading as a woman, I continue to get the feeling that the play protests too much on this score.

The speakers in the masque promise rewards for premarital chastity. As Ceres sings:

> Earth's increase, foison plenty,
> Barns and garners never empty,
> Vines with clust'ring bunches growing,
> Plants with goodly burden bowing,
> Spring come to you at the farthest,
> In the very end of harvest!

(4.1.110–15)

This language echoes that of the earlier scene in which Gonzalo speculates on what he would do, "Had I plantation of this isle" (2.1.140), to make nature bring forth "all foison, all abundance" (2.1.160), in a utopian vision which is at the same time colonialist in so far as the "commonwealth" is subject to his royal command. Sebastian jokes that he will "carry this island home in his pocket and give it his son for an apple," to which Antonio replies: "And sowing the kernels of it in the sea, bring forth more islands" (2.1.87–90), similarly invoking a picture of benign exploitation and a fantasy of magical male fecundity.

The play at times takes the power of the sea to give birth, or rebirth, quite seriously: later in 2.1.245 Antonio refers to all the courtiers as "sea-swallowed, though some cast again," a metaphor repeated by Ariel when, disguised as a harpy, he tells the "men of sin" that Destiny "the never-surfeited sea / Hath caused to belch up you" (3.3.55–56). These are both parodies of birth: birth from the mouth rather than from the uterus. A cruder version of what the body can throw forth arises at 2.2.101, when Stephano sees Trinculo, hiding under Caliban's cloak, as the "seige" or excrement of the "mooncalf." More seriously, in his Medea-inspired speech, Prospero claims the power to resurrect the dead: "Graves at my command / Have waked their sleepers, oped, and let 'em forth" (5.1.48–49), though Ferdinand asserts elsewhere that it is Miranda who "quickens what's dead" (3.1.6). At the end of the play, after Ferdinand's apparent death "mudded in that oozy bed" of the sea (5.1.151), he rhetorically attributes his "second life" to Prospero (5.1.195), although it is Miranda's literal fertility which will, as Gonzalo explains, permit Prospero's "issue" to become kings of Naples (5.1.205–06).

How, then, can a feminist interpret this pattern of references? What is going on in this text which seems, on the one hand, to deny the importance — and even in some cases the presence — of female characters, but which simultaneously attributes enormous power to female chastity and fertility? One noticeable feature of the handling of these themes is the insistence on male control: Prospero must control Miranda's sexuality before he hands her over to Ferdinand. Alonso, her father, formerly controlled Claribel's sexuality, but the play is ambivalent about his decision (a willing version of Desdemona's father Brabantio?) to "lose" or "loose" her to an African rather than to a European suitor (2.1.122),[6] and she herself is said to have been "Weighed between loathness and obedience" in the matter (2.1.127). Men are seen as capable of controlling the fertility of nature, and Prospero even controls Ceres, the goddess of harvests, in so far as the play makes it clear that she is represented in the masque by his servant Ariel (4.1.167). Recent criticism of *The Tempest* suggests two theoretical frameworks for discussing this question of control, the psychoanalytical and the political, both of which can be utilized in a feminist approach.

---

[6]The First Folio's spelling, "loose," was the normal spelling of "lose," but most modern editors, with the exception of Stephen Orgel, print "loose," presumably because it carries an undertone of greater sensuality.

The traditional reading of *The Tempest* prevalent in the nineteenth century and earlier twentieth century interpreted Prospero's control of its events and characters as entirely benign; he was often seen as the representative of Art itself, or even identified with Shakespeare as author. Freudian and post-Freudian psychoanalytic studies of the play have undermined this view, exposing the darker side of the "family romance" by suggesting that Prospero's control might be more problematic and that his concern with his daughter's sexuality might indicate an incestuous desire for her. In David Sundelson's essay " '"So rare a wonder'd father': Prospero's *Tempest*," the play is fraught with anxieties and uncertainties on this level which are only partially resolved by its endorsement of what he calls both Prospero's and the play's "paternal narcissism: the prevailing sense that there is no worthiness like a father's, no accomplishment or power, and that Prospero is the father *par excellence*."[7] Coppélia Kahn, writing on "The Providential Tempest and the Shakespearean Family," agrees in seeing the play as a "fantasy of omnipotence" in which Prospero, coming from Milan to the island, "went from child-like, self-absorbed dependency to paternal omnipotence, skipping the steps of maturation in between." Miranda, like Marina in *Pericles* and Perdita in *The Winter's Tale*, doubles the roles of mother and daughter, uniting chastity and fertility in a non-threatening way. Yet, in so far as Kahn claims that "Prospero's identity is based entirely on his role as father, and his family is never united or complete"— indeed he is left at the end in a state of social and sexual isolation — the "romance" is still a narrative of imperfect wish fulfillment representing the universally ambivalent desire we all have both to escape from our families and to continue to be nurtured by them.[8] Both these readings lay stress on the tensions that arise in the play and the sheer struggle involved in asserting the supposedly natural harmony of patriarchal control: it appears that an "unstanched wench" constitutes a serious threat to this order.

Stephen Orgel has pointed out a danger in the tendency of psychoanalytic readings to treat the play as a case-history, either of the author or of the characters, overlooking the extent to which the reader, playing the role of analyst, is a collaborator in the resultant fantasy. He further

[7] In Murray M. Schwartz and Coppélia Kahn, eds., *Representing Shakespeare: New Psychoanalytic Essays* (Baltimore, MD and London: Johns Hopkins University Press, 1980), pp. 33–53.

[8] In Schwartz and Kahn, *Representing Shakespeare*, pp. 217–43. Passages cited are on p. 238 and p. 240.

notices that while psychoanalysis evokes an unchanging, essential human nature, the theoretical framework does change:

> Recent psychoanalytic theory has replaced Freud's central Oedipal myth with a drama in which the loss of the seducing mother is the crucial trauma. As men, we used to want reassurance that we could successfully compete with or replace or supersede our fathers; now we want to know that our lost mothers will return. (52)[9]

In consequence, his essay, called "Prospero's Wife," transfers the center of interest from the present, dominant father to the absent mother, a strategy comparable to the one employed by Coppélia Kahn in her essay on "The Absent Mother in *King Lear.*"[10] It is, as Orgel acknowledges, a problematic strategy in so far as it deals not with the text itself but with the gaps and blanks that Shakespeare has chosen not to fill in. Indeed, he begins his study with the defensive statement, "This essay is not a reading of *The Tempest,*" and worries about the possible parallels with such currently unfashionable texts as Mary Cowden Clarke's *The Girlhood of Shakespeare's Heroines.* Nevertheless, his work is highly suggestive for feminist critics in its willingness to explore a whole network of feminine allusions and absences, ranging from the obvious one of his title to more obscure issues such as the puzzling references to "widow Dido" at 2.1.74–98, Dido being a "model at once of heroic fidelity to a murdered husband and [of] the destructive potential of erotic passion" (51). He also challenges the traditional view of *The Tempest* as a happy courtship comedy, remarking that while the play does move towards marriage, the relationships are "ignorant at best, characteristically tense, and potentially tragic." He sees this as typical of the author:

> relationships between men and women interest Shakespeare intensely, but not, on the whole, as husbands and wives. The wooing process tends to be what it is here: not so much a prelude to marriage and a family as a process of self-definition. (56)

Current political approaches to *The Tempest* often have links with psychoanalytic approaches. Orgel exemplifies one such link as he moves from his discussion of the missing wife, by way of speculations about Shakespeare's own family experiences, to an analysis of power and authority in the play in terms of the ways these issues were conceived in

[9]"Prospero's Wife," in Margaret W. Ferguson, Maureen Quilligan and Nancy J. Vickers, eds., *Rewriting the Renaissance: The Discourses of Sexual Difference in Early Modern Europe* (Chicago and London: University of Chicago Press, 1986), pp. 50–64. This essay was first published in *Representations* 8 (1984): 1–13.
[10]In Ferguson, Quilligan, and Vickers, *Rewriting the Renaissance,* pp. 33–49.

Jacobean England. He points out that in setting up the contest for the island between Caliban, who claims his inheritance from his mother, and Prospero, whose authority is self-created, Shakespeare is representing positions which were available — indeed, normative — at the time. Further, in his edition of *The Tempest*, Orgel goes on to consider the real-life significance of political marriages like the one in the play where Prospero goes to considerable trouble to marry his daughter to the son of his chief enemy, thereby staging a counter-usurpation of Naples by Milan.

The fact that *The Tempest* was performed at court in 1613 during the wedding festivities of King James's daughter Elizabeth and Frederick the Elector Palatine gives a further resonance to such speculations. This historical circumstance is the starting point for Lorie Jerrell Leininger's feminist reading, "The Miranda Trap: Sexism and Racism in Shakespeare's *Tempest*."[11] She imagines the sixteen-year-old princess as the real-life equivalent of Miranda: beautiful, loving, chaste, and above all obedient to her all-powerful father. Miranda's role as the dependent female is crucial to the play's dynamics of power in so far as Caliban's enslavement is justified by his attempt to rape her: "Prospero needs Miranda as sexual bait, and then needs to protect her from the threat which is inescapable given his hierarchical world" (289). Shakespeare's play allows Miranda no way out of this situation, but Leininger invents an epilogue for a modern Miranda who refuses to participate in the play's assumptions that Prospero is infallible, that Caliban is a "natural" slave, and that a daughter is a "foot" in a family organism of which the father is the head.

Most political readings of *The Tempest*, however, center on the issue of colonialism. This is the focus of Francis Barker and Peter Hulme's essay "'Nymphs and Reapers Heavily Vanish': The Discursive Con-texts of *The Tempest*,"[12] and of Paul Brown's essay "'This thing of darkness I acknowledge mine': *The Tempest* and the Discourse of Colonialism."[13] Both employ the technique of intertextuality to relate the play to nascent seventeenth-century European colonialism, reassessing the "sources" in the context of New World voyage materials and arguing that anxiety and ambivalence result from the struggle to create a self-justifying, colonialist discourse. We are encouraged in these readings to be deeply suspicious of Prospero and to sympathize with Caliban as the representative of an

[11]In Carolyn Ruth Swift Lenz, Gayle Greene, and Carol Thomas Neely, eds., *The Woman's Part* (Urbana and Chicago: University of Illinois Press, 1980), pp. 285–94.

[12]In John Drakakis, ed., *Alternative Shakespeares* (London and New York: Methuen, 1985), pp. 191–205. [Reprinted in this volume, p. 292.]

[13]In Dollimore and Sinfield, *Political Shakespeare*, pp. 48–71. [Reprinted in this volume, p. 268.]

exploited Third World. Brown draws on Freudian theory to point out an analogy between the political operations of colonialism and the modes of psychic repression, and he uses the Freudian concept of "dreamwork" to discuss the way in which Prospero's discourse subordinates that of the other inhabitants of the island, as, for example, when he imposes his memory of earlier events on both Caliban and Ariel in 1.2.

An explicitly feminist version of this kind of reading, and one which is moreover undertaken from a Third World viewpoint, is performed by the Indian critic Ania Loomba as the final chapter of her book *Gender, race, Renaissance Drama*.[14] Loomba is critical of the tendency of "alternative" readings of *The Tempest* to seize upon Caliban as a symbol of exploitation and potential rebellion, and points out that some anti-colonialist or anti-racist readings have been unthinkingly sexist: the specific repression of Miranda has been neglected. Setting out to delineate the limits of the text's supposed "radical ambivalence," she discusses the myth of the black rapist, the significance of Sycorax as "Prospero's other," and the contradictory position of Miranda as typical of that of all white women in the colonial adventure: the nature of her participation confirms her subordination to white men.

Both psychoanalytic and political theoretical approaches nevertheless deny some of the pleasures experienced by earlier generations of audiences and readers who were apparently able to identify more readily with the viewpoint of Prospero as white male patriarch and colonizer. Today, white male critics in Britain and the United States understandably feel uncomfortable and guilty about participating in these attitudes. Reading the play as a woman and as a feminist, it is possible to feel good about delineating and rejecting its idealization of patriarchy, and one can go beyond the play to consider the conscious and unconscious sexism of its critical and stage history. Reading as a white British person, my conscience is less clear: women as well as men benefited (and still benefit) from the kind of colonialism idealized in *The Tempest*.

The current situation as I have sketched it above seems to leave two major questions unanswered (and unanswerable within the scope of this essay): first, is it possible for a staging of *The Tempest* to convey anything approaching a feminist reading of the text (without rewriting it or adding something like Leininger's epilogue); and secondly, what kind of pleasure can a woman and a feminist take in this text beyond the rather grim one of mapping its various patterns of exploitation? Must a feminist reading necessarily be a negative one?

[14]Manchester: Manchester University Press, 1989, pp. 142–58. [Reprinted in this volume, p. 389.]

Writing about Critical Controversy and *The Tempest*

In our introductory essay, we have discussed *why* it makes sense to study critical controversies, suggesting that such study can enhance your engagement with literary texts and with the world of literary criticism in which your teachers and many other readers live. In this essay, we offer some suggestions about *how* to contribute to the debates yourselves. We will focus our advice primarily on how to contribute to those debates in *writing*, because, if you are like most people, you find writing more challenging than speaking, but we believe that our advice can also be useful for participating in class discussion. Our advice will cover some general principles and some specific techniques not just for managing a literary critical argument, but for doing so in response to the arguments of others.

GETTING DIALOGIC

Let us suppose that your teacher, after discussing with you and your classmates the essays in this book on the controversy over postcolonial readings of *The Tempest*, gives you an assignment to write a five-page paper making your own contribution to that debate. How should you proceed? Consider the following responses to the assignment by two different students. Student A decides that the most important thing to do is say something original; therefore, she declares her interpretation early in the paper and then spends the rest of the paper presenting the textual evidence that supports it. Along the way she drops in footnotes that indicate which critics in this book support her interpretation and which do not. Student B decides that the most important thing to do is to show the complexity of the debate, so he spends most of the paper summarizing what others have said, withholding his own interpretation for the last few paragraphs. Indeed, thinking he will impress his teacher, Student B goes to the library to find more essays on the play and he includes their views in his summary.

Although both approaches have some merit, each, in our view, has a major flaw. Student A's, which we will call the *solo flyer model,* mentions and occasionally quotes or summarizes several critics but does not really grapple with their ideas or with their debate. Her references to that debate are not integral to her argument but something added on, perhaps because she has heard that English teachers like secondary sources and footnotes. Since her solo flyer paper fails to relate her ideas to those of other critics, it is unlikely to be received as a substantial contribution to the debate even if the paper has original things to say. Student B's approach, which we will call the *shrinking violet model,* is at the opposite extreme from Student A's. Like Student A, Student B fails to put himself into dialogue with other critics. In addition, by substituting summaries of other critics' arguments for productive engagement with them, he also fails to make an argument of his own. Consequently, although Student B's approach may require more hours of work than Student A's, his paper, too, is unlikely to be a substantial contribution to the debate.

Although the solo flyer and the shrinking violet models are, in one sense, very different, they have something important in common: Both are insufficiently *dialogic,* by which we mean that both student authors do a poor job of relating their own ideas to those of other critics. Critical debates, as difficult as they sometimes look, are really not all that different from the conversations you have in your social life. To be a good conversationalist you need to do two interrelated things: make what you say responsive to what others in the conversation are saying; and have something worthwhile to add to the conversation. The best way to ensure that you have something worthwhile to add is to listen closely to others (or closely read their texts) and try to be as responsive as you can to their arguments. We suspect that you've often had the experience of joining a conversation on a topic that at first you didn't think you had much of an opinion about, only to discover to your surprise, after listening to others offer their views, that you actually had some strong beliefs about the topic and were inspired by the conversation to express them. Of course not all conversations, literary or otherwise, work in exactly this way, but such experiences do underline the point that a good way to find something worthwhile to say is to "get dialogic," letting what others are saying stimulate what you say in response. To put the point another way, making a good argument of your own becomes easier if you can develop your ideas in relation to the arguments of others.

CHOOSING A POSITION: AGREEING, DISAGREEING, DOING BOTH

In one sense, then, making a critical argument is very simple. If you think about situating your ideas in relation to others' along a spectrum from complete agreement to complete disagreement, you can see that you have three main options: strongly agree, strongly disagree, or partially agree and disagree. We think you'll be helped if you can decide at some point, perhaps after some trial and error, which option your essay will best conform to and stick to that plan as you write and revise it. If you find yourself shifting to one of the other options, that's a good sign — as long as you make sure you revise your essay so it indicates clearly to readers which option you have picked.

At the same time — and this makes things more complicated — each of these three simple positions — agree, disagree, do both — is open to countless variations. To illustrate, here are just a few of the variations that are possible for each of the three positions. And these variations are rarely mutually exclusive; they can often be combined within a single response.

1. You can strongly disagree with another critic's argument. You can go on to develop the disagreement by (a) arguing for an opposing interpretation of the critic's main evidence; (b) arguing that there's significant relevant evidence in *The Tempest* that the critic's argument neglects, evidence that would support a different interpretation of the play; or (c) arguing that the context within which the critic reads the evidence is not appropriate. Deborah Willis's essay "Shakespeare's *Tempest* and the Discourse of Colonialism" (p. 321 in this volume), for example, strongly disagrees with Paul Brown's argument in " 'This Thing of Darkness I Acknowledge Mine': *The Tempest* and the Discourse of Colonialism" that Shakespeare's play is a "reflection of colonialist practices" and an example of colonialist discourse. (p. 268). Willis's main strategy is to argue for a different interpretation of Brown's main evidence, Prospero's narrative of himself as ruler of the island and of Miranda, Ariel, and especially Caliban. Where Brown argues that Prospero's narrative fits the pattern in which the colonizer (Prospero) produces a threatening other (Caliban) and then controls or contains that threat as a way to assert the colonizer's power, Willis reexamines Prospero's speeches and contends that the play itself calls attention to "problematic aspects of Prospero's rule on the island" and "raises questions about his view of Caliban" (pp. 325–26). Consequently, in Willis's interpretation, *The Tempest* does not conform to the pattern of colonialist discourse Brown identifies, but instead questions it.

David Scott Kastan, to take another example, in "'The Duke of Milan / And His Brave Son': Old Histories and New in *The Tempest*," also strongly disagrees with the postcolonialist readings that view the play as exemplifying the imperialism inherent in England's efforts to establish colonies in the New World. He develops his case by contending that such readings fail to do justice to a context more relevant to the play's setting on an island in the old world namely, more European power struggles that were closer to home: "the critical emphasis upon the new world not only obscures the play's more dominant discourses of dynastic politics but also blinds us to disturbances in the text that should alert us to this aspect of the play's engagement with its own historical moment" (p. 340).

2. *You can say "Yes, but . . ."* What is often, though not always, more satisfactory to readers than black-and-white agreement or disagreement is to partially agree with another critic and partially disagree. You can partially agree by (a) pointing to convincing aspects of the critic's argument such as his or her use of evidence or (b) applying the critic's argument to some part of the text or some issue that the critic has not addressed. Ania Loomba, in the excerpt from *Gender, race, Renaissance Drama* included in this volume (p. 389), adopts this strategy, agreeing with those who read the play politically but arguing that such readings need to go even further by paying more attention to the play's underlying assumptions about both black male sexuality and relations between the genders.

3. *You can say "Yes, and . . ."* That is, you can agree with another critic and develop the agreement along the lines of 2 (b), above. In this response, you both build on the critic's case and add your own contribution to the debate by pointing out something that he or she (or the critical approach he or she employs) has neglected or failed to explore sufficiently. Ann Thompson in "'Miranda, Where's Your

Sister?': Reading Shakespeare's *The Tempest*" (p. 402), for example, endorses psychoanalytic and political interpretations of the play, and then builds on their insights as she develops her feminist reading of it.

DEALING WITH MULTIPLE OTHERS

As the above examples indicate, you may respond to a single critic, but sometimes you need to respond to several critics who disagree or agree with each other in complicated ways. At other times you may need to put several critics who do not mention each other into conversation. Here are some ways to do these things:

1. After summarizing the critics' positions, you can identify and focus on something significant that they have in common: For example, you can focus on a view of a certain part of *The Tempest,* an assumption about what is important in the play or in the criticism of it, or some other such issue. You can be explicit and straightforward about the underlying issue and your relation to it: "Despite their different concerns, both critics X and Y identify feature Z as a crucial element of the play, and their views of it are largely the same. However, by considering evidence from the play that both essays neglect, I will argue for a different view of Z." Meredith Anne Skura's essay "Discourse and the Individual: The Case of Colonialism in *The Tempest*" is an excellent example of this strategy as she expresses her partial agreement and disagreement with postcolonial critics of the play. After grouping together many different critics who analyze *The Tempest* as an instance of colonialist discourse and assessing their interpretations as "salutary . . . in correcting New Critical 'blindness' to history and ideology" (p. 357), Skura contends that the postcolonialist approach is "in danger of fostering blindness of its own" (p. 357). "The recent criticism not only flattens the text into the mold of colonialist discourse and eliminates what is characteristically 'Shakespearean' in order to foreground what is 'colonialist,' but it is also — paradoxically — in danger of taking the play further from the particular historical situation in England in 1611 even as it brings it closer to what we mean by 'colonialism' today" (pp. 357–58). Skura then goes on to offer her corrective to these problems by addressing the relation between Shakespeare as the individual creator and as a reflector of his culture's discourse of colonialism at the time he wrote. Attending to both the political and psychological dimensions of the play, Skura argues that "the recognition of the individuality of the play, and of Shakespeare, does not counter but rather enriches the understanding" (p. 358) of the play's relation to its historical context.

2. After identifying a generally shared critical practice or interpretation, you can suggest that some different approach represents a critical advance. This strategy is employed by another essay that exemplifies the "yes, but" approach, Francis Barker and Peter Hulme's "Nymphs and Reapers Heavily Vanish: The Discursive Con-texts of *The Tempest*" (p. 292). Barker and Hulme applaud the poststructuralist view of literary texts as participating in networks of other texts and social discourses. But they contend that this move goes too far when it fails to attend to the context of the "still crucially important *first* inscription of the text" (p. 296), that is, what the play probably meant in its original context, a view that, interestingly, puts them into partial agreement with traditional historical critics like Tillyard and Kermode.

As with any art, the best way to become more skillful at entering critical conversations is through practice. The more you get accustomed to developing your ideas in relation to those of others, the more proficient you will become at both reading and writing critical arguments. Your reading skills will advance as you notice the moves other critics make, and this awareness in turn will enhance your own ability to make similar moves in your own writing. Furthermore, the more you practice, the more you will realize that, whether you agree or disagree with other critics, your engagement with their ideas will help you develop your own.

About the Editors

Gerald Graff is professor of English and Education at the University of Illinois at Chicago. He developed and refined his pedagogy of "teaching the conflicts" at Northwestern University, where he was professor of English, and at the University of Chicago, where he was George M. Pullman Professor of English and Education. He is one of the most eminent figures in literary studies and education today, as his election as President of the Modern Language Association (2008) attests. His influential books include *Literature Against Itself* (1979), *Professing Literature* (1987), *Beyond the Culture Wars* (1992), and *Clueless in Academe* (2003). With Cathy Birkenstein, he has authored the writing textbook *"They Say/I Say": The Moves That Matter in Academic Writing* (2005). With James Phelan, he is coeditor of *Adventures of Huckleberry Finn: A Case Study in Critical Controversy*, now in its second edition (2004).

James Phelan is Distinguished University Professor of English at the Ohio State University. Editor of the award-winning journal *Narrative* and coeditor of the Ohio State University Press series on the Theory and Interpretation of Narrative, he has written five books on narrative theory: *Worlds from Words* (1981), *Reading People, Reading Plots* (1989), *Narrative as Rhetoric* (1996), *Living to Tell about It* (2005), and *Experiencing Fiction* (2007). With Peter J. Rabinowitz, Phelan is coeditor of *Understanding Narrative* (1995) and the

Blackwell *Companion to Narrative Theory* (2005). With Jakob Lothe and Jeremy Hawthorn, he is coeditor of *Joseph Conrad: Voice, Sequence, History, Genre* (2008). With Gerald Graff, he is coeditor of *Adventures of Huckleberry Finn: A Case Study in Critical Controversy*, now in its second edition (2004).

(continued from p. ii)

Francis Barker and Peter Hulme. "Nymphs and Reapers Heavily Vanish: The Discursive Con-texts of *The Tempest.*" From *Alternative Shakespeare*, edited by John Drakakis, 1988. Reprinted by permission of Taylor & Francis, Cengage Learning Services (UK).

David Bevington. "The Tempest" from *The Complete Works of Shakespeare,* Fourth Edition, edited by David Bevington. Copyright © 1997 Addison Wesley Educational Publishers. Reprinted by permission of Addison Wesley Longman.

Reuben A. Brower. "The Mirror of Analogy: *The Tempest.*" From *The Fields of Light: An Experiment in Critical Reading* by Reuben Arthur Brower. Copyright © 1951 by Oxford University Press, Inc. Used by permission of Oxford University Press, Inc.

Paul Brown. " 'This Thing of Darkness I Acknowledge Mine': *The Tempest* and the Discourse of Colonialism." From *Political Shakespeare: New Essays in Cultural Materialism*, Second Edition, edited by Jonathan Dollimore and Alan Sinfield. Used by permission of the publisher, Cornell University Press.

Bartolome De Las Casas. From "Letter to Phillip, Great Prince of Spain." From *In Defense of the Indians*, edited by Stafford Poole. Copyright © 1974. Reprinted by permission of Northern University Press.

Aimé Césaire. Scenes from *A Tempest.* Copyright © 1969 by Editions du Seuil. English translation copyright © 1985 by Richard Miller. Reprinted by permission of Georges Borchardt, Inc.

Stephen Greenblatt. "The Best Way to Kill Our Literary Inheritance Is to Turn It into a Decorous Celebration of the New World Order." Originally published in the *Chronicle of Higher Education*, June 12, 1991, Volume XXXVIII, No. 39. Reprinted by permission of the author.

David Scott Kastan. " 'The Duke of Milan/And His Brave Son': Old Histories and New in *The Tempest.*" From *Shakespeare After Theory* by David Kastan. Reproduced by permission of Taylor & Francis/Routledge, Inc.

Frank Kermode. From *Shakespeare: The Final Plays.* Excerpts from the Preface to the Arden edition of *The Tempest*, by Frank Kermode, edited by Frank Kermode. Copyright © 1957. Reprinted with permission from Thomas Nelson and Sons Ltd.

Ania Loomba. From *Gender, race, Renaissance Drama.* Reprinted by permission from Ania Loomba.

Leah Marcus. "The Blue-Eyed Witch." From *Unediting the Renaissance* by Leah Marcus. Used by permission of the author.

Meredith Anne Skura. "Discourse and the Individual: The Case of Colonialism in *The Tempest.*" *Shakespeare Quarterly* 40: 1 (Spring 1989): 42–69. Reprinted by permission of Shakespeare Quarterly.

Ronald Takaki. "The 'Tempest' in the Wilderness." From *A Different Mirror: A History of Multicultural America* by Ronald Takaki. Copyright © 1993 by Ronald Takaki. By permission of Little, Brown and Company (Inc.).

Ann Thompson. " 'Miranda, Where's Your Sister?': Reading Shakespeare's *The Tempest.*" From *Feminist Criticism: Theory and Practice*, edited by Susan Sellers. Published by the University of Toronto Press, 1991. Reprinted by permission of Ann Thompson.

E. M. W. Tillyard. From *The Great Chain of Being.* From *The Elizabethan World Picture* by Eustace Madeville Wenenhall (E. M. W.) Tillyard, pp. 3–4, 9–17, 29–31, 34–35. Copyright © 1959. Reprinted with permission of Jesus College, Cambridge, UK, owners of the literary estate of E. M. W. Tillyard.